THE DLM EARLY CHILDHOOD EXPRESS

Pam Schiller • Douglas Clements • Julie Sarama • Rafael Lara-Alecio

Teacher's Edition D

A Division of The McGraw-Hill Companies

Columbus, Ohio

www.sra4kids.com

SRA/McGraw-Hill

A Division of The McGraw-Hill Companies

Send all inquiries to:
SRA/McGraw-Hill
8787 Orion Place
Columbus, OH 43240-4027

Printed in the United States of America.

ISBN 0-07-572192-9

1 2 3 4 5 6 7 8 9 WEB 07 06 05 04 03 02

WELCOME TO

THE DLM EARLY CHILDHOOD EXPRESS

The DLM Early Childhood Express . . . Your Route To Learning Success!

The DLM Early Childhood Express is a holistic, child-centered program that nurtures each child by offering carefully selected and carefully sequenced learning experiences. It provides a wealth of materials and ideas to foster the social-emotional, intellectual, and physical development of children. At the same time, it nurtures the natural curiosity and sense of self that can serve as the foundation for a lifetime of learning.

The lesson format is designed to present information in a way that makes it easy for children to learn. The cycle is modeled on knowledge gained from the latest neuroscience research. Intelligence is, in large part, our ability to see patterns and build relationships out of those patterns, which is why ***The DLM Early Childhood Express*** is focused on helping children see the patterns in what they are learning. It builds an understanding of how newly taught material resembles what children already know. Then, it takes the differences in the new material and helps the children convert them into new understanding.

Every aspect of ***The DLM Early Childhood Express*** is designed to make learning instinctive. Circle Time at the beginning and end of each day helps children focus on the learning process, reflect on new concepts, and make important connections. The practice portions of the lessons are designed to allow children to apply what they have learned.

Neuroscience research reveals that unless knowledge is applied within twenty-four hours of its introduction, it will probably have to be relearned.

The early years, birth to age six, are the most fertile years in an individual's life for developing language skills. So lessons in The DLM Early Childhood Express are focused on language acquisition and those all-important early reading skills. With the right foundation, reading success is only a matter of maturation.

For children to grow intellectually, they must feel confident in their abilities and secure in their relationships with teachers, family members, and peers. ***The DLM Early Childhood Express*** addresses social-emotional development in a number of ways. It is included in every lesson (via positive reinforcement), built into content connections (via interactive activities), and inherent in the way families are actively involved in ***The DLM Early Childhood Express*** classrooms.

Welcome to ***The DLM Early Childhood Express***. Add your own ideas. Mix and match activities. Our program is designed to offer you a variety of activities on which to build a full year of exciting and creative lessons. Happy learning to you and the children in your care!

Key Findings in Brain Research

The knowledge gained from recent brain research makes it possible to give children the strongest possible foundation for learning. Here are some important facts:

- At birth each child has already developed a complex brain circuitry. The way the circuitry is "wired" depends upon such external forces as nutrition, environment, and degree of sensory stimulation.
- Early experiences contribute significantly to the structure of the brain and its capabilities. Children learn in the context of relationships. Early interactions are critical.
- Brain development is not a step-by-step process. It is more like a spiral with waves or windows of opportunity. Certain periods of a child's development are especially conducive to developing specific skills.

During the first three years of life, a child forms an estimated one thousand trillion synapses. However, neuron connections form only when a child interacts with his or her environment. The richer the child's environment is and the more he or she interacts with it, the more neuron connections the brain will create.

Young children are biologically predisposed to learn. With ***The DLM Early Childhood Express***, they can do it more effectively than ever before.

Your Day Takes Shape

When it comes to scheduling, flexibility is key. With ***The DLM Early Childhood Express***, it's easy to fit lessons into your day.

These suggested schedules can (and should) be altered to reflect:

- Lunch, recess, and other assigned periods
- Your individual teaching style
- The length of your day (half or full)

Both of these sample schedules begin with a Morning Circle. Beginning your day this way:

- Helps you and your class settle in and get organized
- Allows children time to adjust to the transition from home to school
- Provides an opportunity for building a sense of community

TYPICAL FULL-DAY SCHEDULE

8:00 – 8:30	Morning Circle: Begin the Day & Literacy
8:30 – 9:00	Literacy Learning Centers
9:00 – 9:15	Story Circle: Reading Together
9:15 – 9:30	Music and Movement
9:30 – 10:00	Group Activity: Math
10:00 – 10:20	Active Play (outdoors if possible)
10:20 – 10:40	Group Activity: Content Connection or Story Circle
10:40 – 11:15	Learning Centers
11:15 – 12:00	Lunch
12:00 – 12:15	Story Circle: Reading Together
12:15 – 12:45	Rest
12:45 – 1:00	Music and Movement
1:00 – 1:30	Group Activity: Revisit Literacy Lesson or Content Connections
1:30 – 2:20	Learning Centers
2:20 – 2:45	Active Play (outdoors if possible)
2:45 – 3:00	Closing Circle: Reflect on the Day

THE DLM EARLY CHILDHOOD EXPRESS

TYPICAL HALF-DAY SCHEDULE

8:00 – 8:30	Morning Circle: Begin the Day & Literacy
8:30 – 9:00	Literacy Learning Centers
9:00 – 9:15	Story Circle: Reading Together
9:15 – 9:30	Music and Movement
9:30 – 10:00	Group Activity: Math
10:00 – 10:20	Active Play (outdoors if possible)
10:20 – 10:40	Group Activity: Content Connection or Story Circle
10:40 – 11:15	Learning Centers
11:15 – 11:30	Closing Circle: Reflect on the Day

A Typical Weekly Lesson Plan

To help you understand how the weekly lesson plan is organized, each section of the lesson is defined and the location of specific activities within each lesson is described.

Day	Morning Circle	Learning Centers	Storytime	Group Activity	Learning Centers	Music & Movement	Closing Circle
Monday	Begin the Day Literacy Focus and Develop	Literacy Practice	Literacy Reflect "What Makes Me Happy?" /¿Cómo te sientes hoy?	Math Lesson Focus, Develop, Practice & Reflect	Math Practice Theme Centers Content Connection: Science	"The Wonderful Thing About Tiggers" from *Four Baby Bumblebees* CD	Reflect on the Day
Tuesday	Begin the Day Literacy Focus and Develop	Literacy Practice	Literacy Reflect "The Many Faces of Me"/ "La muchas caras de mi persona"	Math Lesson Focus, Develop, Practice & Reflect	Math Practice Theme Centers Content Connection: Health & Safety	"If You're Happy and You Know It" and "Vamos a cantar"	Reflect on the Day
Wednesday	Begin the Day Literacy Focus and Develop	Literacy Practice	Literacy Reflect "Keiko's Good Thinking"/ "El buen pensamiento de Keiko"	Math Lesson Focus, Develop, Practice & Reflect	Math Practice Theme Centers Content Connection: Literacy/Social Studies	*Making Music with Thomas Moore CD*	Reflect on the Day
Thursday	Begin the Day Literacy Focus and Develop	Literacy Practice	Literacy Reflect *Itsy Bitsy Spider/ La araña pequeñita*	Math Lesson Focus, Develop, Practice & Reflect	Math Practice Theme Centers Content Connection: Fine Arts	Hopscotch	Reflect on the Day
Friday	Begin the Day Literacy Focus and Develop	Literacy Practice	Literacy Reflect *How Happy I Would Be!/Me gustaria tener*	Math Lesson Focus, Develop, Practice & Reflect	Math Practice Theme Centers Content Connection: Science	Circle 'Round the Zero Circulo alrededor de cero	Reflect on the Day

Circle: Literacy or Math

These are whole-group activities that include songs, poems, stories, and part or all of a Literacy or Math lesson. Notice that there are several Circle activities for each day. The first Circle of the day, or Morning Circle (see suggestions on page 1), helps children organize their day, get focused, and make that all-important transition from home to school. The Closing Circle lets children recap their day and reflect on applications of what they have learned.

Group Activity: Literacy or Math

This may be a whole- or small-group activity (depending on your preference and the nature of the activity). You can find group activities in Literacy or Math lessons – or use suggestions from Content Connections (see pages xiv and xv).

Learning Centers

These are small-group activities that provide time for practicing skills and concepts taught in the lessons. Suggestions for learning center practice are found in each Literacy and Math Lesson as well as in the Content Connections. The Learning Centers presented on the first pages of theme and are intended to remain open for the entire week. These centers provide the opportunity for children to explore a wide range of curricular areas.

Music/Movement

This section recommends large- or small-group games and dances from the Teacher Resource Anthology, or songs and dances from the program's Music CDs.

Second Language Learners

This section includes suggestions for ways to adapt the lessons to the specific needs of second language learners.

School/Home

Ideas to help tie a lesson to the home come from the Home Connection feature in the lesson.

SRA understands the important role families play in the learning process. By keeping them informed and involved, ***The DLM Early Childhood Express*** helps to reinforce what is taught in the classroom.

Tools for Teaching

The DLM Early Childhood Express is packed full of the components you'll need to teach each theme and enrich your classroom. The Teacher Resource Package is the heart of the program, because it contains all the necessary materials. Plus, the Anthology contains all the fun components that you'll love to teach. You'll find letters, bears, puppets, and instruments in the Manipulative Package to connect learning skills with play.

Teacher Resource Package

This package contains all the essential tools for the teacher. It includes the Teacher's Resource Anthology, 550 pages of the things you love most about teaching Early Childhood, such as songs, patterns, finger plays, and feltboard stories. This package also contains Teacher's Editions, CDs and other resources no teacher would want to be without.

Teacher's Edition A
Teacher's Edition B
Teacher's Edition C
Teacher's Edition D
Teacher's Resource Anthology
Resource Guide, CD ROM & Pattern Blocks – Math
Resource Guide – Phonics (English)
Resource Guide – Phonics (Spanish)
Photo Library
Photo Library User's Guide and CD-ROM
Resource Guide – Home Connections
3 English CDs (1 Instrumental)
Alphabet Wall Cards
Sequencing Cards
Oral Language Development Cards

Manipulative Package

Rhythm band instruments, counters, puppets, and more to be used in lessons as well as to enhance learning center activities.

Uppercase Letters, 42/Set
Lowercase Letters, 44/Set
Spanish Letters, 18/Set
Dinosaurs Counters, 108/Set
Light Brown, Plush Bear Puppet with Shirt
Dark Brown, Plush Bear Puppet with Shirt
1 Set Wood Maracas
4 Hand Bells
1 Drum

Hurray for Pre-K!
Available in English and Spanish

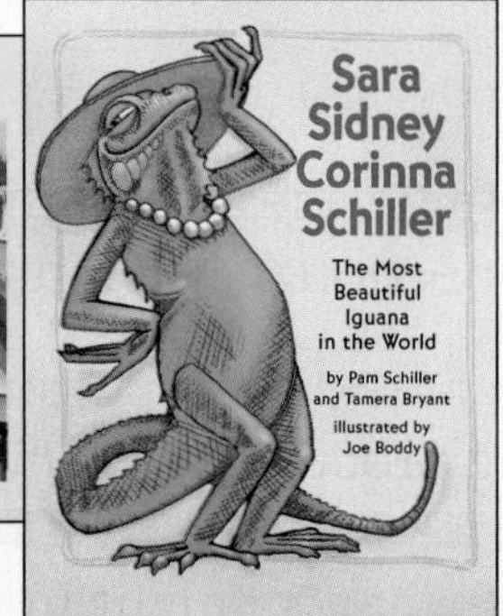

Sara Sidney – The Most Beautiful Iguana in the World
Available in English and Spanish

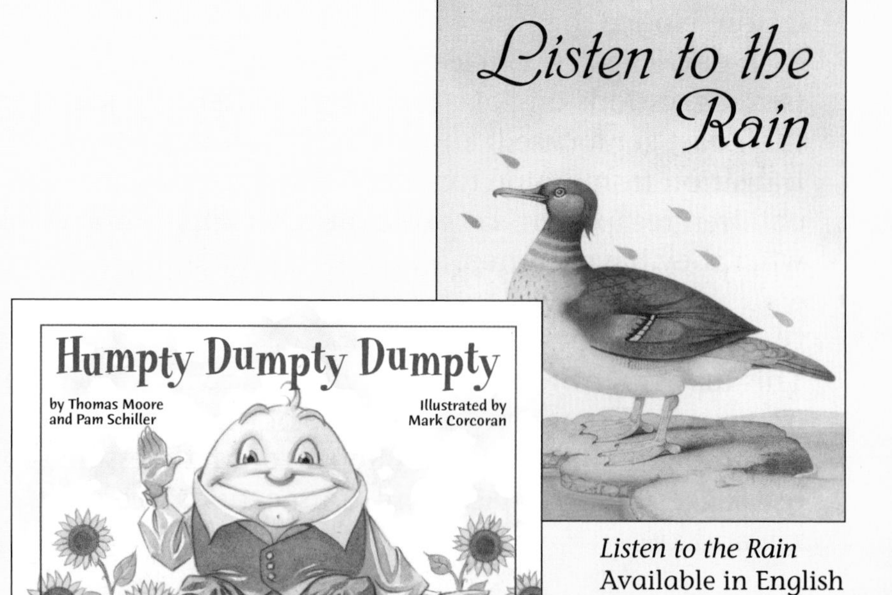

Humpty Dumpty Dumpty
Available in English and Spanish

Listen to the Rain
Available in English and Spanish

In ***The DLM Early Childhood Express*** the Big Books support the literacy lessons, offer storytime suggestions, and are often used in content connections. The Listening Center Package puts books directly into children's hands.

With ***The DLM Early Childhood Express***, children can feel the excitement of turning the pages themselves as they follow along with the story that is being read on the audiocassette.

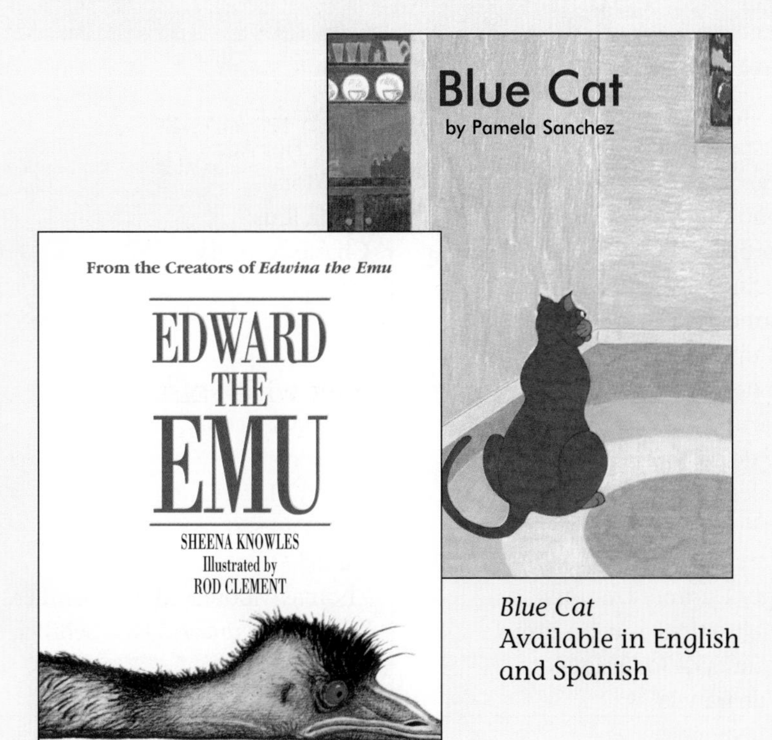

Blue Cat
Available in English and Spanish

Edward the Emu
Available in English and Spanish

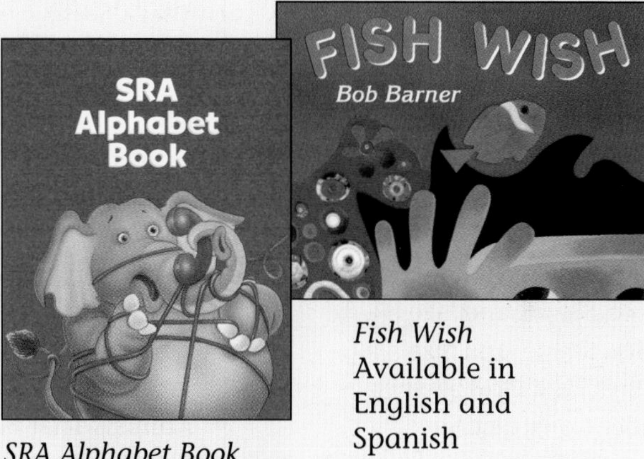

SRA Alphabet Book
Available in English and Spanish

Fish Wish
Available in English and Spanish

Listening Center Package

This package puts books in the hands of children, allowing them to turn the pages themselves as they listen to the stories.

73 Little Books (2 copies of each title)
18 Audiocassettes

Big Book Package

Big Books offer read to and sharing reading experiences for children.

37 Big Books

The ***DLM Early Childhood Express*** program is also available in an English/Spanish edition.

Themes That Help Children Grow

Theme	CORE LITERATURE		
	English	Spanish	Author
School Days	Hurray for Pre-K!	¡Qué viva el preescolar!	Ellen B. Senisi
Physical Me	Here Are My Hands	Aquí están mis manos	Bill Martin Jr
Thinking and Feeling Me	How Happy I Would Be!	Me gustaría tener...	Alma Flor Ada
My Family	A Birthday Basket for Tía	Una canasta de cumpleaños para Tía	Pat Mora
Fall/Autumn	Fall	El otoño	Maria Rius
Friends	Ginger	Jengibre	Charlotte Voake
Pets	Sara Sidney: The Most Beautiful Iguana in the World	Sara Sidney: la iguana más bella del mundo	Pam Schiller and Tamera Bryant
Opposites	Sing a Song of Opposites	Canta una canción de opuestos	Pam Schiller
Color, Shape, and Size	The Color Bear	El oso de colores	Barbara Brenner
Color, Shape, and Size	Blue Cat	Gato azul	Pamela Sanchez
Things That Go Together	Wordsong	Canto de palabras	Bill Martin Jr
Under Construction	Animals That Build Their Homes	Animales que construyen sus nidos	Robert M. McClung
Growing Things	The Tortilla Factory	La tortillería	Gary Paulsen
Food and Nutrition	Martí and the Mango	Martí y el mango	Daniel Moreton
Nursery Rhymes	Humpty Dumpty Dumpty	Humpty Dumpty Dumpty	Thomas Moore and Pam Schiller
Sound and Movement	This Old Man Is Rockin' On	Este viejito tiene mucho ritmo	Tracy Moncure and Pam Schiller
Music	Animal Orchestra	La orquesta de los animales	Scott Gustafson
Winter	Flannel Kisses	Besos de franela	Linda Crotta Brennan
Community Workers	Guess Who?	Adivina quién...	Margaret Miller
Traditional Tales	The Little Red Hen	La gallinita roja	Retold by Rebecca Allen
Traditional Tales	A Bicycle for Rosaura	Rosaura en bicicleta	Daniel Barbot
Cowgirls and Cowboys	The Cowboy Mouse	El ratón vaquero	Beverly J. Irby and Rafael Lara-Alecio
Travel	Little Rabbit's Journey	El viaje del conejito	Beverly J. Irby and Rafael Lara-Alecio
Travel	The Zebra on the Zyder Zee	Una aventura en alta mar	Pam Schiller
Celebrations	¡Fiesta!	¡Fiesta!	Ginger Foglesong Guy
Spring	De Colores	De colores	traditional from Mexico
Weather	Listen to the Rain	Escucha la lluvia	Bill Martin Jr
Real and Make-Believe	The Dragon's Coming After You	El dragón te está persiguiendo	Sally Farrell Odgers
Bugs	Insect Picnic	El picnic de los insectos	Anne Rockwell
Bugs	The Itsy Bitsy Spider	La araña pequeñita	Retold by Tracy Moncure and Pam Schil
Animals	SRA Book of Animals	SRA El libro de los animales	
Zoo Animals	Edward the Emu	Eduardo el emú	Sheena Knowles
Farm Animals	The Farm	La granja	traditional from Mexico
Ocean Life	Fish Wish	Deseos de un pez	Bob Barner
Big Things	Who Is the Beast?	¿Quién es la bestia?	Keith Baker
Summer Fun	The Little Ants	Las hormiguitas	traditional from Mexico

Young children love to learn about themselves. But as they grow, their interests expand to include family, friends, their communities, and the wider world.

Anthology Stories

"I Like School"/"Me gusta la escuela" action story
"I Can, You Can!"/"¡Yo puedo, tú puedes!" flannel board story
"Keiko's Good Thinking"/"El buen pensamiento de Keiko" flannel board story
"Mi abuelo"/"My Grandfather" flannel board story
"The Fall of the Last Leaf"/"La cáida de la última hoja" action story
"Mr. Wiggle and Mr. Waggle"/"Señor Wiggle y Señor Waggle" action story
"A Pet of my Own"/"Mi propia mascota" flannel board story
"El burrito enfermo"/"My Sick Little Donkey" flannel board story
"Rafita and Pepita: Dance of Opposites"/"Rafita y Pepita: un baile de opuestos" action story
"The Color Song"/"Los colores" flannel board story

"Freddie the Snake"/"Braulio, la culebra" flannel board story
"Animal Homes"/"Hogares de animales" flannel board story
"This Is the House That Jack Built"/"Esta es la casa que Juan construyó" flannel board story
"A Special Surprise"/"Una sorpresa especial" prop story
"Let's Pretend to Bake a Cake"/"Pretendamos como que horneamos un pastel" action story
"Little Miss Muffet"/"La Señorita Mufete" flannel board story
"Tortoise Wins a Race"/"La tortuga gana la carrera" flannel board story
"The Traveling Musicians"/"Los músicos viajeros" flannel board story
"The Snow Child"/"La niña de nieve" listening story

"My Father Picks Oranges"/"Mi papá recoge naranjas" listening story
"Henny-Penny"/"Gallinita-Nita" flannel board story
"The Little Red Hen"/"La gallinita roja" flannel board story
"Little Annie Oakley"/"La pequeña Annie Oakley" flannel board story
"Wheels On the Bus"/"Ruedas del bus" flannel board story
"Roll On, Roll On"/"Rueda, rueda" flannel board story
"La piñata"/"The Piñata" action story
"A Spring Walk"/"Una caminata en primavera" action story
"Sing Me a Rainbow"/"Cántame un arco iris" flannel board story

"Candy Land Journey"/"Un viaje a la tierra del dulce" action story
"Ms. Bumblebee Gathers Honey"/"La avispa Zumbi lleve miel" prop story
"Las hormiguitas"/"The Little Ants" flannel board story
"Dog: A Mayan Legend"/"Perro: Una leyenda maya" flannel board story
"Party at Daisy's"/"Fiesta en casa de Daisy" flannel board story
"Old MacDonald"/"El viejo MacDonald" flannel board story
"Going On a Whale Watch"/"Vamos a mirar ballenas" action story
"Lion's Haircut"/"El corte de pelo del león" prop story
"Summer at the Beach"/"Verano en la playa" listening story

In ***The DLM Early Childhood Express***, lesson content is integrated into themes that reflect the world from children's evolving perspective. Organizing lessons in this way helps children to make connections and expand upon the knowledge and skills they have already achieved.

To find the topics that touch home with children the most, we turned to the real experts: their teachers. We held focus groups to learn what works in real Pre-K classrooms. We consulted national research studies and surveys on early childhood education, and we used our years of educational experience to bring it all together.

Developed with the Whole Child in Mind

With ***The DLM Early Childhood Express***, children develop concrete skills through experiences with music, art, storytelling, and teacher-directed lessons that, in addition to skills development, emphasize practice and reflection.

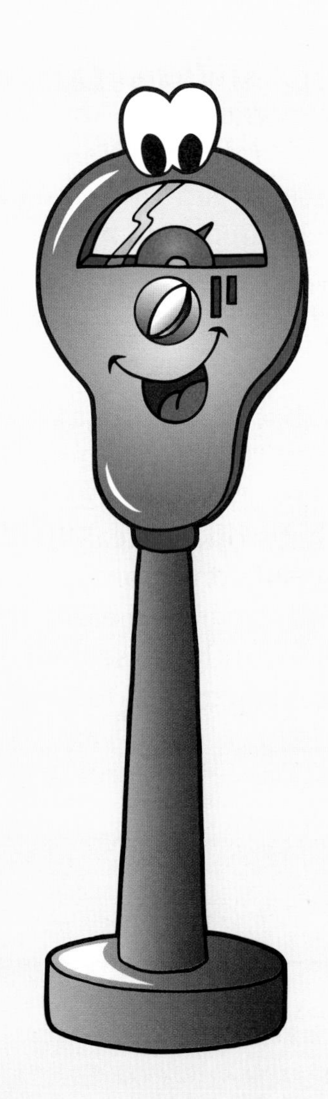

Literacy concepts, including:

- Listening Comprehension
- Vocabulary
- Verbal Expression
- Phonological Awareness
- Print and Book Awareness
- Letter Knowledge and Early Word Recognition
- Motivation to Read
- Developing Knowledge of Literary Form
- Written Expression

Math concepts, including:

- Number Concepts and Operations
- Patterns
- Geometry and Spatial Relations
- Measurement
- Classification and Data Collection

Theme
School Days
Physical Me
Thinking and Feeling Me
My Family
Fall/Autumn
Friends
Pets
Opposites
Color, Shape, and Size
Color, Shape, and Size
Things That Go Together
Under Construction
Growing Things
Food and Nutrition
Nursery Rhymes
Sound and Movement
Music
Winter
Community Workers
Traditional Tales
Traditional Tales
Cowgirls and Cowboys
Travel
Travel
Celebrations
Spring
Weather
Real and Make-Believe
Bugs
Bugs
Animals
Zoo Animals
Farm Animals
Ocean Life
Big Things
Summer Fun

Literacy Focuses		Math Focuses
Listening Comprehension		Classification and Data Collection
Listening Comprehension		Number and Operations
Vocabulary	Verbal Expression	Geometry and Spatial Sense
Print and Book Awareness	Developing Knowledge of Literary Forms	
Vocabulary	Verbal Expression	Geometry and Spatial Sense
Developing Knowledge of Literary Forms	Letter Knowledge and Early Word Recognition	
Phonological Awareness		
Verbal Expression	Listening Comprehension	Number and Operations
Phonological Awareness		
Verbal Expression	Developing Knowledge of Literary Forms	Number and Operations
Print and Book Awareness		
Phonological Awareness	Development of Knowledge of Literary Forms	Number and Operations
Vocabulary	Verbal Expression	
Vocabulary	Listening Comprehension	Number and Operations
Vocabulary	Listening Comprehension	Geometry and Spatial Sense
Verbal Expression	Print and Book Awareness	Classification and Data Collection
Phonological Awareness	Vocabulary	Geometry and Spatial Sense
Speech Production and Speech Discrimination		
Vocabulary		Number and Operations
Vocabulary		Geometry and Spatial Sense
Listening Comprehension		Number and Operations
Print and Book Awareness		Number and Operations
Phonological Awareness		Geometry and Spatial Sense
Verbal Expression	Listening Comprehension	Patterns
Print and Book Awareness	Motivation to Read	
Vocabulary		Patterns
Verbal Expression	Phonological Awareness	Geometry and Spatial Sense
Listening Comprehension	Verbal Expression	Number and Operations
Developing Knowledge of Literary Forms		Number and Operations
Letter Knowledge and Word Recognition	Verbal Expression	Measurement
Developing Knowledge of Literary Forms	Print and Book Awareness	
Verbal Expression	Listening Comprehension	Measurement
Verbal Expression	Vocabulary	Geometry and Spatial Sense
Vocabulary	Listening Comprehension	Patterns
Verbal Expression		Geometry and Spatial Sense
Verbal Expression		Number and Operations
Print and Book Awareness	Listening Comprehension	
Written Expression	Verbal Expression	Number and Operations
Speech Production and Speech Discrimination		
Phonological Awareness	Verbal Expression	Geometry and Spatial Sense
Developing Knowledge of Literary Forms	Verbal Expression	Number and Operations
Vocabulary; Letter Knowledge & Early Word Recognition	Developing Knowledge of Literary Forms	Number and Operations
Listening Comprehension	Print and Book Awareness	
Developing Knowledge of Literary Forms	Verbal Expression	Number and Operations
Vocabulary	Written Expression	
Motivation to Read	Written Expression	Number and Operations
Letter Knowledge and Early Word Recognition		
Print and Book Awareness	Written Expression	Classification and Data Collection
Phonological Awareness		
Phonological Awareness	Listening Comprehension	Classification and Data Collection
Developing Knowledge of Literary Forms		Patterns
Listening Comprehension	Vocabulary	Geometry and Spatial Sense
Developing Knowledge of Literary Forms	Phonological Awareness	
Verbal Expression		
Listening Comprehension	Vocabulary	Geometry and Spatial Sense
Developing Knowledge of Literary Forms	Written Expression	
Vocabulary	Listening Comprehension	Geometry and Spatial Sense
Print and Book Awareness		

Forging Connections in the

Objectives set the tone and direction for the lesson.

Vocabulary expands children's language capacity, giving them a better grasp of words.

A choice of **Activities** offers a variety of ways for children to build upon and enhance learning experiences.

A list of **Materials** makes preparation a snap.

Content Connection

Science

Objectives

To use one or more senses to observe and learn about objects, events, and organisms

To become increasingly sensitive to the sounds of spoken words

Vocabulary

drip-drop, pitter patter, splash, swoosh, swirl

goteo, golpeteo, salpicar, silbar, girar

DLM Materials

- *Teacher's Resource Anthology*
  "The Rain"/"La lluvia"
  "The Wind"/"El viento"

Materials to Gather

spray bottle, cookie sheet, water, sponge, baster, straws, paper plates, small paper sack

Activity 1

- Read "The Rain"/"La lluvia." Discuss the sounds of rain.
- Hand out a spray bottle, a cookie sheet, a tub of water, a sponge, and a baster. Invite the children to explore water sounds by spraying the water on the cookie sheet and into the tub. Challenge them to describe the sounds. Are the words they use examples of onomatopoeia? Encourage the children to splash the water and use the sponge and the baster to drip water.

  How does the water from the baster sound when it hits the surface of the water in the tub?

  ¿Cómo suena el agua cuando choca contra la superficie del agua en la bañera?

  Are the sounds examples of onomatopoeia (splish-splash, drip-drop, pitter patter)?

  ¿Los sonidos son ejemplos onomatopéyicos (plin plin, pun pun)?

Activity 2

- Read "The Wind"/"El viento." Discuss the sounds of wind.
- Provide a small sack, straws, paper plates, and a baster. Invite the children to make sounds that sound like wind. Challenge them to describe the sounds. Are the words they use examples of onomatopoeia? Encourage them to fill the bags with air and pop them. Have them fan the air with paper plates and blow through the straws.

World of Learning

Early learners are constantly making connections between what they know and what they have just learned. Cross-curricular connections are a powerful way to reinforce lesson concepts and expose children to the full spectrum of knowledge.

The challenge for teachers is to consistently integrate these connections into their lessons, and that can be a time-consuming task.

The DLM Early Childhood Express was designed to make it easy. Each lesson contains the most relevant cross-curricular Content Connections, presented as miniature lessons. You get everything you need to teach them effectively – all in one place.

Content Connection areas include:

Fine Arts:

Through art, children learn to express their thoughts, feelings, and ideas in symbolic ways.

Music & Movement:

Children learn to sing, play simple instruments, listen, and respond to music. They also begin to create and recreate moods and experiences in order to express their feelings through increasingly coordinated movement.

Science:

Science teaches children to observe, investigate, and draw conclusions about the world in a systematic way.

Social Studies:

Social studies teaches them to share, cooperate, and participate with others.

Health or Safety:

Lessons in health or safety help children make life choices that will enhance their physical well-being.

Physical Development:

Specially designed movement activities help children practice and improve their gross and fine motor skills as well as maintain personal space.

Personal and Social Development

Interwoven throughout the entire program, these activities enable children to develop a sense of who they are and their own capabilities to establish positive relationships with others.

Giving Children

Scaffolding Strategies

More Help Every child learns at a different pace, which is why flexible lesson plans are a must. This section offers suggestions, such as specific stories you can read, to help bring all children up to speed.

Extra Challenge Our ladder icons make scaffolding easy. Wherever they appear, you'll find strategies on how to adjust the pace or content of a lesson. When children are learning quickly, this section suggests additional activities to keep their interest engaged, such as thinking divergently about a specific topic (i.e., putting yourself in another person's place).

Teaching in a Diverse Classroom

Today's classrooms are diverse and exciting places to teach. Our children come from a range of ethnic and economic backgrounds and family situations. They bring to the classroom a wealth of culture and tradition.

As educators, we want all our children to see themselves in the activities we provide. The DLM Early Childhood Express:

Nurtures and celebrates children's cultural and ethnic heritages

Encourages children to share their traditions with each other

That is why we:

Actively support the continued development of children's home languages

Guide children as they learn English or Spanish as a second language

Make sure we are sensitive to all, so that every child feels comfortable in the classroom

a Sense of Community

There are many ways to create a positive home/school connection that will help support second-language learners. One is to let parents know how important it is to provide a rich language environment in their children's home languages. Encourage parents to talk, sing, read, and discuss books with their children in their home language – and to participate in community activities where the home language is spoken.

Another key strategy is to get parents (and families) involved in class activities. Take the time to get to know them. Listen to parents' ideas and share your positive comments about their children. Display the children's work, photos of them at school, and videotape the classroom activities to make parents feel at ease. Once they feel comfortable with you, parents can become powerful allies in addressing such issues as cultural conflict before they progress too far.

To effectively teach a second language, we must be able to make ourselves understood. In this, common sense is your best guide. Speak clearly at a natural pace. Use short, simple sentences, and pause between sentences to allow children to process your language. Link words and concepts with concrete objects, and paraphrase if children do not understand the first time around. Above all, remain alert and responsive to each child's needs. Acknowledge their attempts to communicate verbally or non-verbally in a conversational tone.

Diverse and multilingual classrooms are the way of the future. With the right approach, we can make them rich, supportive, and rewarding places to learn.

Teacher Editions That Simplify Your Day

The DLM Early Childhood Express Teacher Editions are easy to use. They provide a wealth of flexible and adaptable activities that help you customize lessons to fit the specific needs of your children.

Most themes are taught over a period of five days. Each day features circle group time that emphasizes Literacy and Math. Each Literacy and Math lesson is followed by a Content Connection that ties other curriculum areas, such as science, social studies, fine arts, physical development, health and safety, and personal and social

Every theme has an overview that provides a short description of what you and the children will encounter during the theme.

Each theme has three suggestions for Learning Centers that are intended to remain on-going for the duration of the theme. We often provide suggestions for altering the focus of children's play without altering the setup of the center.

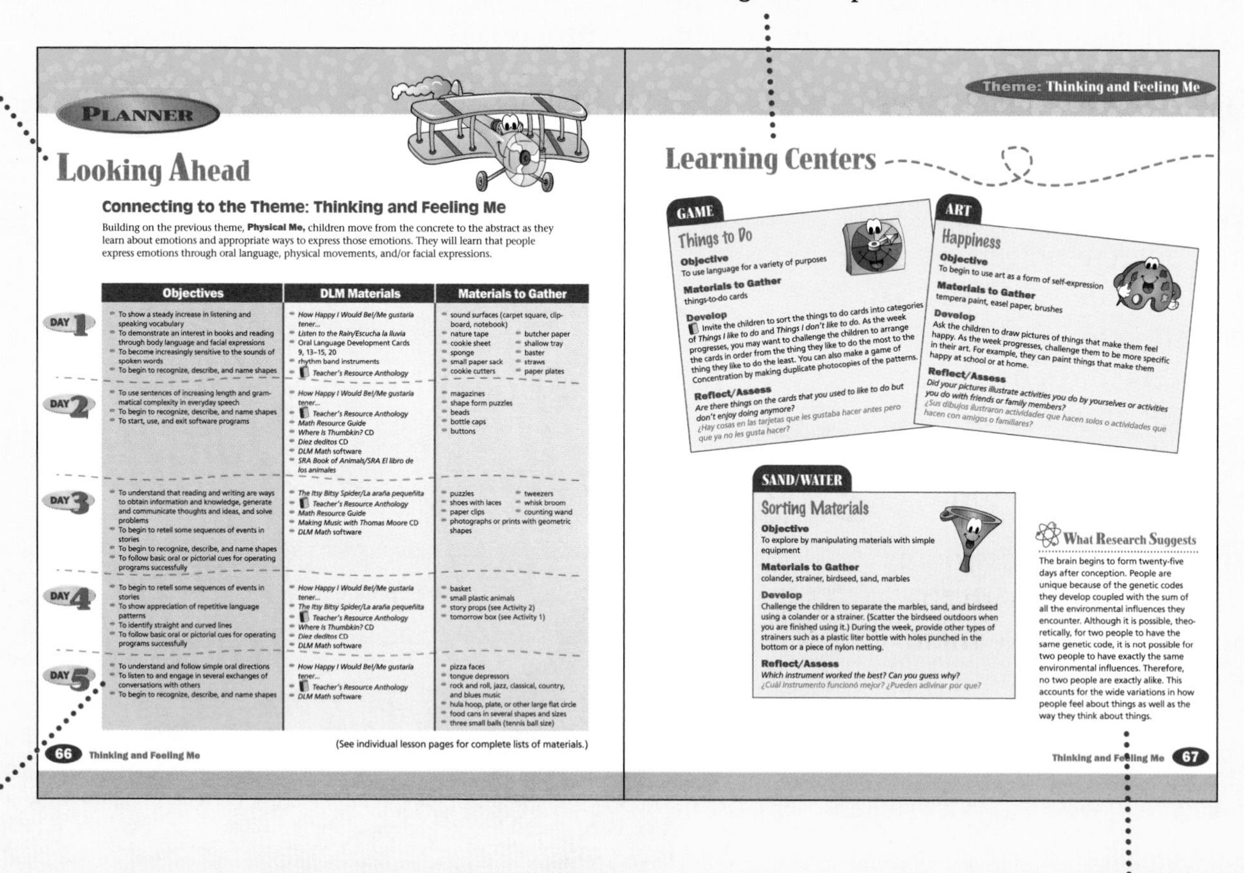

PLANNER

Looking Ahead

Connecting to the Theme: Thinking and Feeling Me

Building on the previous theme, **Physical Me,** children move from the concrete to the abstract as they learn about emotions and appropriate ways to express those emotions. They will learn that people express emotions through oral language, physical movements, and/or facial expressions.

	Objectives	DLM Materials	Materials to Gather
DAY 1	To show a steady increase in listening and speaking vocabulary To demonstrate an interest in books and reading through body language and facial expressions To become increasingly sensitive to the sounds of spoken words To begin to recognize, describe, and name shapes	*How Happy I Would Be!/Me gustaría tener...* *Listen to the Rain/Escucha la lluvia* Oral Language Development Cards 9, 13–15, 20 rhythm band instruments *Teacher's Resource Anthology*	sound surfaces (carpet square, clip-board, notebook) nature tape cookie sheet sponge small paper sack cookie cutters butcher paper shallow tray baster straws paper plates
DAY 2	To use sentences of increasing length and grammatical complexity in everyday speech To begin to recognize, describe, and name shapes To start, use, and exit software programs	*How Happy I Would Be!/Me gustaría tener...* *Teacher's Resource Anthology* *Math Resource Guide* *Where Is Thumbkin?* CD *Diez deditos* CD *DLM Math* software *SRA Book of Animals/SRA El libro de los animales*	magazines shape form puzzles beads bottle caps buttons
DAY 3	To understand that reading and writing are ways to obtain information and knowledge, generate and communicate thoughts and ideas, and solve problems To begin to retell some sequences of events in stories To begin to recognize, describe, and name shapes To follow basic oral or pictorial cues for operating programs successfully	*The Itsy Bitsy Spider/La araña pequeñita* *Teacher's Resource Anthology* *Math Resource Guide* *Making Music with Thomas Moore* CD *DLM Math* software	puzzles shoes with laces paper clips photographs or prints with geometric shapes tweezers whisk broom counting wand
DAY 4	To begin to retell some sequences of events in stories To show appreciation of repetitive language patterns To identify straight and curved lines To follow basic oral or pictorial cues for operating programs successfully	*How Happy I Would Be!/Me gustaría tener...* *The Itsy Bitsy Spider/La araña pequeñita* *Teacher's Resource Anthology* *Where Is Thumbkin?* CD *Diez deditos* CD *DLM Math* software	basket small plastic animals story props (see Activity 2) tomorrow box (see Activity 1)
DAY 5	To understand and follow simple oral directions To listen to and engage in several exchanges of conversations with others To begin to recognize, describe, and name shapes	*How Happy I Would Be!/Me gustaría tener...* *Teacher's Resource Anthology* *DLM Math* software	pizza faces tongue depressors rock and roll, jazz, classical, country, and blues music hula hoop, plate, or other large flat circle food cans in several shapes and sizes three small balls (tennis ball size)

(See individual lesson pages for complete lists of materials.)

66 Thinking and Feeling Me

Theme: Thinking and Feeling Me

Learning Centers

GAME

Things to Do

Objective
To use language for a variety of purposes

Materials to Gather
things-to-do cards

Develop
Invite the children to sort the things to do cards into categories of *Things I like to do* and *Things I don't like to do.* As the week progresses, you may want to challenge the children to arrange the cards in order from the thing they like to do the most to the thing they like to do the least. You can also make a game of Concentration by making duplicate photocopies of the patterns.

Reflect/Assess
Are there things on the cards that you used to like to do but don't enjoy doing anymore?
¿Hay cosas en las tarjetas que les gustaba hacer antes pero que ya no les gusta hacer?

ART

Happiness

Objective
To begin to use art as a form of self-expression

Materials to Gather
tempera paint, easel paper, brushes

Develop
Ask the children to draw pictures of things that make them feel happy. As the week progresses, challenge them to be more specific in their art. For example, they can paint things that make them happy at school or at home.

Reflect/Assess
Did your pictures illustrate activities you do by yourselves or activities you do with friends or family members?
¿Sus dibujos ilustraron actividades que hacen solos o actividades que hacen con amigos o familiares?

SAND/WATER

Sorting Materials

Objective
To explore by manipulating materials with simple equipment

Materials to Gather
colander, strainer, birdseed, sand, marbles

Develop
Challenge the children to separate the marbles, sand, and birdseed using a colander or a strainer. (Scatter the birdseed outdoors when you are finished using it.) During the week, provide other types of strainers such as a plastic liter bottle with holes punched in the bottom or a piece of nylon netting.

Reflect/Assess
Which instrument worked the best? Can you guess why?
¿Cuál instrumento funcionó mejor? ¿Pueden adivinar por que?

What Research Suggests

The brain begins to form twenty-five days after conception. People are unique because of the genetic codes they develop coupled with the sum of all the environmental influences they encounter. Although it is possible, theoretically, for two people to have the same genetic code, it is not possible for two people to have exactly the same environmental influences. Therefore, no two people are exactly alike. This accounts for the wide variations in how people feel about things as well as the way they think about things.

Thinking and Feeling Me 67

An overview of the theme's objectives and materials allows you to see at a glance what the children will be learning and the materials you will need to gather.

Each theme has a statement from emerging neuroscience research that connects or supports the lessons and activities the children will encounter as the theme unfolds.

development, to the lesson using theme and lesson objectives. The Connections provide meaningful context that helps children make sense of what they are learning.

In addition to the Teacher Editions, ***The DLM Early Childhood Express*** includes a **Teacher's Resource Anthology** with more than 500 pages of thematic songs, recipes, patterns, and finger plays. The DLM system is further enhanced by the Resource Guides–**Spanish Phonics**, **English Phonics**, **Math**, and **Home Connections**. See the ladder icon for simple **Scaffolding Strategies** that help you meet the individual needs of your children.

The **Second Language Learners** section offers teaching strategies that help children of all language backgrounds and abilities meet the lesson objectives.

Use the **Anthology Support** to find additional resources to enhance your lessons.

Our **Teacher Editions** are organized by theme and by day. **Objectives** set the direction of the lesson. **Begin the Day** gives children time to adjust to the environment and develop a sense of community with classmates. It also provides an opportunity for a daily literacy activity such as singing about the days of the week or writing the news of the day.

Each theme contains easy to follow literacy lessons that always follow the same four steps: Focus, Develop, Practice, and Reflect/Assess.

Our English/Spanish **Vocabulary** section highlights words that may be new. This helps expand children's ability to use both languages.

The **Materials** section tells you everything you need to gather (and assemble) in advance. No more last-minute surprises!

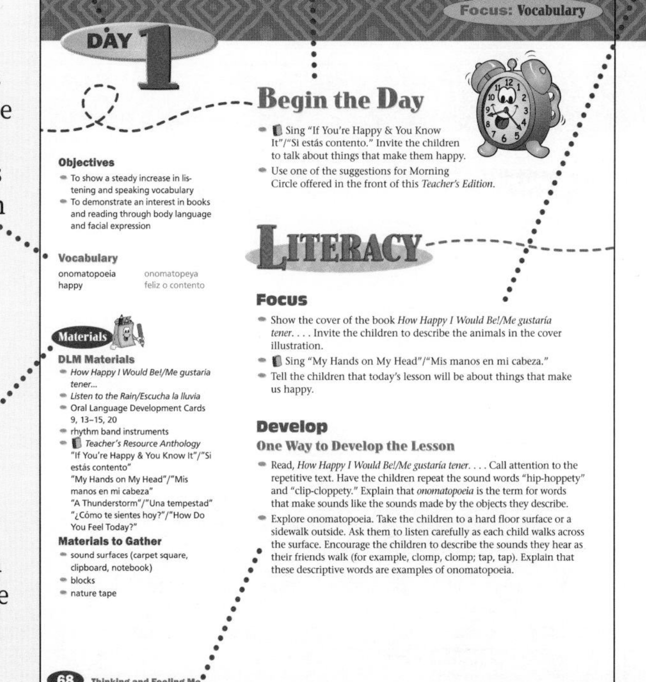
Focus: Vocabulary

DAY 1

Objectives
- To show a steady increase in listening and speaking vocabulary
- To demonstrate an interest in books and reading through body language and facial expression

Vocabulary

onomatopoeia — onomatopeya
happy — feliz o contento

Materials

DLM Materials
- *How Happy I Would Be!/Me gustaria tener...*
- *Listen to the Rain/Escucha la lluvia*
- Oral Language Development Cards 9, 13–15, 20
- rhythm band instruments
- *Teacher's Resource Anthology*
  "If You're Happy & You Know It"/"Si estás contento"
  "My Hands on My Head"/"Mis manos en mi cabeza"
  "A Thunderstorm"/"Una tempestad"
  "¿Cómo te sientes hoy?"/"How Do You Feel Today?"

Materials to Gather
- sound surfaces (carpet square, clipboard, notebook)
- blocks
- nature tape

Begin the Day
- Sing "If You're Happy & You Know It"/"Si estás contento." Invite the children to talk about things that make them happy.
- Use one of the suggestions for Morning Circle offered in the front of this *Teacher's Edition*.

LITERACY

Focus
- Show the cover of the book *How Happy I Would Be!/Me gustaría tener. . . .* Invite the children to describe the animals in the cover illustration.
- Sing "My Hands on My Head"/"Mis manos en mi cabeza."
- Tell the children that today's lesson will be about things that make us happy.

Develop

One Way to Develop the Lesson
- Read, *How Happy I Would Be!/Me gustaría tener. . . .* Call attention to the repetitive text. Have the children repeat the sound words "hip-hoppety" and "clip-cloppety." Explain that *onomatopoeia* is the term for words that make sounds like the sounds made by the objects they describe.
- Explore onomatopoeia. Take the children to a hard floor surface or a sidewalk outside. Ask them to listen carefully as each child walks across the surface. Encourage the children to describe the sounds they hear as their friends walk (for example, clomp, clomp; tap, tap). Explain that these descriptive words are examples of onomatopoeia.

68 Thinking and Feeling Me

Theme: Thinking and Feeling Me

Another Way to Develop the Lesson
- Write the rhyme "A Thunderstorm"/"Una tempestad" on chart paper and read it.
- Ask the children how they feel during thunderstorms. Explore their answers. If any children express fear of storms, discuss this calmly, reassuring them that their fears are natural. Emphasize that they needn't be afraid.

  Why do you think thunder is so loud?

  ¿Por qué creen que el trueno hace tanto ruido?
- Tell the children that the rhyme is full of examples of onomatopoeia. Ask them to help you identify the words that sound like the things they describe. Use a marker to underline those words.

Practice
- Invite the children to explore sounds by providing several different surfaces (for example, a carpet square, clipboard, notebook, piece of wood, and so on) and asking the children to tap on them. Encourage them to describe how the sounds change with each surface. Do their descriptions of the sounds include examples of onomatopoeia?
- Provide Oral Language Cards 9, 13, 14, 15, and 20. Challenge the children to describe the sounds that each animal makes with its mouth or when it moves.
- Give the children the rhythm band instruments. Have them think of onomatopoeic words to describe the sounds the instruments make.
- Have the children draw pictures of how they feel during thunderstorms.
- Place a nature tape in the listening center. Encourage the children to listen for sounds that are examples of onomatopoeia.

Preparation
- Prepare the "¿Cómo te sientes hoy?"/"How Do You Feel Today?" flannel board story.

Scaffolding Strategies

More Help Encourage children to think of sound words. Read some of the selections in the *Anthology* that use onomatopoeia such as "Six White Ducks"/"Los seis patos blancos" or "Clickety, Clickety, Clack."

Extra Challenge Brainstorm a list of words that illustrate onomatopoeia.

Second Language Learners

After children have sorted the things-to-do cards, ask open-ended questions. *Who reads to you at home?/¿Quién lee contigo en casa?* If children have a more basic level of second language proficiency, try using two choices: *Does Trinh or your mom read to you?*

Anthology Support

"Smart Cookie's Best Friend, Gabby Graham"
"Gabby Graham, la mejor amiga de Smart Cookie"
"Clickety, Clickety Clack"
"Old MacDonald"
"El viejo MacDonald"

Day 1 69

The **Preparation** section points out what needs to be done in advance of the lesson.

See the ladder icon for simple **Scaffolding Strategies** that help you meet the individual needs of the children.

The **Second Language Learners** section offers teaching strategies that help children of all language backgrounds and abilities meet the lesson objectives.

A choice of strategies allows you to adjust each lesson to fit your schedule. You can select the method that most appeals to you or use both for added support. If you teach in a dual-language classroom, teach one activity in each language. If you teach in a full day program, do one in the morning and the other in the afternoon.

Practice activities – vitally important to the success of our lessons – provide opportunities for children to apply the information they have just learned. You can choose which of these you want to use or try them all.

Visit **Anthology Support** for additional resources to enrich your lessons.

Teacher Edition

The DLM Early Childhood Express Teacher Editions are easy to use. They provide a wealth of flexible and adaptable activities that help you customize lessons to fit the specific needs of your children.

Some examples of items that will help customize your literacy lessons are shown on this spread.

Letter Knowledge addresses the first four weeks, when schoolchildren are introduced to the alphabet. Then, continuing with the fifth week's unit, there's a focus on individual letters.

Reflect/Assess questions help children think about possible applications of what they have learned in the lesson.

Teacher Notes provide special information about the lesson that may help you better understand its content or format.

Letter Knowledge provides suggestions for helping children learn to recognize the letters of the alphabet.

Reflect/Assess questions are part of every lesson.

Suggested Reading provides a list of books that tie to the theme or the objective of the day's lesson.

Teacher's Notes

Focus: Vocabulary

DAY 1

Letter Knowledge

English/Spanish

- Sing "The ABC Song" or "La canción del abecedario."
- Encourage the children to play with the magnetic letters.
- Display *Alphabet Wall Cards*.

Suggested Reading

Barnyard Banter by Denise Fleming
The Snowy Day by Ezra Jack Keats
La felicidad tiene sabor a miel by Giles Andreae and Vanessa Cabban

Teacher's NOTE

Don't hesitate to introduce the word *onomatopoeia*. Children love the sound of it and will learn it easily.

Reflect/Assess

- *How did the sounds change when you tapped on different surfaces?*
  ¿Cómo cambiaron los sonidos cuando golpearon diferentes superficies?
- *What sounds might we make when we run? Are these examples of onomatopoeia?*
  ¿Qué sonidos podemos producir cuando corremos? ¿Son ejemplos onomatopéyicos?
- *Can you think of some sounds you make when you're happy? What are some onomatopoeic words that can be used for laughing? (ha-ha, tee-hee)*
  ¿Pueden pensar en algunos sonidos que hacen cuando están contentos? ¿Cuáles son algunas palabras onomatopéyicas que se pueden usar para la risa? (ja ja ja, ji ji ji)

Literacy Circle

Storytime 1

- Read *Listen to the Rain/Escucha la lluvia. What does it smell like outdoors after it rains?*
  ¿A qué huele afuera después de llover?
  How does it feel outdoors after it rains?
  ¿Cómo se siente afuera después de llover?
- Reread the story. Ask the children to help you find examples of onomatopoeia.

Storytime 2

- Present the "¿Cómo te sientes hoy?"/"How Do You Feel Today?" flannel board story. Ask the children to add lines to the story.

70 Thinking and Feeling Me

Theme: Thinking and Feeling Me

Content Connection

Science

Objectives

To use one or more senses to observe and learn about objects, events, and organisms
To become increasingly sensitive to the sounds of spoken words

Vocabulary

drip-drop, pitter patter, splash, swoosh, swirl
goteo, golpeteo, salpicar, silbar, girar

DLM Materials

- *Teacher's Resource Anthology*
  "The Rain"/"La lluvia"
  "The Wind"/"El viento"

Materials to Gather

spray bottle, cookie sheet, water, sponge, baster, straws, paper plates, small paper sack

Activity 1

- Read "The Rain"/"La lluvia." Discuss the sounds of rain.
- Hand out a spray bottle, a cookie sheet, a tub of water, a sponge, and a baster. Invite the children to explore water sounds by spraying the water on the cookie sheet and into the tub. Challenge them to describe the sounds. Are the words they use examples of onomatopoeia? Encourage the children to splash the water and use the sponge and the baster to drip water.
  How does the water from the baster sound when it hits the surface of the water in the tub?
  ¿Cómo suena el agua cuando choca contra la superficie del agua en la bañera?
  Are the sounds examples of onomatopoeia (splish-splash, drip-drop, pitter patter)?
  ¿Los sonidos son ejemplos onomatopéyicos (plin plin, pun pun)?

Activity 2

- Read "The Wind"/"El viento." Discuss the sounds of wind.
- Provide a small sack, straws, paper plates, and a baster. Invite the children to make sounds that sound like wind. Challenge them to describe the sounds. Are the words they use examples of onomatopoeia? Encourage them to fill the bags with air and pop them. Have them fan the air with paper plates and blow through the straws.

Day 1 71

Content Connections are mini-lessons or center ideas that tie the lesson to other areas of the curriculum such as physical development, science, social studies and fine arts.

Literacy Circle has two storytime suggestions. Choose one or use both.

Teacher Edition

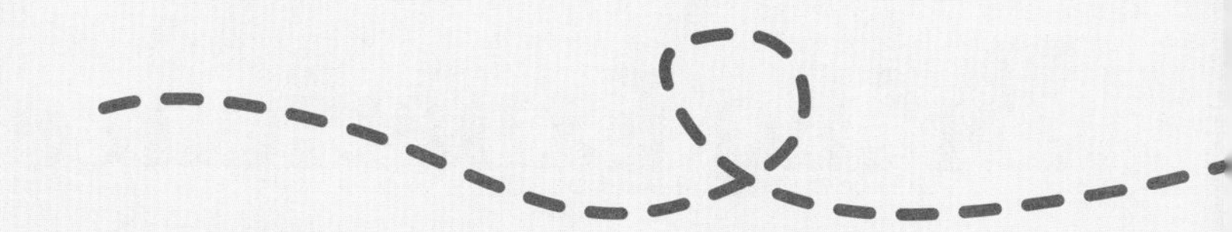

The content of Math lessons throughout the program is supported by research. To help plan your lesson further, **Objectives**, **Vocabulary** and **Preparation** tips are provided. And when new games and activities on the *DLM Math* software are introduced, suggestions for helping the children navigate the software appear in the **Develop** portion of the lesson.

Two suggestions for **Music and Movement** are offered for every day. You can choose one or both. **Content Connections** tie the math lesson to other areas of the curriculum, such as fine arts, science, social studies, health and safety, and physical development. And to finish up the lesson, **Reflect on the Day** helps the children recap the day, think about what has been learned, and discuss applications of the new information.

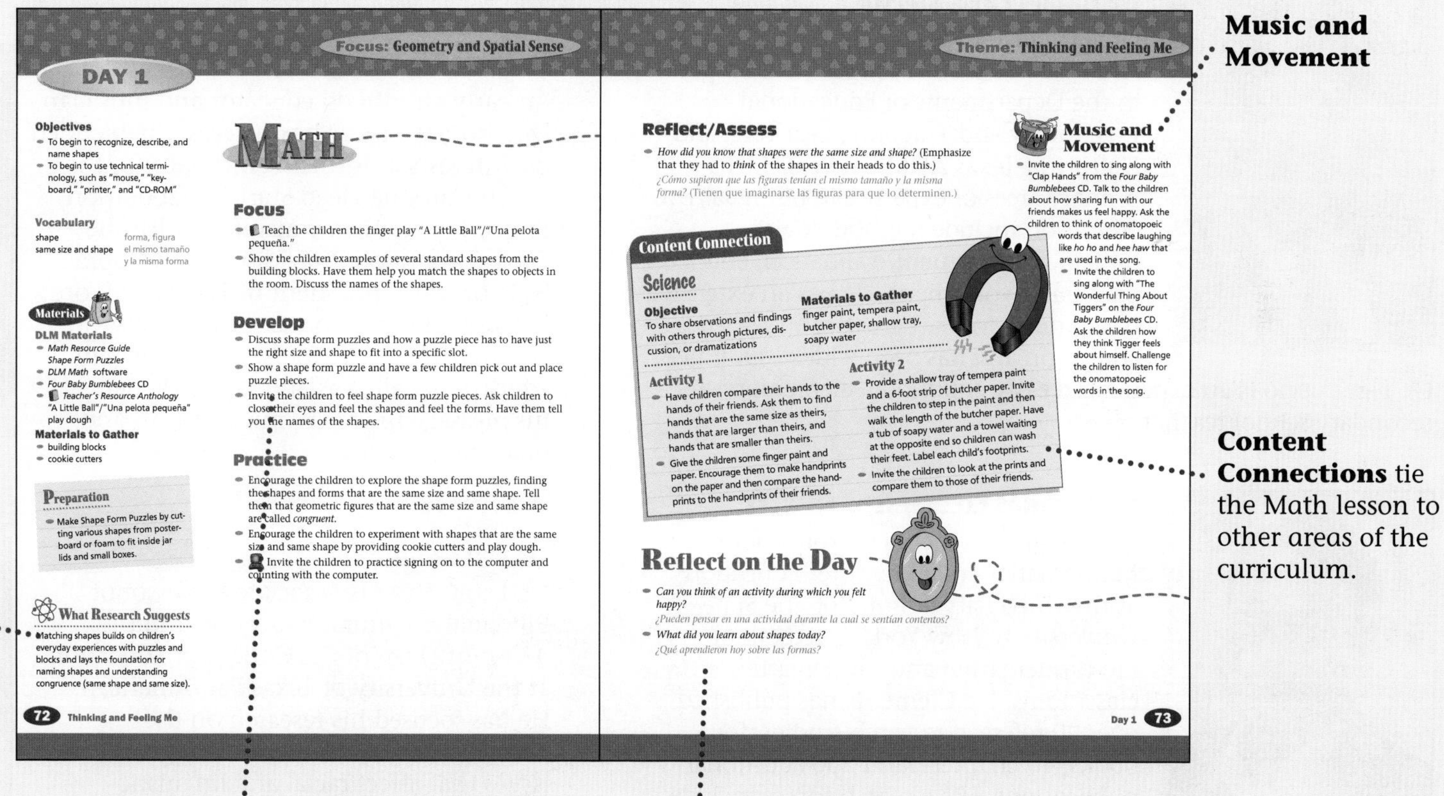

Focus: Geometry and Spatial Sense

DAY 1

Objectives
- To begin to recognize, describe, and name shapes
- To begin to use technical terminology, such as "mouse," "keyboard," "printer," and "CD-ROM"

Vocabulary

shape	forma, figura
same size and shape	el mismo tamaño y la misma forma

Materials

DLM Materials
- *Math Resource Guide*
  Shape Form Puzzles
- *DLM Math* software
- *Four Baby Bumblebees* CD
- *Teacher's Resource Anthology* "A Little Ball"/"Una pelota pequeña" play dough

Materials to Gather
- building blocks
- cookie cutters

Preparation
- Make Shape Form Puzzles by cutting various shapes from posterboard or foam to fit inside jar lids and small boxes.

What Research Suggests
- Matching shapes builds on children's everyday experiences with puzzles and blocks and lays the foundation for naming shapes and understanding congruence (same shape and same size).

MATH

Focus
- Teach the children the finger play "A Little Ball"/"Una pelota pequeña."
- Show the children examples of several standard shapes from the building blocks. Have them help you match the shapes to objects in the room. Discuss the names of the shapes.

Develop
- Discuss shape form puzzles and how a puzzle piece has to have just the right size and shape to fit into a specific slot.
- Show a shape form puzzle and have a few children pick out and place puzzle pieces.
- Invite the children to feel shape form puzzle pieces. Ask children to close their eyes and feel the shapes and feel the forms. Have them tell you the names of the shapes.

Practice
- Encourage the children to explore the shape form puzzles, finding the shapes and forms that are the same size and same shape. Tell them that geometric figures that are the same size and same shape are called *congruent*.
- Encourage the children to experiment with shapes that are the same size and same shape by providing cookie cutters and play dough.
- Invite the children to practice signing on to the computer and counting with the computer.

72 Thinking and Feeling Me

Theme: Thinking and Feeling Me

Reflect/Assess
- *How did you know that shapes were the same size and shape?* (Emphasize that they had to *think* of the shapes in their heads to do this.)
  ¿Cómo supieron que las figuras tenían el mismo tamaño y la misma forma? (Tienen que imaginarse las figuras para que lo determinen.)

Content Connection

Science

Objective
To share observations and findings with others through pictures, discussion, or dramatizations

Materials to Gather
finger paint, tempera paint, butcher paper, shallow tray, soapy water

Activity 1
- Have children compare their hands to the hands of their friends. Ask them to find hands that are the same size as theirs, hands that are larger than theirs, and hands that are smaller than theirs.
- Give the children some finger paint and paper. Encourage them to make handprints on the paper and then compare the handprints to the handprints of their friends.

Activity 2
- Provide a shallow tray of tempera paint and a 6-foot strip of butcher paper. Invite the children to step in the paint and then walk the length of the butcher paper. Have a tub of soapy water and a towel waiting at the opposite end so children can wash their feet. Label each child's footprints.
- Invite the children to look at the prints and compare them to those of their friends.

Music and Movement
- Invite the children to sing along with "Clap Hands" from the *Four Baby Bumblebees* CD. Talk to the children about how sharing fun with our friends makes us feel happy. Ask the children to think of onomatopoeic words that describe laughing like *ho ho* and *hee haw* that are used in the song.
- Invite the children to sing along with "The Wonderful Thing About Tiggers" on the *Four Baby Bumblebees* CD. Ask the children how they think Tigger feels about himself. Challenge the children to listen for the onomatopoeic words in the song.

Reflect on the Day
- *Can you think of an activity during which you felt happy?*
  ¿Pueden pensar en una actividad durante la cual se sentían contentos?
- *What did you learn about shapes today?*
  ¿Qué aprendieron hoy sobre las formas?

Day 1 73

Music and Movement

The research that supports the content of ***The DLM Early Childhood Express*** math lessons is provided throughout the program.

Content Connections tie the Math lesson to other areas of the curriculum.

The **Develop** portion of the Math lesson provides information, demonstrations, and activities to help teach the lesson objectives.

Reflect on the Day appears every day.

Bring Experience and Research

Dr. Pam Schiller

Dr. Pam Schiller is Senior National Early Childhood Consultant for SRA/McGraw-Hill and a past president of the Southern Early Childhood Association. She is the author of numerous award-winning teacher resource materials and children's books. Her areas of expertise include applications of neuroscience research, charter education, and curriculum development. She shares her extensive knowledge through workshops, radio and television interviews, and keynote speeches.

Dr. Rafael Lara-Alecio

Dr. Rafael Lara-Alecio is Associate Professor and Director of the Bilingual/ESL Programs in the Departments of Educational Psychology and Teaching, Learning, and Culture at Texas A&M University. His primary areas of expertise in bilingual/ESL education include methodologies, biliteracy, assessment/evaluation, and parental involvement. He has an extensive background in mathematics and science education and has been widely published. Dr. Lara-Alecio is an experienced early childhood, elementary, and secondary school teacher.

Dr. Douglas Clements

Dr. Douglas Clements is Professor of Mathematics and Computer Education at the University at Buffalo, The State University of New York. A veteran of Pre-Kindergarten and Kindergarten classrooms, Dr. Clements has published over 90 refereed research studies, four books, 40 chapters, and 250 additional publications. His research topics include the early development of mathematical ideas, the effects of social interactions on learning, and the use of computer applications in mathematics education. He is currently working on several National Science Foundation projects.

Dr. Julie Sarama

Dr. Julie Sarama is an Assistant Professor of Mathematics Education at the University at Buffalo, The State University of New York. She is currently the Principal or Co-Principal Investigator for projects funded by the National Science Foundation on professional development, research-based materials development, and Pre-Kindergarten math. Dr. Sarama has taught mathematics enrichment classes at the Pre-Kindergarten and Kindergarten levels. She is also co-author of the award-winning *Turtle Math*.

Thomas Moore

An early childhood educator and musician, Dr. Thomas Moore has successfully blended his interests as former coordinator of the North Carolina Head Start Collaboration Project, on-camera consultant with the Early Childhood Professional Development Network, and president of Thomas Moore Records. He has produced numerous children's learning tools, including eight educational albums and tapes. He delivers his message in words, music, print, and practice.

Dr. Leo Gómez

Dr. Leo Gómez is Associate Professor of Bilingual-Bicultural Education and the Assistant Dean of the College of Education at the University of Texas Pan American. He has focused his research on the curriculum, assessment, and language issues that affect racial and linguistic minority populations. Dr. Gómez has been extensively involved in the development, implementation and assessment of two-way bilingual education programs in Texas.

Into Your Classroom

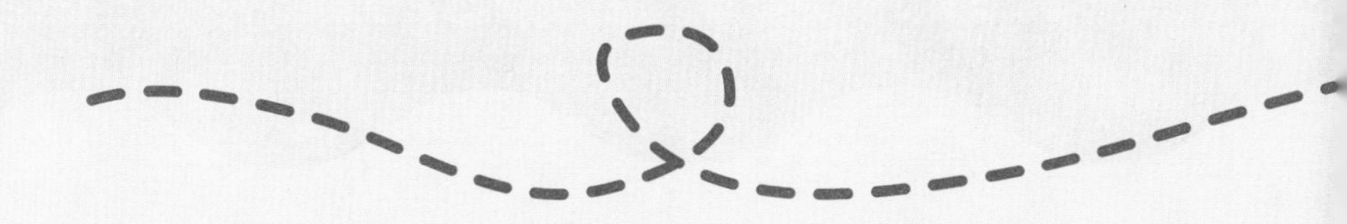

Dr. Beverly J. Irby
Dr. Beverly J. Irby is Professor and Director of the Center for Research and Doctoral Studies in the Department of Educational Leadership and Counseling at Sam Houston State University. She has held several leadership positions in bilingual education. In her research, writing, and presentations, Dr. Irby has explored issues in administration, curriculum development, and gifted and early childhood education.

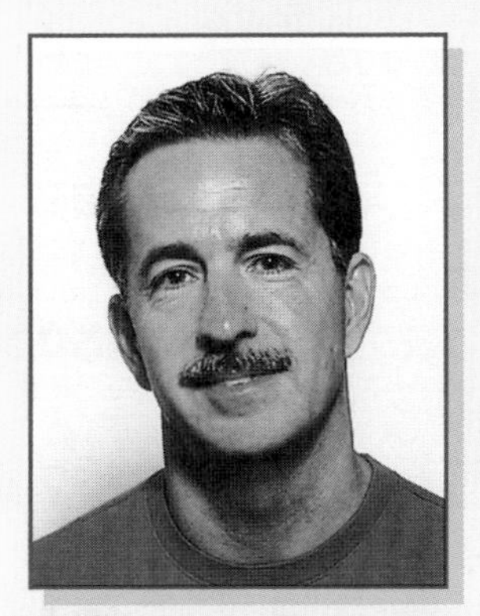

John Funk
John Funk is Adjunct Professor of Children's Literature at the University of Utah. He has extensive teaching expertise in Pre-Kindergarten, Kindergarten, and Grades 1 and 2. He is past president of the Utah Association for the Education of Young Children, and in 1996 he became the first Kindergarten teacher to be named Utah Teacher of the Year.

Dr. Patricia Phipps
Dr. Patricia Phipps is the Executive Director of the California Association for the Education of Young Children. She has served as a faculty member in the Graduate School of Education at George Mason University and the College of Education at the University of Houston. Her areas of expertise include multiple intelligences, brain research implications, multicultural and cross-cultural issues, and family/school/community connections in the early childhood field.

Contributing Writers

Dr. Amie Mitchell Beckett
Dr. Amie Mitchell Beckett is a Professor of Early Childhood Education at the University of Texas at San Antonio. She has served as an early childhood specialist at the state and national levels, with the Texas Education Agency, the U.S. Department of Education, and various professional organizations.

Maria Galindo
Maria Galindo has served as a teacher, educational psychologist and assistant principal in Mexico. She is now Early Literacy Specialist in the Head Start program at Houston's Aldine Independent School District.

Dr. Linda Rodriguez
Dr. Linda Rodriguez has been an educator for 16 years, and for the past four years she has served as principal of a Pre-Kindergarten school in Houston's Aldine Independent School District. Her areas of expertise include curriculum alignment and the early identification of talent among Pre-Kindergarten children.

Dr. Alma Flor Ada
Dr. Alma Flor Ada is Director of Doctoral Studies for the Multicultural Program, School of Education, University of San Francisco, California. She received her doctorate from Pontificia Universidad Catolica del Peru, Lima, Peru. Dr. Ada was the founder and the first Editor-in-Chief of the Journal of the National Association for Bilingual Education. She is a widely published author and frequent speaker about topics concerning bilingual education.

Program Reviewers

Sue Bredekamp - Council for Professional Recognition, Washington, DC • **Mary Carr-Wilt** - Director of 21st Century Grant, Longview, WA • **Peggy Freedson-Gonzalez** - University of Texas, Austin, TX Center for Reading and Language Arts • **Charlotte Hollarn** - Director, Center for Early Childhood Professional Development, Moore, OK • **Jodi Martin** - Children's World, CO • **Nancy Mayes** - Richardson ISD, Richardson, TX • **Cherene McDonald** - Channelview ISD, Houston, TX • **Ruth Meza** - Dallas ISD, Dallas, TX • **Lizette Rodriguez** - Judson ISD, San Antonio, TX • **Gail Rowe** - Program Director of Head Start Programs Dayton, OH • **Robin Stephenson** - Director, The Association for Christian Schools International, Colorado Springs, CO

Table of Contents

Teacher's Edition 

Morning Circle Suggestions

Below are a few suggestions for the Begin the Day Morning Circles. You might use them on a rotation basis, or use one of them for a while and then change to a new approach. You might also want to develop your own strategy by mixing and matching the suggestions below.

#1 Ask the children what day of the week it is. When they respond, tell them that you are going to write a sentence that tells everyone what day of the week it is. Print "Today is Monday" on a piece of chart paper or on a chalkboard. Look on your Helper Chart to find the name of today's helper. Let the children help you locate the name. Print another sentence: "Today's helper is Miguel." Ask the helper to come forward and find the magnetic letters that spell his or her name.

As the year progresses, you might want to have the helper find the magnetic letters that spell the day of the week. Eventually some children may be able to copy the entire sentence with magnetic letters.

When writing your sentences, you might want to make capital letters that begin sentences green (to indicate that they start the sentence) and periods red (to indicate that they stop the sentence).

#2 Print "Today is ______" on the chalkboard or on a piece of chart paper. Ask the children to help you fill in the blank. Print the day of the week in the blank. Invite the children to look at a calendar to determine today's date. Write the date under the sentence that tells what day of the week it is. Invite the children to clap out the syllables of both the sentence and the date.

#3 Make happy- and sad-face puppets for each child by cutting yellow circles from construction paper and drawing happy and sad faces on them. Laminate the faces, and glue them to tongue depressors. Cover two large coffee cans. On one can glue a happy face, and write the sentence "I feel happy today." Glue the sad face to the second can, and write the sentence "I feel sad today."

Give each child a happy- and a sad-face puppet. Encourage the children to tell how they feel today and to hold up the appropriate puppet. Encourage the children to come forward and place their puppets in the can that represents their feelings. For example, if Gabrielle says she feels happy today, she will place her puppet in the can with the happy face. Later in the year you can add puppets to represent other emotions.

You can vary this activity by using a graph titled "How I Feel Today"/"Como me siento hoy." Have the children place their puppets in the appropriate column on the graph instead of in the cans.

#4 Print the words to the "Days of the Week Song"/"Canción de los dias de la semana" on a piece of chart paper. Sing it with the children. Ask a volunteer to tell what day of the week it is. As the children become more familiar with the written days, you can ask the volunteer to show you on the chart what day of the week it is.

#5 Provide a large calendar. Ask the children what day of the week it was yesterday. When they respond, ask them what day it is today. Place a seasonal sticker on today's date. Have the children follow your lead and recite: "Yesterday was Monday, September 12. Today is Tuesday, September 13. Tomorrow will be Wednesday, September 14."

Ask the children how many days are in the month of September. Count the squares on the September calendar. You may want to use a Weather Wheel with this activity and sing the "Weather Song"/"Canción del tiempo."

You can also sing "Months of the Year"/"Los meses del año."

Looking Ahead

Connecting to the Theme: Real and Make-Believe

Although pre-kindergartners typically have a well-functioning imagination, it is vital to help them recognize the difference between reality and fantasy. Through discussions of various literature selections, children should begin to think about what makes certain events in these stories true or false.

	Objectives	DLM Materials	Materials to Gather
DAY 1	• To connect information and events in books to real-life experiences • To ask questions and make comments about the information and events from books • To put together puzzles of increasing complexity • To begin to investigate and predict the results of putting together two or more shapes • To use a variety of software packages with audio, video, and graphics	• *Guess Who?/Adivina quién . . .* • *Hurray for Pre-K!/¡Qué viva el preescolar!* • *The Zebra on the Zyder Zee/Una aventura en alta mar* • *Teacher's Resource Anthology* • *DLM Math* software • *Where Is Thumbkin?* CD • *Diez deditos* CD	• two posterboards • magazines • basket of real and imaginary items • chenille wires cut • geoboards and rubber bands (optional) • overhead projector and sets of translucent shapes (optional) • beanbags
DAY 2	• To ask questions and make comments related to the current topic of discussion • To become increasingly familiar with narrative forms and its elements by identifying characters and predicting events, plot, and the resolution of a story • To put together puzzles of increasing complexity • To begin to recognize, describe, and name shapes	• Oral Language Cards 6, 8, 18, 22, 28 • *The Dragon's Coming After You/El dragón te está persiguiendo* • *Teacher's Resource Anthology* • *Math Resource Guide* • *Four Baby Bumblebees* CD • *Diez deditos* CD	• coat hanger tubes • yarn • sheet • green powdered drink mix • fabric scraps • plastic zoo animals • masking tape in different colors
DAY 3	• To ask questions and make comments about the information and events from books • To put together puzzles of increasing complexity • To begin to recognize, describe, and name shapes	• *The Dragon's Coming After You/El dragón te está persiguiendo* • *Teacher's Resource Anthology* • *Math Resource Guide* • *DLM Math* software • *Wordsong/Canto de palabras*	• empty green soda bottle • hook and loop tape • rock salt • funnel • food coloring • masking tape in different colors
DAY 4	• To begin to retell some sequences of events in stories • To become increasingly familiar with narrative form and its elements by identifying characters and predicting events, plot, and the resolution of a story • To begin to recognize, describe, and name shapes	• *Teacher's Resource Anthology* • pattern blocks • *Math Resource Guide* • *DLM Math* software • *Where Is Thumbkin?* CD • *Esta es mi tierra* CD	• one-half liter bottle • brown felt donkey ears • glitter • headband • pillows • dried peas • family traditional tales tapes from Traditional Tales • masking tape in different colors • straws
DAY 5	• To become increasingly familiar with narrative form and its elements by identifying characters and predicting events, plot, and the resolution of a story • To begin to investigate and predict the results of putting together two or more shapes	• *The Dragon's Coming After You/El dragón te está persiguiendo* • *Teacher's Resource Anthology* • pattern blocks • *Math Resource Guide* • *DLM Math* software	• blank puzzles from white poster board • basket of small items • clothespins • masking tape in different colors • reproductions of works of art

(See individual lesson pages for complete lists of materials.)

Learning Centers

DRAMATIC PLAY

Dressing Up

Objective
To begin to engage in dramatic play with others

Materials to Gather
costumes

Develop
Fill the center with a variety of costumes. If possible, include a full-length mirror. Encourage the children to mix and match costumes. Observe whether they experiment with many costumes or continue to play with the same costumes every day.

Reflect/Assess
Who did you pretend to be when you tried on the different costumes?
¿A quién imitaban cuando se probaron diferentes disfraces?

ART

Imaginary Creatures

Objective
To use different colors, surface textures, and shapes to create form and meaning

Materials to Gather
tempera paints
beads, buttons, pipe cleaners, rickrack, and so on
play dough

Develop
Invite the children to spend the week creating imaginary creatures on paper as well as making them out of play dough. Invite them to name their creatures and have them make up personalities for them.

Reflect/Assess
What types of creatures did you make? How do your creatures act?
¿Qué tipos de criaturas hicieron? ¿Cómo se comportan las criaturas?

MUSIC AND MOVEMENT

Making Shadows

Objective
To begin to create or re-create stories, moods, or experiences through dramatic representations

Materials to Gather
light source

Develop
Set up a light source such as an overhead projector. Invite the children to create imaginary creatures on the wall by making shadows with their bodies in the space between the projector and the wall. Discuss the concept of shadows. Observe the children's creativity and whether they try to work together to create a creature shadow.

Reflect/Assess
What kinds of creature shadows did you make? Describe them.
¿Qué tipos de sombras de criaturas hicieron? Descríbanlos.

What Research Suggests

The ability to recognize patterns is related to the use of people's imaginations. The better a person's understanding of patterns, the greater is one's ability to rearrange those patterns into make-believe patterns. The greater one's understanding of spatial relationships, the better he or she is able to manipulate them into new and creative works of art. The better one's understanding of patterns of physical movement, the greater is one's ability to create new and unusual

DAY 1

Objectives

- To connect information and events in books to real-life experiences
- To ask questions and make comments about the information and events from books

Vocabulary

real	real
make-believe	de mentira o imaginario
imaginary	imaginario
imagination	imaginación
fiction	ficción
nonfiction	no ficción o didáctica(o)

DLM Materials

- *Guess Who?/Adivina quién . . .*
- *Hurray for Pre-K!/¡Qué viva el preescolar!*
- *The Zebra on the Zyder Zee/Una aventura en alta mar*
- *Teacher's Resource Anthology*
  "Catalina Magnalina"/"Catalina Magnalina"
  "Three Little Kittens"/"Los tres gatitos"

Materials to Gather

- drawing paper
- two posterboards
- magazines
- basket of objects or pictures that represent real and imaginary items

Begin the Day

- Sing "Catalina Magnalina"/"Catalina Magnalina." Ask: *Is Catalina a real person or a make-believe person?*
  ¿Catalina es una persona real o de mentira?
- Use one of the suggestions for Morning Circle offered in the front this *Teacher's Edition.*

LITERACY

Focus

- Tell the children an exaggerated tale about something you did last night. You might, for example, tell them you took a ride on a magic carpet or that you turned into a fish when you took your bath. Ask the children if the story you told them was real or make-believe.
  ¿La historia que leyeron era real o de mentira?
- Tell the children that this week they will study things that are real and things that are make-believe.

Develop

One Way to Develop the Lesson

- Discuss the concepts of reality and make-believe. Emphasize that when people make things up, they are using their imaginations. Present several scenarios and ask the children to evaluate each to determine whether it is real or make-believe. For example, you might say, *Cats have fur and whiskers. Is that a true statement or is it make-believe? In the "Three Little Kittens"/"Los tres gatitos," the kittens tell their mother they lost their mittens. Is it possible for kittens to have and to lose mittens, or is it make-believe? Why?*
  ¿Es posible que los gatitos tengan o pierdan unos mitones o es algo imaginario? ¿Por qué?
  Continue with other examples.

Another Way to Develop the Lesson

- Tell the children that you are going to share a book with them that can be read as a real story and as a make-believe story. Tell them that when a story is true it is called *nonfiction* and when it is make-believe it is called *fiction*.
- Read *Guess Who?/Adivina quién* . . . . Read the first question in the book about children and the potential answers, and then the answer the book provides. Ask the children if the book answer is true.
- Now read the question again and let the children choose one of the four possible answers to the question. Let them talk about it for a while. For example, if they choose puppies as the answer, discuss the humor in puppies at school. Then ask if their answer is real or make-believe.
- Point out the fun in pretending that an incorrect answer is a correct answer. Tell the children that this is why make-believe is so enjoyable: it stretches our imaginations.
- Read additional selections from the book using the same procedure for as long as the children remain interested.

Practice

- Place the *Guess Who?/Adivina quién* . . . book and listening tape in the Listening Center.
- Invite the children to fold pieces of drawing paper in half and draw pictures of things that are real on one side and things that are make-believe on the other side.
- Provide two posters, one that says *real/real* and another that says *make-believe/de mentira*. Encourage the children to look through magazines and cut out pictures of things that are real and things that are make-believe. Have them glue the pictures onto the appropriate posters.
- Give the children a small basket of items representing things that exist and things that are imaginary. Invite them to sort the items into real and make-believe categories.
- Invite the children to look through books in the Library Center for books that are about real things and books that are about imaginary or make-believe things. Reinforce the concept that factual books are nonfiction and make-believe books are fiction.

Preparation

- Make two posters for sorting. On one poster write the word *real* and glue on or draw a picture of something that is real. On the other poster, write *make-believe* and glue on or draw a picture of something that represents make-believe.
- Prepare a basket of items representing things that exist and things that are imaginary (for example, a toy horse and a toy unicorn).

Scaffolding Strategies

More Help Ask the children questions related specifically to them. For example, you might say, *You are a cute little kitten; right? Oh, I see. You are not a kitten, you are a boy. You can pretend to be a kitten. Can you show me how you can do that?*
Eres un gatico muy lindo, ¿verdad? Oh, ya veo. No eres un gatico sino un niño. Puedes pretender que eres un gatico. ¿Puedes mostrarme cómo puedes hacer eso?

Extra Challenge Encourage the children to think of a favorite story that is fiction and a favorite story that is nonfiction.

DAY 1

Letter Knowledge

English

- Introduce the letter *x* using the story "Xavier" from the *English Phonics Resource Guide*.

Spanish

- Introduce the letter *y* using the story "Yola" from the *Spanish Phonics Resource Guide*.

Suggested Reading

The Cat in the Hat by Dr. Suess
Abuela by Arthur Dorros

Second Language Learners

In some cultures it is considered an insult for a human to behave like an animal, and as a result children may not have engaged in this type of play. Most children, however, have portrayed human activities in play. Give one child a toothbrush and ask him or her to demonstrate its use. Stress that the volunteer isn't really brushing his or her teeth. Ask the other children to make believe they are brushing their teeth. Repeat the activity with a comb, a pair of scissors and paper, and so on.

Anthology Support

"Humpty Dumpty Sat on a Wall"
"Humpty Dumpty se sentó en la pared"
"El burrito enfermo"
"My Sick Little Donkey"

Reflect/Assess

- *Tell me about something that really happened to you today.*

  Cuéntenme algo que realmente haya pasado hoy.
- *Now, use your imagination and make up something that happened to you today.*

  Ahora, usen su imaginación e inventen algo que les haya pasado hoy.

Literacy Circle

Storytime 1

- Read *Hurray for Pre-K!/¡Qué viva el preescolar! Is the story real or make-believe? Is it fiction or nonfiction?*

  ¿La historia es real o de mentira? ¿Es ficción o didáctica?

Storytime 2

- Read *The Zebra on the Zyder Zee/Una aventura en alta mar. Is the story real or make-believe?*

  ¿La historia es real o de mentira?

  Invite the children to point out the make-believe things in the story.

Content Connection

Personal and Social Development

Objective
To begin to be responsible for individual behavior and actions

Vocabulary
truth, lie
verdad, mentira

DLM Materials
- *Teacher's Resource Anthology* "The Boy Who Cried Wolf"/"El niño y el lobo"

Activity 1

- Discuss with the children the concept of telling the truth. Explain that while it is fun to pretend and to use our imaginations, it is important that we tell the truth. Explain that the truth is what is real, and it is not what people make up in their heads. Nor is it what people wish it would be.
  La verdad es lo que es real y no lo que las personas inventan. Tampoco es verdad los deseos de las personas.

Activity 2

- Present the listening story "The Boy Who Cried Wolf"/"El niño y el lobo." Discuss the consequences the boy in the story faced for not telling the truth.

Teacher's NOTE

Children may have a difficult time determining which things are real and which things are make-believe. This is, in part, because adults fill their world with magical and make-believe things such as Santa Claus and the Tooth Fairy. Their ability to maintain a clear delineation between reality and make-believe is an evolving process that will not be completed until approximately the age of seven.

DAY 1

MATH

Objectives

- To put together puzzles of increasing complexity
- To use a variety of software packages with audio, video, and graphics

Vocabulary

length	longitud, largo
angle	ángulo
slanted	inclinada
all shape names, including *triangle*	nombres de todas las figuras incluido *el triángulo*

DLM Materials

- pattern blocks
- *Math Resource Guide*
  Building Straws
  Shape Step/Paso de figuras
  Feely Box
  Guessing Bag
- *DLM Math* software
- *Where Is Thumbkin?* CD
- *Diez deditos* CD

Materials to Gather

- building blocks

Preparation

- Place a theme-related object, such as a magic wand or a star, in the Guessing Bag.
- For Shape Step/Paso de figuras, use masking tape to outline several large shapes on the floor or the playground.

Focus

- Show the children a square and a right triangle from the pattern blocks. Hide them both and secretly put 1 in the Feely Box. Display a second, identical square and triangle.
- Have 1 child touch the shape in the Feely Box, describe it, and guess which shape you hid using the displayed shapes as a reference.
- Remind the children that the shapes must have the right parts (attributes) to be triangles—3 straight sides.
- Repeat using a large square and a small square, a rectangle and an equilateral triangle.

Develop

- Play Shape Step/Paso de figuras. Show the children the shapes you taped to the floor and ask them to touch a triangle with their toes. Ask them to step on a side of a triangle, the corner of a triangle, and so forth. Discuss why their choices are or are not triangles.
- Continue the activity until all the children have identified at least 2 or 3 triangles.
- Tell children they will be playing Shape Puzzles again this week; challenge them to try more challenging puzzles!

Practice

- Encourage the children to play Shape Step/Paso de figuras with friends, using the shapes on the floor.
- Allow the children to work in pairs, identifying shapes in the Feely Box and/or Guessing Bag.
- Have the children make shapes using Building Straws or building blocks. Children may discover that some collections of 3 straws will not always create a triangle. Help the children think about why this happens. (If 1 straw is longer than the other 2 combined, they will not connect).
- Invite the children to work on Shape Puzzles (no assigned level).

Reflect/Assess

- *How did you figure out which parts of shapes are sides and which are corners?*

  ¿Cómo determinaron qué partes de las figuras son lados y qué partes son esquinas?

Music and Movement

- Play the "Crocodile Song" from the *Where Is Thumbkin?* CD. *Could someone ride on the back of a crocodile? Would someone ride on the back of a crocodile?*

  ¿Alguien puede montarse en el lomo de un cocodrilo? ¿Alguien se montaría en el lomo de un cocodrilo?

- Play "Aserrín, asserán" from the *Diez deditos* CD. *Can termites do any of these things?*

  ¿Las termitas pueden hacer algunas de estas cosas?

Content Connection

Physical Development

Objectives

To begin to throw or kick an object in a particular direction
To begin to coordinate arms and legs

Materials to Gather

beanbags

Activity 1

- Invite the children to toss a beanbag into the triangles you have outlined on the floor with masking tape. Discuss their choice. Are they triangles? Why?

  ¿Son triángulos? ¿Por qué?

Activity 2

- Invite the children to think of ways to make triangles using their bodies.

Suggested Reading

Simon and His Boxes by Gilles Tibo
A Box Can Be Many Things by Dana Meachen Rau

Reflect on the Day

- *What did you learn about what is real and what is make-believe?*

  ¿Qué aprendieron sobre lo que es real y lo que es de mentira?

- *What can you share with your families about real and make-believe things?*

  ¿Qué pueden compartir con sus familias sobre las cosas reales y las de mentira?

Home Connection

Send a note home to families suggesting they use this week as an opportunity to point out the differences between real and make-believe things to their children.

Objectives

- To ask questions and make comments related to the current topic of discussion
- To become increasingly familiar with narrative form and its elements by identifying characters and predicting events, plot, and the resolution of a story

Vocabulary

pretend	pretender o fingir
make-believe	de mentira o imaginario
real	real
imaginary	imaginario
dragon	dragón

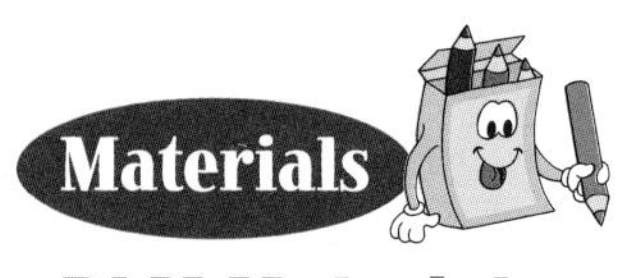

DLM Materials

- Oral Language Development Cards 6, 8, 18, 22, 28
- *The Dragon's Coming After You/El dragón te está persiguiendo*
- *Teacher's Resource Anthology*
  "Five Little Monkeys"/"Cinco monitos"
  "Five Little Speckled Frogs"/"Cinco ranitas manchadas"
  "Let's Pretend to Bake a Cake"/"Pretendamos como que horneamos un pastel"
  "Candy Land Journey"/"Un viaje a la tierra del dulce"

Begin the Day

- Invite the children to act out "Five Little Monkeys"/"Cinco monitos." Ask the class if the children who played the parts of monkeys were really monkeys or just pretending to be monkeys.

  ¿Los niños que representaron los papeles de monos eran monos de verdad o solo pretendían ser monos?
- Use one of the suggestions for Morning Circle offered in the front of this *Teacher's Edition.*

LITERACY

Focus

- Sing "Five Little Speckled Frogs"/"Cinco ranitas manchadas." Select five volunteers to be the frogs. Ask the class if the volunteers are real frogs or pretend frogs.
- Tell the children that today we will be learning more about real and make-believe things.

Develop

One Way to Develop the Lesson

- Place Oral Language Cards 6, 8, 18, 22, and 28 facedown. Invite a volunteer to pick a card and, without showing it to anyone else, pretend to be the animal on the card. Encourage the class to guess what animal the volunteer is pretending to be. After the children have guessed correctly, point out that the volunteer was only pretending to be that animal. Continue with new volunteers until all the cards have been turned over.

Another Way to Develop the Lesson

- Tell the children you are going to read them a book about pretending. Have them listen for all the things that the children in the story are pretending to be.
- Read *The Dragon's Coming After You/El dragón te está persiguiendo.*

  Make a list of all the different animals the children in the story pretended to be.
- If you are reading the book in English, read it again and ask the children to focus on listening to the rhyming word clues to predict which animals will appear next.

  ¿Qué animales van a aparecer luego?

Materials to Gather

- construction paper
- stuffed animal props
- coat hanger tubes
- medium-size cardboard box
- sheet
- green powdered drink mix
- craft materials
- small boxes
- fabric scraps
- graham crackers, icing, small decorative candies, and a small milk carton (optional)

Practice

- Place the *The Dragon's Coming After You/ El dragón te está persiguiendo* book and tape in the Listening Center.
- Provide a sheet and a box for a dragon's head and have the children pretend to be dragons. Provide stuffed animal props and have the children reenact the story.
- Encourage the children to play Catch the Dragon with the cut-out dragons. Have them fish for the matching rhyming word picture pairs.
- Invite the children to mix a green dragon powdered drink mix. Serve this for snack.
- Give the children arts and crafts materials, small boxes, and scarves or squares of fabrics. Encourage them to make dragon puppets.

Preparation

- Prepare the Catch the Dragon game by cutting dragon shapes out of construction paper. Paste rhyming word pictures on pairs of cut-out dragons. Attach paper clips to the dragons' noses and lay them on the floor. Provide a fishing pole made from a coat hanger tube that has a magnet attached to the end of a yarn line.
- Make a dragon's head out of a cardboard box.

Technology Support

Assuming your class has progressed in its computer skills and knowledge, allow time for the children to ask questions. Discuss their questions.

DAY 2

Letter Knowledge

English

- Read "Maxie and the Taxi" from the *SRA Alphabet Book*.

Spanish

- Read the *y* selection "Yego y yaya" from the *Los niños alfabéticos*.

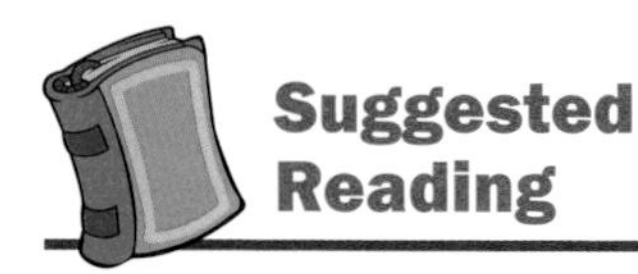

Suggested Reading

Pretend You're a Cat by Jean Marzollo

Second Language Learners

In "Let's Pretend to Bake a Cake"/"Pretendamos como que horneamos un pastel," wait to model the actions until you have noted children's responses to your language. Do they readily pantomime the actions without looking at more proficient children? This is an indication of their levels of understanding.

Anthology Support

"Weather"
"El tiempo"
"Rafita and Pepita"
"Rafita y Pepita"
"Have You Been to Candy Land?"
"¿Has visitado la ciudad de dulce?"

Reflect/Assess

- *What are the differences between something we pretend and something that is real?*

  ¿Cuáles son las diferencias entre algo que imaginamos o algo que es real?
- *Will you ever see a real dragon? Why not?*

  ¿Algún día podrán ver un dragón de verdad? ¿Por qué no?

Literacy Circle

Storytime 1

- Invite the children to participate in the action story "Let's Pretend to Bake a Cake"/"Pretendamos como que horneamos un pastel." Have the children compare this make-believe experience to the real experience of baking a cake.

Storytime 2

- Invite the children to participate in the action story "Candy Land Journey"/"Un viaje a la tierra del dulce." *Is this a real experience or is it make-believe?*

  ¿Ésta es una experiencia real o de mentira?
- You may want to provide graham crackers, icing, small decorative candies, and a small milk carton and invite the children to build a candy house.

Content Connection

Fine Arts

Objective
To begin to create or re-create stories, moods, or experiences through dramatic representation

Materials to Gather
plastic zoo animals, paper sack, animal crackers (optional)

Vocabulary
imagination
imaginación

Activity 1

- Pretend to go on a safari. Place animals in strategic locations around the room and invite the children to watch for them as you take a tour of the room. Emphasize that this is pretend and that the children are using their imaginations.

Vean los animales en el salón de clases. Esto que estamos haciendo es pretender. Estamos usando nuestra imaginación.

Activity 2

- Take a pretend trip to the zoo. Sit the children in a circle and give them a paper sack filled with plastic zoo animals or zoo animal crackers. Invite them to pass the bag around the circle and have each child reach in the bag and draw out an animal that the class will visit. Ask each child to name his or her animal and describe it to the other zoo visitors. Have each child pretend to be that animal.

¿Pueden nombrar su animal y describirlo a otros visitantes del zoológico? ¿Pretendan que son ese animal?

DAY 2

Objectives
- To put together puzzles of increasing complexity
- To begin to recognize, describe, and name shapes

Vocabulary

angle	ángulo
length	longitud/largo
all shape names, including *triangle*	nombres de todas las figuras incluido *el triángulo*

DLM Materials
- pattern blocks
- *Math Resource Guide*
- See Day 1
- *DLM Math* software
- *Four Baby Bumblebees* CD
- *Diez deditos* CD

Materials to Gather
- masking tape in different colors
- building blocks

Preparation
- For the tape shapes activity, draw several large shapes of various kinds (e.g., the Shape Set shapes) on paper; duplicate 1 of each for each child. The children will cover the shapes with tape for a tactile experience.

MATH

Focus
- Using the figures from yesterday's game of Shape Step/Paso de figuras, ask the children to touch a triangle with their toes, reminding them that the shapes must have the right parts: 3 straight sides and 3 corners.
- Ask children to step on shapes that are not triangles.
- Talk about why shapes are and especially are not triangles.

Develop
- Show the children a large triangle drawn on paper.
- Demonstrate making a tape shape by tearing off just the right length of masking tape for each side of the shape and sticking the tape right over each side.

Practice
- Invite the children to make tape shapes with masking tape. Emphasize that as they work on tape shapes, they have to tear off tape that is just the right length for each side. Encourage them to use different colors for different length sides.
- Encourage the children to practice identifying various shapes in the Feely Box or Guessing Bag.
- Invite the children to continue playing Shape Step/Paso de figuras from yesterday's lesson. Ask them to identify the attributes of triangles.
- Invite the children to work on Shape Puzzles (no level assigned).

Reflect/Assess

- *How did you figure out which shapes to use for the puzzles?*
  ¿Cómo determinaron qué figuras usar para los rompecabezas?

Content Connection

Fine Arts/Physical Development

Objectives

To participate in classroom music activities
To begin to coordinate arms and legs

DLM Materials

Teacher's Resource Anthology
Square Dance/Baile de figuras

Activity 1

- This activity requires children to look at and visualize lines from a different perspective. Demonstrate each line as you introduce it.
- Have 4 children form a straight line. Ask them to hold hands and move while remaining in a straight line. Ask them to move so they make a curved line.
- Ask 2 new groups to make straight lines that are parallel.
- Invite the children to help you make up a dance they can do in 2 parallel lines.

Activity 2

- Do a Square Dance/Baile de figuras with the children.

Music and Movement

- Play "On the Good Ship Lollipop" from the *Four Baby Bumblebees* CD. *Is the song about a real or make-believe experience? How do you know?*
  ¿La canción es sobre una experiencia real o una fantasía? ¿Cómo lo saben?
- Play "Pimpón" from the *Diez deditos* CD. *Is Pimpón real or make-believe? Can he really wash his face?*
  ¿Pimpón es real o fantasía? ¿Puede él realmente lavarse la cara?

Suggested Reading

Dance Tanya by Patricia Lee Gauch
Barn Dance by John Archambault and Bill Martin Jr.

Reflect on the Day

- *What did you learn about pretending?*
  ¿Qué aprendieron sobre fingir?
- *Which activity did you enjoy most?*
  ¿Qué actividad disfrutaron más?

Home Connection

Ask families to help collect boxes and egg cartons that will be used next week to build insects. Also, ask families about any insect allergies their children may have, because they will be going outdoors to look for insects.

Begin the Day

- Sing "Down by the Bay"/"Junto a la bahía." Make up fanciful creatures doing fanciful things. For example, you might say, *Did you ever see a grumba doing the rumba, or a thingamajig riding a pig?*

  ¿Alguna vez vieron una grumba bailando la rumba o un cerdo bailando plantilla?

  Have the children invent additional sentences.
- Use one of the suggestions for Morning Circle offered in the front of this *Teacher's Edition.*

Objectives

- To ask questions and make comments about the information and events from books
- To become increasingly familiar with narrative form and its elements by identifying characters and predicting events, plot, and the resolution of a story

Vocabulary

pretend	pretender
make-believe	de mentira o imaginario
imagination	imaginación
dragons	dragones
monsters	monstruos
giants	gigantes
trolls	duendes

Materials

DLM Materials

- *The Dragon's Coming After You/El dragón te está persiguiendo*
- magnetic letters
- *Teacher's Resource Anthology*
  "Down by the Bay"/"Junto a la bahía"
  "Who Is Traipsing on My Bridge?"/"¿Quién cazcalea por mi puente?"
  "The Three Billy Goats Gruff"/"Los tres chivitos Gruff"
  "Oh, My Monster Bobari"/"Ay, mi monstruo Buldoso"
  "Jack and the Beanstalk"/"Jaime y los frijoles mágicos"

LITERACY

Focus

- Encourage the children to chant "Who Is Traipsing on My Bridge?"/"¿Quién cazcalea por mi puente?"
- Tell the children that we will continue to learn about real and make-believe things today.

Develop

One Way to Develop the Lesson

- Discuss trolls, dragons, giants, and monsters. If you have books that feature each type of character, share the illustrations.
- Ask if these creatures are real or make-believe. Emphasize that each of these creatures is used in stories and songs to stimulate imaginations.
- Invite the children to dramatize "The Three Billy Goats Gruff"/"Los tres chivitos Gruff." Discuss which parts of the story could be real and which parts could not be real.
- Assist a volunteer in using the magnetic letters to spell the name of the creature *(troll)*. Have another volunteer count the billy goats pictured on different pages of the book.

Another Way to Develop the Lesson

- Sing "Oh, My Monster Bobari"/"Ay, mi monstruo Buldoso." Ask the children to talk about monsters. *What is a monster? Are they real or are they make-believe?*

  ¿Qué es un monstruo? ¿Son reales o de mentira?
- Write a monster story with the children. Give them the beginning of the story . . . *The monster came to my room every night. He was big and dark. He had green eyes and . . .*

  El monstruo aparecía todas las noches en mi cuarto. Era grande y oscuro. Tenía ojos verdes y . . .
- After the story is finished, read it to the class. Emphasize that the monster in the story is one they made up using their imaginations.

Practice

- Place the *The Dragon's Coming After You/El dragón te está persiguiendo* book and tape in the Listening Center.
- Place "The Three Billy Goats Gruff"/"Los tres chivitos Gruff" flannel board story in the Language Center. Invite the children to retell the story or make up a new story.
- Place the monster chart story you wrote during the lesson in the Art Center and invite the children to illustrate it.
- Give them an empty spray bottle with a label that says *Monster Spray*. Provide colored water in three or four colors, a funnel, an eye-dropper, and some rock salt. Invite them to create monster spray to keep pretend monsters away.
- Invite the children to play Ring the Dragon in the Gross Motor Center.
- Encourage them to play Monster Eye Toss in the Blocks Center.
- Provide the words *dragons, monsters, giants,* and *trolls* on index cards. Invite the children to copy the names using magnetic letters.

  Copien los nombres dragones, monstruos, gigantes *y* duendes *en tarjetas.*

Materials to Gather

- chart paper
- bulletin board paper
- plastic coffee can lids
- empty green soda bottle
- sand
- poster board
- hook and loop tape
- ping-pong balls
- spray bottle
- rock salt
- eyedropper
- funnel
- food coloring
- books about dragons, trolls, giants, and monsters (optional)

Preparation

- Make the flannel board stories.
- Cut out giant footprints from bulletin board paper and make a trail from your classroom door to the circle area.
- Write the words *monsters, dragons, trolls,* and *giants* on index cards.
- Make the Ring the Dragon game. Place sand in an empty green soda bottle. Draw a dragon face to attach to the bottle. Make plastic ringers by cutting the centers out of coffee can lids.
- Make the Monster Eye Toss game. Draw a monster face on posterboard. Glue one side of hook and loop tape where the eyes should be. Glue the other side of the hook and loop tape around ping-pong balls.

DAY 3

Letter Knowledge

English

- Invite the children to shape the letter *x* with modeling dough.

Spanish

- Invite the children to shape the letter *y* with modeling dough.

Second Language Learners

When "The Three Billy Goats Gruff"/ "Los tres chivitos Gruff" is placed in the Language Center, invite the children to tell the story in pairs. A child who is proficient in the language can work with a second language learner. Note the language the second language learner uses. Does the proficient child help the second language learner by asking questions and providing important details? During the proficient child's story, does the second language learner also interact? In what ways?

"The Strange Visitor"
"Extraña compañía"

Reflect/Assess

- *Have you ever been afraid of monsters, giants, or trolls? When? How did you become unafraid?*

  ¿Alguna vez han sentido miedo debido a monstruos, gigantes o duendes? ¿Cuándo? ¿Cómo dejaron de sentir miedo?
- *How are dragons like dinosaurs?*

  ¿Los dragones son como dinosaurios?

Storytime 1

- Reread *The Dragon's Coming After You/El dragón te está persiguiendo. What other stories do you know about dragons?*

  ¿Qué otros cuentos de dragones conocen?

Storytime 2

- Present the "Jack and the Beanstalk"/"Jaime y los frijoles mágicos" flannel board story. *What other stories do you know about giants? Which parts of this story might be true? Which parts cannot be true?*

  ¿Qué otros cuentos de gigantes conocen? ¿Qué partes de este cuento podrían ser ciertas? ¿Qué partes no podrían ser ciertas?

Content Connection

Fine Arts

Objective
To begin to engage in dramatic play with others

Vocabulary
dinosaurs
dinosaurios

DLM Materials
Teacher's Resource Anthology
"The Smallest Dragon"/"El diminuto dragón"
"Five Huge Dinosaurs"/"Cinco enormes dinosaurios"

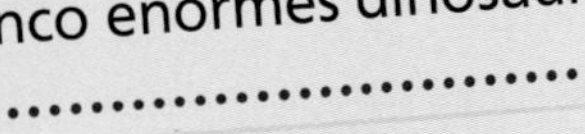

Activity 1

- Invite the children to act out "The Smallest Dragon"/"El diminuto dragón."

Activity 2

- Invite the children to act out "Five Huge Dinosaurs"/"Cinco enormes dinosaurios."

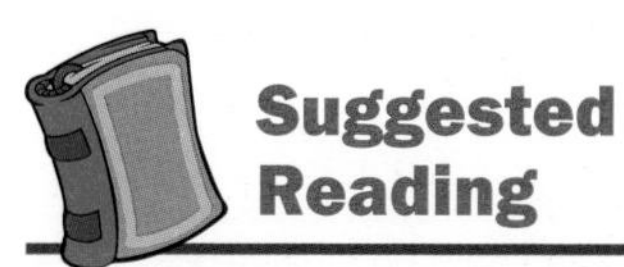

Suggested Reading

The Judge: An Untrue Tale by Margot and Harve Zemach
There's a Monster Under My Bed by James Howe
David's Father by Robert N. Munsch

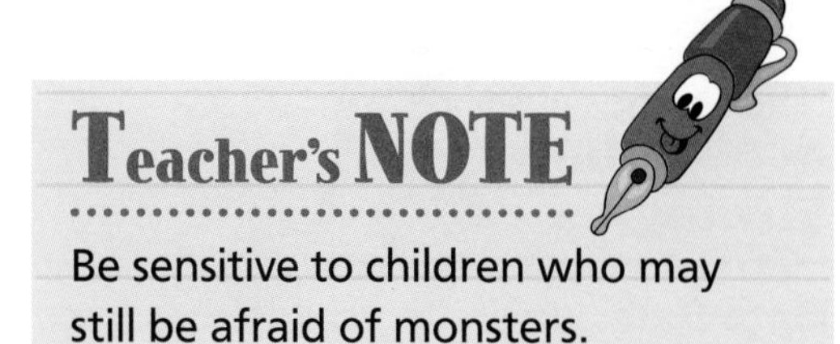

Teacher's NOTE

Be sensitive to children who may still be afraid of monsters.

DAY 3

Objectives

- To put together puzzles of increasing complexity
- To begin to recognize, describe, and name shapes

Vocabulary

angle	ángulo
length	longitud/largo
all shape names, including *triangle*	nombres de todas las figuras incluido *el triángulo*

DLM Materials

- *Math Resource Guide* Shape Set
- See Day 1
- *DLM Math* software

Materials to Gather

- masking tape in different colors
- green and brown bulletin board paper
- See Day 1

Scaffolding Strategies

More Help Invite the children to trace triangles in the Shape Set with their fingers.

Extra Challenge Encourage the children to make different shapes within each category (e.g., different size squares, or equilateral or right triangles).

MATH

Focus

- Have each child put a hand on 1 hip. Ask them what shape is made by their arms and their sides (triangle).
- Ask the children to name other ways they could make a triangle using their bodies.
- Tell children that *triangle* means "three angles."
- Draw a triangle and challenge the children to duplicate that triangle using their bodies. Discuss how they make the sides and angles. Draw different triangles. Make 1 with 2 long sides the same length and 1 short side (isosceles). Make another with all 3 sides the same length (equilateral), and another with a right angle (right).

Develop

- Hold up a triangle from the Shape Set. Challenge the children to make a shape like that one using Building Straws.
- Challenge them to make 1 of each of the triangles from the Shape Set using Building Straws.

Practice

- Encourage the children to make shapes like those in the Shape Set using Building Straws or building blocks.
- Continue the Practice activities from Days 1 and 2 of this week.
- Invite the children to work on Shape Puzzles (no level assigned).

Reflect/Assess

- *How did you tell one shape from another in the Feely Box?*
  ¿Cómo diferenciaron una figura de otra en la Feely Box?
- *How did you know which straw or block to use to make the shape you made?*
  ¿Cómo sabían qué pajita o bloque usar para hacer la figura que hicieron?

Music and Movement

- Play Dragons, Trolls, and Giants. Play a piece of classical music and have the children move or dance like the creature whose name you call out. For example, when you call out *giant,* the children will dance like a giant. You might want to rehearse some movements for each creature before starting the game.
- Twist green and brown bulletin board paper into a beanstalk that reaches from the floor to the ceiling. Have the children march around Jack's beanstalk. Ask all the children who have names that start with the letter *P* to march up to the beanstalk and pretend to climb it. Change the criteria as you continue to play the game. For example, you may call children forward by clothing color, shoe type, or names that rhyme with a word you provide.

Content Connection

Fine Arts

Objective
To begin to show interest in the artwork of others

DLM Materials
Wordsong/Canto de palabras

Vocabulary
shape names
nombres de figuras

Activity 1

- Read *Wordsong/Canto de palabras* with the children. Discuss the role of the illustrator.
- Review the illustrations in the book looking specifically at the shapes and lines used by the illustrator. *What shapes do you see?*
  ¿Qué figuras ven?

Activity 2

- Invite the children to draw a picture of 1 of the items mentioned in *Wordsong/Canto de palabras.* Ask them what shapes and lines they used in their illustrations.
  ¿Qué figuras y líneas usaron en su ilustración?

Reflect on the Day

- *What other make-believe things can you add to the class monster story?*
  ¿Qué otras cosas de fantasía pueden agregar al cuento del monstruo de la clase?
- *What did you learn about monsters, trolls, giants, and dragons?*
  ¿Qué aprendieron sobre monstruos, duendes, gigantes y dragones?

Begin the Day

- Sing "White Coral Bells" or say the chant "Pimpón."
- Use one of the suggestions for Morning Circle offered in the front of this *Teacher's Edition*.

Objectives

- To begin to retell some sequences of events in stories
- To become increasingly familiar with narrative form and its elements by identifying characters and predicting events, plot, and the resolution of a story

Vocabulary

real	real
make-believe	de mentira o imaginario
magic	mágico
wish	deseo
fairies	hadas
fairy tales	cuentos de hadas

DLM Materials

- *Teacher's Resource Anthology*
  "White Coral Bells"
  "Pimpón"
  "Fairies in the Air"/"Duendes en el aire"
  "The Princess and the Pea"/"La princesa y la arveja"
  "Three Wishes"/"Tres deseos"
  "Frog Went a-Courtin'"/"El sapo fue a cortejar"
  "Little Red Riding Hood"/"Caperucita Roja"

LITERACY

Focus

- Sing "Fairies in the Air"/"Duendes en el aire." Ask the children if they have ever seen a fairy. *What do you know about fairies?*

  ¿Qué saben de las hadas?

  Most children will mention the Tooth Fairy here. Be careful not to shatter that piece of magic.
- Tell the children that we will continue to learn about real and make-believe things.

Develop

One Way to Develop the Lesson

- Discuss fairy tales and traditional tales. Tell the children that fairy tales were originally called fairy tales because the stories were about fairies and elves. Most fairy tales are filled with magical make-believe characters such as princesses, dwarves, and talking animals. They contain make-believe plots such as wishes that come true and waking a princess who has slept a hundred years.

  Los cuentos de hadas contienen tramas imaginarias, como deseos que se hacen realidad o despertar a una princesa que ha dormido por cien años.
- Invite the children to name fairy tales with which they are familiar. List the story names on chart paper. Show some books that are examples of fairy tales.
- Read the listening story "The Princess and the Pea"/"La princesa y la arveja." After the children have heard the story once, invite them to re-enact it. Provide a few pillows and a dried pea as props.

Another Way to Develop the Lesson

- Tell the children that you are going to share a fairy tale/traditional tale that comes from Puerto Rico.

  Vamos a leer un cuento de hadas/cuento popular de Puerto Rico.
- Present the listening story "Three Wishes"/"Tres deseos." Discuss the elements of the story. Remind them about the discussion in One Way to Develop the Lesson. *What makes the story a fairy tale?*

  ¿Qué hace que este cuento sea de hadas?
- Ask the children which parts of the story could really happen and which parts could not really happen. *Did the family use their wishes wisely?*

  ¿La familia usó los deseos de forma sensata?

Practice

- Provide the props from "The Princess and the Pea"/"La princesa y la arveja" and "Three Wishes"/"Tres deseos" and encourage the children to re-enact the stories.
- Give the children the magic wish bottle. Encourage them to shake the bottle and make pretend wishes.
- Invite each child to dictate three wishes he or she would make.

  Agiten la botella y pidan deseos de mentira.
- Encourage the children to illustrate their wishes. Display their wishes on a wall of wishes.
- Fill the Library Center with fairy tales.
- Invite the children to make pea pictures. Provide a shallow box. Place a sheet of paper in the bottom of the box. Place two or three peas in some paint and then put them into the box. Encourage the children to roll the peas around in the box to create pea pictures.
- Place family tapes of traditional tales from the Traditional Tales themes in the Listening Center.

Materials to Gather

- fairy tale books
- one-half liter bottle
- glitter
- food coloring
- brown felt donkey ears
- headband
- chart paper
- pillows
- dried peas
- shallow box
- tempera paint
- family traditional tales tapes from Traditional Tales

Preparation

- Make the flannel board stories.
- Make a magic wish bottle. Place four teaspoons of glitter in an empty one-half liter bottle, add a few drops of food coloring, and fill with water. Glue the lid to the bottle.
- Make a pair of donkey ears by attaching two large brown felt ears to a headband.

Second Language Learners

Encourage parents to share traditional tales from their home countries. You might also check the library for versions of the Cinderella/Cenicienta story from the children's home cultures. Examples include the Mexican *Estrellita de oro/ Little Gold Star, A Cinderella cuento* by Joe Hayes; an African version: *Mufaro's Beautiful Daughters* by John Steptoe; and *Yeh-Shen: A Cinderella Story from China* by Ai-Ling Louie.

DAY 4

Letter Knowledge

English

- Invite the children to think of ways to make the letter *x* with their bodies. Use the Think, Pair, Share game/Piensa, aparea, comparte with this activity.

Spanish

- Invite the children to think of ways to make the letter *y* with their bodies. Use the Think, Pair, Share game/Piensa, aparea, comparte with this activity.

Suggested Reading

The Frog Princess by Laura Cecil
Favorite Tales from Hans Christian Andersen

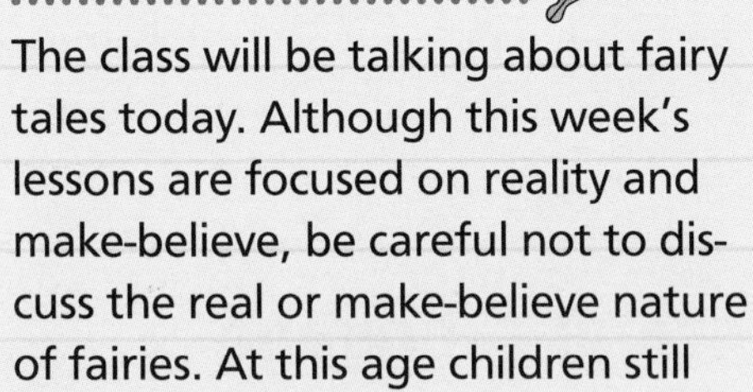

Teacher's NOTE

The class will be talking about fairy tales today. Although this week's lessons are focused on reality and make-believe, be careful not to discuss the real or make-believe nature of fairies. At this age children still believe in the Tooth Fairy.

Anthology Support

"Three Bears Rap"
"El rap de los tres osos"
"There Once Were Three Brown Bears"
"Había una vez tres osos café"
"Los animales de Amelia "
"Amelia's Pets"

Reflect/Assess

- *Which fairy tale is your favorite? Why?*
  ¿Cuál cuento de hadas es su favorito? ¿Por qué?
- *What wishes did you make?*
  ¿Qué deseos pidieron?

Storytime 1

- Present the "Frog Went a-Courtin'"/"El sapo fue a cortejar" flannel board story. Discuss the parts of the story that might be real or make-believe. Most of this story is make-believe. Discuss the humor and fun in the story.
  La mayor parte de este cuento es imaginaria. ¿Qué les hace reír en este cuento?

Storytime 2

- Present the "Little Red Riding Hood"/"Caperucita Roja" flannel board story. *What makes this story a fairy tale? Which parts of the story could really happen and which parts could not?*
  ¿Qué hace que este cuento sea de hadas? ¿Qué partes del cuento podrían suceder de verdad y qué partes no podrían suceder?

Content Connection

Personal and Social Development

Objective

To begin to be responsible for individual behavior and actions

Vocabulary

plan

plan

Activity 1

- Discuss the nature of wishes. Explain that people cannot wish on any particular object like a star, a lucky penny, or a four-leaf clover and expect that their wishes will come true.

  ¿Qué tipo de deseos piden ustedes? No podemos pedirle a una estrella, una moneda sortaria o un trébol de cuatro hojas que haga realidad nuestros deseos.

- Tell the children that the way to make a wish come true is to identify the wish and to make a plan to help make the wish come true. For example, a person might wish he or she could take a trip. This person can start working on that wish by developing a plan of how to save enough money for the trip. People make their wishes come true by making plans that will bring about the results they desire.

  Cuando la gente pide un deseo, hace planes que ayudan a que se cumpla.

Activity 2

- Invite the children to make realistic wishes about school. Have them make wishes for which they can develop plans to begin working toward. For example, they may wish for a new piece of playground equipment. Discuss with them the plans they might make for accomplishing that goal.

  ¿Qué planes tienen para lograr esa meta?

DAY 4

Objectives

- To put together puzzles of increasing complexity
- To begin to recognize, describe, and name shapes

Vocabulary

angle	ángulo
length	longitud/largo
slanted	inclinada
all shape names, including *triangle*	nombres de todas las figuras incluido *el triángulo*

DLM Materials

- *Math Resource Guide* Shape Set
- See Day 1
- *DLM Math* software
- *Where Is Thumbkin?* CD
- *Esta es mi tierra* CD

Materials to Gather

- masking tape in different colors
- See Day 1

MATH

Focus

- Have a child secretly put 1 of the shapes from the pattern blocks in the Feely Box. Describe the sides and angles of the shape you are feeling. Challenge the children to identify what shape you are feeling by listening to the descriptions you are providing. After they have guessed, pull the shape out to check.
- Repeat with new shapes.

Develop

- Display a shape from the Shape Set that the children have not yet made and challenge them to build 1 with the Building Straws.

Practice

- Continue the Practice activities from previous days this week.
- Have the children work on Shape Puzzles (no level assigned). If they like a certain shape puzzle they have made, have them print it and then construct it using physical shapes. They can also make designs with physical manipulatives, copy them on a computer, and save them as puzzles.

Reflect/Assess

- *How did you tell one shape from another in the Feely Box?*
  ¿Cómo diferenciaron una figura de otra en la Feely Box?
- *How did you know which straw or block to use to make the shape you made?*
  ¿Cómo sabían qué pajita o bloque usar para hacer la figura que hicieron?

Music and Movement

- Play "The Frog Went A-Courtin'" from the *Where Is Thumbkin?* CD. Discuss the real versus make-believe elements in the song.
- Play "La monedita"/ "Magic Penny" from the *Esta es mi tierra* CD.

Content Connection

Physical Development

Objectives

To begin to use scissors
To begin to develop pincer control in picking up objects

Materials to Gather

straws, masking tape, scissors, building blocks

Activity 1

- Invite the children to create straw structures. Provide masking tape, scissors, and straws and encourage them to build. Discuss the lines of the structures. *What shapes are formed as straws are taped together? How tall can they build their structure without it falling?*

  ¿Qué figuras se forman cuando se pegan las pajitas? ¿De qué altura pueden construir su estructura sin que se caiga?

Activity 2

- Invite the children to build structures in the Blocks Center using only the triangular blocks.

Suggested Reading

Building a House by Byron Barton
Bridges Connect by Lee Sullivan Hill

Reflect on the Day

- *Which activity did you like best?*
  ¿Qué actividad les gustó más?
- *What did you learn about fairy tales?*
  ¿Qué aprendieron sobre cuentos de hadas?

Home Connection

Send home four take-home book packs.

What Research Suggests

Children can get frustrated with puzzles that use rhombuses and squares because of the different angles involved. It is important that they use these shapes early.

Begin the Day

- Sing "Down by the Bay"/"Junto a la bahía." Use your imagination to create new verses.
- Use one of the suggestions for Morning Circle offered in the front of this *Teacher's Edition.*

Objectives

- To become increasingly familiar with narrative form and its elements by identifying characters and predicting events, plot, and the resolution of a story
- To use language for a variety of purposes

Vocabulary

imagination imaginación

DLM Materials

- *The Dragon's Coming After You/El dragón te está persiguiendo*
- *Teacher's Resource Anthology*
  "Down by the Bay"/"Junto a la bahía"
  "I Wish I Were"
  "Goldilocks and the Three Bears"/"Goldilocks y los tres osos"
  "The Three Billy Goats Gruff"/"Los tres chivitos Gruff"
  "Jack and the Beanstalk"/"Jaime y los frijoles mágicos"

Materials to Gather

- red crayons, paper, and paint
- blank puzzles from white poster board
- basket of small items

LITERACY

Focus

- Sing "I Wish I Were." *What would life be like if you were any of the things mentioned in the song?*

  ¿Cómo sería la vida si fueran una de las cosas mencionadas en la canción?

  Take one item and explore it.
- Tell the children that we will continue to learn about real and make-believe things today.

Develop

One Way to Develop the Lesson

- Present some scenarios to the children and invite them to explore each one. *What if everything in the world were red? What would that be like? What would a red banana taste like? What would it feel like to be surrounded by red?*

  ¿Qué pasaría si todas las cosas del mundo fueran rojas? ¿Cómo sería eso? ¿A qué sabría una banana roja? ¿Cómo nos sentiríamos si estuviéramos rodeados de rojo?
- *What if there were only one kind of dog?*

  ¿Qué pasaría si solo hubiera un tipo de perro?
- *What if kids were in charge and adults had to listen to kids? How would you like that? What do you think would happen?*

  ¿Qué pasaría si los niños estuvieran en control y los adultos tuvieran que hacerles caso a los niños? ¿Les gustaría eso? ¿Qué creen que sucedería?
- Have the children create their own scenarios.

Another Way to Develop the Lesson

- Tell the children that you are going to play a game of What if.. Retell the story of "Goldilocks and the Three Bears"/"Goldilocks y los tres osos" by changing the characters and then changing the plot.
- Present the same story using the flannel board illustrations from "The Three Billy Goats Gruff"/"Los tres chivitos Gruff." *Would the goats eat the same things the bears ate or would they prefer to go outside and graze? Would the goats have the same type of chairs? Would Goldilocks be afraid of the goats?*

  ¿Los chivitos comerían lo mismo que los osos o preferirían ir afuera a comer pasto? ¿Tendrían los chivitos el mismo tipo de sillas? ¿Ricitos de Oro tendría miedo de los chivitos?

  Let the children help you retell the story with new characters.
- Now retell the story changing the plot. Have the bears go into Goldilocks' house uninvited.

Practice

- Give the children the flannel board stories and let them intermingle the characters to make up new stories.
- In the Art Center, provide only red paint, red paper, and red crayons. Have the children think about their answers from the first Develop.
- Provide a basket of small items for the children to pick up with their toes. *What if we could pick things up only with our toes?*

  ¿Qué pasaría si solo pudiéramos recoger cosas con los dedos de los pies?
- Give the children white poster board cut into puzzle pieces. *What if all of our puzzles had no pictures on them? Is it easy or difficult to work with puzzles that have no pictures? Why?*

  ¿Qué pasaría si todos nuestros rompecabezas no tuvieran dibujos? ¿Es fácil resolver rompecabezas sin dibujos? ¿Por qué?
- Invite the children to dictate their reactions to being told that the only food they will ever have to eat is broccoli. Encourage them to illustrate their reactions.

Preparation

- Prepare the flannel board stories.
- Cut one-fourth sheets of white poster board into puzzles.
- Prepare basket of small items.

Scaffolding Strategies

More Help Ask the children direct questions. *Would your orange juice taste different if it were purple?* *¿Sabría diferente el jugo de naranja si fuera morado?*

Extra Challenge Ask the children to create a list of "what if" questions. Have them ask each other questions.

Second Language Learners

Make a picture chart comparing two stories: Brinton Turkle's *Deep In the Forest,* a wordless book, and a traditional version of Goldilocks and the Three Bears/Ricitos de oro. Compare WHO went in the house, WHAT they did, WHO came home to find them, and WHAT HAPPENED. Note the children's responses. Do they understand the terms WHO, WHAT, and WHAT HAPPENED? Can they tell you or show you on the chart why the stories are the same or not the same?

DAY 5

Letter Knowledge

English

- Encourage the children to find and circle the letter *x* in magazine and newspaper articles.

Spanish

- Encourage the children to find and circle the letter *y* in magazine and newspaper articles.

Suggested Reading

Petite Rouge by Mike Artell
Bored Nothing to Do by Peter Spier

Teacher's NOTE

This can be a humorous day. Go with the theme of "what if" throughout the day. You may be surprised at where you end up.

Anthology Support

"The Three Little Pigs"
"Los tres cerditos"
"Catalina Magnalina"

Reflect/Assess

- *Did changing the characters from the flannel board stories change the story of Goldilocks and the Three Bears? What things changed?*
  ¿Cambió el cuento al cambiar los personajes? ¿Qué cosas cambiaron?
- *What have you learned about pretending and using your imagination?*
  ¿Qué han aprendido sobre pretender y usar la imaginación?

Literacy Circle

Storytime 1

- Present "The Three Billy Goats Gruff"/"Los tres chivitos Gruff" flannel board story with a change of characters. Have Little Red Riding Hood be the one who is trying to cross the bridge on her way to grandmother's house.

Storytime 2

- Present the "Jack and the Beanstalk"/"Jaime y los frijoles mágicos" flannel board story with one alteration: Jack's beans do not grow.
- Reread *The Dragon's Coming After You/El dragón te está persiguiendo.* This time have the children make up imaginary names for animals that rhyme with the word clues.
  Inventen nombres de animales que rimen con estas palabras.

Content Connection

Personal and Social Development/Science

Objectives

To express interests and self-direction in learning

To show an interest in investigating unfamiliar objects, organisms, and phenomena

Vocabulary

imagination, creative thinking

imaginación, razonamiento creativo

Materials to Gather

clothespins

Activity 1

- Discuss creative thinking. Tell the children that when a person thinks about "what if" and unusual things, he or she is using his or her imagination. Explain that this is called creative thinking. Creative thinking is often at the heart of new things that are invented.

  Cuando se inventan cosas nuevas se hace a través del razonamiento creativo.

- Explain that the Wright brothers had to think in a creative way to come up with the first airplane. *What do you think gave them the idea? Watching birds?*

  ¿Qué creen que les dio la idea? ¿Observar los pájaros?

Activity 2

- Invite the children to brainstorm some things they could use a clothespin for besides hanging up clothes.

  ¿Para qué otra cosa pueden usar una pinza de ropa aparte de tender ropa?

DAY 5

Objectives

- To put together puzzles of increasing complexity
- To begin to investigate and predict the results of putting together two or more shapes

Vocabulary

angle	ángulo
length	longitud/largo
puzzle	rompecabezas
line	línea/recta
horizontal	horizontal
vertical	vertical
slanted	inclinada
all shape names, including *triangle*	nombres de todas las figuras incluido *el triángulo*

DLM Materials

- pattern blocks
- *Math Resource Guide*
- See Day 1
- *DLM Math* software
- *Teacher's Resource Anthology* Mother, May I?/Mamá, ¿puedo?

Materials to Gather

- See Day 1

MATH

Focus

- Place a mystery object in the Guessing Bag. Have the children tell what they think the object is and why. Accept any descriptions. After everyone has brainstormed, let 1 child pull the object out. Guide them to focus on geometric attributes.

Develop

- Have several children share a favorite puzzle that they completed or a favorite shape they made from parts this week.
- Complete a task from Shape Puzzles with the children. Talk about the different ways to solve, and to figure out how to solve, the puzzle, emphasizing how and why shapes fit.

Practice

- Continue the Practice activities from previous days this week.
- Have the children work on Shape Puzzles. Are they moving toward higher levels in the computer program, and in their knowledge and skills?

Reflect/Assess

- *How did you figure out which lengths to use to make this shape?*
  ¿Cómo determinaron qué longitudes usar para hacer esta figura?
- Computer Show: *How did you figure out how to solve the computer shape puzzle?*
  ¿Cómo determinaron cómo resolver el rompecabezas de figuras de computadora?

Music and Movement

- Challenge the children to do things backwards such as walking, crawling, hopping, and skipping.
  Hagan cosas al revés como caminar, gatear, saltar y brincar.
- Play Mother, May I?/Mamá, ¿puedo? in a circle instead of a line.

Suggested Reading

I Spy Two Eyes: Numbers in Art by Lucy Micklethwait

Content Connection

Fine Arts

Objective
To begin to show interest in the artwork of others

Materials to Gather
reproductions of works of art

Activity 1

- Display works of art and ask the children to find all the shapes, parts of shapes, and combinations of shapes they can. The children should be able to see the parts of shapes and combinations of shapes with more visual literacy and insight than when this activity was done in prior lessons.

Activity 2

- Take the children to the library and have the librarian share books with collections of artwork in them. Ask the children to identify shapes, parts of shapes, and combinations of shapes they see in the illustrations.
  Identifiquen figuras, partes de ellas y combinaciones en las ilustraciones.

Reflect on the Day

- *What have you learned this week about what is real and what is make-believe?*
  ¿Qué aprendieron esta semana sobre lo que es real y lo que es fantasía?
- *Tonight, play a game of What if. . . with your families. Ask them, What if animals could talk?*
  Esta noche jueguen con sus familias un juego de Qué pasaría si . . . Pregúntenles, ¿qué pasaría si los animales hablaran?

Looking Ahead

Connecting to the Theme: Bugs

Most children are curious about insects. It is important when discussing insects not to reinforce any child's fear of them. Children should begin to recognize the roles that insects play in our world. This lesson addresses some insects and their body parts, how different insects move or fly, and where certain insects live.

	Objectives	DLM Materials	Materials to Gather
DAY 1	• To link new learning experiences and vocabulary to what is already known about a topic • To understand that illustrations carry meaning but cannot be read • To combine, separate, and name "how many" concrete objects • To count by ones to 10 or higher	• *Insect Picnic/El picnic de los insectos* • *The Dragon's Coming After You/El dragón te está persiguiendo* • *Teacher's Resource Anthology* • dinosaur counters • *Math Resource Guide* • *DLM Math* software • *Four Baby Bumblebees* CD	• bug puzzles • index cards • chenille wires • plate or tray • 24-inch pieces of yarn • coffee can or similar can • plastic bugs or counters • magnifying lens • egg cartons • sticky notes
DAY 2	• To identify 10 or more printed alphabet letters • To begin to recognize the association between spoken and written words by following the print as it is read aloud • To describe observations • To combine, separate, and name "how many" concrete objects	• Oral Language Development Card 30 • *The Little Ants/Las hormiguitas* • *Insect Picnic/El picnic de los insectos* • *Teacher's Resource Anthology* • *Math Resource Guide* • *SRA Book of Animals/SRA El libro de los animales*	• celery sticks • raisins • shovel • sticks • bug puzzles (see Day 1) • index cards with insect names • coffee can or similar can • peanut butter • jar • straws • clay
DAY 3	• To begin to retell some sequences of events in stories • To understand that print carries a message by recognizing labels, signs, and other print forms in the environment • To count by ones to 10 or higher • To describe observations • To participate in classroom music activities	• Oral Language Cards 29 & 35 • *Insect Picnic/El picnic de los insectos* • *Animals That Build Their Homes/Animales que construyen sus nidos* • *Teacher's Resource Anthology* • *Math Resource Guide* • *DLM Math* software • *Four Baby Bumblebees* CD	• bug puzzles • salt or sand • play dough • wiggle eyes • waxed paper • fish-shaped crackers (10 per child) • copies of Ms. Bumblebee • paper plates (2 for each child) • tongue depressors • cookie sheet • chenille wires • toothpicks • counters
DAY 4	• To listen with increasing attention • To understand and follow simple oral directions • To combine, separate, and name "how many" concrete objects • To count by ones to 10 or higher • To use a variety of software packages with audio, video, and graphics	• Oral Language Development Card 29 • *Insect Picnic/El picnic de los insectos* • *The Dragon's Coming After You/El dragón te está persiguiendo* • *Teacher's Resource Anthology* • *DLM Math* software • *Four Baby Bumblebees* CD	• bug puzzles • chenille wires • black pen • magazines • no-hinge clothespin • fifteen-inch crepe paper streamers • fish-shaped crackers (10 per child) • paper towel tubes • waxed paper • stamp pads • counters
DAY 5	• To begin to identify rhymes and rhyming sounds in familiar words, participate in rhyming games, and repeat rhyming songs and poems • To combine, separate, and name "how many" concrete objects	• *Insect Picnic/El picnic de los insectos* • *Animals That Build Their Homes/Animales que construyen sus nidos* • *Teacher's Resource Anthology* • Oral Language Cards 27, 29, & 30 • *Math Resource Guide*	• large eyedropper • egg cartons • connecting cubes • decorations such as beads, sequins, rickrack, paint, and so on • insect puzzles • pitcher of juice • chenille wires

(See individual lesson pages for complete lists of materials.)

Learning Centers

SCIENCE

Looking for Bugs

Objective
To describe properties of objects and characteristics of living things

Materials to Gather
photographs and pictures of insects, magazines, books, magnifying lenses

Develop
Fill the center with photos, magazines, and books involving insects and bugs. Encourage the children to browse the books and magazines. Suggest that they use magnifying lenses to get a closer look. If you can capture an insect each day, place it in the center. Be sure that you release it at the end of the day and make sure that you let the children know that you are doing this. It is important that you model respect for all living things.

Reflect/Assess
Can you identify the body parts of the bugs?
¿Pueden identificar las partes del cuerpo de los insectos?
Who can describe his or her favorite bug?
¿Quién puede describir su animalito favorito?

ART

Building Bugs

Objective
To use a variety of materials to create original work

Materials to Gather
boxes, chenille wires, wiggle eyes (optional), tempera paint, egg cartons, index cards, blocks

Develop
Provide a variety of scrap material and encourage the children to build insects. Provide wiggle eyes, if you have them. Encourage the children to make real bugs and imaginary bugs. Encourage them to name their creatures and provide a caged area, possibly made out of blocks, where they can display their bugs. Have them use index cards to label their creatures.

Reflect/Assess
What type of insect did you build?
¿Qué tipo de insecto construyeron?

DRAMATIC PLAY

Let's Go Camping

Objective
To begin to create or re-create stories, moods, or experiences through dramatic representations

Materials to Gather
sheet to make a tent or, if available, a small tent; pretend fire (logs and red, yellow, and orange tissue paper); cookout pots and pans; bed rolls; empty bottle of insect repellent; plastic insects, if available

Develop
Set up a camp area. Encourage the children to pretend to be on an overnight cookout. Suggest plots for their dramatic play.

Reflect/Assess
Invite the children to describe their cookout experiences. *What kinds of bugs did you encounter?*
¿Qué tipo de insectos encontraron?

What Research Suggests

Research shows that repetition is critical to storing information in long-term memory. People have a ten percent chance of remembering what they repeat once in thirty days and a ninety percent chance of remembering what they repeat six times in thirty days. This is one reason why briefly summarizing previously learned facts facilitates greater memory retention.

Begin the Day

- Sing "Five Little Speckled Frogs"/ "Cinco ranitas manchadas."
- Use one of the suggestions for Morning Circle offered in the front of this *Teacher's Edition.*

Objectives

- To link new learning experiences and vocabulary to what is already known about a topic
- To understand that illustrations carry meaning but cannot be read

Vocabulary

insect	insecto
thorax	tórax
abdomen	abdomen
antennae	antenas

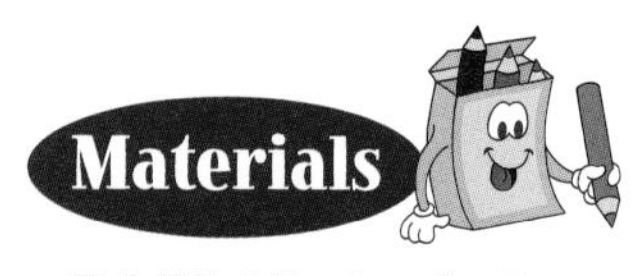

DLM Materials

- *Insect Picnic/El picnic de los insectos*
- *The Dragon's Coming After You/El dragón te está persiguiendo*
- magnetic letters
- *Teacher's Resource Anthology*
  "Five Little Speckled Frogs"/"Cinco ranitas manchadas"
  "Baby Bumblebee"/"Abejorro bebé"
  "The Insect Song"/"La canción del insecto"
  "A Spring Walk"/"Una caminata en primavera"
  bug patterns
  Bug Concentration game

Materials to Gather

- 24-inch pieces of yarn
- magnifying lens
- index cards
- egg cartons
- chenille wires
- wiggle eyes (optional)

LITERACY

Focus

- Sing "Baby Bumblebee"/"Abejorro bebé." Discuss the different endings to the song. In this version, the child does not kill the bumblebee. *What does the girl do with the bumblebee? Why?*
  ¿Qué hace la niña con el abejorro? ¿Por qué?
- Tell the children that they are going to study bugs for the next two weeks. Tell them that this week they will discuss insects. Insects are types of bugs.

Develop

One Way to Develop the Lesson

- Encourage the children to talk about bugs and insects. Have them describe insects they have seen and tell where they have seen them.
- Show the cover of *Insect Picnic/El picnic de los insectos.* Ask the children what they think the book will be about.
- Read the book without stopping at this point to discuss the various insects.
- Ask the children to recall the insects mentioned in the book. Make a list on a piece of chart paper.

Another Way to Develop the Lesson

- Ask the children to recall what *Insect Picnic/El picnic de los insectos* is about. Tell them that you are going to look at some of the insects in the book to gather information to write on your chart.
- Turn to page 5. Call attention to the ant under the magnifying glass. Ask the children to count the body parts. After they count, name the parts for them: head, thorax, and abdomen. Explain that most insects have three body parts. Write *three body parts* on your chart. Now count the legs, and tell the children that most insects have six legs. Write *six legs* on your chart. Finally, count the antennae and tell the children that most insects have two antennae. Write *two antennae* on your chart.
- Show the children the picture of the wasp on page 10 and have them check the criteria: three body parts, two antennae, and six legs. Ask: *Is the wasp an insect?/¿La avispa es un insecto?* Have them closely look at the wasp. What other body parts do they notice? Discuss the fact that many but not all insects have wings. Now check the cricket on page 1. *Is the cricket an insect? Does the cricket have wings?*

  ¿El grillo es un insecto? ¿El grillo tiene alas?
- Sing "The Insect Song"/"La canción del insecto." Tell the children that singing the song will help them remember the body parts a bug needs to have to be called an insect.

  La canción los va a ayudar a recordar las cosas que debe tener un animalito para considerarse un insecto.

Practice

- Place the *Insect Picnic/El picnic de los insectos* book and tape in the Listening Center.
- Invite the children to play the Bug Concentration game.
- Encourage the children to complete the bug puzzles.
- Encourage the children to draw pictures of the insects they found on the playground or insects they have seen before.
- Give each child three crates of an egg carton, wiggle eyes if available, and chenille wires. Encourage the children to create insects. Remind them about the number of body parts that insects have. Have them give their insects names and have them describe how their insects move.
- Give the children the chart of insect names and encourage them to copy the names using magnetic letters. Give them index cards with the names of insects printed on them and encourage them to trace the names.

Preparation

- Make a Bug Concentration game using two photocopies of the bug patterns. Color them, cut them out, and laminate them.
- Make and enlarge two more photocopies of the bug patterns. Color them, cut them out, mount them on different colored construction paper, laminate them, and cut them into puzzles so that you have two puzzles of each bug.
- Write the names of the insects on index cards.

Scaffolding Strategies

More Help Talk about personal experiences the children may have had with insects. *Have you ever been bitten by a mosquito or a bumblebee? Have you ever had to shoo a fly away from your food?*

¿Alguna vez los ha picado un mosquito o un abejorro?

¿Alguna vez han tenido que espantar una mosca de su comida?

Extra Challenge Invite the children to examine the other pictures in *Insect Picnic/El picnic de los insectos. Are all the pictures of insects? What should the title of the book actually be?*

¿Todas las ilustraciones son de insectos?

¿Cuál debía ser el título del libro?

Letter Knowledge

English

- Introduce the letter *y* by reading the story "Yasmeen" in the *English Phonics Resource Guide.*

Spanish

- Introduce the letter *h* by reading the story "Hilario" in the *Spanish Phonics Resource Guide.*

Teacher's NOTE

ALLERGY WARNING Be sensitive to children who may be fearful of insects. Check to make sure that none of the children suffer from allergies to insects before allowing them to search for insects on the playground.

Second Language Learners

Ask parents to send live nonpoisonous insects or dead specimens to school in clear jars with lids. Provide magnifying lenses to promote in-depth investigation, and listen to the children as they examine the insects. Respond to all the statements they make. Restate to clarify, ask questions, or expand on what children say as needed. Encourage the children to compare and contrast the insects, noting attributes such as color, size, and distinguishing characteristics. Provide labels when necessary.

Reflect/Assess

- *What kinds of insects did you find outside?*
  ¿Qué tipos de insectos encontraron afuera?
- *What do insects have in common?*
  ¿Qué tienen en común los insectos?

Storytime 1

- Invite the children to participate in the action story "A Spring Walk"/"Una caminata en primavera." *Which insects are mentioned in the story?*
  ¿Qué insectos se mencionan en el cuento?
  Ask the children to think of other insects they might see on a walk.

Storytime 2

- Read *The Dragon's Coming After You/El dragón te está persiguiendo*. Ask the children to name the two insects mentioned in the story. Go back to the pages that mention the bee and the fly. Have the children check to make sure that both the fly and the bee are insects.

Content Connection

Health and Safety

Objective
To know about safe behavior around bugs and insects

Vocabulary
sting, bite
picar, picar

Activity 1

- Discuss the ways that insects defend themselves. Remind the children of the song about the baby bumblebee. Ask them to name insects that bite or sting. Explain the importance of staying away from anthills and beehives and of not picking up insects.

  ¿Se acuerdan de la canción del abejorro bebé? ¿Pueden nombrar insectos que piquen?

Activity 2

- Talk about what to do if a child gets stung or bitten by an insect. Tell the children that they should tell an adult immediately. Discuss using baking soda for stings and ointments for bites.

  Si alguna vez los pica un insecto, deben decírselo a un adulto inmediatamente. Pueden usar bicarbonato de sodio si el insecto los pica con un punzón o una crema si es simplemente una picada sin punzón.

Anthology Support

"There Was an Old Woman Who Swallowed a Fly"
"Había una anciana que se tragó una mosca"

Suggested Reading

An Insect's Body by Joanna Cole
La luciérnaga Luci by Jesús Ballaz Zabalza

DAY 1

Objectives

- To combine, separate, and name "how many" concrete objects
- To use a variety of software packages with audio, video, and graphics to enhance learning experiences

Vocabulary

add sumar
adding sumar

DLM Materials

- dinosaur counters (2 types)
- *Math Resource Guide*
  Places Scenes (dinosaur backgrounds with 2 counting areas)
  Listen and Count/Escucha y cuenta
  Make It Right: Dinosaur Shop version/Hazlo bien: versión la tienda de los dinosaurios
  Compare Game: Adding version/ Juego de comparar: versión suma
  Counting cards (1–4)
  Numeral cards (1–4)
  Counting Jar (filled with 2 colors of dinosaur counters)
- *DLM Math* software
- *Four Baby Bumblebees* CD
- *Teacher's Resource Anthology*
  Duck, Duck, Goose/Pato, pato, ganso

Materials to Gather

- coffee can or similar can
- sticky notes
- plate or tray
- Dinosaur Shop props (cash register, play money, boxes with labels, and so on)

MATH

Focus

- Play Listen and Count/Escucha y cuenta. Emphasize that the children are adding. Slowly drop counters or cubes into a coffee can; be sure to pause between sets of the drops (e.g. drop, drop . . . (pause) . . . drop, drop.) Start with 1 to 4 drops, then add 2 more. Have them tell how many items have been dropped into the can.
- Ask them to explain how they knew. Ask them how many dropped first, then, how many more. How many in all? Have the children count out loud. Dump out the contents to check.

Develop

- Teach the children Make It Right: Dinosaur Shop version/Hazlo bien: versión la tienda de los dinosaurios. Show the children a box containing 4 dinosaurs. Tell them that you wanted 5 dinosaurs. Ask them to help you make it 5. Follow their suggestions and count to check. Have them put 2 dinosaurs in their hands. Tell them the customer now wants 3 dinosaurs. Ask them how they can make it 3. Repeat, changing to other numbers.
- Introduce and demonstrate the activity Dinosaur Shop, Level 4 and Dinosaur Shop, Level 5 (Free Explore).

Practice

- Reintroduce and have the children play the Compare Game: Adding version/Juego de comparar: versión suma with cards from 1 to 4.
- Encourage the children to play Make It Right: Dinosaur Shop version/Hazlo bien: versión la tienda de los dinosaurios.
- Give the children the Places Scenes: Adding version background with 2 counting areas (see Spring, Day 1). Have them label their sheets with Numeral cards.
- Start a new emphasis with the Counting Jar. If the children haven't already started recording their counts (with pictures or numerals), help them write and post their counts, along with their names.
- Invite the children to work on Dinosaur Shop, Level 4 and Dinosaur Shop, Level 5. Help pairs of children cooperate to play Dinosaur Shop, Level 5 (Free Explore).

Reflect/Assess

- *How did you make sure there was the right number of dinosaurs in the box?*
  ¿Cómo se aseguraron de que había el número correcto de dinosaurios en la caja?

Music and Movement

- Play "Shoo! Fly, Don't Bother Me" from the *Four Baby Bumblebees* CD.
- Play Ant, Ant, Bee/Hormiga, hormiga, abeja as you would Duck, Duck, Goose/Pato, pato, ganso.

Suggested Reading

The Icky Bug Counting Book by Jerry Pallotta

Content Connection

Fine Arts

Objectives

To begin to engage in dramatic play with others

To participate in classroom music activities

DLM Materials

Teacher's Resource Guide

"Las hormiguitas"/"The Little Ants"

"Five Little Speckled Frogs"/ "Cinco ranitas manchadas"

Materials to Gather

plastic bugs or counters

Activity 1

- Invite the children to role-play "Las hormiguitas"/"The Little Ants." Divide them into groups of 4: those who walk, those who jump, those who dance, and those who spin. *How many ants are in each group?*
  ¿Cuántas hormigas hay en cada grupo?

Activity 2

- Encourage the children to role-play "Five Little Speckled Frogs"/ "Cinco ranitas manchadas." Use counters or plastic bugs to represent the bugs the frogs eat. Make it a one-to-one correspondence. Have the children match bugs to frogs. Then ask the children how many frogs there are and how many bugs there are.

Reflect on the Day

- *What did you learn about insects today?*
  ¿Qué aprendieron sobre los insectos hoy?
- *What are some of the kinds of insects we talked about today?*
  ¿Cuáles son algunos de los tipos de insectos de los que hablamos hoy?

Begin the Day

- Sing "The Insect Song"/"La canción del insecto."
- Use one of the suggestions for Morning Circle offered in the front of this *Teacher's Edition.*

Objectives

- To identify 10 or more printed alphabet letters
- To begin to recognize the association between spoken and written words by following the print as it is read aloud

Vocabulary

ants	hormigas
queen	reina
anthill	hormiguero
worker	obrera
colony	colonia

DLM Materials

- Oral Language Development Card 30
- magnetic letters
- *The Little Ants/Las hormiguitas*
- *Insect Picnic/El picnic de los insectos*
- *Teacher's Resource Anthology*
  "The Insect Song"/"La canción del insecto"
  "The Ants Go Marching"/"Las hormiguitas marchan"
  Bug Concentration game
  "The Ram in the Chile Patch"/"El carnero en el sembrado de chiles"
  "The Ant and the Grasshopper"/"La hormiguita y el grillo"
  Ants on a Log

Literacy

Focus

- Sing "The Ants Go Marching"/"Las hormiguitas marchan." Ask the children what they know about ants.
- Tell the children that today they will be studying ants.
  Hoy vamos a estudiar las hormigas.

Develop

One Way to Develop the Lesson

- Show Oral Language Card 30 (ant). Use the suggestions on the back of the card to stimulate conversation. Write the word *ant* on a piece of chart paper. Ask a volunteer to copy the word with magnetic letters.
- Ask the children to check the body parts of the ant in the picture against the criteria for insects. *Does the ant have wings?*
  ¿La hormiga tiene alas?
  Tell the children that the queen ant is the only ant that has wings and that she rubs her wings off before she lays her eggs.
- Explain that ants live in colonies. They are social insects like bees. They spend their entire lives working to build their home and gather food for the colony. They can tunnel fifteen feet under the ground.
- Explain that ants have specific jobs. The ones who build are called *worker ants*. The ant that lays the eggs is called the *queen*.
- Tell the children that some ants live in trees. Ask if anyone has ever found an ant in his or her house. Ask the children where else they see ants.
  ¿Dónde más pueden ver hormigas?

Another Way to Develop the Lesson

- Show the cover of the book *The Little Ants/Las hormiguitas*. Read the title. Ask what letters are in the title. Ask the children what they think the book will be about. Explain that this book is based on a traditional Spanish song about ants.

  ¿Qué letras aparecen en el título? ¿De qué creen que tratará el libro? Este libro se basa en una canción popular española.
- Read the story. Move your hand under the text as you read. Read it a second time and have the children act out the movements of the ants.

Practice

- Place the *Insect Picnic/El picnic de los insectos* book and tape in the Listening Center.
- Provide celery sticks, peanut butter, and raisins in the Cooking Center and encourage the children to make Ants on a Log. You may want to create a simple rebus direction card for them to follow.
- Make thumb print ants. Encourage the children to make thumbprints using finger paint. Remind them to make three body parts. Encourage them to draw legs and antennas.
- Invite the children to play the Bug Concentration game.
- Encourage the children to work on the insect puzzles.
- Give the children the index cards with insect names written on them to trace or copy with magnetic letters.

Materials to Gather

- insect puzzles (see Day 1)
- tracing paper
- index cards with insect names
- celery sticks
- peanut butter
- raisins
- finger paint

Preparation

- Prepare the flannel board story.

Scaffolding Strategies

More Help Have the children count their body parts. *How many arms do humans have? How many legs? How many body parts?*

¿Cuántos brazos tiene el ser humano? ¿Cuántas piernas? ¿Cuántas partes tiene su cuerpo?

Extra Challenge Encourage the children to think of a list of bugs that do not have three body parts.

Second Language Learners

Create a rebus card for children to follow as they make Ants on a Log. Ask them to describe how to make the snack and note the language they use. Are they able to describe each step? Restate to clarify, ask questions, and expand on what the children say, as needed.

Letter Knowledge

English

- Read "Yickity-Yackity, Yickity-Yak" in the *SRA Alphabet Book*.

Spanish

- Read "Hormigas" in *Los niños alfabéticos*. Point out that the name of the bug the children are studying today starts with the letter *h*.

Suggested Reading

Hey, Little Ant by Phillip M. and Hannah Hoose
Inside an Ant Colony by Allan Fowler
La hormiguita que iba a Jerusalén by Grancesca Garberí

Anthology Support

"Little Anthill"
"La hormiguita y Ratón Pérez"
"Baby Bumblebee"
"Abejorro bebé"

Reflect/Assess

- *What do you think ants like to eat?*
  ¿Por qué creen que a las hormigas les gusta comer?
- *Have you ever seen an ant carrying something larger than itself?*
  ¿Alguna vez han visto una hormiga cargando algo más grande que ella?

Literacy Circle

Storytime 1

- Present the "The Ram in the Chile Patch"/"El carnero en el sembrado de chiles" flannel board story. *How was such a small creature able to get such a large creature to move?*
  ¿Cómo pudo esa criatura tan pequeña hacer mover a una criatura tan grande?

Storytime 2

- Read the listening story "The Ant and the Grasshopper"/"La hormiguita y el grillo." *How are the ant and the grasshopper alike? How are they different?*
  ¿En qué se parecen la hormiga y el grillo? ¿En qué se diferencian?

Content Connection

Science/Health and Safety

Objectives
To describe observations
To know safe behavior around bugs and insects

Materials to Gather
shovel, jar, magnifying lens, straws, sticks, clay

Vocabulary
ant, anthill, colony
hormiga, hormiguero, colonia

Activity 1
- Go on a nature walk in search of an anthill. Use a shovel to dig up some of the ants as well as part of their home. Place the contents in a jar.
- Place the jar of ants in the Science Center and encourage the children to observe the behavior of the ants. Provide a magnifying lens. Encourage the children to observe the ants communicating with each other (which they do by touching antennae). Ask the children how they think it would feel to work all the time.

  Observen cómo se comportan las hormigas. Fíjense si ellas hablan entre sí. ¿Cómo creen que se sentirían si tuvieran que trabajar todo el día?
- Give the children clay and let them build an ant colony. Provide straws and sticks for them to use to create tunnels.
- Remind the children about safe behavior around bugs.

Activity 2
- Take the children outdoors. Give each child a 24-inch piece of yarn and a magnifying lens. Have them choose spots on the playground to be their investigation spots. Show them how to make circles with their yarn and encourage them to use the magnifying lenses to look for insects inside their circled spots.

DAY 2

Objectives

- To combine, separate, and name "how many" concrete objects
- To count by ones to 10 or higher
- To use a variety of software packages with audio, video, and graphics to enhance learning experiences

Vocabulary

add	sumar
adding	sumar
number names	nombres de números

DLM Materials

- rhythm band instruments
- *Math Resource Guide*
- See Day 1
- *DLM Math* software
- *Teacher's Resource Anthology* Follow the Leader/Sigue al líder

Materials to Gather

- See Day 1

MATH

Focus

- Have the children capture pretend bugs as they count up to 6 (or higher), then let them go while counting back down to 0.
- Give the children a word problem to act out and solve. A bug scientist captures 6 bugs in a net (have children act as bugs). He counts them to make sure he has 6 (do so). Then the bugs begin to escape out of a hole in the net. Count one by one backwards as each bug escapes.

Develop

- Demonstrate Make It Right: Dinosaur Shop version/Hazlo bien: versión la tienda de los dinosaurios. Give the children their own box (or they can simply use their cupped hands) and toy dinosaurs (or other counters). Have them put 2 dinosaurs in their hands. Tell them the customer now wants 3 dinosaurs. Ask them how they can make it 3. Repeat the activity, changing to other numbers.
- Have the children play the Compare Game: Adding version/Juego de comparar: versión suma with cards from 1 to 4.
- Reintroduce and demonstrate the activity Dinosaur Shop, Level 4 and Dinosaur Shop, Level 5 (Free Explore).

Practice

- Invite the children to play Make It Right: Dinosaur Shop version/ Hazlo bien: versión la tienda de los dinosaurios. Be sure the children understand the task is to make the right number by putting in items to create the requested total.
- Encourage the children to continue to work on Places Scenes: Adding version. Have them label their sheets with Numeral cards.
- Invite the children to explore the Counting Jar.
- Invite the children to work on Dinosaur Shop, Level 4 and Dinosaur Shop, Level 5.

Reflect/Assess

- *How did you figure out who was the winner in the Compare Game: Adding version/Juego de comparar: versión suma?*

  ¿Cómo determinaron quién fue el ganador del Juego de comparar: versión suma?

Music and Movement

- Give the children rhythm band instruments and challenge them to create a musical beat that matches the quick pace of the ant's movement.
- Play Follow the Leader/Sigue al líder. Encourage the children to pretend they are ants on the trail of a sugary treat.

Content Connection

Science

Objectives

To describe observations

To compare objects and organisms and identify similarities and differences

Vocabulary

bug, insects, legs

insecto, insectos, patas

DLM Materials

SRA Book of Animals/SRA El libro de los animales

Teacher's Resource Anthology

"The Insect Song"/"La canción del insecto"

Activity 1

- Read "Spiders"/"Arañas" from the *SRA Book of Animals/SRA El libro de los animales.* Discuss the illustrations. Count the legs on the spider and on the fly. *Which bug has more legs? How many more legs?*

  ¿Qué insecto tiene más patas? ¿Cuántas patas más?

Activity 2

- Sing "The Insect Song"/"La canción del insecto." Check the spider and the fly in the story "Spiders"/"Arañas" in the *SRA Book of Animals/SRA El libro de los animales. Which bug in the story is an insect?*

  ¿Qué animal del cuento es un insecto?

Suggested Reading

The Grouchy Ladybug by Eric Carle

What Research Suggests

Children who have not yet developed counting strategies can still be successful at counting very small numbers.

Reflect on the Day

- *What did you learn about ants today?*

  ¿Qué aprendieron sobre las hormigas hoy?
- *Who can help me spell the word* ant?

  ¿Quién me puede ayudar a deletrear la palabra hormiga?

Begin the Day

- Sing "The Insect Song"/"La canción del insecto."
- Use one of the suggestions for Morning Circle offered in the front of this *Teacher's Edition.*

Objectives

- To begin to retell some sequences of events in stories
- To understand that print carries a message by recognizing labels, signs, and other print forms in the environment

Vocabulary

bee	abeja
beehive	colmena
queen bee	abeja reina
worker	obrera
wasp	avispa
wasp nest	avispero

DLM Materials

- Oral Language Development Cards 29 & 35
- *SRA Photo Library* software
- *Insect Picnic/El picnic de los insectos*
- *Animals That Build Their Homes/ Animales que construyen sus nidos*
- magnetic letters
- *Teacher's Resource Anthology*
  "The Insect Song"/"La canción del insecto"
  "Baby Bumblebee"/"Abejorro bebé"
  "Ms. Bumblebee Gathers Honey"/ "La avispa Zumbi lleva miel"
  Bug Concentration game
  "Animal Homes"/"Hogares de animales"
  bug card patterns (bee)

LITERACY

Focus

- Sing "Baby Bumblebee"/"Abejorro bebé." Ask the children if they remember discussing why the child let the bumblebee go. *What would you do if you got stung by a bumblebee?*

  ¿Recuerdan haber hablado sobre por qué el niño dejó escapar el abejorro? ¿Qué harían si los picara un abejorro?
- Tell the children that today they are going to discuss bumblebees and wasps.

  Hoy vamos a hablar de los abejorros y las avispas.

Develop

One Way to Develop the Lesson

- Show the picture of the wasp from *Insect Picnic/El picnic de los insectos* or page 20 of *Animals That Build Their Homes/Animales que construyen sus nidos.* Write the word *wasp* on a piece of chart paper and invite a volunteer to copy the word using magnetic letters.
- Ask the children to look closely at the wasp. *Does it have all the necessary body parts to be called an insect?*

  ¿El cuerpo de la abeja tiene todas las partes necesarias para considerarse un insecto?
- A female potter wasp makes a clay pot for each of her eggs. She puts live caterpillars into each pot, so that the baby wasp has food when it hatches.
- Ask: *How are wasps like bees? How are they different?*

  ¿En qué se parecen las avispas a las abejas? ¿En qué se diferencian?

Another Way to Develop the Lesson

- Show Oral Language Cards 29 and 35. Use the suggestions on the backs of the cards to stimulate conversation. Write the words *bee* and *beehive* on a piece of chart paper and invite a volunteer to copy the words using magnetic letters. Ask the children if they can find the word *bee* in *beehive*.
- Ask the children to look closely at the bee. *Does the bee have all the necessary body parts to be called an insect?*

  ¿El cuerpo de la abeja tiene todas las partes necesarias para considerarse un insecto?
- Explain that bumblebees, like ants, are social insects. They each have specific jobs to perform. There are worker bees, guard bees, and queen bees. The workers collect nectar and pollen from flowers. The guard bees watch the nest and protect it from intruders. The queen bee helps to reproduce new bees.

Practice

- Place the Ms. Bumblebee puppet and props in the Language Center and encourage the children to retell the story.
- Invite the children to play the Bug Concentration game.
- Encourage the children to work on the bug puzzles.
- Give the children copies of Ms. Bumblebee and have them color her, cut her out, and glue her to tongue depressors to make their own puppets.
- Place the index cards with insect names in the Writing Center. Provide bee pollen (salt or sand colored yellow by powdered tempera paint) on a cookie sheet and invite the children to write the names of insects in the pollen.
- Give the children yellow and black strips of construction paper and encourage them to make striped yellow and black bee patterns.
- Encourage the children to find insects in the Animal category on the *SRA Photo Library* software.

Materials to Gather

- tongue depressors
- salt or sand
- yellow tempera paint
- cookie sheet
- yellow and black construction paper
- insect name index cards

Preparation

- Make the flannel board story.
- Make a copy of Ms. Bumblebee for every child.
- Mix yellow tempera paint with salt or sand.

Second Language Learners

For "The Beehive," make paper bees and tape them to your fingers. Show how they can be hidden/escondidas to familiarize second language learners with the new vocabulary. Show a picture of the beehive and demonstrate how your hands are clasped to look like a hive. Recite the entire poem as you model the finger play. Then invite the children to complete the finger play as you repeat the poem and do the motions. Some children will begin to recite some of the words as they complete the motions. Note the language they use.

DAY 3

Letter Knowledge

English

- Invite the children to shape the letter *y* with play dough.

Spanish

- Invite the children to shape the letter *h* with play dough.

Suggested Reading

Berlioz the Bear by Jan Brett
Esteban Pio, Pio by Rita Culla
La abejita coja by Tapia de González

Anthology Support

"The Beehive"
"Big Brown Bee"
"Los mosquitos"

Technology Support

Type simple addition problems on the computer so the answers increase by 1. For example: 0+1, 1+1, 2+1, 2+2, and 2+3. Have volunteers type answers. Discuss the number progression (1, 2, 3, 4, 5).

Reflect/Assess

- *How are bumblebees like ants? How are they different?*
  ¿En qué se parecen las abejas a las hormigas? ¿En qué se diferencian?
- *Can someone demonstrate the waggle dance?*
  ¿Alguien me puede demostrar el baile del meneo?

Literacy Circle

Storytime 1

- Read the pages in *Animals That Build Their Homes/Animales que construyen sus nidos* that pertain to bees, hornets, and wasps.

Storytime 2

- Present the "Animal Homes"/"Hogares de animales" flannel board story. Review the types of homes bees and wasps build.

Content Connection

Fine Arts

Objective

To use a variety of materials to create original work

DLM Materials

Teacher's Resource Anthology
"Ms. Bumblebee Gathers Honey"/"La avispa Zumbi lleva miel," Rafita and Pepita puppets

Materials to Gather

yellow and black tempera paint, play dough, chenille wires, wiggle eyes, toothpicks, waxed paper

Activity 1

- Ask the children who remembers how ants communicate with each other. If no one remembers, remind the children that ants communicate by touching antennas. Explain that bees communicate by wagging their tails at each other and by flying in circles. Bees do what is called a *waggle dance.* In this dance, the direction in which the bee moves in relationship to the hive communicates the location of food and pollen to the rest of the bees. Demonstrate this movement or ask a child to demonstrate it.
- Present the puppet story "Ms. Bumblebee Gathers Honey"/"La avispa Zumbi lleva miel." Ask the children to help you tell the story. *Who remembers the color of the flower Ms. Bumblebee visited first? Who tried to steal Ms. Bumblebee's honey? What did Ms. Bumblebee do?* Use Rafita and Pepita to defend the bear's actions.

  ¿Quién recuerda qué color de flor visitó primero la avispa Zumbi? ¿Quién trató de robar la miel de la avispa Zumbi? ¿Qué hizo la avispa Zumbi?

Activity 2

- Invite the children to shape bees out of play dough. Encourage them to make the three body parts. Provide chenille wires for legs and antennae. Use waxed paper for wings and let the children use wiggle eyes, if available. If wiggle eyes are not available, encourage them to use toothpicks to draw the eyes on their bees.
- Provide yellow and black paint and encourage the children to paint large bumblebees.

DAY 3

Objectives

- To combine, separate, and name "how many" concrete objects
- To count by ones to 10 or higher
- To use a variety of software packages with audio, video, and graphics to enhance learning experiences

Vocabulary

add	sumar
adding	sumar
number names	nombres de números

DLM Materials

- dinosaur counters
- *Math Resource Guide*
  Feely Box
  Gone Fishing/De pesca
- See Day 1
- *DLM Math* software
- *Four Baby Bumblebees* CD
- *Teacher's Resource Anthology*
  Waggle Dance/El baile del meneo

Materials to Gather

- fish-shaped crackers (10 per child)
- connecting cubes
- paper plates (2 for each child)

Preparation

- Place a tower of 2 connecting cubes and a separate single cube in the Feely Box.

MATH

Focus

- Play Gone Fishing/De pesca. Tell the children that they will be dinosaurs that eat fish. Pass out containers of fish crackers. Have the children use their cupped hands as their lake. Encourage them to act out a fish story.
- Ask how many fish they have in their lake (0). Say that 2 fish swam near the dinosaur. Have them put 2 fish in their lake. Say that 3 more swam near. Have them add 3. Ask how many fish they have in all. Say the dinosaur was so happy to have 5 fish, it ate them all! Ask them how many fish are now in the lake (0 again).
- When the children are ready, you can decrease/subtract the number of fish in the lake by having them eat some of what they have and asking them how many are still in the lake.

Develop

- Secretly hide 2 towers of 2 connecting cubes each in the Feely Box. Have a child feel both and tell how many there are in all. Encourage the children to tell how they figured out how many cubes they were feeling. Repeat with different, small numbers of cubes. Tell them they can play the same game with each other in the centers.
- Have the children play Places Scenes: Adding version. Have them label their sheets with a Numeral card.

Practice

- Invite the children to guess with a friend what is in the Feely Box.
- Invite the children to continue to count counters on their Places Scenes sheet.
- Encourage the children to continue to play Make It Right: Dinosaur Shop version/Hazlo bien: versión la tienda de los dinosaurios.
- Have the children explore the Counting Jar.
- Invite the children to work on Dinosaur Shop, Level 4 and Dinosaur Shop, Level 5. Ask the children how they figured out how to give the customer the number he or she wanted.

Reflect/Assess

- *If you were a dinosaur with 3 fish in your lake, then 3 more swam in, how would you figure out how many there were in all?*
  Si fueran un dinosaurio con 3 peces en su lago y luego llegaran 3 más, ¿cómo determinarían cuántos hay en total?

Music and Movement

- Give each child 2 paper plates to use as wings and encourage them to fly like bumblebees to classical music. If available, play "Flight of the Bumblebee" by Rimsky-Korsakov, which makes a great accompaniment for their movements.
- Teach the children how to do the Waggle Dance/El baile del meneo. Play "Be My Little Baby Bumblebee" from the *Four Baby Bumblebees CD*.

Content Connection

Science/Fine Arts

Objectives

To describe observations

To participate in classroom music activities

Vocabulary

bugs, insects, counting words

insectos, insectos, palabras para contar

DLM Materials

Insect Picnic/El picnic de los insectos

Teacher's Resource Anthology

"There Was an Old Woman Who Swallowed a Fly"/"Había una anciana que se tragó una mosca"

Activity 1

- Have the children count the bugs on each page of *Insect Picnic/El picnic de los insectos*. When appropriate, count a small collection in 1 area of the page and additional insects in a second area of the page. For example, on page 4 there are 2 bees in the air and 1 on a flower for a total of 3 bees.

Activity 2

- Sing "There Was an Old Woman Who Swallowed a Fly"/"Había una anciana que se tragó una mosca." Use the flannel board illustrations with the song. Count the things the old woman swallowed. Then count the things she swallowed before the spider and after the spider.

Suggested Reading

The Icky Bug Counting Book by Jerry Pallotta

Reflect on the Day

- *What did you learn about bees today?*
  ¿Qué aprendieron de las abejas hoy?
- *Which do you like best, bees or ants? Why?*
  ¿Cuál les gusta más, las abejas o las hormigas? ¿Por qué?

Begin the Day

- Sing "The Insect Song"/"La canción del insecto."
- Use one of the suggestions for Morning Circle offered in the front of this *Teacher's Edition*.

Objectives

- To listen with increasing attention
- To understand and follow simple oral directions

Vocabulary

fly	mosca
dragonfly	libélula

DLM Materials

- Oral Language Development Card 29
- *Insect Picnic/El picnic de los insectos*
- *The Dragon's Coming After You/El dragón te está persiguiendo*
- magnetic letters
- *Teacher's Resource Anthology*
  "The Insect Song"/"La canción del insecto"
  "There Was an Old Woman Who Swallowed a Fly"/"Había una anciana que se tragó una mosca"
  Bug Concentration game

Materials to Gather

- bug puzzles
- index cards with insect names
- fifteen-inch crepe paper streamers
- paper towel tubes
- chart paper

Preparation

- Make the flannel board story, if not already made.

LITERACY

Focus

- Sing "There Was an Old Woman Who Swallowed a Fly"/"Había una anciana que se tragó una mosca." Ask the children to listen to the story and guess which one of the bugs mentioned in the story will be in the lesson today.
  ¿De cuál insecto del cuento hablaremos hoy?
- Tell the children that today they will discuss flying insects: flies, dragonflies, and termites.
  Hoy hablaremos de insectos voladores: moscas, libélulas y termitas.

Develop

One Way to Develop the Lesson

- Show Oral Language Card 29 (dragonfly). Use the questions on the back of the card to stimulate conversation. Show another photo of a dragonfly on page 15 in *Insect Picnic/El picnic de los insectos*. Ask the children if they have ever seen a dragonfly. If so, where and what was it doing? Write the word *dragonfly* on a piece of chart paper. Invite a volunteer to copy the insect's name using magnetic letters.
  ¿Alguna vez han visto una libélula? ¿Dónde y qué estaba haciendo?
- Encourage the children to count the legs, body parts, and antennae of the dragonfly to verify that it is an insect.
- Have the children look carefully at the dragonfly's wings. They are transparent. Tell the children that the dragonfly is the fastest flying insect. It can fly as fast as people drive their cars. It flies over ponds, streams, and rivers, hunting other insects to eat.

Another Way to Develop the Lesson

- Show the photo of a fly on page 13 in *Insect Picnic/El picnic de los insectos*. Ask the children if they have ever seen a fly. If so, where and what was it doing? Write the word *fly* on the chart paper under the word *dragonfly*. Ask the children if they can find the word *fly* in *dragonfly*.

  ¿Pueden encontrar la palabra fly *en* dragonfly?

  Invite a volunteer to copy the insect's name using magnetic letters.
- Encourage the children to count the legs, body parts, and antennae of the fly to verify that it is an insect.
- Ask the children to look closely at the wings of the fly. Do they notice the black veins running through the wings?

  ¿Pueden ver las venas negras en las alas?
- Share that flies have eyes that cause them to see multiple images. They also have eyes that allow them to see in all directions. Like the dragonfly, the fly is a fast-moving insect.
- Ask the children if they have ever heard someone say, *I wish I could be a fly on the wall/Desearía ser una mosca en la pared.* Discuss the meaning of this sentence. Explain that this kind of expression is called a *cliché.* Give some other examples such as *quiet as a mouse/silencioso como un ratón* or *big as a horse/grande como un caballo.*

Practice

- Place the *Insect Picnic/El picnic de los insectos* book and tape in the Listening Center.
- Invite the children to play the Bug Concentration game.
- Encourage the children to work on bug puzzles.
- Invite each child to make dragonfly wings by taping two 10- to 15-inch crepe paper streamers to a paper towel tube. Have the children save their dragonflies to use during Music and Movement.
- Give the children index cards with insect names written on them. Encourage them to copy or trace the names.
- Give the children the "There Was an Old Woman Who Swallowed a Fly"/"Había una anciana que se tragó una mosca" flannel board story and have them sequence the things the old woman swallowed.
- Provide a prism to replicate the construction of a fly's eye. Ask the children to look at pictures through the prism. Tell them that this is similar to how a fly sees. Ask them to describe what happens to the pictures as they look through the prism.

  ¿Qué les sucede a los dibujos cuando los ven por el prisma?

Scaffolding Strategies

More Help Take the children outdoors in search of flies and dragonflies.

Extra Challenge Encourage the children to help create a Venn diagram comparing flies to dragonflies.

Second Language Learners

Place an audiotape of "There Was an Old Woman Who Swallowed a Fly"/"Había una anciana que se tragó una mosca" in the Language Center with the flannel board story. Have the children use the flannel board story pieces to help them sequence the things she swallowed. When the children are able to sequence the story independently, ask them to retell the story using the figures; note the language they use. It may also help if children sing the story.

Anthology Support

"Jump or Jiggle"
"Baby Bumblebee"
"Abejorro bebé"
"La pulga"
"A un caracol"

Letter Knowledge

English

- Invite the children to think of ways to make the letter *y* with their bodies. Play the Think, Pair, Share game with this activity.

Spanish

- Invite the children to think of ways to make the letter *h* with their bodies. Play the Piensa, aparea, comparte game with this activity.

Suggested Reading

Discovery of the Dragonflies by Jim Patton

Reflect/Assess

- *How are dragonflies and flies alike? How are they different?*

  ¿En qué se parecen las libélulas y las moscas? ¿En qué se diferencian?
- *Which insect flies the fastest, the fly or the dragonfly?*

  ¿Qué insecto vuela más rápido, la mosca o la libélula?

Literacy Circle

Storytime 1

- Present the "There Was an Old Woman Who Swallowed a Fly"/ "Había una anciana que se tragó una mosca" flannel board story. *What other bug did the old woman swallow?*

  ¿Qué otro insecto se tragó la anciana?

Storytime 2

- Invite the children to help write a story about a little elf who rode on the back of a dragonfly. *Where did they go? What did they do?/¿Adónde fueron? ¿Qué hicieron?* Or read *The Dragon's Coming After You/El dragón te está persiguiendo* and ask the children to listen for the line in the story about a fly.

Content Connection

Fine Motor Development

Objectives

To begin to develop pincer control in picking up objects
To begin to use scissors

Materials to Gather

no-hinge clothespin, chenille wires, construction paper

Activity 1

- Invite the children to make dragonflies using no-hinge clothespins. Have them paint and decorate the heads of the dragonflies and then add chenille wires for antennas. Provide a template for them to trace to make wings. After they have decorated the wings, have them slip the wings into the slits in the clothespins.

Activity 2

- Tell the children that dragonflies have eyes that can see in all directions. The dragonfly's head is almost entirely eyes. Demonstrate the dragonfly's ability to see in all directions by playing a direction game. Stand behind the children where they can't see you and give a direction that includes a visual clue. For example, *Move your hand like this/Muevan su mano así.* When the children cannot follow your directions, ask them why. When they respond that they could not see you, tell them that a dragonfly could see you because its eyes allow it to see in all directions, even behind it. *¿Por qué no pueden seguir mis instrucciones?*

DAY 4

Objectives

- To combine, separate, and name "how many" concrete objects
- To count by ones to 10 or higher
- To use a variety of software packages with audio, video, and graphics to enhance learning experiences

Vocabulary

add sumar
adding sumar

DLM Materials

- dinosaur counters
- *Math Resource Guide*
  Feely Box
  Gone Fishing/De pesca
- See Day 1
- *DLM Math* software
- *Four Baby Bumblebees* CD

Materials to Gather

- fish-shaped crackers (10 per child)
- connecting cubes
- See Day 1

Scaffolding Strategies

More Help Decrease the total number of counters the children use on their Places Scenes backgrounds.

Extra Challenge Increase the total number of counters the children use on the Places Scenes backgrounds.

MATH

Focus

- Pretend to be a dinosaur capturing fish as you count up to 6 (or higher), then eat them while you count back down to 0.
- Play Gone Fishing/De pesca again.

Develop

- Have the children make numbers with their fingers. Have them put their hands in their laps between each task. Tell them to show 3 fingers on their right hand. Ask them, how many fingers are up and how many are down. Repeat several times with other numbers.

Practice

- Invite the children to guess with a friend what is in the Feely Box. Have 1 child secretly hide 2 small towers of connecting cubes in the Feely Box for a friend and see if he or she can feel it and tell how many cubes are in the box.
- Invite the children to continue to count counters on their Places Scenes: Adding version sheet. Encourage them to label their scenes with the numeral that shows how many they have altogether.
- Have the children play the Compare Game: Adding version/Juego de comparar: versión suma.
- Encourage the children to continue playing Make It Right: Dinosaur Shop version/Hazlo bien: versión la tienda de los dinosaurios.
- Have the children explore the Counting Jar.
- Invite the children to work on Dinosaur Shop, Level 4 and Dinosaur Shop, Level 5.

Reflect/Assess

- *If you have 1 finger up on one hand, how many fingers are down? How do you know?*

  Si levantan 1 dedo de su mano, ¿cuántos dedos tienen abajo? ¿Cómo lo saben?

Music and Movement

- Play "Shoo! Fly, Don't Bother Me" from the *Four Baby Bumblebees* CD. Invite the children to do the dance that goes with the song. The instructions on how to do the dance are on the CD cover.
- Play classical music and encourage the children to fly the dragonflies they made.

Suggested Reading

The Icky Bug Counting Book by Jerry Pallotta

Content Connection

Fine Arts/Math

Objectives

To use a variety of materials to create original work

To sort objects into groups by an attribute and begin to explain how the grouping was done

Materials to Gather

stamp pads, markers, magazines, drawing paper, crayons

Activity 1

- Encourage the children to fold a piece of paper in half and using a stamp pad, make fingerprint bugs on each half of their paper. When they have finished, have them count the bugs on each half of their paper and tell you how many bugs they have drawn in all.

Activity 2

- Provide magazines that have pictures of bugs. Encourage the children to cut out the bugs and then glue them to a mural in a position that denotes whether they are flying or walking. After the mural is finished, count the bugs in the air and the bugs on the ground. *How many bugs are there in all?*

  ¿Cuántos insectos hay en total?

Reflect on the Day

- *What did you learn about insects today?*

  ¿Qué aprendieron sobre insectos hoy?
- *Who can help me spell the word* fly?

  ¿Quién me puede ayudar a deletrear la palabra mosca?

Home Connection

Send home a take-home book pack with four children. You will find the directions and a recording sheet for this activity in the *Home Connections Resource Guide.*

Begin the Day

- Sing "The Insect Song"/"La canción del insecto."
- Use one of the suggestions for Morning Circle offered in the front of this *Teacher's Edition.*

Objectives

- To begin to recognize the association between spoken and written words by following the print as it is read aloud
- To begin to identify rhymes and rhyming sounds in familiar words, participate in rhyming games, and repeat rhyming songs and poems

Vocabulary

mosquito	mosquito
termite	termita
pest	plaga

DLM Materials

- *Insect Picnic/El picnic de los insectos*
- *Animals That Build Their Homes/ Animales que construyen sus nidos*
- *Teacher's Resource Anthology*
  "The Insect Song"/"La canción del insecto"
  "Mosquitoes"/"Mosquitos"
  Bug Concentration game
  "The Evil King"/"El rey malvado"

Materials to Gather

- chart paper
- insect puzzles
- large eyedropper
- pitcher of juice
- egg cartons
- chenille wires
- index cards with insect names
- decorations such as beads, sequins, rickrack, paint, and so on

LITERACY

Focus

- Sing "Mosquitoes"/"Mosquitos." Ask the children if they have been bitten by mosquitoes. Explain that a mosquito sucks human and animal blood. It uses its sharp mouthparts to pierce the skin and suck the blood through a tube.
- Tell the children that today they will learn about mosquitoes and termites.

  Hoy aprenderán sobre mosquitos y termitas.

Develop

One Way to Develop the Lesson

- Create a word web. Write the word *mosquito* in the center of a piece of chart paper. Show the children the picture of the mosquito in *Insect Picnic/El picnic de los insectos.* Ask them to determine if the mosquito is an insect by looking closely at its body parts. Encourage the children to tell you what they know about mosquitoes.
- Print the poem below on a piece of chart paper. Read it to the children a few times, moving your hand beneath the words. Have the children read the poem with you. Invite a volunteer to point to the word *mosquitoes.* For the English version, ask the children which word rhymes with *yummy. Which part of the poem is funny?*

  ¿Qué parte del poema es divertido?

  Don't try to eat mosquitoes
  They really aren't that yummy
  And if they get inside you
  They'll bite you in the tummy.

  No intentes comer mosquitos
  porque no son muy sabrosos.
  Y si los dejas entrar
  tu barriguita van a picar.

Another Way to Develop the Lesson

- Show the children pages 26 and 27 of *Animals That Build Their Homes/Animales que construyen sus nidos*. Discuss termites. Ask the children what other insect looks like a termite. Ask the children to determine if the termite is an insect by using the same criteria they have been using all week.

  ¿La termita es un insecto?
- Explain that termites eat wood and that people have to be careful that they don't eat the wood in their houses. Termites are usually found in damp, dark places.

  Las termitas comen madera y tenemos que tener cuidado de que no se coman la madera de nuestras casas. Por lo general, se encuentran en sitios húmedos y lugares oscuros.
- Print the chant below on a piece of chart paper. Read it to the children a couple of times. Have them read it with you. Invite a volunteer to point to the word *termite*. Ask the children which other words in the chant start with the same letter as *termite*. Ask the children which words in the chant rhyme with *door*. Ask inferential questions about the rhyme. *Why does the author of the poem want the bugs to leave?*

  ¿Por qué el autor del poema quiere que los insectos se vayan?

  Testy termites tapping at my door,
  Testy termites rapping on my floor,
  You're much too noisy to ignore,
  Fly away! Fly away! Return no more.
- Print the chant below on a piece of chart paper. Read it a couple of times. Then ask the children to read it with you. Ask a volunteer to find the word *termita*. Find another word that has the same beginning letter. Ask the children what words rhyme with *vez* or *más*. *Why does the author say the termites should go away?*

  ¿Por qué el autor dice que las termitas se deben alejar?

  Termita, termita comiendo mi puerta otra vez,
  termita, termita golpeando con tus pies.
  Lárgate de aquí y no vuelvas más
  porque sí vuelves, mucho pagarás.

Preparation

- Print the English and Spanish termite chant and mosquito poem on chart paper.
- Construct a pair of bug glasses for each child.

Second Language Learners

Encourage the children to name the insects they uncover as they play Bug Concentration. This will help them to recall the location of the insect on the next trial and promote vocabulary development.

Anthology Support

"My Pet Mosquito"
"Mosquito, mi mascota"
"Little Anthill"
"La hormiguita"
"Los mosquitos"

DAY 5

Letter Knowledge

English

- Invite the children to find and circle the letter *y* in newspapers and magazines.

Spanish

- Invite the children to find and circle the letter *h* in newspapers and magazines.

Suggested Reading

Why Mosquitoes Buzz in People's Ears by Verna Aardema
Gotcha by Gail Jorgensen
La canción del mosquito by Alma Flor Ada

Practice

- Invite the children to play the Bug Concentration game.
- Encourage the children to work on bug puzzles.
- Provide a pitcher of juice, juice cups, and a large eyedropper. Invite the children to fill their juice cups using the mosquito mouthpiece eyedropper. *How long does it take to get a cup of juice?*

  ¿Cuánto tiempo toma obtener una taza de jugo?
- Give the children the index cards with names of insects on them and a tray of damp sand to simulate the damp places where mosquitoes and termites are found. Encourage the children to use sticks to write the insect names in the wet sand.
- Encourage the children to construct bug eyes. Give each child two connected crates from a foam egg carton. Cut a small hole in the bottom of each crate and hook a chenille wire to each side to make glasses. Provide paint, beads, sequins, and rickrack to decorate the bug eyes.

Reflect/Assess

- *How are mosquitoes and termites alike? How are they different?*

  ¿En qué se parecen los mosquitos y las termitas? ¿En qué se diferencian?
- *How are termites like ants? How are they different?*

  ¿En qué se parecen las termitas y las hormigas? ¿En qué se diferencian?

Literacy Circle

Storytime 1

- Read the listening story "The Evil King"/"El rey malvado." Ask the children how such a tiny creature could help get rid of such a mean king.

  ¿Cómo una criatura tan pequeña pudo ayudar a deshacerse de un rey tan malo?

Storytime 2

- Read *Insect Picnic/El picnic de los insectos*. Stop and discuss each of the insects the children have studied this week.

Content Connection

Social Studies

Objectives

To cooperate with others in a joint activity

To identify animals and plants as living things

Vocabulary

decomposition, fertilization, pollinate, bacteria

descomposición, fertilización, polinización, bacteria

DLM Materials

Insect Picnic/El picnic de los insectos

Oral Language Development Cards 27, 29, & 30

Activity 1

- Review all the insects studied this week. Display Oral Language Cards 27, 29, and 30. Use *Insect Picnic/El picnic de los insectos* to show pictures of the wasp, the mosquito, and the fly. Ask the children if they have ever turned over a rock or pile of wet leaves and found ants, spiders, and other bugs underneath.
- Work with the children to create a list of ways that insects help people. They aid in decomposition, pollinate flowers, consume bacteria, destroy other insects, improve the fertilization of the earth and, in some cultures, serve as food.

Activity 2

- Encourage the children to look at the list of the ways insects help people. Have them make a list of ways people can be kinder to insects, such as leaving them in their natural habitats and not harming them. Discuss the children's ideas. Emphasize that all living things play a role in making Earth a good place to live.

Podemos ser más cariñosos con los insectos al dejarlos en su hábitat natural y no hacerles daño. Todos los seres vivos juegan un papel al hacer de la Tierra un mejor lugar para vivir.

DAY 5

Objectives

- To combine, separate, and name "how many" concrete objects
- To count by ones to 10 or higher
- To use a variety of software packages with audio, video, and graphics to enhance learning experiences

Vocabulary

add	sumar
adding	sumar
number names	nombres de números

DLM Materials

- Rafita and Pepita/Rafita y Pepita puppets
- *Math Resource Guide*
  Feely Box
  How Many Now?: Hidden version/ ¿Cuántos hay ahora?: versión de esconder
- See Day 1
- *DLM Math* software
- *Teacher's Resource Anthology*
  Simon Says/Simón dice

Materials to Gather

- connecting cubes
- See Day 1

MATH

Focus

- Examine the children's displayed recordings of how many are in the Counting Jar. Do they remember how many of each type (e.g., color)? Dump the objects and count them to check.

Develop

- Play How Many Now?: Hidden version/¿Cuántos hay ahora?: versión de esconder. Show 2 cubes of 1 color and ask the children to tell you how many you have. Close your hand (or put the cubes under a container), hiding the cubes.
- Add 2 cubes of a second color to your closed hand. Ask the children how many there are now altogether. Have them figure out how to solve the problem. Open your hand and count all the cubes to check.
- Repeat with different numbers, only adding 1, 2, or at most 3, cubes to your closed hand.
- Play Dinosaur Shop, Level 5, with the children.

Practice

- Invite the children to guess with a friend what is in the Feely Box. Have 1 child secretly hide 2 small towers of connecting cubes in the Feely Box for a friend and see if the friend can feel it and tell how many cubes are in the box.
- Invite the children to continue to count counters on their Places Scenes: Adding version sheet. Encourage them to label their scene with the Numeral card that shows how many they have altogether.
- Have the children play the Compare Game: Adding version/Juego de comparar: versión suma.
- Encourage the children to continue playing Make It Right: Dinosaur Shop version/Hazlo bien: versión la tienda de los dinosaurios.
- Have the children explore the Counting Jar.
- Invite the children to work on Dinosaur Shop, Level 4 and Dinosaur Shop, Level 5. Can you see signs of progress in their thinking in Level 4? Are they able to answer without a lot of trial and error?

Reflect/Assess

- *How did you know how many objects there were in the Feely Box?*
  ¿Cómo sabían cuántos objetos había en la Feely Box?
- Computer Show: Have the children show their work in Dinosaur Shop, Level 4.

Content Connection

Science

Objectives
To describe observations
To share observations and findings with others through pictures, discussions, or dramatizations

DLM Materials
Oral Language Development Cards 29 and 30

Materials to Gather
crayons, number words, drawing paper

Activity 1

- Use Oral Language Cards 29 and 30 and count the legs on one side and then on the other side of the insects. Ask the children how many legs are on each side of the insects and how many legs in all.

Activity 2

- Encourage the children to record their observations about the number of body parts of insects by drawing an insect of their choice. Encourage them to check their drawings for accuracy to make sure they have added the correct number of legs on each side of the insect body. Provide Oral Language Cards 29 and 30 for models.

Music and Movement

- Play Mr. Mosquito/Señor Mosquito as you would Simon Says/Simón dice.
- Divide the class in half. Tell one-half of the children that they are mosquitoes and the other half that they are termites. Give the mosquitoes toilet paper tubes to make a buzzing sound through and give the termites two craft sticks to hit together. Play some music and let your insect musicians play along. Let Rafita and Pepita/Rafita y Pepita each play with one of the groups.

Suggested Reading

The Icky Bug Counting Book by Jerry Pallotta

Reflect on the Day

- *What have you learned about insects this week?*
  ¿Qué aprendieron sobre los insectos esta semana?
- *What can you tell your families about insects?*
  ¿Qué les pueden decir a sus familias sobre los insectos?

Looking Ahead

Connecting to the Theme: Bugs

Continuing the previous theme, these lessons include topics such as ladybugs, fireflies, caterpillars, and worms. Again, children should begin to understand that insects are important to the world in which we live. Through various literature selections and activities, children will have the opportunity to compare and contrast various insects.

	Objectives	DLM Materials	Materials to Gather
DAY 1	• To show appreciation of repetitive language patterns • To begin to notice beginning letters in familiar words • To combine, separate, and name "how many" concrete objects • To enjoy listening to and discussing storybooks and information books read aloud	• Oral Language Development Card 36 • magnetic letters • *Insect Picnic/El picnic de los insectos* • *Teacher's Resource Anthology* • counters (10 per child) • *Math Resource Guide* • *DLM Math* software	• bug puzzles • plastic combs • craft sticks • index cards with insect names • ping-pong balls • green spray paint • three-inch pieces of yarn • paper plates to use as cookies
DAY 2	• To use language for a variety of purposes • To begin to dictate words, phrases, and sentences to an adult recording on paper • To cooperate with others in a joint activity • To combine, separate, and name "how many" concrete objects • To count concrete objects to five or higher • To begin to use scissors	• *Insect Picnic/El picnic de los insectos* • *Teacher's Resource Anthology* • counters (10 per child) • *Math Resource Guide* • *DLM Math* software	• flashlights • fluorescent markers • paper plates • plastic knife • apples • bananas • raisins • whipping cream • templates • plastic bugs or paper bugs
DAY 3	• To use language for a variety of purposes • To listen for different purposes • To use different colors, surface textures, and shapes to create form and meaning • To use a variety of materials to create original work • To combine, separate, and name "how many" concrete objects • To count concrete objects to five or higher	• Oral Language Development Cards 25 & 26 • Metamorphosis sequence cards • *Insect Picnic/El picnic de los insectos* • *Teacher's Resource Anthology* • counters (10 per child) • *Math Resource Guide* • *DLM Math* software	• tray of sand or salt • caterpillar and butterfly puzzles • food coloring • coffee filters • clothespins • chenille wires • raisins (10 per child) • number cube (3–8 dots) • streamers
DAY 4	• To refine and extend understanding of known words • To link new learning experiences and vocabulary to what is already known about a topic • To combine, separate, and name "how many" concrete objects • To count concrete objects to five or higher • To begin to share and cooperate with others in group activities	• Oral Language Development Cards 25-31 & 36 • magnetic letters • *Teacher's Resource Anthology* • counters (10 per child) • *Math Resource Guide* • *DLM Math* software • *Making Music with Thomas Moore* CD	• finger paint • yarn or string • chenille wires • light source • connecting cubes (blue and yellow) • raisins (10 per child) • two number cubes (1–3) • cloth
DAY 5	• To understand that writing is used to communicate ideas and information • To begin to dictate words, phrases, and sentences to an adult recording on paper • To begin to create or re-create stories, moods, or experiences through dramatic representations • To count concrete objects to five or higher	• Oral Language Development Card 24 • *Teacher's Resource Anthology* • counters (10 per child) • *Math Resource Guide* • *DLM Math* software • *Esta es mi tierra* CD	• white yarn • play dough or clay • elastic thread • chenille wires • black chenille wires • raisins (10 per child) • yarn • large white sheet

(See individual lesson pages for complete lists of materials.)

Learning Centers

SCIENCE

Looking for Bugs

Objective
To begin to use scientific words and phrases to describe objects, events, and living things

Materials to Gather
photographs and pictures of insects, magazines, books, magnifying glasses, bug cages

Develop
This weekly center builds on the Science center from last week. Change the books and photographs, and continue looking for live insects and bugs to put on display for a day. Be sure that you release any live insects at the end of each day. Remind the children that they should not take the insects from their natural homes. Interact with the children as they browse through the magazines, books, and photographs.

Reflect/Assess
Can you tell me the names of the bugs' body parts?
¿Pueden decirme los nombres de las partes del cuerpo de los insectos?
Can you tell me where the bugs live?
¿Pueden decirme dónde viven los insectos?

ART

Building Bugs

Objective
To use different colors, surface textures, and shapes to create form and meaning

Materials to Gather
boxes, pipe cleaners, wiggle eyes (optional), tempera paint, egg cartons, hose, socks, foam balls, tissue paper, clear plastic wrap, waxed paper, index cards

Develop
Continue this center from last week and add new materials. This week the children will be learning more about insects and will also learn about worms and spiders. You may want to put socks and hose in the center and provide newspaper to stuff them with to make worms. Provide pipe cleaners and yarn for spider legs and plastic foam balls for heads and bodies. Add wiggle eyes, if available. Encourage the children to name their creatures and provide a caged area where they can display their collection. Provide index cards for labeling creatures.

Reflect/Assess
What insect did you make?
¿Qué insecto hicieron?
What did you name your insect?
¿Cómo llamaron a su insecto?

DRAMATIC PLAY

Let's Go On a Picnic

Objective
To begin to create or recreate stories, moods, or experiences through dramatic representations

Materials to Gather
tablecloth; picnic basket; plastic fruits, vegetables, and other foods; empty bottle of insect repellent; plastic insects, if available

Develop
Change your camping area to a picnic area. Encourage the children to pretend to be at a family picnic. Suggest plots for their dramatic play. Invite them to describe their picnic experiences.

Reflect/Assess
What kinds of bugs did you see?
¿Qué tipos de insectos vieron?
What kinds of bugs did you see most often?
¿Qué tipos de insectos vieron más?

What Research Suggests

Wiring for vision is connected during the first two years of life. It is important for children to have many opportunities to refine their visual discrimination. Between the ages of two and five, the vision wiring is enhanced through repetitive examination of visual images.

Begin the Day

- Sing "The Insect Song"/"La canción del insecto."
- Use one of the suggestions for Morning Circle found in the front of this *Teacher's Edition.*

Objectives

- To show appreciation of repetitive language patterns
- To begin to notice beginning letters in familiar words

An entomologist is a scientist who studies insects.

Vocabulary

cricket	grillo
grasshopper	saltamontes
flea	pulga
hop	brincar
jump	saltar
entomologist	entomólogo

DLM Materials

- Oral Language Development Card 36
- magnetic letters
- *Insect Picnic/El picnic de los insectos*
- *Teacher's Resource Anthology*
  "The Insect Song"/"La canción del insecto"
  "Grasshopper"
  "El saltamontes"
  Bug Concentration game
  "The Ant and the Grasshopper"/"La hormiguita y el grillo"
  "The Traveling Flea"/"El viaje de la pulguita coqui"

LITERACY

Focus

- Sing "Grasshopper" or say "El saltamontes." Ask the children if they have ever seen a grasshopper.
- Tell the children that this week they will continue studying bugs and that they are becoming entomologists. Tell them that today they will study hopping insects, such as grasshoppers, crickets, and fleas.
  Esta semana vamos a seguir el estudio de los insectos. Ustedes se van a convertir en unos verdaderos entomólogos.

Develop

One Way to Develop the Lesson

- Show Oral Language Card 36 and the picture of the cricket on page two of *Insect Picnic/El picnic de los insectos*. Use the suggestions on the back of Oral Language Card 36 to stimulate discussions. *Are grasshoppers and crickets insects? How do you know?*
  ¿Los saltamontes y los grillos son insectos? ¿Cómo lo saben?
- Write *grasshopper* on a piece of chart paper. Invite a volunteer to copy the word using the magnetic letters. Ask the children what they know about grasshoppers and list their comments on the chart.
  Tell the children that grasshoppers
  - are vegetarians, eating mostly grass and leaves
  - are considered pests; they can destroy entire crops in a few days
  - move in swarms
  - sing by using two different methods: rubbing their legs against their wings or rubbing their forewings together
  - can grow to be three inches long

Another Way to Develop the Lesson

- If you are teaching the lesson in English, tell the children you are going to share a poem about how insects and bugs move. Read the grasshopper poem from the chart, and move your hand under the words as you read.
- Have the children read the poem with you. Name the animal and see if they can remember the movement that goes with that animal.

  Grasshoppers jump. Caterpillars hump.
  Worms wiggle. Bees jiggle.
  Inchworms plop. Fleas hop.
  Mosquitoes stalk—but I walk.
- Discuss the rhyming words in the poem. Ask volunteers to demonstrate the insects' movements.
- If you are teaching the lesson in Spanish, tell the children that you are going to share a poem called "El saltamontes." Read the poem from the chart paper and move your hand under the words as you read. Invite the children to read the poem with you.
- Ask a volunteer to show you the words in the poem that begin with the letter *s*. Ask a second volunteer to show you words beginning with the letter *v*. Ask a volunteer to share the movements of the grasshopper.

  ¿Quién quiere mostrarme las palabras del poema que comienzan con la letra s*? ¿Quién quiere mostrarme las palabras que empiezan con* v*? ¿Quién quiere demostrar los movimientos del saltamontes?*

Practice

- Invite the children to play a game of Bug Concentration.
- Encourage the children to work on the bug puzzles.
- Make grasshopper hoppers by spray painting ping-pong balls green and using markers to draw big eyes. Challenge the children to make the hoppers bounce once and land in a basket.
- Give the children three-inch pieces of yarn that represent the length of a large grasshopper. Encourage them to find things in the room that are the length of a large grasshopper.
- Invite the children to rub craft sticks on the teeth of plastic combs to see if they can make sounds similar to those of grasshoppers.
- Give the children green tempera paint and encourage them to paint a grasshopper.
- Provide an index card with *grasshopper* written on it and encourage the children to spell it with magnetic letters.

Materials to Gather

- chart paper
- bug puzzles
- plastic combs
- craft sticks
- basket
- index cards with insect names
- green tempera paint
- ping-pong balls
- green spray paint
- three-inch pieces of yarn

Preparation

- Write *jump* or *jiggle* on a piece of chart paper for a lesson in English.
- Write the words to "El saltamontes" on chart paper for a lesson in Spanish. Also on chart paper, write the text for the grasshopper poem in Another Way to Develop the Lesson.
- Write names of insects on index cards.

Scaffolding Strategies

More Help Take the children outdoors to look for grasshoppers, if they are indigenous to your area.

Extra Challenge Encourage the children to write their own poems using the predictable text of either poem from the lesson.

DAY 1

Letter Knowledge

English

- Read the story "Zack" from the *English Phonics Resource Guide* or use the *z* activities.

Spanish

- Read the story "La zorra y el zacate" from the *Spanish Phonics Resource Guide* or use the *z* activities.

Suggested Reading

Grasshoppers on the Road by Arnold Lobel
The Very Quiet Cricket by Eric Carle
Saltamontes va de viaje by Arnold Lobel
El piojo y la pulga by Jordi Cots

Second Language Learners

Children of Mexican heritage are more likely to know the word *chapulín* to refer to grasshoppers. The word *chapulín* is of nahuatl origin, as are a number of words in the Mexican Spanish. Also in Mexico, *cri-cri* is the sound made by crickets. A popular children's singer also bears the name Cri-Cri.

Anthology Support

"Calico Pie"
"Way Down South"
"La pulga"
"Pulgarcito y las botas"

Reflect/Assess

- *How are grasshoppers and crickets alike? How are they different?*
  ¿En qué se parecen los saltamontes y los grillos? ¿En qué se diferencian?
- *How are grasshoppers like ants and bees? How are they different?*
  ¿En qué se parecen los saltamontes a las hormigas y las abejas? ¿En qué se diferencian?

Literacy Circle

Storytime 1

- Read "The Ant and the Grasshopper"/"La hormiguita y el grillo." *What is different about ants and grasshoppers in real life?*
  ¿En qué se diferencian las hormigas y los saltamontes en la vida real?

Storytime 2

- Read the listening story "The Traveling Flea"/"El viaje de la pulguita coqui." If you have a picture of a flea, show it to the children. Ask a volunteer to demonstrate how a flea moves according to the poem.

Content Connection

Science

Objectives

To show an interest in investigating unfamiliar objects, organisms, and phenomena

To become more able to move from one space to another in different ways

Vocabulary

catapulting, catapult

catapultar o disparar, catapulta

Materials to Gather

masking tape

Activity 1

- Discuss the movements of grasshoppers. Tell the children that when grasshoppers move they use a catapulting motion, like people use when they bounce and jump or warm up to throw a ball. Demonstrate the movement. Let the children try the bounce-and-jump movement several times.

Activity 2

- Go outdoors and let the children try grasshopper jumps. Show them how to run a few steps, bounce (catapult), and take a jump. If this is too challenging for some children, encourage them to try broad jumping. Place a piece of masking tape on the ground. Take a running start and jump as far as possible from the masking tape line.

DAY 1

Objectives

- To combine, separate, and name "how many" concrete objects
- To start, use, and exit software programs

Vocabulary

number names — nombres de números

DLM Materials

- counters (10 per child)
- *Math Resource Guide*
  Feely Box
  Counting cards (1 to 4)
  Counting Jar
  Make It Right: Double Trouble version/Hazlo bien: versión problema doble
  Places Scenes: Adding version (party or food backgrounds)
  Compare Game: Adding version/Juego de comparar: versión suma
- *DLM Math* software
- *Teacher's Resource Anthology*
  "Who Took the Cookie from the Cookie Jar?"/"¿Quién se comió la galleta?"

Materials to Gather

- connecting cubes
- paper plates to use as cookies
- sticky notes
- small boxes

Preparation

- Fill the Counting Jar with 5 to 10 pretend cookies of 2 different types or colors.

MATH

Focus

- Play "Who Took the Cookie from the Cookie Jar?"/"¿Quién se comió la galleta?" with the numerals 1 to 10.

Develop

- Demonstrate Make It Right: Double Trouble version/Hazlo bien: versión problema doble. Give each child pretend chips (counters) and a pretend cookie (paper plate). Instruct them to make a cookie with 3 chips. Then tell them that they have to change the cookie so it has 5 chips. Ask them to explain how they figured out how many chips to add.
- Repeat this activity, making different changes.
- Introduce and demonstrate the activity Double Trouble, Level 5. Children count to fix a cookie that has too few chips; for example, making a 4-chip cookie into a 7-chip cookie.
- Introduce Double Trouble, Level 6 (Free Explore). Children make cookie problems for each other. Children can challenge each other at any of the previous levels.

Practice

- Invite the children to play the Compare Game: Adding version/Juego de comparar: versión suma.
- Have the children work in pairs to identify how many connecting cubes are in the Feely Box.
- Encourage the children to work on Places Scenes: Adding version. Children do not need to label the sum of the counters they are using since they are always counting out that number.
- Have the children explore the Counting Jar. Have them record their counts on sticky notes.
- Invite the children to work on Double Trouble, Level 5 and Double Trouble, Level 6. Help pairs of children cooperate to play Double Trouble, Level 6 (Free Explore).

Reflect/Assess

- *How did you make sure there was the right number of chips on the cookie?*
  ¿Cómo se aseguraron de que había el número correcto de chispas en la galleta?

Music and Movement

- Create a maze of small boxes. Challenge the children to jump through the maze like a grasshopper.
- Play music with a quick tempo and invite the children to try hopping like fleas.

Content Connection

Language and Literacy

Objectives

To enjoy listening to and discussing storybooks and information books read aloud

To understand that reading and writing are ways to obtain information and knowledge, generate and communicate thoughts and ideas, and solve problems

DLM Materials

- *Teacher's Resource Anthology*
  "The Runaway Cookie Parade"/"El desfile de la galleta fugitiva" flannel board story
  "Smart Cookie's Clever Idea"/"La inteligente idea de Smart Cookie" flannel board story

Activity 1

- Present "The Runaway Cookie Parade"/"El desfile de la galleta fugitiva" flannel board story. Count the cookies that escape from the cookie jar.

Activity 2

- Present "Smart Cookie's Clever Idea"/"La inteligente idea de Smart Cookie" flannel board story. *How many cookies did Smart Cookie use to make the pattern on her tray?*
  ¿Cuántas galletas usó Smart Cookie para hacer el patrón en su bandeja?

Suggested Reading

How Many Bugs in a Box? by David A. Carter

The Doorbell Rang by Pat Hutchins

What Research Suggests

When children talk about the strategy they use to solve a problem, and listen to others tell what they do, they learn more about the specific skill. They also learn how to represent and communicate their thinking.

Reflect on the Day

- *What have you learned about grasshoppers or fleas today?*
  ¿Qué aprendieron sobre los saltamontes o las pulgas hoy?
- *Which activity was your favorite activity?*
  ¿Cuál fue su actividad favorita?

Begin the Day

- Sing "The Insect Song"/"La canción del insecto."
- Use one of the suggestions for Morning Circle offered in the front of this *Teacher's Edition.*

Objectives

- To use language for a variety of purposes
- To begin to dictate words, phrases, and sentences to an adult recording on paper

Vocabulary

ladybug	mariquita
pill bug	cochinilla de humedad
fireflies	luciérnagas

DLM Materials

- *Insect Picnic/El picnic de los insectos*
- *SRA Photo Library* software
- *Teacher's Resource Anthology*
  "The Insect Song"/"La canción del insecto"
  "Five Little Ladybugs"/"Cinco mariquitas"
  bug card patterns
  Bug Concentration game (see Day 1)
  "My Grandmother's Garden"/"El jardín de mi abuela"

Materials to Gather

- picture of a firefly (optional)
- flashlights
- bug puzzles
- index cards with insect names
- tracing paper
- fluorescent markers
- paper plates
- plastic knife
- apples
- bananas
- raisins
- whipping cream

Literacy

Focus

- Introduce "Five Little Ladybugs"/"Cinco mariquitas." Ask: *Have you ever seen a ladybug? Where? What was it doing?*
  ¿Alguna vez han visto una mariquita? ¿Dónde? ¿Qué estaba haciendo?
- Tell the children that today they are going to discuss ladybugs and fireflies.

Develop

One Way to Develop the Lesson

- Show the ladybug on page sixteen of *Insect Picnic/El picnic de los insectos*. Ask the children if they think the ladybug is an insect. This will be difficult for the children to decipher because the ladybug's wings are not transparent, and therefore they hide two of the three body parts the children will be looking for.
- Tell the children about ladybugs. Ladybugs are a form of beetle and are not considered pests. They are friends of the gardener because they eat other insects that are hazardous to crops. Ladybugs are usually red with black spots, but they fade with age and may appear orange.
  Las mariquitas son una forma de escarabajo y no se consideran peste. Son amigos de los agricultores porque comen otros insectos que perjudican los cultivos. Las mariquitas por lo general son rojas con manchas negras, pero éstas desaparecen con el tiempo viéndose anaranjadas.

Another Way to Develop the Lesson

- Turn your flashlight off and on a few times. Ask the children if they can guess which insects you are going to talk about next.

  ¿Saben de qué insectos voy a hablar?
- Show a picture of a firefly, if you have one. If not, tell the children that a firefly looks like a small termite. It is an insect that can display a light in its tail, but not like the light from flashlights or ceiling lights. A mixture of chemicals creates the light in a firefly's tail.

  Una luciérnaga se parece a una termita pequeña. Es un insecto que puede exhibir luz en su cola. Pero esta luz no es como la luz de una linterna o de una lámpara. Una mezcla de sustancias químicas produce la luz de las luciérnagas.
- Ask the children to help you write a poem about a firefly. Start with *Firefly, firefly light up the night.*

  ¿Quieren escribir un poema conmigo sobre las luciérnagas?

Practice

- Invite the children to play the Bug Concentration game.
- Encourage the children to work on the bug puzzles.
- Make a ladybug snack. Cut apples in half and place them with the cut side down on paper plates. Encourage the children to use a plastic knife to cut off a small piece of a banana and place it at one edge of their apples (where the ladybug's head should go.) Provide raisins to use as eyes. Give the children each a small amount of whipping cream to hold the eyes in place.
- Give the children markers to draw ladybugs and fireflies. Provide fluorescent markers to make the fireflies' tails.
- Give the children the index cards with insect names on them. Provide tracing paper and florescent markers to trace the insect names.
- Have the children look for bugs and insects in the Animal category of the *SRA Photo Library* software.

Preparation

- Gather ingredients for ladybug snacks.

Scaffolding Strategies

More Help Take the children outdoors to look for ladybugs.

Extra Challenge Invite the children to write a new chant about the ladybug.

Second Language Learners

Create a rebus card for children to follow as they make the ladybug snack. Describe the steps as you demonstrate the process, referring to the cards as you go. After the children eat their snacks, ask them to describe the steps of making the ladybug snack using the rebus cards, so they can make a snack at home. Note the language they use. Do the children describe things they don't know the name for, or ask the name of unfamiliar objects? These are good strategies for second language learners.

Anthology Support

"Calico Pie"
"Five Little Speckled Frogs"
"Cinco ranitas manchadas"
"Five Little Ladybugs"
"Cinco mariquitas"

DAY 2

Letter Knowledge

English

- Read "Zeppelin" in the *SRA Alphabet Book.*

Spanish

- Read "Zayda la zorra" in *Los niños alfabéticos.*

Suggested Reading

The Grouchy Ladybug by Eric Carle
La mariquita malhumorada by Eric Carle
Fireflies for Nathan by Shulamith Oppenheim
El cocuyo y la mora by Jesús Zatón

Technology Support

Invite the children to find Grandmother's favorite flower in the Plant category on the *SRA Photo Library* software.

Reflect/Assess

- *How are fireflies and ladybugs alike? How are they different?*
  ¿En qué se parecen las luciérnagas y las mariquitas? ¿En qué se diferencian?
- *Who can tell me why the ladybug is the gardener's friend?*
  ¿Quién me puede decir por qué la mariquita es una amiga de los agricultores?

Literacy Circle

Storytime 1

- Read *Insect Picnic/El picnic de los insectos*. Discuss the insects in the story.

Storytime 2

- Write a group story about a firefly that uses the light of its tail to rescue someone lost in the dark. Or read the listening and participation story "My Grandmother's Garden"/"El jardín de mi abuela." Ask the children to tell you why Grandmother likes the ladybugs in her garden.
  ¿Por qué a la abuela le gustan las mariquitas en su jardín?

Content Connection

Social Studies

Objectives

To cooperate with others in a joint activity

To know about safe behavior around bugs and insects

Vocabulary

ants, bees, mosquitoes, fireflies, ladybugs, grasshoppers

hormigas, abejas, mosquitos, luciérnagas, mariquitas, saltamontes

Materials to Gather

chart paper

Activity 1

- Tell the children that they are close to the end of their study of insects and that they will soon move on to study other bugs. Ask the children to recall some of the insects they have studied.

  Ya casi estamos terminando nuestro estudio de los insectos. Pronto vamos a comenzar a estudiar otros animalitos. ¿Quién me puede decir qué insectos hemos estudiado?

- Tell them that they are going to make a graph of their favorite insects. Write the names of six insects on a piece of chart paper. Let each child tell the class which of the six he or she likes best and why. Mark their answers on the graph.
- Help the children read the chart to determine which insect the class has chosen as the favorite and which is the least favorite.

Activity 2

- Remind the children that some insects are considered beneficial because they help pollinate plants, destroy crop-eating insects, or provide products such as honey. Insects are considered harmful if they bite, sting, spread germs, or destroy plants. *Into which category does the insect chosen as the class favorite fit?*

  ¿A qué categoría pertenece el insecto escogido por la clase?

- Remind the children about safe behavior around bugs.

DAY 2

Objectives

- To combine, separate, and name "how many" concrete objects
- To count concrete objects to five or higher

Vocabulary

add	sumar
adding	sumar
number names	nombres de números

Materials

DLM Materials

- counters (10 per child)
- *Math Resource Guide*
  Make It Right: Cookie version/Hazlo bien: versión galleta
- See Day 1
- *DLM Math* software

Materials to Gather

- pretend paper cookies
- flashlight
- See Day 1

Preparation

- Make a paper cookie for each child. Write a numeral (from 3 to 6) on each paper cookie and glue on some chips (buttons, colored dots). The number of chips should be fewer than indicated by the numeral.

MATH

Focus

- Play Make It Right: Double Trouble version/Hazlo bien: versión problema doble. Give each child pretend chips and a cookie. Pose several problems. Encourage the children to solve the problem and then tell how they solved it.
- Remind the children that this game is like Make It Right: Dinosaur Shop/Hazlo bien: versión la tienda de los dinosaurios. This may seem obvious, but making connections is an important part of learning mathematics.

Develop

- Demonstrate how to play Make It Right: Cookie version/Hazlo bien: versión galleta. Tell the children the baker needs help getting the right number of chips on each cookie. Tell them they will fix the cookie by gluing on chips so it has the right number of chips as indicated by the numeral written on it. Let the children know that they can keep the cookie they make during center time.
- Remind the children that the Counting Jar is a cookie jar this week. Ask them how many of each color cookie is in the jar and how many in all.
- Re-introduce Double Trouble, Level 5 and Double Trouble, Level 6 (Free Explore).

Practice

- Invite the children to play Make It Right: Cookie version/Hazlo bien: versión galleta.
- Encourage the children to play the Compare Game: Adding version/ Juego de comparar: versión suma.
- Have the children work in pairs to identify objects in the Feely Box.
- Have the children work on Places Scenes: Adding version.
- Encourage the children to explore the Counting Jar. Have them record their count.
- Invite the children to work on Double Trouble, Level 5 and Double Trouble, Level 6.

Reflect/Assess

- *How did you fix the cookie and make it the right number?*
  ¿Cómo arreglaron la galleta y la hicieron el número correcto?

Music and Movement

- Play Find the Firefly. Give whoever is *It* a flashlight. Turn off the lights. Have the person who is *It* hide and then flash the light quickly. Whoever finds the person who is *It* is the next firefly.
- Play Ladybug, Ladybug, Fly Away Home as you would Musical Chairs. Have the children sit in a circle on carpet squares. Tell them that when you say the first part of the rhyme, they are to get up and run away from the circle. While they are gone, remove one of the carpet squares. Then say, *Ladybug, ladybug, come home*. The children should return to the circle and sit on any carpet square. Children who do not have a seat must sit in the middle of the circle until the end of the game.

Content Connection

Physical Development

Objectives

To begin to hold writing tools with fingers instead of with a fist

To begin to use scissors

DLM Materials

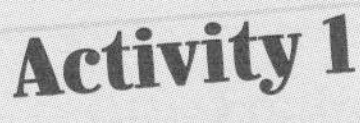

- *Teacher's Resource Anthology* "Five Little Ladybugs"/"Cinco mariquitas"

Materials to Gather

templates, crayons, scissors, red construction paper, drawing paper, black markers, plastic bugs or paper bugs

Activity 1

- Give the children red construction paper and templates for ladybug wings. Encourage them to trace around the templates on red construction paper to make a set of wings. Have them cut out the wings and glue them on a piece of paper.
- Encourage them to use crayons to make a head with antennae and a black marker to place 2 dots on each wing. Ask the children how many dots are on each wing and how many dots are on the ladybug.
  ¿Cuántos puntos hay en cada ala y cuántos hay sobre la mariquita?

Activity 2

- Review the finger play, "Five Little Ladybugs"/"Cinco mariquitas" and encourage them to count the bugs on their fingers.

Suggested Reading

How Many Bugs in a Box? David A. Carter

The Grouchy Ladybug by Eric Carle

Reflect on the Day

- *Tell me something you learned today about fireflies.*
  Díganme algo de lo que aprendieron sobre las luciérnagas hoy.
- *What will you share with your family about ladybugs and fireflies?*
  ¿Qué compartirán con su familia sobre las mariquitas y las luciérnagas?

Begin the Day

- Ask the children why they think the leaves are on the floor. *Can you think of an insect that eats lots of green leaves?*

  ¿Pueden pensar en algún insecto que coma muchas hojas verdes?
- Sing "A Fuzzy Caterpillar"/"Una oruga peluda." Use the butterfly puppet with this song.
- Use one of the suggestions for Morning Circle offered in the front of this *Teacher's Edition.*

Objectives

- To use language for a variety of purposes
- To listen for different purposes

Vocabulary

caterpillar	oruga
butterfly	mariposa
metamorphosis	metamorfosis

DLM Materials

- Oral Language Development Cards 25 & 26
- Metamorphosis sequence cards
- *Insect Picnic/El picnic de los insectos*
- *Teacher's Resource Anthology*
  "A Fuzzy Caterpillar"/"Una oruga peluda"
  "Little Caterpillar"/"La oruga"
  butterfly puppet
  bug card patterns
  Bug Concentration game (see Day 1)
  "A Spring Walk"/"Una caminata en primavera"

Materials to Gather

- green construction paper leaves
- tray of sand or salt
- yellow tempera paint
- caterpillar and butterfly puzzles

LITERACY

Focus

- Introduce "Little Caterpillar"/"La oruga."
- Tell the children that today they will learn about caterpillars and butterflies.

  Hoy vamos a aprender sobre las orugas y las mariposas.

Develop

One Way to Develop the Lesson

- Show Oral Language Cards 25 and 26. Use the suggestions on the backs of the cards to stimulate conversation.
- Invite the children to tell you what they know about caterpillars. Show pages six and seven of *Insect Picnic/El picnic de los insectos.*
- Ask the children to look at the picture of the caterpillar. Is it an insect? Have the children check what they see in the photo against what they know about insects.
- Explain that caterpillars will become butterflies, which are insects. The caterpillars go through a process called *metamorphosis*. Have the children repeat the word *metamorphosis*. Tell them it is a long word and ask them to clap out the syllables.

  Aplaudan con cada sílaba.

Another Way to Develop the Lesson

- Discuss metamorphosis. Have the children clap out the syllables again. Count the syllables. Ask what other long words they know that might be as long as *metamorphosis*. Clap out their suggestions and count the syllables.
- Explain that there are four stages in the metamorphosis of a caterpillar. Show the Metamorphosis sequence cards. Let the children help you put them in order.
- Invite the children to act out the stages of metamorphosis beginning with the egg. You may want to use your puppet. Have the children hold out fists to represent eggs. When the eggs hatch, out come caterpillars. Have the children wiggle their index fingers to represent this stage. Next, the caterpillars make cocoons and wrap themselves inside. Have them wrap the opposite hands around the caterpillars (their index fingers). Finally, out of the cocoons come beautiful butterflies. Encourage the children to flap their arms like wings.

Practice

- Give the children the Metamorphosis sequence cards and let them practice telling the story of the metamorphosis of a caterpillar.
- Let the children use the butterfly puppet to practice the cycle.
- Provide a tray of sand or salt that has been colored yellow with powdered tempera paint to resemble pollen. Invite the children to write the word *butterfly* in the pollen.
- Encourage the children to work on the caterpillar and butterfly puzzles.
- Invite the children to sort the Bug Concentration game cards into the following categories: bugs that crawl, bugs that fly, bugs that swim, and bugs that move in more than one way.

Preparation

- Cut leaves out of green construction paper and make a trail of them from the doorway to the circle area.
- Make a butterfly puppet.

Scaffolding Strategies

More Help Read *The Very Hungry Caterpillar/La oruga muy hambrienta* or another simple metamorphosis story to the children.

Extra Challenge Encourage the children to draw the stages of metamorphosis.

Second Language Learners

Find a caterpillar. Place it in a large jar with air holes in the lid. Read *The Very Hungry Caterpillar/La oruga muy hambrienta* by Eric Carle or tell the children a story about a hungry caterpillar. Ask the children to identify what the caterpillar ate in the story. Place some of these objects (an apple, plums, pears, leaves, etc.) in the large jar with the caterpillar. Each day after this lesson, check with the children to see what the caterpillar ate. Ask the children which elements of the story were real and which were make believe, according to their observations.

DAY 3

Letter Knowledge

English/Spanish

- Invite the children to shape the letter *z* with modeling dough.

Suggested Reading

The Very Hungry Caterpillar by Eric Carle
La oruga muy hambrienta by Eric Carle
Waiting for Wings by Lois Ehlert
Olmo y la mariposa azul by Alma Flor Ada

Teacher's NOTE

Teach the word *metamorphosis* with this lesson. You might be surprised how quickly children pick up this big word.

Anthology Support

"Fuzzy, Wuzzy Caterpillar"
"Está la mariposa"
"My Grandmother's Garden"
"El jardín de mi abuela"

Reflect/Assess

- *Are caterpillars insects? Why? Why not?*
  ¿Las orugas son insectos? ¿Por qué sí? ¿Por qué no?
- *What do caterpillars become? How?*
  ¿En qué se convierten las orugas? ¿Cómo?

Storytime 1

- Invite the children to participate in the action story, "Little Caterpillar"/"La oruga." *What do we call the "silk blanket" that covers a caterpillar?*
  ¿Cómo llamamos a la "sábana de seda" que cubre a una oruga?

Storytime 2

- Read *Insect Picnic/El picnic de los insectos* or the action story "A Spring Walk"/"Una caminata en primavera." Let the children write a new part to the story that involves finding a caterpillar forming a cocoon, or a butterfly bursting out of a cocoon.

Content Connection

Fine Arts

Objectives

To use different colors, surface textures, and shapes to create form and meaning

To use a variety of materials to create original work

Materials to Gather

white drawing paper, construction paper, tempera paint, food coloring, eyedroppers, coffee filters, clothespins, chenille wires

Activity 1

- Fold sheets of white drawing paper in half and draw one half of a butterfly using the fold as the center. Encourage the children to cut around the lines. When they open their papers, they will find butterfly shapes.
- Provide several colors of thick tempera paint. Have the children place teaspoons of two or three colors of paint on one side of their butterfly wings and then refold their papers. Show them how to smooth the wings with their hands to spread the paint. When they open their paper this time, they will have colorful butterflies. Provide construction paper and crayons for the children to use to add details.

Activity 2

- Have the children use eyedroppers to drop food coloring (diluted with some water) onto coffee filters to create designs. Call attention to how the colors spread through the filters. Remind the children that this is called *absorption*. When the filters are dry, help the children thread the filter into the slots of clothes-pins to make butterflies. Provide markers for the children to use to add eyes, and chenille wires to use for antennae.

DAY 3

Objectives

- To combine, separate, and name "how many" concrete objects
- To count concrete objects to five or higher

Vocabulary

add	sumar
adding	sumar
number names	nombres de números

DLM Materials

- counters (10 per child)
- *Math Resource Guide*
  Cookie Game 2/Juego de la galleta 2 with activity sheet
  Make It Right: Cookie version/Hazlo bien: versión galleta
  Monsters and Raisins/Monstruos y pasas
  Dot cube (3–8 dots)
- See Day 1
- *DLM Math* software
- *Teacher's Resource Anthology* "Metamorphosis"

Materials to Gather

- pretend paper cookies
- raisins (10 per child)
- streamers
- See Day 1

MATH

Focus

- Play Monsters and Raisins/Monstruos y pasas. This game is similar to the Gone Fishing game/Juego de pesca. Tell the children they will be monsters that love eating the raisins off cookies. Pass out containers of raisins and a cookie (plate) for each child. Have children act out the story.
- Ask how many raisins they have on their cookies (0). Say that the monster put 2 raisins on her cookie. Then the monster put on 3 more. Ask, how many are on the cookie now. Say the monster couldn't stand it . . . and ate 1 raisin! Ask how many raisins there are now.
- Continue the story, adding and subtracting various amounts.

Develop

- Demonstrate how to play Cookie Game 2/Juego de la galleta 2. For this game, 5 is the target number.
- Each player needs a copy of the Cookie Game 2 activity sheet, 1 Dot cube, and small counters for chocolate chips. Player 1 rolls a cube and puts that many chips on her plate. Player 2 must agree that she is correct. If so, player 1 puts the chips on her cookies, trying to get 5 on each (e.g., if she rolled 6, she could put 5 on 1 cookie and start another cookie with 1 chip). Players take turns. The winner is the first player to get 5 chips on each cookie.

Practice

- Have the children play Cookie Game 2/Juego de la galleta 2.
- Have the children continue the Practice activities from Day 1 and Day 2.
- Invite the children to work on Double Trouble, Level 5 and Double Trouble, Level 6. Ask the children how they figured out how to add just enough to fill the order correctly.

Reflect/Assess

- *Pretend you are a monster with 4 raisins on your cookie, and then you eat 2. How would you figure out how many you still have?*

  Imagínense que son un monstruo con 4 pasas en su galleta y luego se comen 2. ¿Cómo determinarían cuántas les quedan todavía?

Music and Movement

- Invite the children to do the action rhyme, "Metamorphosis."
- Give the children streamers and encourage them to dance like butterflies to classical music.

Suggested Reading

How Many Bugs in a Box? by David A. Carter

Content Connection

Personal and Social Development

Objectives

To begin to share and cooperate with others in group activities

To begin to coordinate arms and legs

DLM Materials

Teacher's Resource Anthology

Leap Frog/Pídola

Materials to Gather

plastic bugs

Activity 1

- Tell the children that you are hiding bugs in each hand (3 or less in each hand). Ask them to tell you how many are in both hands. Show the bugs for 2 seconds. Then ask them how many you have in all. Repeat.
- Encourage the children to play the game with a friend.

Activity 2

- Play Leap Flea as you would Leap Frog/Pídola. Divide the children into groups of 5. Have 4 children get on the floor on all fours pretending to be dogs and have the fifth child in the group be a flea jumping over the backs of the dogs. Ask the *flea* to count the dogs as he or she jumps over them.

Reflect on the Day

- *What did you learn today about caterpillars?*

  ¿Qué aprendieron sobre las orugas hoy?
- *Who can tell me the name of the process a caterpillar goes through in order to become a butterfly?*

  ¿Quién me puede decir el nombre del proceso por el que pasa una oruga para convertirse en una mariposa?

Begin the Day

- Sing "A Fuzzy Caterpillar"/"Una oruga peluda." Ask a volunteer to tell what he or she learned yesterday about caterpillars.
- Use one of the suggestions for Morning Circle offered in the front of this *Teacher's Edition.*

Objectives

- To refine and extend understanding of known words
- To link new learning experiences and vocabulary to what is already known about a topic

Vocabulary

worm gusano o lombriz
earthworm lombriz de tierra
centipede ciempiés
arthropods artrópodos

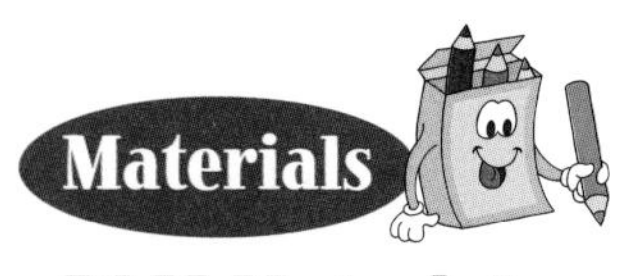

DLM Materials

- Oral Language Development Cards 25–31 & 36
- magnetic letters
- *Teacher's Resource Anthology*
  "A Fuzzy Caterpillar"/"Una oruga peluda"
  "Nobody Likes Me"/"A nadie le gusto"
  "Wally Worm's World"/"El mundo del gusano Wally"
  play dough

Materials to Gather

- finger paint
- yarn or string
- chenille wires
- light source
- candy worms (optional)
- chocolate cookies (optional)

LITERACY

Focus

- Sing "Nobody Likes Me"/"A nadie le gusto."
- Tell the children that today's activities will be about worms and centipedes.

Develop

One Way to Develop the Lesson

- Show Oral Language Card 28. Use the suggestions on the back of the card to stimulate conversations. *Is the worm an insect?* Have the children apply the information they have learned about insects.
  ¿El gusano es un insecto?
- Worms often eat crops, which makes them pests to farmers. *Can you think of creatures that eat worms? (birds)*
  ¿Pueden pensar en otras criaturas que coman gusanos?
- Invite the children to make a list of adjectives that describe worms, such as *slimy, wiggly, grimy, jiggly, squashy,* and *smashy*. Nonsense words are fine.
- Discuss words that describe. Tell the children that these words help people add details to what they are trying to tell others. Give an example.

Another Way to Develop the Lesson

- Show Oral Language Card 31. Use the suggestions on the back of the card to stimulate conversation. Find out what children know about centipedes. *Is the centipede an insect?*

  ¿El ciempiés es un insecto?
- Centipedes come in many colors. They can be red, orange, black, and variations of these colors. They will bite if provoked. Their stings are dangerous to people who are allergic to their venom. Centipedes eat other insects. They live in the soil and in damp places such as under rocks.
- Tell the children centipede means "one hundred legs." Ask if they think it is a good descriptive word for the bug.
- Ask the children to help make a list of descriptive words for the centipede. *Is it more difficult or less difficult to think of descriptive words for the centipede than it is for the worm?*

  ¿Es más difícil o menos difícil pensar en palabras descriptivas para los ciempiés que para el gusano?

Practice

- Invite the children to use string or yarn to paint tracks like those a worm makes as it moves along the ground.
- Invite the children to fingerpaint. Show them how to make worm tracks in the paint.
- Encourage the children to roll worms out of play dough.
- Invite the children to spell *worm* using the magnetic letters. Provide a model.
- Provide a light source, such as an overhead projector. Invite the children to use their index fingers to make shadow worms on the wall. Encourage them to make up a worm puppet show.
- Give the children the Oral Language Cards 25–31 and 36. Encourage them to sort the insects by color, size, number of legs, and movement.
- Serve candy worms and crumbled chocolate cookies for snack.

Preparation

- Gather candy worms and chocolate cookies, if you provide a snack.

Scaffolding Strategies

More Help Go outside and dig up some worms. Bring the worms and some damp dirt inside the classroom for observation. Be sure to return the worms to the soil outdoors. They cannot live long outside of their environment.

Extra Challenge Invite the children to think of descriptive words that rhyme with *worm*. Nonsense words are fine.

Second Language Learners

Bring a worm to class and compare it to the caterpillar. Use vocabulary describing length, color, shape, texture, and design. If a magnifying glass is available, this will help children to observe finer points of similarity and difference. Listen to the children's descriptions. Do they make a statement about only the worm or the caterpillar? If so, ask, "Is the caterpillar (long), as the worm is?" If they say, "Yes," then say, "Oh, the caterpillar AND the worm are (long)." If they point out a difference, reply, "Oh. The caterpillar (has feet), BUT the worm (does) not." Model these language patterns throughout the activity.

DAY 4

Letter Knowledge

English

- Invite the children to think of ways to make the letter *z* with their bodies. Use the Think, Pair, Share game with this activity.

Spanish

- Invite the children to think of ways to make the letter *z* with their bodies. Use the Piensa, aparea, comparte game with this activity.

Suggested Reading

Inch by Inch by Leo Lionni
Earthworms by Chris Henwood

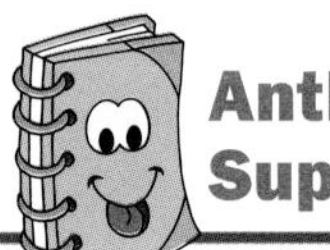

Anthology Support

"The Little Worm"
"The Caterpillar"
"La oruga"
"Fuzzy, Wuzzy Caterpillar"
"Mariposa Linda"

Reflect/Assess

- *How are the centipede and the worm alike? How are they different?*
  ¿En qué se parecen los ciempiés y los gusanos? ¿En qué se diferencian?
- *Is the caterpillar a centipede? Why or why not?*
  ¿La oruga es un ciempiés? ¿Por qué o por qué no?

Literacy Circle

Storytime 1

- Read the listening story "Wally Worm's World"/"El mundo del gusano Wally." *What did Wally find out about his home?*
  ¿Qué descubrió Wally de su hogar?

Storytime 2

- Encourage the children to help you write a story about a centipede looking for tennis shoes. *How many pairs of shoes would the centipede need? How many skates would a centipede need?*
  ¿Cuántos pares de zapatos necesitaría el ciempiés? ¿Cuántos patines necesitaría un ciempiés?

Content Connection

Personal and Social Development

Objectives

To begin to share and cooperate with others in group activities

To begin to show self-control by following classroom rules

Materials to Gather

Oral Language Development Cards 25–31 & 36

Activity 1

- Display the Oral Language Cards. Ask the children to provide a few descriptive words for each bug. Tell the children that they are going to play a game. They must listen closely to the clues before deciding which bug you are describing. When you give a clue that rules an insect out, they should tell you which card to turn over. When they hear a clue that makes them believe they know which bug is being described, they should raise their hands and tell you which bug it is. For example, if you say this insect flies, a child should tell you to cover up the centipede, worm, ant, and caterpillar. If you say, this bug isn't green, someone should tell you to turn over the grasshopper. If you say this bug has clear wings, someone should tell you that the bug is a dragonfly. Continue the game for as long as the children enjoy it.

Activity 2

- Play the game again and this time encourage the children to give the clues.

MATH

Objectives

- To combine, separate, and name "how many" concrete objects
- To count concrete objects to five or higher

Vocabulary

add	sumar
adding	sumar
number names	nombres de números

DLM Materials

- *Math Resource Guide*
  Hidden Chips/Chispas escondidas
  Making Towers/Hacer torres
  Make It Right: Cookie Version/Hazlo bien: versión galleta
  Cookie Game 2/Juego de la galleta 2 with activity sheet
  Dot cube (3–8 dots)
  2 Numeral cubes (1–3)
- See Day 1
- *DLM Math* software
- *Teacher's Resource Anthology*
  Follow the Leader/Sigue al líder

Materials to Gather

- connecting cubes (blue and yellow)
- pretend paper cookies
- raisins (10 per child)
- cloth
- See Day 1

Focus

- Teach the children the game Hidden Chips/Chispas escondidas. Tell them that you are Ms. or Mr. Double, and you have some cookie problems for them.
- Show them 3 chips on your cookie and then hide them under a cloth and add 1 more under the cloth. Ask them how many there are and how they figured it out. Uncover the chips and count to check. Repeat with new numbers.

Develop

- Demonstrate Making Towers/Hacer torres. Give the children connecting cubes in 2 colors. Roll 2 Numeral cubes (1–3) and have them make a tower with that many blue cubes. Then have the children add enough yellow cubes to make a tower of 6.

Practice

- Invite the children to play Making Towers/Hacer torres.
- Have the children play Cookie Game 2/Juego de la galleta 2.
- Encourage the children to play Make It Right: Cookie version/Hazlo bien: versión galleta.
- Invite the children to continue playing the Compare Game: Adding version/Juego de comparar: versión suma.
- Have the children work in pairs to identify objects in the Feely Box. Have 1 child secretly hide 2 small towers of connecting cubes in the Feely Box for a friend and see if he or she can feel it and tell how many in all.
- Encourage the children to play Places Scenes: Adding version.
- Have the children to explore the Counting Jar. Encourage them to record their count.
- Invite the children to work on Double Trouble, Level 5 and Double Trouble, Level 6. The free explore level can be a wonderful chance to get children to cooperate, making cookies together with the same number, or posing hidden cookie problems for each other. Adult guidance will help the children start inventing such possibilities.

Reflect/Assess

- *Pretend you are a monster with 4 raisins on your cookie, and then you eat 2. How would you figure out how many you still have?*

  Imagínense que son un mosntruo con 4 pasas en su galleta y luego de comen 2. ¿Cómo determinarían cuántas les quedan todavía?

Music and Movement

- Worms move by lengthening the front part of their body, then pulling up the back part. Encourage the children to move like worms.
- Encourage the children to grab hold of each other's waists to make a long worm. Then have them worm their way through the classroom in a Follow the Leader/Sigue al líder game.

Suggested Reading

One Tortoise, Ten Wallabies: A Wildlife Counting Book by Jakki Wood

Content Connection

Physical Development

Objectives

To begin to share and cooperate with others in group activities

To begin to throw or kick an object in a particular direction

DLM Materials

Teacher's Resource Anthology

Cooperative Musical Circle/Círculo musical cooperativo

Materials to Gather

butcher paper, knee-high hose

Activity 1

- Play Musical Leaves as you would Cooperative Musical Circle/Círculo musical cooperativo. Cut several big leaves out of green butcher paper and lay them on the floor. Divide the children into groups of 4. Have each group crawl around a leaf like worms. When the music stops, the children are to crawl on the leaf that belongs to their group. When each group is settled, have them count how many worms are on the leaf and how many are off the leaf.

Activity 2

- Stuff 4 knee-high panty hose with crumpled paper to make 4 worms. Cut a large green leaf from butcher paper and lay it on the floor. Make a throw line on the floor with masking tape about 6 feet from the leaf. Invite the children to toss the worms. Have each child count the number of worms on the leaf and off the leaf and then how many worms in all.

Reflect on the Day

- *What did you learn about worms today? What will you share with your family?*

  ¿Qué aprendieron sobre los gusanos hoy? ¿Qué compartirán con su familia?

Home Connection

Send home a take-home book pack with four children.

Begin the Day

- When the children come to the Morning Circle, ask them which bug they think you will be discussing today.

  ¿Qué animalito creen que vamos a estudiar hoy?
- Sing or say "Little Miss Muffet"/"Señorita Mufete." *Why did Miss Muffet run away? Are you afraid of spiders?*

  ¿Por qué la señorita Mufete se fue? ¿Ustedes le tienen miedo a las arañas?
- Use one of the suggestions for Morning Circle in the front of this *Teacher's Edition.*

Objectives

- To understand that writing is used to communicate ideas and information
- To begin to dictate words, phrases, and sentences to an adult recording on paper

Vocabulary

spider — araña
arthropods — artrópodos

DLM Materials

- Oral Language Development Card 24
- *SRA Book of Animals/SRA El libro de los animales*
- *Teacher's Resource Anthology*
  "Little Miss Muffet"/"Señorita Mufete"
  "Itsy Bitsy Spider"/"La araña pequeñita"
  "Spiders"
  "There Was an Old Woman Who Swallowed a Fly"/"Había una anciana que tragó una mosca"
  play dough

Materials to Gather

- white yarn
- black and other shades of construction paper
- play dough or clay
- pipe cleaners
- chart paper

LITERACY

Focus

- Sing "Itsy Bitsy Spider"/"La araña pequeñita." Invite the children to share experiences they have had with spiders.
- Tell the children that today's lesson will be about spiders.

  La lección de hoy tratará de las arañas.

Develop

One Way to Develop the Lesson

- Show Oral Language Card 24. Use the suggestions on the back of the card to stimulate discussions. *Is the spider an insect? Why not?*

  ¿La araña es un insecto? ¿Por qué no?
- Explain that most spiders spin sticky webs using their spinnerets. They use their webs to catch prey. They primarily eat insects. Some spiders live in holes in the ground and in the bark of trees.
- Tell the children that spiders come in all sizes. Some are as big as ten inches in diameter, while others are so small you can barely see them.
- Ask the children to think of the things you have told them about spiders. Write their comments on chart paper for the Science Center.

Another Way to Develop the Lesson

- Present the "Little Miss Muffet"/"La Señorita Mufete" flannel board story. Tell only the original verse. *Why do you think Miss Muffet was afraid of the spider? Should she have been afraid? Will spiders hurt you if you don't bother them? What was Miss Muffet eating? What is a tuffet? Which word rhymes with* tuffet? *How would the rhyme be different if Miss Muffet didn't run away?*

  ¿Por qué creen que la señorita Mufete le tenía miedo a la araña? ¿Debía tenerle miedo? ¿Las arañas les harían daño si no las molestaran? ¿Qué comía la señorita Mufete? ¿Qué es un taburete? ¿Qué palabra rima con taburete? *¿Cómo cambiaría la rima si la señorita Mufete no se fuera?*
- Ask the children to help you rewrite the last two lines of the rhyme. Write lines one and two on a piece of chart paper and encourage the children to help write lines three and four.
- After you have written two new lines with the children, present the alternate version of "Little Miss Muffet"/"La Señorita Mufete" offered in the Anthology.

Practice

- Place the list of spider facts in the Art Center and encourage the children to illustrate it.
- Encourage the children to draw pictures to illustrate their version of "Little Miss Muffet"/"La Señorita Mufete."
- Place the "Little Miss Muffet"/ "La Señorita Mufete" flannel board story in the Language Center and encourage the children to retell the story.
- Give the children three-dimensional spider webs and encourage them to make crayon rubbings. Suggest they use crayons or markers to add spiders to their webs. Suggest they name their spiders. Help them write their spiders' names on the bottoms of their pictures.
- Encourage the children to make spider hats. Cut pieces of construction paper to make into headbands. Give the children one-inch by twelve-inch strips of black construction paper. Have them fold the strips of paper as they would a fan and glue them onto their headbands.
- Give the children play dough and have them fashion spiders. Provide chenille wires for legs.

Preparation

- In your circle area, make a big spider web out of white yarn. Encourage the children to sit on the web during circle time.
- Make three-dimensional webs. Draw a web and trace it with glue. Let it dry.

Second Language Learners

When discussing similarities and differences of ants and spiders, bring models of ants and spiders or real examples. Model the use of *and/y* and *but/pero*, as you did in activities on Day 4.

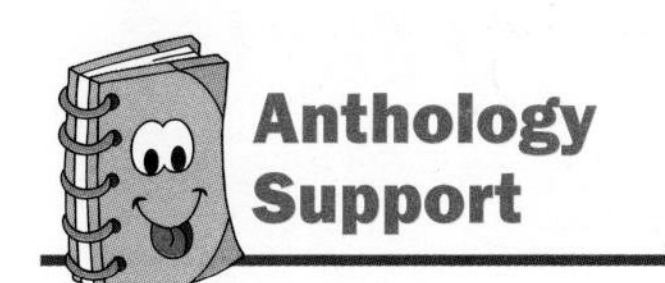

"We've Got the Whole World in Our Hands"
"Tenemos todo el mundo en nuestras manos"
"Earth Is Our Home"
"La tierra es nuestro hogar"

DAY 5

Letter Knowledge

English/Spanish

- Invite the children to find and circle the letter *z* in newspapers and magazines.

Suggested Reading

Be Nice to Spiders by Margaret Bloy Graham
The Very Busy Spider by Eric Carle
Tono, el hilo y la araña by Antonio Cuadrench
El gigante que tenía un secreto by Liliana Santirso

Reflect/Assess

- *How are spiders like ants? How are they different?*
  ¿En qué se parecen las arañas y las hormigas? ¿En qué se diferencian?
- *Is a spider an insect? How do you know?*
  ¿Una araña es un insecto? ¿Cómo lo saben?

Storytime 1

- Read "Spiders" on page 32 of the *SRA Book of Animals/SRA El libro de los animales. Which insects are mentioned in the story?*
  ¿Qué insectos se mencionan en el cuento?

Storytime 2

- Tell the "There Was an Old Woman Who Swallowed a Fly"/"Había una anciana que se tragó una mosca" flannel board story. *What other insect did the old woman swallow? What did the spider do inside the old woman?*
  ¿Qué otro insecto se tragó la anciana? ¿Qué hizo la araña dentro de la anciana?

Content Connection

Fine Arts

Objectives

To use a variety of materials to create original work

To begin to create or re-create stories, moods, or experiences through dramatic representations

Materials to Gather

black chenille wires, elastic thread

Activity 1

- Show the children how to make wiggle spiders. Twist four chenille wires together and then shape them into eight-legged spiders. Attach the spiders to pieces of elastic thread. Show the children how to bounce their spiders.

Activity 2

- Encourage the children to create a puppet show with their spiders.

DAY 5

Objectives

- To combine, separate, and name "how many" concrete objects
- To count concrete objects to five or higher

Vocabulary

add	sumar
adding	sumar
number names	nombres de números

DLM Materials

- counters (10 per child)
- *Math Resource Guide*
  Hidden Chips/Chispas escondidas
  Monsters and Raisins/Monstruos y pasas
  Making Towers/Hacer torres
  Make It Right: Cookie version/Hazlo bien: versión galleta
  Cookie Game 2/Juego de la galleta with activity sheet
  Dot cube (3–8 dots)
  2 Numeral cubes (1–3)
- See Day 1
- *DLM Math* software
- *Esta es mi tierra* CD
- *Teacher's Resource Anthology*
  Spider Walk/Camina como la araña

Materials to Gather

- connecting cubes (blue and yellow)
- pretend paper cookies
- raisins (10 per child)
- yarn
- See Day 1

MATH

Focus

- Examine the Counting Jar. Review the children's displayed recordings of how many are in the Counting Jar. Do they remember how many of each type (e.g., color)? Dump the objects and count them to check.
- Review Hidden Chips/Chispas escondidas.

Develop

- Play Monsters and Raisins/Monstruos y pasas. Have the children act out a few story problems.
- Play Double Trouble, Level 6, with the children.

Practice

- Invite the children to play Making Towers/Hacer torres.
- Have the children play Cookie Game 2/Juego de la galleta 2.
- Encourage the children to play Make It Right: Cookie version/Hazlo bien: versión galleta.
- Invite the children to continue playing the Compare Game: Adding version/Juego de comparar: versión suma.
- Have the children work in pairs to identify objects in the Feely Box. Have 1 child secretly hide 2 small towers of connecting cubes in the Feely Box for a friend and see if he or she can feel it and tell how many in all.
- Encourage the children to play Places Scenes: Adding version.
- Invite the children to work on Double Trouble, Level 5 and Double Trouble, Level 6. Encourage the children to use the free explore level to make cookies with the same number of chips.

Reflect/Assess

- Computer Show: Have the children show their work in Double Trouble, Level 5 or 6.
- *How did you figure out how to make it the right number in Double Trouble, Level 5?*

  ¿Cómo determinaron cómo hacerlo el número correcto en Double Trouble, Nivel 5?

Content Connection

Physical Development/Science

Objectives
To begin to coordinate arms and legs

Materials to Gather
large white sheet

Activity 1

- Take a large white sheet (spider web) outdoors and use it like a parachute. Have the children pretend to be spiders. Instruct spiders wearing red to run under the web. Ask how many spiders are under the web. *¿Cuántas arañas hay debajo de la telaraña?* Continue sending spiders (children) in other colors under the web, asking questions about how many are under the web each time.

Activity 2

- Discuss the number of legs on a spider. Ask the children how many pairs of shoes a spider would need if it wore shoes. *How many pairs of skates? ¿Cuántos pares de patines?* Do they think in terms of 2 shoes and skates in a pair or do they answer 8?

Reflect on the Day

- *What have you learned about bugs? Which bugs do you like best? Why?*

  ¿Qué aprendieron sobre los insectos? ¿Qué insectos les gusta más? ¿Por qué?
- *Tell me one thing you remember about the spider.*

  Díganme una cosa que recuerden sobre la araña.

Music and Movement

- Teach the children how to do the Spider Walk/Camina como la araña. Have 4 children stand back-to-back and lock arms. Ask them to see if they can get their 8 legs going in the right direction to walk. *Is it difficult to move? Why? Do you think the spider has trouble moving with its eight legs?* *¿Es difícil caminar? ¿Por qué? ¿Creen que la araña tiene problemas moviéndose con ocho patas?*
- Use yarn to make a big spider web. Anchor it with table legs and chair legs. Encourage the children to navigate their way through the web by crawling, scooting, walking, and jumping. Remind them that they can't touch the web, or they will be food for the spider. Or play "La rana" from the *Esta es mi tierra* CD.

Suggested Reading

Miss Spider's Tea Party: The Counting Book by David Kirk

Looking Ahead

Connecting to the Theme: Animals

This theme continues to sensitize children to the many living things with which we share our world by focusing on animals such as llamas, whales, iguanas, and fish. Children will also learn about some differences between mammals and reptiles. This theme also presents an opportunity to address the proper care and treatment of animals.

	Objectives	DLM Materials	Materials to Gather
DAY 1	• To enjoy listening to and discussing storybooks and information books read aloud • To begin to identify some high-frequency words • To identify similarities and differences among objects and organisms • To combine, separate, and name "how many" concrete objects • To start, use, and exit software programs	• *SRA Book of Animals/SRA El libro de los animales* • *Martí and the Mango/Martí y el mango* • *The Zebra on the Zyder Zee/Una aventura en alta mar* • *Teacher's Resource Anthology* • Oral Language Cards 6–14 & 19–21 • *Where Is Thumbkin?* CD • *Diez deditos* CD	• magazines • tray of sand or salt • books about animals • number cube with 3 to 8 dots • tray or paper plate • toothpicks (10 per child) • animal shape sponges • animal cookie cutters
DAY 2	• To understand that writing is used to communicate ideas and information • To combine, separate, and name "how many" concrete objects • To begin to demonstrate part of and whole with real objects	• Oral Language Cards 6–14 • *Teacher's Resource Anthology* • *DLM Math* software • *Where Is Thumbkin?* CD • *Esta es mi tierra* CD • *Diez deditos* CD	• cardboard strips • yarn • tray or paper plate • toothpicks (10 per child) • felt shapes • parquetry blocks (optional)
DAY 3	• To use language for a variety of purposes • To begin to retell the sequence of a story • To combine, separate, and name "how many" concrete objects • To begin to demonstrate part of and whole with real objects	• *Sara Sidney* • *English/Spanish Phonics Resource Guides* • *Teacher's Resource Anthology* • *Math Resource Guide* • *DLM Math* software • *Where Is Thumbkin?* CD	• rope or yarn • ribbon • animal pattern cards (see Day 2) • tongue depressors • potato masher • toothpicks • tray or paper plate
DAY 4	• To begin to identify some high-frequency words • To identify 10 or more printed alphabet letters • To combine, separate, and name "how many" concrete objects • To begin to demonstrate part of and whole with real objects	• Oral Language Development Card 22 • *Fish Wish/Deseos de un pez* • Teacher's Resource Anthology • pattern blocks • *Math Resource Guide* • *DLM Math* software • *The SRA Book of Animals/SRA El libro de los animales*	• coat hanger tube • clear sequins • colored acetate • fish bowl • colored tissue paper • resealable plastic bags (one per child) • blue hair gel • laminating film
DAY 5	• To ask questions and make comments related to the current topic of discussion • To describe properties of objects and characteristics of living things • To combine, separate, and name "how many" concrete objects • To begin to demonstrate part of and whole with real objects	• Oral Language Cards 11 & 15–18 • *A Bicycle for Rosaura/Rosaura en bicicleta* • *Teacher's Resource Anthology* • *DLM Math* software • *Where Is Thumbkin?* CD • *Making Music with Thomas Moore* CD • *Diez deditos* CD	• feathers • cotton balls • buttons • animal pattern cards (see Day 2) • nature tapes of bird calls • toothpicks (10 per child) • cups, counters, and pieces of colored paper • beads • leaves

(See individual lesson pages for complete lists of materials.)

Learning Centers

DRAMATIC PLAY

Caring for Animals

Objective
To begin to create or re-create stories, moods, or experiences through dramatic representations

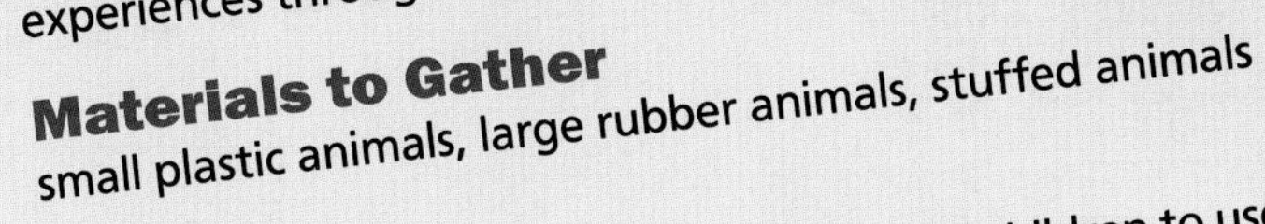

Materials to Gather
small plastic animals, large rubber animals, stuffed animals

Develop
Add animals to the center and encourage the children to use them in their play. Make suggestions for ways to include the animals during the week. For example, the children might build animal cages for a zoo or set up an animal care center. You might want to limit the animals to mammals on Tuesday and Wednesday when they study mammals; to reptiles on Thursday when they study reptiles; and to birds on Friday when they focus on birds.

Reflect/Assess
Which animal did you like best?
¿Qué animal les gustó más?
Which animals were mammals?
¿Qué animales eran mamíferos?

SCIENCE

Animal Observations

Objective
To describe properties of objects and characteristics of living things

Materials to Gather
animal magazines, animal posters, animal books, live animal (optional)

Develop
Fill the center with pictures of animals and books and magazines about animals. If you have access to a live animal, keep it in the center. During the week, visit this center and encourage the children to look for details. If they are allowed to cut the animal pictures out of magazines, suggest they classify them in different ways, such as big or small, water or land, fur or feathers, and so on. If you have a live animal in the center, suggest that they keep journals recording the animal's diet and habits.

Reflect/Assess
Who can name an animal that has feathers?
¿Quién puede decirme el nombre de un animal que tenga plumas?
Which animals live in the water?
¿Qué animales viven en el agua?

ART

Animal Representations

Objective
To use a variety of materials to create original work

Materials to Gather
animal stencils, animal templates, animal-shaped sponges, animal construction paper cutouts, animal cookie cutters, play dough, clay, tempera paint, markers

Develop
Encourage the children to use the materials to create a variety of animal pictures and dough or clay creations.

Reflect/Assess
Which material did you like working with?
¿Con qué material les gustó trabajar más?
Which material was the easiest to work with?
¿Con cuál material fue más fácil trabajar?

What Research Suggests

Children love to hear a story again and again. Rereading familiar stories coincides with the way children learn. The repetition improves their vocabulary, sequencing, and memory skills. Research shows that children often ask as many questions, and sometimes the same questions, after a dozen readings as they do after the first reading. This is because they are learning language in increments. During each reading, the children connect more meaning to the story.

DAY 1

Begin the Day

- Sing "Animal Fair" or read "El burrito enfermo"/"My Sick Little Donkey."
- Use one of the suggestions for Morning Circle in the front of this *Teacher's Edition.*

Objectives

- To enjoy listening to and discussing storybooks and information books read aloud
- To begin to identify some high-frequency words

Vocabulary

raccoon	mapache
cubs	crías o cachorros
hippopotamus	hipopótamo
zebra	cebra
mice	ratones
frog	rana
turtles	tortugas
alligator	caimán
robin	petirrojo
kangaroo	canguro

DLM Materials

- *SRA Book of Animals/SRA El libro de los animales*
- *Martí and the Mango/Martí y el mango*
- *The Zebra on the Zyder Zee/Una aventura en alta mar*
- magnetic letters
- *Teacher's Resource Anthology*
  "Animal Fair"
  "El burrito enfermo"/"My Sick Little Donkey"
  "Los animales de Amelia"/"Amelia's Pets"
  "Muévete como yo"

LITERACY

Focus

- Sing "Los animales de Amelia"/"Amelia's Pets" or "Muévete como yo."
- Tell the children that they will be studying animals this week.

Develop

One Way to Develop the Lesson

- Show the cover of the book the *SRA Book of Animals/SRA El libro de los animales*. Ask the children to predict what the book might be about. Read the title and tell the children the book is a collection of nonfiction stories about animals. Read "Raccoons" and "Baby Animals" from the *SRA Book of Animals/SRA El libro de los animales*. Use the focus questions that accompany the selections.
- When you have finished reading each selection, ask the children questions about the animals. *What are baby raccoons called? Do all animals look like their mothers when they are born? Which animals don't need their mothers to take care of them? Which animals do need their mothers to take care of them?*
  ¿Cómo se llaman los mapaches bebés? ¿Todos los animales se parecen a sus mamás cuando nacen? ¿Qué animales no necesitan de sus mamás para cuidarlos? ¿Qué animales necesitan que sus mamás los cuiden?

- Ask the children to help you make a list of all the animals that are mentioned in the story. Say and spell each name as you write it. At the end of the list write the word *mother.* Ask if anyone can read the word. If no one recognizes the word, tell them the word is *mother* and that they will work on learning to read this word today.
- Invite the children to make up an imaginary baby animal that has characteristics of several animals they like. For example, they may conjure up an animal that flies like a bird but carries its baby like a kangaroo.

Another Way to Develop the Lesson

- Read "Munch Crunch: The Foods Animals Eat" from the *SRA Book of Animals/SRA El libro de los animales*. Use the focus questions at the beginning of the selection to get the children interested in the story.
- Ask questions. Reread the first four lines of the story. Ask the children if they can remember what words that make the sounds they describe are called. If the children don't remember that it is *onomatopoeia,* tell them the word. Ask the children to name some of the animals that only eat plants. *Which animals eat fish?*

  ¿Se acuerdan cuál es la palabra que describe los sonidos de algo? (onomatopeya) *Nombren algunos animales que solo coman plantas. ¿Qué animales comen peces?*
- Let the children help you read page 29 using the picture clues. Show enthusiasm for their ability to read.
- Ask a volunteer to show you the word *mother* on pages 18 and 19 of the book.

Materials to Gather

- index cards
- magazines
- chart paper
- tray of sand or salt
- books about animals

Preparation

- Write the names of the animals listed in the vocabulary list on index cards to make word cards. Add the word *mother* to the word cards.

Teacher's NOTE

Sight words will be added to the lessons this week. Not all children will be ready, but those who are will catch on quickly.

DAY 1

Scaffolding Strategies

More Help Encourage the children to understand that recognizing their names is reading sight words. Point out the names of friends they are able to recognize.

Extra Challenge Invite the children to search the text of the book for the names that are on their word cards.

Technology Support

Encourage the children to find the animals we are focusing on each day on the *SRA Photo Library* software in the Animals category.

Practice

- Invite the children to draw pictures of their imaginary animals. With their permission, write the names of the animals on their drawings. *What kind of skin cover does your animal have? How big is it? How many tails does it have? How does it move?*

  ¿Qué tipo de pelaje tiene su animal? ¿De qué tamaño es? ¿Cuántas colas tiene? ¿Cómo se mueve?
- Place the *SRA Book of Animals/SRA El libro de los animales* book and listening tape in the Listening Center.
- Invite the children to look through magazines for pictures of animals that were mentioned in the stories.
- Write the name of each animal in the book on an index card. Provide a tray of sand. Invite the children to practice writing the names in a tray of sand.
- Let the children copy the word *mother* from the chart paper using magnetic letters.
- Fill the Library Center with books about animals.

Reflect/Assess

- *Which of the animals mentioned in the story do you like best? Why?*

  ¿Cuáles de los animales mencionados en el cuento les gusta más? ¿Por qué?
- *How are baby turtles and alligators alike?*

  ¿En qué se parecen las tortuguitas y los caimanes?

Literacy Circle

Storytime 1

- Read *Martí and the Mango/Martí y el mango. Which animals appear in this story and in the stories from the* SRA Book of Animals/SRA El libro de los animales?

  ¿Qué animales aparecen en este cuento y en los cuentos de SRA El libro de los animales?

Storytime 2

- Read *The Zebra on the Zyder Zee/Una aventura en alta mar.* Name some of the rhyming words in this story. *What kind of animals did the zebra take on his trip across the sea?*

  ¿Qué tipos de animales se llevó la cebra en su viaje por el mar?

Content Connection

Science

Objective
To identify similarities and differences among objects and organisms

Vocabulary
reptiles, mammals
reptiles, mamíferos

DLM Materials
Oral Language Development Cards 6–14 and 19–21
 *SRA Photo Library* software

Activity 1

- Discuss mammals and reptiles. Tell the children that mammals are warm-blooded animals that have skin coverings that are either fur or hair. Most mammals give birth to live babies. Examples of mammals are dogs, cats, elephants, monkeys, giraffes, and human beings. The biggest mammal is the blue whale.

  Los mamíferos son animales de sangre caliente que tienen cubiertas de piel o de pelaje. La mayoría de los mamíferos reproduce crías vivas. Algunos ejemplos de mamíferos son perros, gatos, elefantes, monos, jirafas y seres humanos. El mamífero más grande es la ballena azul.

- Reptiles are cold-blooded animals that have dry, scaly skin. Their babies hatch from eggs. Most reptiles live in warm areas. Some live in water and some live on land. Examples of reptiles include lizards, snakes, turtles, alligators, and crocodiles.

  Los reptiles son animales de sangre fría que tienen una piel escamosa. Sus crías salen de huevos. La mayoría de los reptiles vive en países cálidos. Algunos viven en agua y otros en tierra. Algunos ejemplos de reptiles son lagartijas, serpientes, tortugas, caimanes y cocodrilos.

Activity 2

- Show Oral Language Cards 6–14 and 19–21. Invite the children to evaluate each animal and decide if it is a mammal or a reptile.
- Have the children identify the reptiles and mammals on the *SRA Photo Library* software in the Animals category.

DAY 1

Objectives

- To combine, separate, and name "how many" concrete objects
- To start, use, and exit software programs

Vocabulary

add	sumar
adding	sumar

DLM Materials

- *Animal Orchestra/La orquesta de los animales*
- *Math Resource Guide*
  Numeral cards (1–4)
  Counting cards (1–4)
  Places Scenes: Adding version (animal or natural backgrounds)
  Cookie Game 2/Juego de la galleta 2 with activity sheet
  Counting Jar
  Number Pictures/Dibujos de números
  Compare Game: Adding version/ Juego de comparar: versión suma
  Making Towers/Hacer torres
  Numeral cube (3–8)
  2 Numeral cubes (1–3)
- *DLM Math* software
- *Where Is Thumbkin?* CD
- *Diez deditos* CD

Materials to Gather

- counters (small toy animals)
- counters (to use for chocolate chips)
- sticky notes
- tray or paper plate
- toothpicks (10 per child)
- connecting cubes (blue and yellow)

MATH

Focus

- Show page 2 of *Animal Orchestra/La orquesta de los animales.* Ask the children to show 2 with their fingers. Repeat with other numbers.

Develop

- Show the children how to create Number Pictures/Dibujos de números with toothpicks. Tell them they will be making pictures for 3, so they have to use exactly 3 toothpicks. Show an example.
- Have the children make a 3 picture using exactly 3 toothpicks. Have them describe their pictures, both with words and with numbers. Tell the children they will be making more Number Pictures/Dibujos de números in the centers.
- Introduce and demonstrate the computer activity Number Pictures.

Practice

- Invite the children to make Number Pictures/Dibujos de números. Assign them a number such as 5. Ask them to count out 5 objects (toothpicks today) and make a picture using that number of objects.
- Encourage the children to play Making Towers/Hacer torres. Children roll 2 Numeral cubes (labeled 1–3), take that many blue cubes, then add enough yellow cubes to make 6.
- Invite the children to play Cookie Game 2/Juego de la galleta 2 using the Numeral cube (3–8).
- Have the children continue to play the Compare Game: Adding version/Juego de comparar: versión suma.
- Invite the children to play Places Scenes: Adding version.
- Encourage the children to explore the Counting Jar.
- Invite the children to work on Number Pictures and any other activity they wish.

Reflect/Assess

- *How did you figure out how many were in your number picture?*
  ¿Cómo determinaron cuántos había en sus dibujos de números?

Music and Movement

- Sing "One Elephant" from the *Where Is Thumbkin?* CD.
- Sing "La casa de Peña" from the *Diez deditos* CD.

Suggested Reading

The Three Bears
Los tres ositos

Content Connection

Math A.3
Fine Arts A.2

Fine Arts

Objective
To use a variety of materials to create original work

DLM Materials
Teacher's Resource Anthology
play dough

Materials to Gather
animal shape sponges, animal cookie cutters

Activity 1
- Give the children an animal shape sponge and invite them to create a picture with 3 animals in it.

Activity 2
- Give the children play dough and cookie cutters and invite them to cut 3 animal-shaped cookies from the dough.

Reflect on the Day

- *What did you learn about animals today?*
  ¿Qué aprendieron hoy sobre los animales?
- *Which activity did you most enjoy today?*
  ¿Qué actividad disfrutaron más hoy?

Begin the Day

- Sing "Fiddle-I-Fee"/"Riqui-riqui-ra" or any of the children's favorite animal songs.
- Use one of the suggestions for Morning Circle offered in the front of this *Teacher's Edition.*

Objectives

- To begin to dictate words, phrases, and sentences to an adult recording on paper
- To understand that writing is used to communicate ideas and information

Vocabulary

mammal   mamìfero

DLM Materials

- Oral Language Development Cards 6–14
- magnetic letters
- *SRA Photo Library* software
- *Teacher's Resource Anthology*
  "Fiddle-I-Fee"/"Riqui-riqui-ra"
  "Five Little Monkeys"/"Cinco monitos"
  "The Great Big Turnip"/"El nabo gigante"
  zoo card patterns
  farm card patterns
  ocean card patterns
  "Going on a Bear Hunt"/"Vamos a cazar un oso"
  "Dog: A Mayan Legend"/"Perro: Una leyenda maya"
  "Rabbit: A Mayan Legend"/"El conejo: Una leyenda maya"

Materials to Gather

- cardboard strips
- yarn
- chart paper

LITERACY

Focus

- Perform the action rhyme "Five Little Monkeys"/"Cinco monitos."
- Tell the children that they will learn about mammals today.

Develop

One Way to Develop the Lesson

- Ask a volunteer to remind everyone what a mammal is. Write the characteristics on a piece of chart paper (see Day 1).
- Make a word web for animals that are mammals. Invite the children to name animals that they believe are mammals. Before you add them to the word web, check the characteristics of these animals against the characteristics you have listed for mammals. If these animals match, write the names on your word web.
- Use Oral Language Cards 6–14 with this lesson. You may want to discuss each of the animals pictured on the cards individually.

Another Way to Develop the Lesson

- Tell the children that you are going to tell them a make-believe story in which all the characters are mammals. Present "The Great Big Turnip"/"El nabo gigante" flannel board story. If you prefer, you may change the big thing in the story to something more applicable to the time of year or to your geographical location. The important thing is the cast of characters. *Which animals helped little bear? Where did the animals take the big thing? Who told the animals what the big thing was?*

  ¿Qué animales ayudaron al osito? ¿Dónde los animales llevaron la cosa grande? ¿Quién les dijo a los animales lo que era la cosa grande?
- Ask if anyone can remember how to spell *mother/madre*. Let a volunteer spell the word with the magnetic letters. Provide a model if needed.
- After you have told the story, have the children re-enact it. Give each child a necklace name card with the name of the character he or she is representing. Show each card as you hand it out and point out the letters that spell that animal's name.

Practice

- Place the flannel board story in the Language Center and encourage the children to retell the story or make up a new one.
- Place the name necklaces in the Writing Center and encourage the children to copy the names of the characters. You may want to keep the children focused on spelling and recognizing *mother/madre*.
- Invite the children to draw or paint their favorite story characters.
- Give the children the zoo, ocean, and farm animal card patterns. Have them select the animals that are mammals.
- Invite the children to choose one of the animals on the Oral Language Cards and dictate a story about it.
- Encourage the children to find the mammals in the Animal category on the *SRA Photo Library* software.

Preparation

- Make "The Great Big Turnip"/"El nabo gigante" flannel board story.
- Make a necklace for each character in the flannel board story. Write the animal's name on a cardboard strip and add a copy of the animal's picture made from the flannel board patterns. Attach yarn to make each card into a necklace.
- Make copies of the animal card patterns. Color them, cut them out, and laminate them.

Second Language Learners

Audiotape the flannel board story "The Great Big Turnip"/"El nabo gigante" as you tell it to the children. Then place the figures and the flannel board in the Language Center along with the audiotape. Children can place the appropriate items on the flannel board as they listen to the story.

"Little Skunk's Hole"
"The Bear Went over the Mountain"
"Mi mascota"
"My Pet"
"Gray Squirrel"
"La ardilla gris"

DAY 2

Letter Knowledge

English

- Read selections from the *SRA Alphabet Book.*

Spanish

- Read "Gerardo" from *Los niños alfabéticos.*

Suggested Reading

The Whales' Song by Dyan Sheldon
Never Mail an Elephant by Mike Thaler
Oli, el pequeño elefante by Burny Bos
Soy un oso grande y hermoso by Janosch
The Mitten by Jan Brett
Henrietta's First Winter by Rob Lewis
Harquin el zorro que bajó al valle by John Burningham
El gato tragón by Phyllis King

Reflect/Assess

- *What is the most interesting thing you learned about mammals today?*

  ¿Qué fue lo más interesante que aprendieron hoy sobre los mamíferos?
- *Do any mammals live at your house? Name them. Don't forget that humans are mammals.*

  ¿Hay algún mamífero que viva en su casa? Díganme quién es. No se olviden de que los seres humanos son mamíferos.

Literacy Circle

Storytime 1

- Invite the children to participate in the action rhyme "Going on a Bear Hunt"/"Vamos a cazar un oso." Discuss the place in which the bear was found.

Storytime 2

- Read the listening stories "Dog: A Mayan Legend"/"Perro: Una leyenda maya" and "Rabbit: A Mayan Legend"/"El conejo: Una leyenda maya." Discuss the morals of the stories. Ask children to describe the characteristics of dogs and rabbits and to describe their interactions with each animal.

Content Connection

Science

Objective
To describe properties of objects and characteristics of living things

Vocabulary
blue whale
ballena azul

DLM Materials
Teacher's Resource Anthology
"Going on a Whale Watch"/ "Vamos a mirar ballenas"

Materials to Gather
yarn

Activity 1

- Remind the children that the blue whale is the largest living marine animal and is also the largest living mammal. The whale is one of the most intelligent animals, although it has no sense of taste or smell and very poor eyesight. It depends on its senses of touch and sound for survival.
  La ballena azul es el ser marino más grande y el mamífero más grande que existe. La ballena es el ser más inteligente de todos los animales aunque no tiene ni sentido del gusto ni del olfato y muy poca visión. Depende de su sentido del tacto y del sonido para sobrevivir.
- The whale can grow to a length of one hundred feet and can weigh two hundred and twenty short tons. Use a piece of yarn to demonstrate the length of the whale.

Activity 2

- Present the "Going on a Whale Watch"/"Vamos a mirar ballenas" flannel board story. Children have a difficult time classifying the whale as a mammal because they often see it as a big fish. Help them understand why a whale is a mammal and not a fish.

DAY 2

Objectives

- To combine, separate, and name "how many" concrete objects
- To begin to demonstrate part of and whole with real objects

Vocabulary

add	sumar
adding	sumar
number names	nombres de los números

DLM Materials

- *Math Resource Guide*
  Places Scenes: Number Parts version (animal or natural backgrounds) (see Day 1)
  Snapshots: Adding version/ Instantáneas: versión suma
- See Day 1
- *DLM Math* software
- *Where Is Thumbkin?* CD
- *Esta es mi tierra* CD
- *Diez deditos* CD

Materials to Gather

- See Day 1

MATH

Focus

- Play Snapshots: Adding version/Instantáneas: versión suma. Secretly put 2 counters in one of your hands and 2 counters in your other hand. Hold out your closed hands, then open them for 2 seconds, then close them. Ask the children how many counters were in each hand. Ask them how many you had in all. Open both hands again, and count to check.
- Repeat using numbers totaling 5 or fewer.

Develop

- Play Places Scenes: Number Parts version. Give each child a background sheet and counters of 2 types. Have the children put 4 counters on their sheets. Ask them how many of each type they have, and how many altogether.
- Some of the Places Scenes sheets have 2 areas. An alternative would be to use 1 of the scenes that has 2 areas and give the children 4 counters of the same type. Instruct them to put some counters in 1 area and some in the other.
- Reintroduce the computer activity Number Pictures.

Practice

- Encourage the children to play Places Scenes: Number Parts version.
- Have the children play Number Pictures/Dibujos de números.
- Encourage the children to play Cookie Game 2/Juego de la galleta 2.
- Invite the children to play the Compare Game: Adding version/Juego de comparar: versión suma.
- Encourage the children to explore the Counting Jar.
- Invite the children to work on Number Pictures and any other activity they wish.

Reflect/Assess

- *How did you figure out how many would make 4 altogether on the Places Scenes sheets?*
  ¿Cómo determinaron cuántos formaban 4 en total en las hojas de Escenas de lugares?

Music and Movement

- Play "One Elephant" or "Gray Squirrel" from the *Where Is Thumbkin?* CD. Let the children sing and act out the song "One Elephant" without the music.
- Play "La rana" from the *Esta es mi tierra* CD or "La casa de Peña" from the *Diez deditos* CD. Ask the children which of the animals in the songs are mammals.

Suggested Reading

Blue's Felt Friends by Angela C. Santomero
The Shape of Things by Dayle Ann Dodds

Content Connection

Physical Development

Objective
To begin to manipulate play objects that have fine parts

DLM Materials
pattern blocks

Materials to Gather
felt shapes
flannel board
parquetry blocks (optional)

Activity 1

- Give the children parquetry blocks or pattern blocks and encourage them to make a picture using the shapes. Suggest they create an animal. Have them count how many shapes they used to create their designs.

Activity 2

- Give the children felt shapes to create a picture on the flannel board. Suggest they create an animal. Encourage them to count the number of shapes they used to create their pictures.

Reflect on the Day

- *What did you learn about mammals today?*
  ¿Qué aprendieron hoy sobre los mamíferos?
- *What was your favorite activity today? Why?*
  ¿Cuál fue su actividad favorita del día? ¿Por qué?

Begin the Day

Objectives

- To use language for a variety of purposes
- To begin to retell the sequence of a story

Vocabulary

reptiles   reptiles

DLM Materials

- *Sara Sidney: The Most Beautiful Iguana in the World/Sara Sidney: la iguana más bella del mundo*
- *SRA Photo Library* software
- magnetic letters
- *Teacher's Resource Anthology*
  "I'm Being Swallowed by a Boa Constrictor"/"Me está tragando una boa común"
  "Five Little Speckled Frogs"/"Cinco ranitas manchadas"
  "There Was a Little Turtle"/"Había una tortuguita"
  "My Very Own Pet"/"Mi propia mascota"
  "Tortoise Wins a Race"/"La tortuga gana la carrera"
  play dough

- Ask: *Who noticed the long snake stretched from the door to the circle? Why do you think it is there?*
  ¿Quién pudo notar la serpiente larga que se extendía desde la puerta hasta el círculo? ¿Por qué creen que está allí?
  Tell the children that they are going to study reptiles today and that the snake is a reptile.
- Sing or chant "I'm Being Swallowed by a Boa Constrictor"/"Me está tragando una boa común."
- Use one of the suggestions for Morning Circle offered in the front of this *Teacher's Edition.*

LITERACY

Focus

- Let the children act out "Five Little Speckled Frogs"/"Cinco ranitas manchadas" or say the finger play "There Was a Little Turtle"/"Había una tortuguita." Ask the children if the turtle or the frogs are on the list of mammals. *Do turtles or frogs have hair or fur?*
  ¿Las tortugas o las ranas tienen pelo o pelaje?
  Tell the children that the turtle and snake are reptiles.

Develop

One Way to Develop the Lesson

- Remind the children about the characteristics of a reptile. Reptiles are cold-blooded animals that have dry, scaly skin. Their babies hatch from eggs. Most reptiles live in warm areas. Some live in water and some live on land. Examples of reptiles include lizards, snakes, turtles, alligators, and crocodiles. Make a list of reptile characteristics.
- Make a word web for animals that are reptiles. Ask the children to name animals to add to the web.
- Ask the children to think of ways that mammals and reptiles are alike and different.

Another Way to Develop the Lesson

- Tell the children that you are going to tell them a story about a little boy who wants a pet. Some of the pets the little boy wants are reptiles and some are mammals. *Listen carefully so that you can tell me which pets in the story are reptiles.*

  Oigan con cuidado para que me puedan decir cuáles mascotas del cuento son reptiles.
- Present the "My Very Own Pet"/"Mi propia mascota" flannel board story. *What animals did Austin bring home? Which of the animals were reptiles? What did Austin's mother say each time he came home with another pet?*

  ¿Qué animales llevó Austin a la casa? ¿Cuáles de los animales eran reptiles? ¿Qué dijo la mamá de Austin cada vez que él llegaba con otra mascota?

  Call attention to the names written on the backs of the puppets.
- Write the word *mother* on the chalkboard or on a piece of chart paper. Tell the children that *mother* and *mama* mean the same thing but are used and spelled differently. Ask the children to tell you which term they use: *mama, mother,* or something else. Tell the children that today they will practice recognizing and reading the word *mother.*

  Las palabras madre *y* mamá *significan lo mismo pero se escriben de forma diferente. ¿Quién usa la palabra* madre *y quién usa* mamá*? ¿Quién usa una palabra diferente? Hoy vamos a practicar cómo reconocer y poder leer la palabra* madre.
- Give the children the stick puppets you made and invite them to retell the story using the puppets.

Practice

- Place the "My Very Own Pet"/"Mi propia mascota" flannel board story and the puppets in the Language Center and encourage the children to retell the story or make up a new one.
- Invite the children to draw or paint their favorite pets from the story.
- Give the children the zoo, farm animal, and ocean card patterns. Have them select the animals that are reptiles.
- Invite the children to choose one of the animals on the Oral Language Cards to write a story about.

Materials to Gather

- rope or yarn
- ribbon
- animal pattern cards (see Day 2)
- green construction paper
- chart paper
- tempera paint
- tongue depressors
- word cards

Preparation

- Lay a long ribbon or fat piece of rope or yarn from the doorway to the circle area to create a snake. Have the children follow the snake to Morning Circle.
- Make flannel board stories. Make a second enlarged copy of "My Very Own Pet"/ "Mi propia mascota" characters. Color them, cut them out, laminate them, and glue them to tongue depressors to create puppets. Tape the name of the character to the back of each puppet.
- Write *mother* and *madre* on index cards.
- Make spiral lines on green construction paper.

Second Language Learners

Mother/madre and *mama/mamá* refer to the same person, but *mother/madre* is a more formal term. Many people use *mama* (or *mommy/mami*) when addressing their mothers, but they say "my mother/mi madre" or "your

DAY 3

Letter Knowledge

English/Spanish

- Invite the children to make the letter *g* with play dough.

Suggested Reading

Slinky, Scaly, Snakes by Jennifer Dussling
Lyle, Lyle, Crocodile by Bernard Waber
The Day Jimmy's Boa Ate the Wash by Trinka Hakes Noble

Anthology Support

"Hear the Lively Song"
"Oye la alegre canción"
"Crocodile Song"
"Freddie the Snake"
"Braulio, la culebra"

- Place play dough in the Fine Motor Center and encourage the children to roll snakes. Give them a potato masher so they can make baby snakes. Provide toothpicks for etching facial features.
- Use a marking pen to draw spiral patterns (like a coiled-up snake) on pieces of green construction paper. Encourage the children to cut out the spirals to make snakes.
- Give the children the words *mother* and *madre* written on index cards. Provide flannel board letters and let the children copy the words on the flannel board.
- Encourage the children to find the reptiles in the Animal category of the *SRA Photo Library* software.

Reflect/Assess

- *How are reptiles like mammals? How are they different?*

  ¿En qué se parecen los reptiles a los mamíferos? ¿En qué se diferencian?
- *Which reptile is your favorite? Why?*

  ¿Cuál reptil es su favorito? ¿Por qué?

Literacy Circle

Storytime 1

- Present the "Tortoise Wins a Race"/"La tortuga gana la carrera" flannel board story. *Which animal in the story is a reptile? What kind of animal is the hare?*

  ¿Qué animal del cuento es un reptil? ¿Qué tipo de animal es una liebre?

Storytime 2

- Read *Sara Sidney: The Most Beautiful Iguana in the World/Sara Sidney: la iguana más bella del mundo*. Describe the things about Sara Sidney that make her a reptile. Read the fact sheet at the end of the book.

Content Connection

Fine Arts

Objective
To begin to create or re-create stories, moods, or experiences through dramatic representations

DLM Materials
Teacher's Resource Anthology
"Three Little Monkeys"/ "Tres monitos"

Activity 1

- Introduce "Three Little Monkeys"/ "Tres monitos." Let the children act out the rhyme.
- Challenge the children to think of ways the monkeys could have avoided being eaten. Make a list of their ideas.

Activity 2

- Invite the children to write a new rhyme about the monkeys in which the monkeys escape.
- Let the children act out their version of the rhyme.

DAY 3

Objectives

- To combine, separate, and name "how many" concrete objects
- To begin to demonstrate part of and whole with real objects

Vocabulary

add	sumar
adding	sumar
number names	nombres de los números

DLM Materials

- pattern blocks (triangles and squares only)
- *Math Resource Guide*
  Places Scenes: Number Parts version (animal or natural backgrounds)
  Cube Trains/Trenes de cubos
- See Day 1
- *DLM Math* software
- *Where Is Thumbkin?* CD
- *Teacher's Resource Anthology*
  "Five Little Monkeys,"/"Cinco monitos"
  Leap Frog/Pídola

Materials to Gather

- See Day 1
- connecting cubes (2 colors)

MATH

Focus

- Do the finger play "Five Little Monkeys"/"Cinco monitos," but start at 7 or 10!

Develop

- Make Cube Trains/Trenes de cubos. Give the children connecting cubes in 2 colors. Have them make a train of 4 cubes. Ask them to count the number of colors of each cube used in their trains.
- Play Number Pictures/Dibujos de números. Have pattern block triangles and squares available for the children. Challenge them to make a 4 design with the pattern block triangles and squares.

Practice

- Encourage the children to build Cube Trains/Trenes de cubos. Have them make as many different trains of 4 as they can with 2 colors of connecting cubes. You may wish to place the cubes in more than 1 center and use 2 different colors of cubes in each center.
- Have the children make Number Pictures/Dibujos de números. Assign them a number such as 5. Ask them to count out 5 objects and make a picture using that number of objects. Ask them to describe the picture, both with words and with numbers.
- Invite the children to play Places Scenes: Number Parts version.
- Have the children play Cookie Game 2/Juego de la galleta 2.
- Invite the children to continue playing the Compare Game: Adding version/Juego de comparar: versión suma.
- Encourage the children to continue to explore the Counting Jar. Have them record their counts. They should include their names and the amount they counted, using pictures or numerals.
- Invite the children to work on Number Pictures and any other activity they wish.

Reflect/Assess

- *How many different trains of 4 could you make?*
  ¿Cuántos trenes diferentes de 4 podrían hacer?
- *How could you figure out if you made them all?*
  ¿Cómo podrían determinar si los hicieron todos?

Music and Movement

- Play the "Crocodile Song" or "The Frog Went A-Courtin'" from the *Where Is Thumbkin?* CD. Invite the children to sing along.
- Play Leap Frog/Pídola.

Content Connection

Fine Arts

Objective
To participate in classroom music activities

DLM Materials
- *Teacher's Resource Anthology*
  "The Ants Go Marching"/"Las hormiguitas marchan"
  "Five Little Ducks"/"Los cinco patitos"

Activity 1
- Sing "The Ants Go Marching"/"Las hormiguitas marchan."
- Talk about and dramatize the various situations in the song that show how various combinations of 2 can make 2, 4, or 6.

Activity 2
- Sing "Five Little Ducks"/"Los cinco patitos" with a variation. Make it 6 ducks and have them reappear 2 at a time.
- Dramatize the song and discuss how various combinations of 2 can make 2, 4, or 6.

Reflect on the Day

- *What did you learn about reptiles today?*
  ¿Qué aprendieron hoy sobre los reptiles?
- *What will you share with your family about reptiles?*
  ¿Qué compartirán con sus familias sobre los reptiles?

Suggested Reading

Benny's Pennies by Pat Brisson
Five Little Ducks by Raffi

What Research Suggests

The computer helps children connect collections of objects such as shapes to number words and numerals.

Begin the Day

- Sing "Over in the Meadow"/"Sobre la pradera." Invite the children to classify the animals in the song.
- Tell the children that today they will learn about fish and tomorrow they will learn about birds. *Which type of animal isn't mentioned in the song? Can you add a verse about a mammal?*

  ¿Qué tipo de animal no se menciona en la canción? ¿Pueden agregar un verso sobre un mamífero?
- Use one of the suggestions for Morning Circle offered in the front of this *Teacher's Edition.*

Objectives

- To begin to identify some high-frequency words
- To identify 10 or more printed alphabet letters

Vocabulary

reptiles	reptiles
mammals	mamíferos
fish	peces

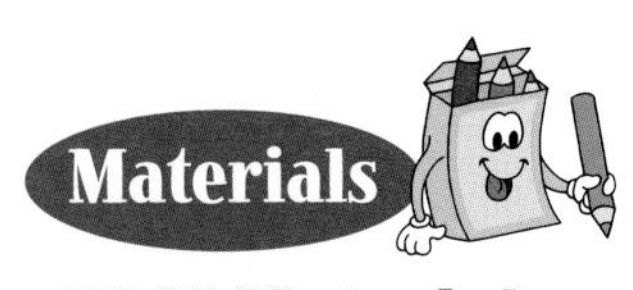

DLM Materials

- Oral Language Development Card 22
- *Fish Wish/Deseos de un pez*
- *SRA Book of Animals/SRA El libro de los animales*
- *SRA Photo Library* software
- *Teacher's Resource Anthology*
  "Over in the Meadow"/ "Sobre la pradera"
  "Counting Rhyme"
  "Pin uno"

Materials to Gather

- coat hanger tube
- yarn
- construction paper
- overhead projector
- chart paper
- fish or fish pictures
- magnifying lens
- clear sequins
- colored acetate
- fish bowl
- fish story starters

LITERACY

Focus

- Say the "Counting Rhyme" or "Pin uno" with the children. Ask if the children have ever been fishing. Let them share their experiences with fish.

Develop

One Way to Develop the Lesson

- Show Oral Language Card 22. Use the suggestions on the back of the card to stimulate discussion.
- Check the fish against the criteria you have established for reptiles and mammals. When the children realize that the fish fits neither of the categories, tell them that the fish is in a category of its own.
- Discuss the characteristics of fish. They live in the water. They breathe through gills. They have tails and fins that move from side to side and are used to direct their course while swimming. Their bodies are covered with scales. Fish have eyes but no eyelids. Make a list of all the characteristics of fish.

Another Way to Develop the Lesson

- Write the words *papa* and *father/padre* on the chalkboard or on a piece of chart paper. Ask if anyone can read the words. If no one recognizes the words, read them. Tell the children that these are new sight words they will learn to recognize.

  ¿Quién puede leer una de las palabras o ambas? Éstas son dos palabras que vamos a aprender a reconocer.
- Lay the fish you made on the floor. Invite a child to use the fishing pole to catch a fish. Ask him or her to read the word or letter on the fish. If he or she is correct, have the child hand the pole to another child. If he or she misses the word or letter, ask a volunteer to help and then let the volunteer catch the next fish. Continue until everyone has had a turn.

Practice

- Place the fishing game in the Language Center and let the children continue to play.
- Cut fish out of colored acetate and invite the children to play with them on the overhead projector. Encourage them to make up a story about the fish they are projecting on the wall.
- Use large clear sequins to represent fish scales. Write the word *fish* on a piece of construction paper. Invite the children to spell *fish* by gluing sequins over the letters.
- Provide a real fish or pictures of fish and a magnifying glass. Invite the children to look at the fish and find the characteristics that you listed on the fish chart.
- Fill a fish bowl with story starters. Let the children draw starters and then dictate stories. Some examples of starters might be: "My Uncle Pat caught a big fish one day when . . ." or "One day when I was feeding my goldfish, something funny happened. . . ."
- Encourage the children to find the fish in the Animal category of the *SRA Photo Library* software.

Preparation

- Make a fishing game. Make a fishing pole by using a coat hanger tube and attaching a piece of yarn with a magnet to the end of it. Cut fish out of construction paper. Write the four sight words *mama, papa, mother/madre,* and *father/padre* on four of the fish. Write some alphabet letters on other fish. Attach paperclips to the fish.
- Cut fish shapes out of colored acetate to use with the overhead projector.
- Write some fish story starters.
- Write the word *fish* on several sheets of colored construction paper.

Second Language Learners

Father/padre and *papa/papá* refer to the same person, but *father/padre* is a more formal term. Many people use *papa/papá* (or *daddy/papi)* to talk to their fathers, but they say "my father/mi padre" or "your father/tu padre" if they are talking about him.

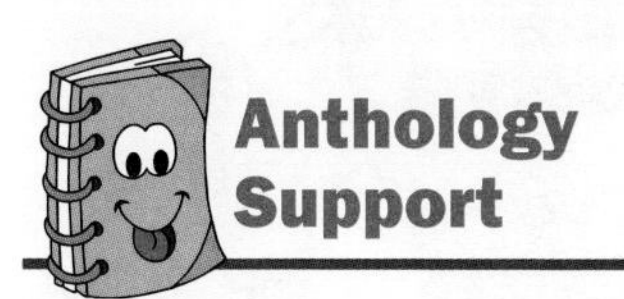

Anthology Support

"My Pet"
"Mi mascota"
"Muévete como yo"
"Fish Games"
"Juegos de peces"

Letter Knowledge

English

- Invite the children to make letter shapes with their bodies. Use the Think, Pair, Share game/Piensa, aparea, comparte with this activity.

Spanish

- Invite the children to make the letter *g* with their bodies. Use the Think, Pair, Share game/Piensa, aparea, comparte with this activity.

Suggested Reading

Swimmy by Leo Lionni
Nadarín by Leo Lionni
Fish Eyes by Lois Ehlert
Turquesita by Silvia Dubovoy
In the Small, Small Pond by Denise Fleming

Reflect/Assess

- *How are fish like reptiles? How are they like mammals? How are they different from both?*

  ¿En qué se parecen los peces a los reptiles? ¿En qué se parecen a los mamíferos? ¿En qué se diferencian de los dos?

- *What would a fish need in order to live on land?*

  ¿Qué necesitaría un pez para poder vivir en tierra?

Literacy Circle

Storytime 1

- Read *Fish Wish/Deseos de un pez. Did you know there were so many beautiful fish? Not everything in the ocean is a fish. Some of the animals in the book are reptiles and mammals. Can you name an animal in the story that is a mammal? Can you name an animal in the story that is a reptile?*

  ¿Sabían que había tantos peces bellos? No todo lo que vive en el mar es un pez. Algunos de los animales del libro son reptiles y mamíferos. ¿Pueden decirme un animal del cuento que sea mamífero? ¿Pueden decirme un animal del cuento que sea reptil?

Storytime 2

- Read "The Hermit Crab"/"El cangrejo hermitaño" from the *SRA Book of Animals/SRA El libro de los animales.* Use the focus questions at the beginning of the selection to get the children interested. When you have finished reading the selection, ask the children questions. *Are hermit crabs and fish friends, or are hermit crabs afraid of fish? Why? How are fish and hermit crabs alike and how are they different?*

  ¿Los cangrejos ermitaños y los peces son amigos o los cangrejos ermitaños tienen miedo de los peces? ¿Por qué? ¿En qué se parecen los peces y los cangrejos ermitaños y en qué se diferencian?

Content Connection

Fine Arts

Objective
To use different colors, surface textures, and shapes to create form and meaning

DLM Materials
Fish Wish/Deseos de un pez

Materials to Gather
poster board fish, colored tissue paper, fish patterns, resealable plastic bags (one per child), blue hair gel, black permanent pens, laminating film

Activity 1

- Remind the children of the brightly colored fish in *Fish Wish/Deseos de un pez.* Give them fish cut out of poster board and an assortment of several colors of tissue paper. Invite the children to collage the tissue paper in an overlapping fashion to create colorful fish.

Activity 2

- Give the children fish patterns to trace onto laminating film and cut out. Have them add details with black pens. Place the fish in a resealable plastic bag with one-third cup of blue hair gel to create an aquarium.

DAY 4

Objectives
- To combine, separate, and name "how many" concrete objects
- To begin to demonstrate part of and whole with real objects

Vocabulary
add	sumar
adding	sumar

DLM Materials
- pattern blocks (triangles and squares only)
- *Math Resource Guide*
  Places Scenes: Number Parts version (animal or natural backgrounds)
  Snapshots: Adding version/ Instantáneas: versión suma
  Off and On/Apaga y prende
  Cube Trains/Trenes de cubos
- See Day 1
- *DLM Math* software
- *Teacher's Resource Anthology*
  Duck, Duck, Goose/Pato, pato, ganso
  Simon Says/Simón dice

Materials to Gather
- connecting cubes (2 colors)
- cups, counters, and pieces of colored paper
- See Day 1

MATH

Focus
- Play Snapshots: Adding version/Instantáneas: versión suma. Repeat this activity with new numbers.

Develop
- Have the children make numbers with their fingers. Ask them to show 3 fingers using 1 or 2 hands. Have several children demonstrate how they did it. Repeat a couple of times.
- Play Off and On/Apaga y prende. Demonstrate this new center activity that shows the numbers hidden inside 4. Have the children place 4 counters in a cup and toss them on a piece of paper on the floor or a table. Ask them to determine how many counters landed on and off the paper, and have them read aloud the combinations. Teach the children to call them *break aparts*. For example, the break aparts might be read aloud as the numbers 1 and 3.

Practice
- Encourage the children to play Off and On/Apaga y prende.
- Invite the children to continue making Cube Trains/Trenes de cubos.
- Have the children make Number Pictures/Dibujos de números.
- Invite the children to play Places Scenes: Number Parts version with an adult.
- Have the children play Cookie Game 2/Juego de la galleta 2.
- Encourage the children to play the Compare Game: Adding version/Juego de comparar: versión suma.
- Have the children explore the Counting Jar.
- Have the children work on Number Pictures and any other activity they wish. Encourage children to notice the number combinations they are making, such as 2 and 2 making 4.

Reflect/Assess

- *How many different trains of 4 could you make?*
  ¿Cuántos trenes diferentes de 4 pueden hacer?
- *How could you figure out if you made them all?*
  ¿Cómo determinarían si los hicieron todos?

Music and Movement

- Play different tempos of music and invite the children to swim like fish. Suggest they swim like fish in a bowl and then like fish in the ocean. Suggest they swim like happy fish, tired fish, scared fish, and baby fish.
- Invite the children to play Duck, Duck, Fish as they would Duck, Duck, Goose/Pato, pato, ganso. Or suggest they play Fish Wishes as they would play Simon Says/Simón dice.

Content Connection

Fine Arts

Objectives

To use a variety of materials to create original work

To share ideas about personal artwork

DLM Materials

SRA Book of Animals/
SRA El libro de los animales

Materials to Gather

strips of paper (various lengths, widths, zigzagged, curved, or straight), paper, glue

Activity 1

- Show the children the painting "Line of Maasai cattle"/"Fila de ganado Maasai" on page 48 of the *SRA Book of Animals/ SRA El libro de los animales.* Discuss the lines and shapes in the borders of the picture. Give the children strips of paper cut in various lengths and widths. Have them create a design and glue it to their papers.
- Have them show and describe what they created to the class or to a friend.

Activity 2

- Invite the children to make a collage from scraps of materials such as rickrack and ribbon. Discuss the lines of each item in the collage. Have the children describe their work to a friend.

Suggested Reading

Harold and the Purple Crayon by Crockett Johnson

Reflect on the Day

- *What did you learn about fish today?*
  ¿Qué aprendieron hoy sobre los peces?
- *What will you share with your family about fish?*
  ¿Qué compartirán con su familia sobre los peces?

Home Connection

Send home a take-home book pack with four children.

Begin the Day

- Ask the children about the feathers that they followed into the room. *Where did they come from? What do they mean?* Tell the children that they will learn about birds today.
- Sing or say "Two Little Blackbirds"/"Dos mirlos."
- Use one of the suggestions for Morning Circle offered in the front of this *Teacher's Edition.*

Objectives

- To ask questions and make comments related to the current topic of discussion
- To link new learning experiences and vocabulary to what is already known about a topic

DLM Materials

- Oral Language Development Cards 11 & 15-18
- *A Bicycle for Rosaura/Rosaura en bicicleta*
- *SRA Photo Library* software
- *Teacher's Resource Anthology*
  "Two Little Blackbirds"/"Dos mirlos"
  "Five Little Ducks"/"Los cinco patitos"
  "Silly Nellie: The Story of One Funny Turkey"/"Clotilde Bobilde: La historia de una pavita muy divertida" story map
  "Amelia's Pets"/"Los animales de Amelia"
  "Henny-Penny"/"Gallinita-Nita"
  animal pattern cards (see Day 2)

Materials to Gather

- feathers
- tempera paint
- nature tapes of bird calls
- paintbrushes

Focus

- Sing "Five Little Ducks"/"Los cinco patitos." *Are ducks birds? ¿Los patos son pájaros?*
- Change the roles of the mother and the father in the song and sing the song again. Write the word *papa* on chart paper or on the chalkboard. Tell the children that this will be their sight word today.
- Tell the children they will learn about birds today.

Develop

One Way to Develop the Lesson

- Show Oral Language Cards 11 and 15–18. Use the suggestions on the backs of the cards to stimulate discussion.
- Check the birds against the criteria you have established for reptiles, mammals, and fish. When the children reach the conclusion that the birds do not fit any of these categories, tell them that birds are in a category of their own.
- Discuss the characteristics of birds. They live in trees and on cliffs. They are covered in feathers. They have beaks and wings. Their babies hatch from eggs. List the characteristics on chart paper.

Another Way to Develop the Lesson

- Show the Oral Language Cards again. Discuss the many types of animals that fit into the category called birds.
- Make a word web for birds. Let the children name all the different kinds of birds they can think of. Be sure that they include birds for which you don't have pictures, such as ducks and turkeys.
- Tell the children that you are going to tell them a story about a silly turkey named Nellie. Present the story "Silly Nellie: The Story of One Funny Turkey"/"Clotilde Bobilde: La historia de una pavita muy divertida." *Who thinks Silly Nellie hung the moon? What does that mean? How does Silly Nellie help her friends?*

  ¿Quién cree que Clotilde Bobilde colgó la Luna? ¿Qué significa eso? ¿Cómo ayudó Clotilde Bobilde a sus amigos?
- Make a story map of the flannel board story. Use one of the samples that allows you to list the characters in the story. Be sure to point out the character names *mother* and *father* on your story map.

Practice

- Place the flannel board story in the Language Center for the children to use to retell the story or to make up a new story.
- Give the children the Animal card patterns. Have them select the animals that are mammals.
- Invite the children to choose one of the birds from the Oral Language Cards to write a story about.
- Play nature tapes with birdcalls on them. Are the children able to hear the slight differences in the sounds the various birds make?
- Encourage the children to use feathers as writing instruments. Give them word cards *(mother/madre, father/padre, mamá, papá)* to copy. Let them use tempera paint for ink.
- Show the children how to use feathers as brushes and invite them to paint pictures.
- Encourage the children to find the photos of birds in the Animal category of the *SRA Photo Library* software.

Preparation

- Spread feathers from your doorway to the Morning Circle area.
- Make the flannel board stories, if not already made.
- Copy a story map.

Scaffolding Strategies

More Help Read books about birds on a one-on-one basis.

Extra Challenge Invite the children to compare birds to airplanes.

Second Language Learners

For "Two Little Blackbirds"/"Dos mirlos," provide illustrations of the birds and their actions. As the children recite the finger play, do they remember all the words, or do they mark the rhythm with sounds, inserting only the most important words in the finger play? This is an appropriate finger play for second language learners because the language and accompanying actions are clear and simple. Provide opportunities throughout the day to practice this finger play.

DAY 5

Letter Knowledge

English

- Select a letter and have the children find and circle the letter in newspapers or magazines.

Spanish

- Invite the children to find and circle the letter *g* in newspapers or magazines.

Suggested Reading

Chickens Aren't the Only Ones by Ruth Heller
Owl Moon by Jane Yolen
El árbol de los pájaros by Jesus Ballaz
El huevo más hermoso del mundo by Helme Heine

Anthology Support

"Six White Ducks"
"Los seis patos blancos"
"Little Polly Parakeet"
"El pajarito"
"Be Kind to Your Web-Footed Friends"
"White Wings"

Reflect/Assess

- *What do you think it would be like to be a bird? Where would you sleep?*
  ¿Cómo creen que sería ser un pájaro? ¿Dónde dormirían?
- *Which of the birds that we discussed today do you like best? Why?*
  ¿Cuáles de los pájaros que estudiamos hoy les gustó más? ¿Por qué?

Literacy Circle

Storytime 1

- Read *A Bicycle for Rosaura/Rosaura en bicicleta*. Discuss what a stranger is. Explain that it is never a good idea to approach a stranger without a trusted adult. Tell the children how to get help if they ever feel unsafe. Talk about the stranger in the story.
- Sing "Los animales de Amelia"/"Amelia's Pets." *Which of Señora Amelia's pets are birds? What are the other pets?*
  ¿Cuáles mascotas de la señora Amelia son pájaros? ¿Qué son las otras mascotas?

Storytime 2

- Present the "Henny-Penny"/"Gallinita-Nita" flannel board story. *How many of the characters in the story are birds?*
  ¿Cuántos de los personajes del cuento son pájaros?
- Invite the children to talk about the rhyming word names. Ask them what a penguin would be named, if there was one in the story.

Content Connection

Science

Objectives

To describe properties of objects and characteristics of living things

To begin to use scientific words and phrases to describe objects, events, and living things

Materials to Gather

feathers, eyedroppers, cotton balls, buttons, beads, leaves

Vocabulary

water repellent, aerodynamic

impermeable, aerodinámico

Activity 1

- Discuss how feathers serve as protection for birds. Give the children feathers and eyedroppers. Have them drop water on the feathers. Call attention to how the feathers repel the water. Tell the children that feathers also protect birds' skin. Feathers act like shields to protect the birds from thorns and other things that could tear skin.

Activity 2

- Let the children test the weight of feathers. Provide several items such as cotton balls, buttons, beads, and leaves that they can toss into the air and watch fall.
- Point out that birds could not fly if they were weighted down with heavier skin coverings. Their feathers and their wings are aerodynamically perfect for flight.

DAY 5

MATH

Objectives
- To combine, separate, and name "how many" concrete objects
- To begin to demonstrate part of and whole with real objects

Vocabulary

add	sumar
adding	sumar
number names	nombres de los números

Materials

DLM Materials
- pattern blocks (triangles, squares, rhombuses, and trapezoids)
- *Math Resource Guide*
  Off and On/Apaga y prende
  Places Scenes: Number Parts version (animal or natural backgrounds)
  Cube Trains/Trenes de cubos
- *DLM Math* software
- *Where Is Thumbkin?* CD
- *Making Music with Thomas Moore* CD
- *Diez deditos* CD

Materials to Gather
- connecting cubes (2 colors)
- cups, counters, and pieces of colored paper

Focus
- Discuss the Counting Jar. Examine the children's displayed recordings. Do they remember how many of each type? Dump the objects and count them to check.
- Have the children make numbers with their fingers. Have them put their hands in their laps between each task. Ask them to show you 4 on one hand. Ask them how many fingers they are holding up and how many they are keeping down. Repeat with other numbers up to 5.

Develop
- Ask the children to talk about their work on Number Pictures/Dibujos de números.
- Have pattern blocks (blue rhombuses and trapezoids only) available for the children. Challenge them to make a 4 design. Show them that there are numbers hidden inside other numbers. For example, 2 and 2 are hidden inside a 4.
- Reintroduce the Off and On/Apaga y prende game.

Practice
- Invite the children to play the Off and On/Apaga y prende game.
- Encourage the children to continue making Cube Trains/Trenes de cubos.
- Have the children make 4 designs with Number Pictures/Dibujos de números. Add the rhombuses and trapezoids to a center today.
- Encourage the children to continue working on the previous activities for this week.
- Invite the children to work on Number Pictures. Use discussions to ensure that they can point out what each numeral is in their number pictures.

Reflect/Assess

- Computer Show: Have the children show their number pictures on the computer. *How did you describe your pictures with numbers?*
  ¿Cómo describieron sus dibujos con números?
- *How can you determine what numbers can be hidden inside 5?*
  ¿Cómo pueden determinar qué números pueden esconderse en 5?

Music and Movement

- Sing "Five Little Ducks" from the *Where Is Thumbkin?* CD or play and do "Chicken Dance" from the *Making Music with Thomas Moore* CD.
- Sing "Sun, sun, ba, ba" or "La pata" from the *Diez deditos* CD, or invite the children to have a feather race.

Suggested Reading

Shadows and Reflections by Tana Hoban

Content Connection

Science

Objective
To show an interest in investigating unfamiliar objects, organisms, and phenomena

DLM Materials
pattern blocks

Materials to Gather
blue or black construction paper

Activity 1

- Take the children outdoors. Encourage them to use the pattern blocks to create an animal on a sheet of construction paper. Tell them that you are going to leave the pictures outdoors for a while to see what will happen to them in the sun.
- Ask the children to predict what they think will happen.
  ¿Qué creen que sucederá?
- After a couple of hours go back outdoors to examine their pictures. Have them remove the pattern blocks. Discuss the sun's effect on the part of the paper not covered by the blocks. Use the pictures for a display, talk about the number of objects, and so on.

Activity 2

- Take the children outdoors to look for designs in shadows. Look particularly at the shadow patterns created by steps.

Reflect on the Day

- *What have you learned about animals this week?*
  ¿Qué aprendieron sobre los animales esta semana?
- *Which activity did you like best today?*
  ¿Qué actividad les gustó más hoy?

Looking Ahead

Connecting to the Theme: Zoo Animals

Extending the previous Animals theme, this lesson focuses specifically on animals we may encounter at the zoo. In reviewing this lesson, please be sensitive to the fact that not all prekindergartners have visited a zoo yet. Children will also learn about people who work at the zoo, safety at the zoo, and how to say some animal names using American Sign Language.

	Objectives	DLM Materials	Materials to Gather
DAY 1	• To understand that reading and writing are ways to obtain information and knowledge, generate and communicate thoughts and ideas, and solve problems • To sort objects into groups by an attribute and to begin to explain how the grouping was done	• *Edward the Emu/Eduardo el emú* • *Teacher's Resource Anthology* • pattern blocks • *Math Resource Guide* • *DLM Math* software	• cups • sticky notes • yarn • zoo puzzles • plastic eggs • plastic animals • toothpicks (10 per child) • envelopes or plastic bags (one per child)
DAY 2	• To understand that writing is used to communicate ideas and information • To begin to make size comparisons between objects • To participate in creating and using real and pictorial graphs • To combine, separate, and name "how many" concrete objects	• Oral Language Development Cards 6 & 7 • *SRA Book of Animals/SRA El Libro de los animales* • *Teacher's Resource Anthology* • pattern blocks • *Math Resource Guide* • *DLM Math* software • Oral Language Cards 8–11, 17–22	• index cards • sponges • inch cubes • paper plates • plastic rings • connecting cubes • sticky notes • cups • empty toilet paper tubes (one per child) • plastic coffee can lids • weighted soda bottle • toothpicks (10 per child)
DAY 3	• To begin to dictate words, phrases, and sentences to an adult recording on paper • To understand that writing is used to communicate ideas and information • To participate in creating and using real and pictorial graphs • To combine, separate, and name "how many" concrete objects	• *Who Is the Beast?/¿Quién es la bestia?* • *Edward the Emu/Eduardo el emú* • *Teacher's Resource Anthology* • pattern blocks • *Math Resource Guide* • *DLM Math* software • *Four Baby Bumblebees* CD	• zoo puzzles • cherries • raisins • KWL chart • paper plates • cups • orange and black ribbon, yarn, or crepe paper • pineapple slices (one per child) • shredded carrots
DAY 4	• To begin to attend to the beginning sounds in familiar words by identifying that the pronunciations of several words all begin the same way • To participate in creating and using real and pictorial graphs • To combine, separate, and name "how many" concrete objects	• Oral Language Development Card 8 • magnetic letters • *Teacher's Resource Anthology* • pattern blocks • *Math Resource Guide* • *DLM Math* software • *Where Is Thumbkin?* CD	• bananas • granola • bear photographs • zoo puzzles • flashlight • berry baskets • yogurt • craft sticks • die • brown sheet • cups • plastic animals • toothpicks (10 per child)
DAY 5	• To understand that different text forms are used for different functions • To participate in creating and using simple data charts • To participate in creating and using real and pictorial graphs • To use a variety of software packages with audio, video, and graphics to enhance learning	• Oral Language Cards 17, 18, & 21 • *Edward the Emu/Eduardo el emú* • *Teacher's Resource Anthology* • Rafita and Pepita • *DLM Math* software • *Diez deditos* CD • *Where Is Thumbkin?* CD • Oral Language Cards 6–22	• raisins • tray of sand • word cards • butcher paper • cups • berry baskets • zoo puzzles • sticks • yarn • magazines • counters • plastic animals • toilet paper tubes • green sugar sprinkles • uncooked breadsticks

(See individual lesson pages for complete lists of materials.)

Learning Centers

BLOCKS

Let's Build a Zoo

Objectives

To begin to share and cooperate with others in group activities

To begin to engage in dramatic play with others

Materials to Gather

berry baskets for cages, brown paint, construction paper, green paint, large sheet of paper, plastic animals, rubber animals

Develop

Provide various props and encourage the children to build a zoo. Allow them to add to the zoo during the week. Help them make cage signs for the animals. The children could also add landscaping to their zoo (trees, flowers, ponds, and so on). Make any paper trees stand up by attaching them to blocks.

Reflect/Assess

What did you like about building a zoo?

¿Qué les gustó acerca de construir un zoológico?

DRAMATIC PLAY

Animal Stories

Objective

To begin to create or re-create stories, moods, or experiences through dramatic representations

DLM Materials

Teacher's Resource Anthology

Materials to Gather

animal costumes, animal masks

Develop

To prepare, make copies of the animal mask patterns and assemble them. Invite the children to use the animal masks for storytelling and retelling, and also for dramatic recreation.

Reflect/Assess

Do you like to use the same story ideas or think of new ideas?

¿Les gusta usar las mismas ideas para los cuentos o les gusta pensar en ideas nuevas?

FINE MOTOR

Animal Figures

Objectives

To begin to develop pincer control in picking up objects

To begin to use scissors

DLM Materials

Teacher's Resource Anthology

Materials to Gather

animal cookie cutters (plastic), chenille wires, play dough, various craft materials

Develop

Have the children shape chenille wires into animals. Invite them to use cookie cutters to make animal shapes out of play dough. Provide various craft materials such as rickrack, sequins, wiggle eyes, construction paper, and so on for the children so they can add details to their work.

Reflect/Assess

Did you remember to put all the parts on your animals?

¿Recordaron ponerles todas las partes a sus animales?

What Research Suggests

Before the emergence of PET (Positron Emission Tomography) scans and MRI (Magnetic Resonance Imaging) machinery, neurological researchers depended heavily on animal research. The advancement of technology has progressed in two ways. First, it has reduced scientific dependency on animals for study. Secondly, technology has provided us with a more accurate picture of how human brains collect, process, and store data.

DAY 1

Begin the Day

- Sing and act out "Muévete como yo." Ask: *Has anyone ever seen any of the animals from this song?*
  ¿Alguien ha visto alguna vez uno de los animales de esta canción?
- Use a suggestion for Morning Circle found in the front of this *Teacher's Edition.*

Objectives

- To understand that reading and writing are ways to obtain information and knowledge, generate and communicate thoughts and ideas, and solve problems
- To understand that a book has a title and an author

Vocabulary

emu	emú
seals	focas
snakes	serpientes, culebras
zoo	zoológico
zookeeper	guardián del zoológico

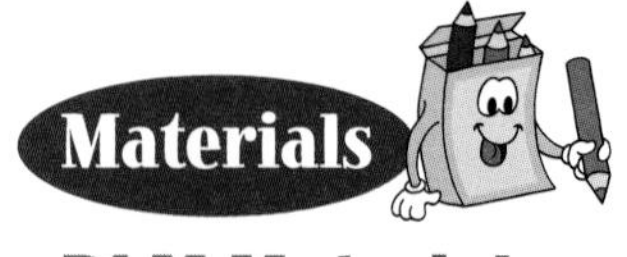

DLM Materials

- *Edward the Emu/Eduardo el emú*
- *SRA Photo Library* software
- *Teacher's Resource Anthology*
  "Muévete como yo"
  "Oh, Do You Want to See the Zoo?"/"¿Al zoológico quieres ver?"
  Zoo card patterns
  "Party at Daisy's"/"Fiesta en casa de Daisy"
  "The Zanzibar Zoo"/"El zoológico de Zanzíbar"

Materials to Gather

- chart paper
- KWL chart (Know, Would like to know, Learned)
- zoo puzzles
- index cards
- plastic eggs

LITERACY

Focus

- Sing "Oh, Do You Want to See the Zoo?"/"¿Al zoológico quieres ver?" Allow the children to share any of their zoo experiences.
- Explain that the children will be learning about zoos and animals at zoos this week.

Develop

One Way to Develop the Lesson

- Zoos and zoo animals are topics about which children generally have a significant amount of prior knowledge. This is a good time to create a KWL chart if you have not used one yet this year.
- Create a KWL chart using three columns. Label the first column *Know,* the second column *Would like to know,* and the third column *Learned.*
- Explain to the children that in the first column, they will list information they already know about the zoo and zoo animals. In the middle column, they will list things that they would like to know about the zoo and its animals. Finally, in the third column, they will list what they have just learned about the zoo and zoo animals.
  En la primera columna harán una lista de la información que ya saben sobre el zoológico. En la columna del medio harán una lista de las cosas que les gustaría saber sobre el zoológico y sus animales. Finalmente, en la tercera columna harán una lista de lo que acaban de aprender sobre el zoológico.

- Set up the KWL chart and show it to the children. Print the word *Zoo* at the top, and point out that *zoo* is an easy word to recognize and that after learning about zoos all week, they might be able to read it on their own. Fill in the chart's first two columns with comments from the children.

Another Way to Develop the Lesson

- Show the cover of *Edward the Emu/Eduardo el emú*. Read the title aloud and explain that authors give their books names or titles. Point out the names of the author and the illustrator. Make sure the children know how each person contributes to the story.
- Read *Edward the Emu/Eduardo el emú*. Discuss the story. Ask: *Why was Edward unhappy? What did he do? What happened at the end of the story that made Edward happy? Did Edward learn anything?*

  ¿Por qué Eduardo estaba infeliz? ¿Qué hizo? ¿Qué pasó al final del cuento que alegró a Eduardo? ¿Aprendió Eduardo algo?
- Continue to complete the KWL chart with any answers the children are discovering, or with any new questions they might have.

Practice

- Place the *Edward the Emu/Eduardo el emú* book and tape in the Listening Center.
- Write the words *zoo* and *zookeeper* on index cards. Provide tracing paper and allow the children to trace each word.
- Have the children play the Zoo Concentration game.
- Place copies of zoo card patterns inside plastic eggs. Have the children choose an egg, open it, and, with your help, write a sentence about the animal. Explain that the written words express their thoughts.
- Invite the children to draw pictures of their favorite parts in the story.
- Give the children zoo puzzles to complete.

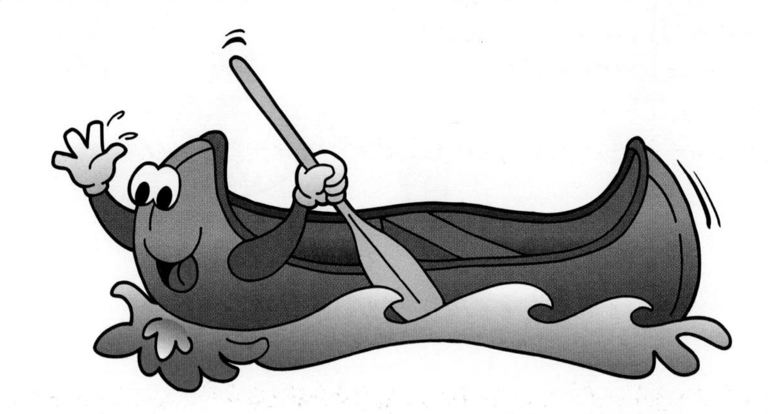

Preparation

- Make the flannel board story.
- Make a KWL chart for zoos and zoo animals.
- Make three copies of the zoo card patterns. Color, laminate, and cut out two of the copies for a Zoo Concentration game. Use the third copy in a story egg.
- Copy and enlarge the zoo card patterns. Color them, laminate them, and then cut them into puzzle pieces.
- Write *zoo* and *zookeeper* on index cards.

Second Language Learners

While other children are in centers, work one-on-one with second language learners. As the children open plastic eggs and find pictures of zoo animals inside, ask them to talk about the animals. Have they ever seen a live animal like this? Where? What do they know about this animal? After a brief discussion, ask them what they want to write. Simplify the sentence so it is manageable, and write it for them. A few children may attempt to write on their own. If so, do not write corrections under their attempted writing. Once it is written, ask the children to read the sentence with you. Note the language they use.

DAY 1

Letter Knowledge

English
- Read any of the letter stories in the *English Phonics Resource Guide*.

Spanish
- Discuss the letter *c* using the "Cecilia" story from the *Spanish Phonics Resource Guide*.

Suggested Reading

At the Zoo by Paul Simon

Anthology Support

"Animal Fair"
"We're Going to the Zoo"
"Vamos al zoo"
"Six White Ducks"
"Los seis patos blancos"

Scaffolding Strategies

More Help Talk with the children about any trips they have taken to a zoo. You might get books or videos about the zoo from the library for any children that have not been to a zoo.

Extra Challenge Help the children think about how it might feel to be an animal living in a confined space.

Reflect/Assess

- *Why do you think we have zoos?*
  ¿Por qué creen que tenemos zoológicos?
- *Why was Edward unhappy at the zoo? Do you think he was lonely?*
  ¿Por qué estaba infeliz Eduardo en el zoológico? ¿Creen que estaba solo?

Literacy Circle

Storytime 1

- Present the "Party at Daisy's"/"Fiesta en casa de Daisy" flannel board story. Ask: *What kind of work does a zookeeper do at the zoo?*
  ¿Qué clase de trabajo hace un guardián en el zoológico?

Storytime 2

- Read the "The Zanzibar Zoo"/"El zoológico de Zanzíbar" listening story. Talk with the children about how this zoo is different from Edward's zoo.

Content Connection

Health and Safety

Objective
To understand about safe behavior in potentially dangerous places

Vocabulary
safety
seguridad

Activity 1

- Discuss how to be safe at the zoo. Have the children help you make a zoo safety list. Be sure to include being respectful of the animals and mindful of the adults and zoo employees. Talk about how it is improper to yell or throw things at the animals. Explain that it is unsafe to feed or chase the animals and to hit their windows or cages. You might address not running, shoving, or littering.

Activity 2

- Take a pretend trip to the zoo. Describe each part of the trip to the children. Then ask them about proper and safe behavior. For example, "Here we are by the ducks." Ask: *Should we run after the ducks?* "Now, we are at the monkey habitat." Ask: *Should we feed some popcorn to the monkeys?* "The zookeeper said to stay away from the fence." Ask: *Should we climb on the fence?* Discuss their responses.

  ¿Debemos correr detrás de los patos? ¿Les debemos dar un poco de palomitas de maíz a los monos? ¿Debemos escalar la cerca?

DAY 1

Objectives

- To combine, separate, and name "how many" concrete objects and record findings
- To start, use, and exit software programs

Vocabulary

add	sumar
adding	sumar
number names	nombres de los números

DLM Materials

- pattern blocks (triangles, squares, blue rhombuses, and trapezoids)
- *Math Resource Guide*
  Pattern Blocks Cutouts (blue rhombuses and trapezoids)
  Train Patterns (3–6, or higher—2 copies per child)
  Counting Jar
  Number Pictures/Dibujos de números
  Off and On/Apaga y prende
- *DLM Math* software
- *Teacher's Resource Anthology*
  Simon Says/Simón dice

Materials to Gather

- construction paper
- toothpicks (10 per child)
- cups
- counters
- sticky notes
- envelopes or plastic bags (one per child, labeled with children's names)

MATH

Focus

- Tell the children the giraffes at the zoo need to be brushed 20 times each day. Count to 20, pretending to brush a giraffe with each count.

Develop

- Tell the children that this week they will continue to work with Number Pictures/Dibujos de números and Cube Trains/Trenes de cubos. They will record and collect their best work during the week in an envelope or plastic bag to use to make Number Books next week.
- Introduce Memory—Number, Level 5.

Practice

- Assign the children a number and have them create Number Pictures/Dibujos de números using toothpicks or any of the following items from the pattern blocks: squares and triangles or rhombuses and trapezoids. Have the children describe their pictures, both with words and with numerals, then choose their favorite picture to record by pasting Pattern Block Cutouts or toothpicks on a piece of construction paper. Have them write the numeral on their recording, or if necessary, write it for them.
- Encourage the children to play Off and On/Apaga y prende (see Animals, Day 4). They record the combination by coloring in the cubes on a Train Pattern and then write the numeral on their recording.
- Encourage the children to explore the Counting Jar and record the number on sticky notes.
- Invite the children to work on Number Pictures and any other activity they wish. Children can print their favorite picture for their Number Books.

Reflect/Assess

- *How did you figure out how many were in your number picture?*
  ¿Cómo determinaron cuántos había en el dibujo de números?

Fine Arts

Objectives
To begin to engage in dramatic play with others
To begin to create or re-create stories, moods, or experiences through dramatic representations

DLM Materials
Teacher's Resource Anthology
"Party at Daisy's"/"Fiesta en casa de Daisy" flannel board story

Materials to Gather
plastic animals, yarn, paper, glue

Activity 1
- Visit the zoo the children have built in the Blocks Center. Encourage dramatic play by making up addition problems using the plastic animals. For example, there are 4 monkeys in the monkey cage. The zookeeper bought 2 more from another zoo. *How many monkeys are in the cage now?*
  ¿Cuántos monos hay ahora en la jaula?

Activity 2
- Use the "Party at Daisy's"/"Fiesta en casa de Daisy" flannel board illustrations to make character necklaces. Make 1 zookeeper, 1 gorilla, 2 elephants, 3 monkeys, 4 snakes, 5 turtles, and 6 lions. Adjust the numbers to fit the size of your class. Have the children act out the story.

Music and Movement

- Teach the children how to move like animals. For example, they can move like an ostrich by bending over to their ankles and then stretching out their necks as they walk. Or for a duck, have them squat and waddle.
- Play Zookeeper Says the same way you would play Simon Says/Simón dice. Make the commands related to zoo animals. For example, the Zookeeper says to walk like an elephant or to roar like a lion.

Suggested Reading

If I Ran the Zoo by Dr. Seuss
1,2,3 to the Zoo by Eric Carle

Reflect on the Day

- *What did you learn about the zoo today?*
  ¿Qué aprendieron hoy sobre el zoológico?
- *What will you share about zoos with your families?*
  ¿Qué compartirán con sus familias sobre los zoológicos?

Home Connection

Send notes home to families asking them to save empty food containers from farm products (milk cartons or jugs, butter bowls, egg cartons, and so on).

Begin the Day

- Sing "Here We Go 'Round the Mulberry Bush"/"Aquí vamos vuelta de la morera" to reflect the tasks of zookeepers. For example, this is the way we feed the seals or clean the cages.
- Use one of the suggestions for Morning Circle found in the front of this *Teacher's Edition*.

Objectives

- To understand that writing is used to communicate ideas and information
- To begin to dictate words, phrases, and sentences to an adult recording on paper

Vocabulary

elephant	elefante
giraffe	jirafa
gorilla	gorila
hippopotamus	hipopótamo
rhinoceros	rinoceronte

DLM Materials

- Oral Language Cards 6 and 7
- *SRA Book of Animals/SRA El libro de los animales*
- *SRA Photo Library* software
- *Teacher's Resource Anthology*
  "The Zebra"/"La cebra"
  American Sign Language patterns
  Zoo Concentration game
  "Party at Daisy's"/"Fiesta en casa de Daisy"
  plastic bag books
  animal mask patterns
  elephant and peanut match patterns

Materials to Gather

- empty toilet paper tubes
- plastic coffee can lids
- plastic rings
- sponges
- weighted soda bottle
- tempera paint

LITERACY

Focus

- Teach "The Zebra"/"La cebra." Ask the children if they have ever seen a zebra.
  ¿Alguna vez han visto una cebra?
- Tell the children that today they will be learning about five zoo animals: elephants, giraffes, gorillas, rhinoceroses, and hippopotamuses.
  Hoy vamos a aprender sobre cinco animales del zoológico: elefantes, jirafas, gorilas, rinocerontes e hipopótamos.
- Teach the children how to say *elephant, giraffe,* and *gorilla* using American Sign Language.

Develop

One Way to Develop the Lesson

- Display Oral Language Cards 6 and 7. Review the suggestions on the backs of the cards.
- Provide some factual information for the following animals.
  1. An elephant's trunk serves many purposes including communication and a way to grasp and hold things.
  2. A giraffe must bend its knees and spread its legs to reach the ground for water since its neck is so long.
  3. A gorilla is the largest of the apes and it does not eat meat. Gorillas eat leaves, roots, and stalks of plants.
  4. A rhinoceros may have very poor eyesight, but it has highly developed senses of smell and sound.

5. A hippopotamus is distantly related to the pig and the word *hippopotamus* means "river horse."

- Have the children help you write a sentence describing the animals. Continue to fill in your KWL chart with any relevant information.

Another Way to Develop the Lesson

- Write a predictable story about today's animals. You may write most of the story except for the names of the animals. Write verses for each of the five animals and then invite the children to fill in their names. For example, you might write:
  I went to the zoo and what did I see.
  I saw a hippo looking at me.
- Once you have finished writing, have the children read the story with you. Explain that they will be drawing pictures for the story during their learning center time. Collect their drawings and copy the story's text into a plastic bag book.

Practice

- Write the words *elephant, giraffe, gorilla, rhinoceros,* and *hippopotamus* on individual index cards. Have the children trace the words. Include the zoo and zookeeper cards for tracing also.
- Have the children put the zoo puzzles together.
- Invite the children to play the Zoo Concentration game.
- Provide yellow and brown paint, sponges, and paper. Have the children use the sponges to paint a giraffe.
- Make a rhino horn by rolling a piece of white construction paper into a cone. Attach it to the top of a weighted soda bottle. With plastic rings, have the children toss the rings onto the rhino horn.
- Give the children the elephant and gorilla masks and encourage them to role-play the appropriate animal behaviors.
- Make a number matching game using several copies of the ele-hant and peanut match patterns. Invite the children to "feed" each elephant the number of peanuts indicated by the numeral printed on the elephant's blanket.
- Find the elephant, giraffe, and gorilla in the Animal category of the *SRA Photo Library* software.

Preparation

- Make the flannel board story, if necessary.
- Make a plastic bag book.
- Roll white construction paper into a cone for a rhino horn.
- Cut circles in the centers of plastic coffee can lids.
- Write animal names on index cards.
- Copy and enlarge the ele-phant and gorilla masks from the animal mask patterns. Color them, glue them to paper plates, and mount them on craft sticks.
- Make five copies of the ele-phant and peanut match pat-terns to make a matching game. Print numerals 1 through 5 on the saddles. Cut them out and laminate them.

Second Language Learners

The words *elephant, giraffe,* and *gorilla,* which the children learned in American Sign Language, are cognates/palabras afines in English and Spanish: *elephant/elefante, giraffe/jirafa,* and *gorilla/gorila.* Ask the children to think of other animals that have similar names in the two lan-guages. Examples include *camel/camello, zebra/cebra,* and *tiger/tigre.* Children can predict zoo animals' names in the new language based on their knowledge of animals' names in the home language.

DAY 2

Letter Knowledge

English

- Read selections from the *SRA Alphabet Book.* You may want to choose selections that feature today's zoo animals.

Spanish

- Read "Cinco cerditos" from *Los niños alfabéticos.*

Suggested Reading

Gorilla by Anthony Browne
When the Elephant Walks by Keiko Kasza
The Giraffe That Walked to Paris by Nancy Milton
El elefante by José García Sanchez
Oli, el pequeño elefante by Burny Bos

Anthology Support

"Muévete como yo"
"We're Going to the Zoo"
"Vamos al zoo"
"Oh, Do You Want to See the Zoo?"
"¿Al zoológico quieres ver?"
"The Elephant Song"

Reflect/Assess

- *Who can show me the American Sign Language sign for any animal that we learned about today?*

  ¿Quién me puede mostrar la seña para cualquiera de los animales de los que aprendimos hoy?
- *Are the animals we learned about today large or small?*

  ¿Los animales de los que aprendimos hoy son grandes o pequeños?

Literacy Circle

Storytime 1

- Present the "Party at Daisy's"/"Fiesta en casa de Daisy" flannel board story. Have the children discuss the various types of housing that the animals need.

Storytime 2

- Review the plastic bag book that you and the children created today.
- Read "Munch Crunch: The Food Animals Eat" from the *SRA Book of Animals/SRA El libro de los animales.*

Content Connection

Math/Science

Objectives

To begin to make size comparisons between objects

To use simple measuring devices to learn about objects and organisms

Materials to Gather

inch cubes, masking tape, paper plates

Vocabulary

feet, inches

pies, pulgadas

Activity 1

- Explain that some giraffes' necks are about six feet long. Put a six-foot strip of masking tape on the floor. As the children walk the line, have them count how many footsteps it takes to cover the length of a giraffe's neck.

Activity 2

- Explain that some elephants' feet are approximately eight inches around. Give the children an eight-inch paper plate. Have them see how many inch cubes it takes to fill the plate.

DAY 2

Objectives

- To combine, separate, and name "how many" concrete objects and record findings
- To sort objects into groups by an attribute and to begin to explain how the grouping was done

Vocabulary

add	sumar
adding	sumar
number names	nombres de los números

DLM Materials

- *Math Resource Guide*
  Cube Trains/Trenes de cubos
- See Day 1
- *DLM Math* software
- *Teacher's Resource Anthology*
  One Elephant/Un elefante

Materials to Gather

- connecting cubes
- crayons in colors matching the cubes
- See Day 1

Preparation

- Make copies of the Train Patterns for the children to use for recording their Cube Train combinations.

MATH

Focus

- Show the children how they can make numbers by sorting people. Have 4 children stand up. Then have them sort themselves into categories of sneakers and no sneakers.
- Record the number combinations (with simple pictures, numerals, or both). Repeat with a different group of 4 children, but with the same sorting rule, until all the children have been included.

Develop

- Demonstrate making Number Pictures/Dibujos de números using only 5 square pattern blocks. Show several spatial arrangements. Have the children label the arrangements by indicating how many total squares they use.
- Tell the children that they will continue working on their Number Books in the centers today. Explain that you will add the square pattern blocks to their options for making Number Pictures/Dibujos de números. Remind the children how to record each Number Picture/Dibujo de números or number combination they make.

Practice

- Assign the children a number and have them create Number Pictures/Dibujos de números. (See Day 1.)
- Invite the children to make Cube Trains/Trenes de cubos. Have them make as many different trains as they can with 2 colors of connecting cubes. Have them record each one on the appropriate Train Pattern with crayons and then have them write the numeral on the pattern. Tell them that this will be included in their Number Books.
- Have the children continue to work with and record the Practice activities from Day 1.
- Invite the children to work on Number Pictures and any other activity they wish. Children can print their favorite picture for their Number Books.

Reflect/Assess

- *Tonight, sort your family members into those wearing sneakers and those not wearing sneakers. Tomorrow, tell me what numbers you have.*

  Esta noche, clasifiquen a sus familiares entre los que llevan zapatos de goma y los que no llevan zapatos de goma. Mañana me dicen qué números obtuvieron.

Content Connection

Science

Objectives

To describe observations

To sort objects and organisms into groups and begin to describe how groups were organized

DLM Materials

Oral Language Cards 8–11, 17–22

Activity 1

- Use the Oral Language Cards and other pictures you find to show animals that have different numbers of legs. Encourage the children to graph the animals by the numbers of legs they have.

Activity 2

- Use the Oral Language Cards to make a graph of animals that have fur and those that do not have fur.

Reflect on the Day

- *What did you learn about zoo animals today?*

  ¿Qué aprendieron hoy sobre los animales del zoológico?
- *Which of today's animals is your favorite? Tell me something you learned today about that animal.*

  ¿Cuál de los animales de hoy es su favorito? Díganme algo que aprendieron hoy sobre ese animal.

Music and Movement

- Play One Elephant/Un elefante.
- Play Elephant Soccer/Fútbol de los elefantes. Have the children stand in a circle with their feet apart. Show them how to put their hands together to represent an elephant trunk. Roll a ball to one of the children. That child must roll it to someone else using only his or her elephant trunk.

Suggested Reading

Good Night, Gorilla by Peggy Rathmann

Color Zoo by Lois Ehlert

What Research Suggests

Using a computer that shows number combinations graphically and provides an audible number word helps children build real understanding.

Begin the Day

- Sing "Oh, Do You Want to See the Zoo?"/"¿Al zoológico quieres ver?"
- Use a suggestion for Morning Circle from the front of this *Teacher's Edition*.

Objectives

- To begin to dictate words, phrases, and sentences to an adult recording on paper
- To understand that writing is used to communicate ideas and information

Vocabulary

lion	león
tiger	tigre

DLM Materials

- *Who Is the Beast?/¿Quién es la bestia?*
- *Edward the Emu/Eduardo el emú*
- *SRA Photo Library* software
- *Teacher's Resource Anthology*
  "Oh, Do You Want to See the Zoo?"/"¿Al zoológico quieres ver?"
  "Three Terrifying Tigers"
  "Tres tristes tigres"
  American Sign Language patterns
  "Lion's Haircut"/"El corte de pelo del león"
  "The Lion and the Mouse"/"El león y el ratón agradecido"
  animal mask patterns (lion)
  Zoo Concentration game

Materials to Gather

- masking tape
- KWL chart
- zoo puzzles
- index cards
- orange and black ribbon, yarn, or crepe paper
- orange and black tempera paint
- word cards

LITERACY

Focus

- Say "Three Terrifying Tigers" or "Tres tristes tigres." Discuss any of the children's tiger experiences.
- Explain that today the children will learn about lions and tigers.
- Teach the children how to say *lion* and *tiger* using American Sign Language. You might review the other signs from Day 2.

Develop

One Way to Develop the Lesson

- Show the children the picture of the tiger from *Who Is the Beast?/¿Quién es la bestia?* Then show them the lion from *Edward the Emu/Eduardo el emú.*
- Make a Venn diagram to compare lions and tigers. Share some information about the animals.
  1. Lions (and tigers) are the largest animals in the cat family. Lions live primarily in Africa. They like to hunt when it is cool (early morning). They eat meat. Lions live in family units called *prides*. They care for their lion cubs until the cubs can care for themselves. Male lions have large manes.
  2. Tigers live primarily in Asia. They eat meat. Tigers hunt but do not like the heat. Their fur has a light and dark striped pattern, which makes them hard to see as they hunt and creep through the grass. Tigers live on their own, unlike lions, which live in prides.
- Help the children arrange this information into the Venn diagram.
- Place today's information on your KWL chart.

Another Way to Develop the Lesson

- Show the cover of *Who Is the Beast?/¿Quién es la bestia?* Help the children predict what the book is about. Read the story.
- When you reach the part where the tiger goes back to the other animals, instruct the children to look closely at the tiger's face. Ask: *Does the tiger look afraid?*

  ¿Parecía que el tigre tenía miedo?
- Help the children make a list of the tiger's physical characteristics from this book.

Practice

- Place the *Who Is the Beast?/¿Quién es la bestia?* book and tape in the Listening Center.
- Using a balance beam or strip of masking tape, have the children walk across it like a cat (like a tiger).
- Provide orange and black paint for the children to paint tigers.
- Invite the children to play the Zoo Concentration game.
- Have the children complete the zoo puzzles.
- Partner up the children to play Catch a Tiger by Its Tail. Place the tails in a box with a small part of each tail hanging out. Have the children pull a tail and try to read the word. If they read it correctly, they keep the tail. Otherwise, the tail goes back into the box. The child with the most tails at the end of the game wins.
- Give the children the lion masks and encourage them to role-play lion behaviors. You may want to make available the gorilla and elephant masks from yesterday.
- Allow the children to look at the lions and tigers in the Animal category of the *SRA Photo Library* software. You might also encourage the children to find other animals from the cat family.

Preparation

- Make the prop story.
- Write *tiger* and *lion* on index cards.
- Prepare a Venn diagram about lions and tigers.
- Make tiger tails by twisting 36-inch long pieces of orange and black ribbon, yarn, or crepe paper together. Attach word cards to tail ends (including *mama, papa, mother, father, zoo,* and *zookeeper*).
- Copy and enlarge the lion mask from the animal mask patterns. Color it and glue it to a paper plate. Mount the mask on a craft stick.

Second Language Learners

To compare and contrast pictures of tigers and lions, use vocabulary describing length, color, shape, texture, and design. Listen to the children's descriptions. Do they make a statement only about the tiger or the lion? If so, ask, "Does the tiger (have a tail), as the lion does?" If they say, "Yes," then say, "Oh, the tiger AND the lion (have a tail)." If they point out a difference, reply, "Oh. The tiger (has stripes), BUT the lion (does) not." Point to the pictured characteristics as you model these language patterns.

Letter Knowledge

English/Spanish

- Have the children shape letters with play dough.

Suggested Reading

Brave as a Tiger by Libuse Palecek
Un león en la nieve (traditional)
El tigre by Dirk Hall

Anthology Support

"My Very Own Pet"
"Mi propia mascota"
"We're Going to the Zoo"
"Vamos al zoo"
"Going on Safari"
"Ir de safari"

Scaffolding Strategies

More Help Read nonfiction books about lions and/or tigers.

Extra Challenge Make a list of lion and tiger characteristics by asking the children to recall the information in the first part of Develop.

Reflect/Assess

- *How are tigers and lions alike? How are they different?*
  ¿En qué se parecen los tigres y los leones? ¿En qué se diferencian?
- *How are tigers and lions different from pet cats? How are they like pet cats?*
  ¿En qué se diferencian los tigres y leones de los gatos domésticos? ¿En qué se parecen a los gatos domésticos?

Storytime 1

- Present the "Lion's Haircut"/"El corte de pelo del león" prop story. Ask: *Why did Leo want his mane to grow long?*
  ¿Por qué Leo quería que su melena creciera?

Storytime 2

- Read "The Lion and the Mouse"/"El león y el ratón agradecido" listening story. Ask the children to discuss the ways the lion and the mouse helped each other.

Content Connection

Fine Arts

Objective
To use a variety of materials to create original work

Materials to Gather
cherries, paper plates, pineapple slices (one per child), raisins, shredded carrots, yellow and brown construction paper

Activity 1

- **(Allergy Warning)** Make lion faces. Give each child a pineapple slice. Have them put shredded carrots around the pineapple slice like a mane. Provide raisins for eyes and a cherry for a nose. Enjoy this yummy snack!

Activity 2

- Help the children make lion faces out of paper plates. Curl yellow and brown construction paper strips using a pencil to make manes. Help them glue the strips to the plate's perimeter. Allow the children to draw on facial features with markers or crayons.

DAY 3

Objectives

- To combine, separate, and name "how many" concrete objects and record findings
- To sort objects into groups by an attribute and begin to explain how the grouping was done

Vocabulary

add	sumar
adding	sumar
number names	nombres de los números

Materials

DLM Materials

- *Math Resource Guide* Cube Trains/Trenes de cubos
- See Day 1
- *DLM Math* software
- *Four Baby Bumblebees* CD

Materials to Gather

- connecting cubes
- crayons in colors matching the cubes
- stickers (optional)
- See Day 1

Scaffolding Strategies

More Help Decrease the number that the children use for their number combinations.

Extra Challenge Increase the number that the children use for their number combinations.

MATH

Focus

- Have the children make numbers with their fingers. Have them put their hands in their laps between each task. Ask the children to show you 4. Then ask them to show you 4 using some fingers on each hand. Ask a volunteer to describe what he or she has done.
- Next, ask the children to show you 4 using the same number of fingers on each hand. Ask a volunteer to describe what he or she has done.

Develop

- Invite the children to make numbers by sorting people as they did yesterday. Have 4 children stand up. Then have them sort themselves into categories of buttons and no buttons.
- Record the number combinations (with simple pictures, numerals, or both). Repeat with a different group of 4 children, but use the same sorting rule, until all the children have been included.

Practice

- Assign the children a number and have them create Number Pictures/Dibujos de números. (See Day 1.)
- Invite the children to make Cube Trains/Trenes de cubos. Have them make as many different trains as they can with 2 colors of connecting cubes. Encourage the children to describe patterns they notice as they make their trains.
- Encourage the children to play Off and On/Apaga y prende and record their tosses.
- Encourage the children to explore the Counting Jar and record the number on sticky notes.
- Invite the children to work on Number Pictures and any other activity they wish. Children can print their favorite picture for their Number Books. To help children think of new ideas, lay out physical shapes next to the computer for them to use.

Reflect/Assess

- *How many different trains of 4 can you make?*
  ¿Cuántos trenes diferentes de 4 pueden hacer?

Music and Movement

- Play "The Wonderful Thing About Tiggers" from the *Four Baby Bumblebees* CD.
- Have the children stretch, jump, leap, run, and stalk like a tiger or a lion, but do so safely.

Suggested Reading

If I Ran the Zoo by Dr. Seuss

Content Connection

Fine Arts

Objectives

To begin to engage in dramatic play with others

To begin to create or re-create stories, moods, or experiences through dramatic representation

DLM Materials

Teacher's Resource Anthology

"Five Little Speckled Frogs"/"Cinco ranitas manchadas"

"Five Little Monkeys"/"Cinco monitos"

Activity 1

- Sing and act out "Five Little Speckled Frogs"/"Cinco ranitas manchadas." Stop after each verse of the song and ask how many frogs are on the log, how many frogs are in the pond, and how many frogs there are in all.
  ¿Cuántas ranas hay en el tronco?
  ¿Cuántas ranas hay en el estanque?
  ¿Cuántas ranas hay en total?

Activity 2

- Say and act out the chant "Five Little Monkeys"/"Cinco monitos." Stop after each verse and ask how many monkeys are on the bed, how many monkeys are off the bed, and how many monkeys there are in all.
  ¿Cuántos monos hay en la cama?
  ¿Cuántos monos no están en la cama?
  ¿Cuántos monos hay en total?

Reflect on the Day

- *What did you learn about tigers and/or lions today?*
  ¿Qué aprendieron hoy sobre los tigres y/o leones?
- *Who can show me how to sign the word* tiger? Lion?
  ¿Quién me puede mostrar cómo hacer por señas la palabra tigre? ¿León?

Begin the Day

- Sing "The Bear Went Over the Mountain." Allow the children to share any bear experiences.
- Use one of the suggestions for Morning Circle found in the front of this *Teacher's Edition.*

Objectives

- To become increasingly sensitive to the sounds of spoken words
- To begin to attend to the beginning sounds in familiar words by identifying that the pronunciations of several words all begin the same way

Vocabulary

alliteration	aliteración
bear	oso
monkey	mono

DLM Materials

- Animal Orchestra/La orquesta de los animales
- Oral Language Development Card 8
- magnetic letters
- Rafita and Pepita puppets
- *Teacher's Resource Anthology*
  "Ten Little Monkeys"/"Los changuitos"
  American Sign Language patterns
  Zoo Concentration game
  animal mask patterns
  "Monkey See, Monkey Do"/"Los monos ven, los monos hacen"
  "Rafita and Pepita"/"Rafita y Pepita"
- bear counters

Materials to Gather

- bananas, yogurt, and granola
- bear photographs
- die
- manila folder
- brown sheet
- flashlight

LITERACY

Focus

- Sing "Ten Little Monkeys"/"Los changuitos."
- Use Rafita and Pepita to help you explain that today the children will learn about monkeys and bears.
- Teach the children how to say *bear* and *monkey* using American Sign Language. You might review other signs from this week.

Develop

One Way to Develop the Lesson

- Display Oral Language Card 8. Use the suggestions on the back of the card for discussion.
- If you have a picture of a bear, show it to the children. Discuss what children already know about either bears or monkeys.
- Share other information about bears and monkeys with the children.
  1. There are several types of bears including black bears and brown bears. Bears are usually harmless unless provoked, threatened, or injured.
  2. There are many types of monkeys. Monkeys use their tails like another hand. Monkeys are swift as they swing and jump from tree to tree.
- Place today's information on your KWL chart with the children's help.
- Help the children think of descriptive words for bears and monkeys that start with the same beginning sound as each animal's name. For monkeys, use *mischievous, marvelous,* or *many*. For bears, use *bashful, brown, black,* or *big*.

Another Way to Develop the Lesson

- Write the following sentences on the board: *Many monkeys make mischief/Monos machan membrillos* and *Brown bear blowing bubbles/El oso belloso bajaba brincando* (the hairy bear came down jumping). Underline the first letter in each word.
- Do one sentence at a time. Instruct the children to look at the sentence. Ask: *What do you notice about the first letter of each word?* *¿Qué notan sobre la primera letra de cada palabra?*
- Explain that the letters are the same. Remind the children that this is an example of alliteration, when words placed together start with the same letter sound.
- Help the children think of alliterative phrases. For example, *mighty monkeys, magic monkeys, beautiful bears,* and *bouncy bears*. Discuss any similar pronunciations.

Practice

- Allow the children to complete zoo puzzles.
- Have the children play the Zoo Concentration game.
- Provide the *bear, monkey, zoo,* and *zookeeper* word cards. Invite the children to copy the words using magnetic letters.
- Make monkey snacks. Use a banana half for each child and put a stick through it. Help the children dip the bananas in yogurt and granola.
- Give the children two bear counters for game pieces, a die, and the zoo game board (see Preparation). Have them play the zoo land game.
- Provide a bear cave reading area. Toss a brown blanket or sheet over a table to create a cave. Provide a flashlight for reading.
- Add the bear and monkey masks to the other masks used this week. Encourage the children to role-play the animal behaviors.
- Encourage the children to find the bears and monkeys in *Animal Orchestra/La orquesta de los animales*.

Preparation

- Make the flannel board story.
- Make a zoo game board on a manila folder. Draw a trail between the start and finish lines. Add zoo decorations.
- Gather ingredients for monkey snacks.

Scaffolding Strategies

More Help Read nonfiction books about bears and/or monkeys.

Extra Challenge Help the children write a story about having a monkey or a bear as a pet.

Second Language Learners

Encourage the children to name the zoo animals as they play Zoo Concentration. This will help them recall the location of the animal the next time they play, as well as promote vocabulary development.

DAY 4

Letter Knowledge

English

- Use the Think, Pair, Share/ Piensa, aparea, comparte game to help the children think of ways to make the letters *b* and *m* with their bodies.

Spanish

- Use the Think, Pair, Share/ Piensa, aparea, comparte game to help the children think of ways to make the letter *g* with their bodies.

Suggested Reading

Caps for Sale by Esphyr Slobodkina
Bear by John Schoenherr
Soy un oso grande y hermoso by Janosh
El parque de Enrique Osos by David McPhail

Anthology Support

"Five Little Monkeys"
"Cinco monitos"
"Three Bears Rap"
"El rap de los tres osos"
"We're Going to the Zoo"
"Vamos al zoo"

Technology Support

Building on today's math lesson, type 10; 20; 30; 40 on the computer (repeat the sequence for more participants). Ask a child how many 10s it takes to make the number and have him or her type it (1, 2, 3, or 4).

Reflect/Assess

- *Tell me something you learned today about monkeys and something you learned today about bears.*

  Díganme algo que aprendieron hoy sobre los monos y díganme algo que aprendieron hoy sobre los osos.
- *Would you like to have a pet monkey or a pet bear? Why?*

  ¿Les gustaría tener un mono o un oso como mascota? ¿Por qué?

Literacy Circle

Storytime 1

- Invite the children to participate in the "Monkey See, Monkey Do"/"Los monos ven, los monos hacen" action story.

Storytime 2

- Present the "Rafita and Pepita"/"Rafita y Pepita" flannel board story. Ask the children if they think Rafita and Pepita/Rafita y Pepita would make good pets. Ask them if they think real bears would make good pets.

  ¿Creen que los osos serían buenas mascotas?

Content Connection

Physical Development

Objectives
To begin to move in rhythm
To explore moving in space

DLM Materials
Teacher's Resource Anthology
"Three Little Monkeys"/"Tres monitos"
"Going on a Bear Hunt"/"Vamos a cazar un oso"

Activity 1
- Invite the children to act out "Three Little Monkeys"/"Tres monitos." Help them think of an alternative ending where the monkeys escape.

Activity 2
- Allow the children to participate in the "Going on a Bear Hunt"/"Vamos a cazar un oso" action story. Ask: *How would the story be different if the bear was friendly?*
  ¿Cómo cambiaría el cuento si el oso fuera amistoso?

DAY 4

Objectives

- To combine, separate, and name "how many" concrete objects and record findings
- To sort objects into groups by an attribute and to begin to explain how the grouping was done

Vocabulary

add	sumar
adding	sumar
number names	nombres de los números

DLM Materials

- *Math Resource Guide* Cube Trains/Trenes de cubos
- See Day 1
- *DLM Math* software
- *Where Is Thumbkin?* CD
- *Teacher's Resource Anthology* "Monkey See, Monkey Do"/"Los monos ven, los monos hacen"

Materials to Gather

- connecting cubes
- crayons in colors matching the cubes
- stickers (optional)
- See Day 1

MATH

Focus

- Tell the children the monkeys in the zoo need to be fed 20 bananas. Have 2 volunteers use their fingers as you help them count to 20 by ones, pretending to feed monkeys, 1 banana at a time with each count.
- Have the children make numbers with their fingers. Ask them to show you 5. Then ask them to show you 5 using some fingers on each hand. Ask a volunteer to describe what he or she has done.

Develop

- Invite the children to make numbers by sorting people as they did yesterday. Have 4 children stand up. Then have them sort themselves into categories of light hair and dark hair.
- Record the number combinations (with simple pictures, numerals, or both). Repeat with a different group of 4 children, but use the same sorting rule, until all the children have been included.

Practice

- Assign the children a number and have them create Number Pictures/Dibujos de números. (See Day 1.)
- Invite the children to make Cube Trains/Trenes de cubos. Have them make as many different trains as they can with 2 colors of connecting cubes.
- Encourage the children to play Off and On/Apaga y prende and record their tosses.
- Encourage the children to explore the Counting Jar and record the number on sticky notes.
- Invite the children to work on Number Pictures and any other activity they wish.

Reflect/Assess

- *How can you figure out which numbers can be hidden inside 6?*
  ¿Cómo determinaron qué números pueden esconderse en el 6?

Music and Movement

- Play Monkey See, Monkey Do/Los monos ven, los monos hacen. Invite the children to mimic your monkey movements.
- Sing "Three Little Monkeys" from the *Where Is Thumbkin?* CD.

Suggested Reading

My Camera: At the Zoo by Janet Perry Marshall

Content Connection

Science

Objectives

To sort objects and organisms into groups and begin to describe how groups were organized

To begin to recognize that living things have similar needs for water, food, and air

DLM Materials

Teacher's Resource Anthology

"Party at Daisy's"/"Fiesta en casa de Daisy" flannel board story

Materials to Gather

berry baskets, plastic animals

Activity 1

- Encourage play in the Blocks Center by giving the children some math problems to work on. First discuss the needs of animals for water, food, air, and shelter. Then tell the children that you have 5 monkeys. Ask them how you could arrange the monkeys into 2 cages. Ask how you will be sure that the monkeys all have enough food and water in their cages.

Activity 2

- Give the children some of the animals from the "Party at Daisy's"/"Fiesta en casa de Daisy" flannel board story. Propose the scenario that you want to put the animals into 2 different cages. Ask the children to help you make different arrangements of the animals. Ask them how many elephants are in each cage and then how many elephants there are in all.

Reflect on the Day

- *What did you learn about monkeys and/or bears today?*
  ¿Qué aprendieron hoy sobre los monos y/o los osos?
- *Which activity did you enjoy most today? Why?*
  ¿Qué actividad disfrutaron más hoy? ¿Por qué?

Home Connection

Send home a take-home book pack with four children.

Begin the Day

- Sing "I'm Being Swallowed by a Boa Constrictor"/"Me está tragando una boa común." Discuss any snake experiences.
- Use a suggestion for Morning Circle from the front of this *Teacher's Edition.*

Objective

- To understand that different text forms are used for different functions

Vocabulary

aviary	pajarera
birds	pájaros
duck	pato
geese	ganso
iguana	iguana
reptiles	reptiles
snake	serpiente, culebra
turkey	pavo
turtle	tortuga

DLM Materials

- Oral Language Development Cards 17, 18, 21
- *Edward the Emu/Eduardo el emú*
- *Teacher's Resource Anthology*
  "I'm Being Swallowed by a Boa Constrictor"/"Me está tragando una boa común"
  "Little Ducky Duddle"/"El patito Tito"
  American Sign Language patterns
  "Freddie the Snake"/"Braulio, la culebra"
  Zoo Concentration game
  "My Very Own Pet"/"Mi propia mascota"
  play dough

LITERACY

Focus

- Sing "Little Ducky Duddle"/"El patito Tito." Allow the children to share any of their duck experiences with the class.
- Explain that the children will learn about birds and reptiles today.
- Teach the children how to say *snake* and *bird* using American Sign Language. Review other animal signs they learned this week.

Develop

One Way to Develop the Lesson

- Tell the children that most zoos have a bird area (aviary) and a reptile house. Let them share any experiences with either zoo area.
- Display Oral Language Cards 21, 17, and 18. Use the suggestions on the backs of the cards to stimulate conversation.
- Make word webs for reptiles and for birds. This can be a good review of last week's lessons. Encourage the children to recall lizards, snakes, iguanas, turtles, crocodiles, and alligators on the reptile word web. The bird web should include ducks, chickens, turkeys, robins, seagulls, sparrows, crows, and parakeets.
- Place today's information on your KWL chart.

Another Way to Develop the Lesson

- Present the "Freddie the Snake"/"Braulio, la culebra" flannel board story. Help the children name all of the shapes that Freddie/Braulio becomes.
- Display the cover of *Edward the Emu/Eduardo el emú*. Ask a volunteer to remind the class what the character of the book is (an emu).
- Discuss how the two stories are similar. Then ask: *How are the stories different?*

  ¿En qué se diferencian los cuentos?

Practice

- Place the *Edward the Emu/Eduardo el emú* book and tape in the Listening Center.
- Place the flannel board story in the Language Center. Invite the children to retell the story or to make up a new story.
- Allow the children to play the Zoo Concentration game.
- Have the children work on zoo puzzles.
- Provide the word cards for *zoo, zookeeper, snake, iguana,* and *bird*. With a tray of damp sand, have the children use a stick to copy the words.
- Give the children empty toilet paper tubes to decorate. Explain that they are making a class snake. String their finished tubes on yarn to create the snake. Make the snake's head by pressing one end of the tube together to form a mouth, and then add eyes.
- Make breadstick snakes. Give each child a breadstick to shape into a letter *s* (as if the snake is moving). Help each child stick two raisins in the dough for eyes. Allow them all to sprinkle their dough with green sprinkles. Bake in an oven and enjoy this slithery snack.
- Supply play dough. Have the children make the letter *s* (like a snake) or have them make the first letters of their names with the dough.

Materials to Gather

- KWL chart
- zoo puzzles
- green sugar sprinkles
- raisins
- tray of sand
- sticks
- toilet paper tubes
- uncooked breadsticks
- word cards
- yarn

Preparation

- Make the flannel board story if necessary.
- Gather ingredients for breadstick snakes.
- Make several snake shapes from different colors of play dough.

Second Language Learners

Practice alliterative tongue twisters, using pictures or a sock puppet boa to aid comprehension. Speak slowly and act out the tongue twisters allowing children to hear each word. Then encourage the children to repeat the sentences with you several times. Some may then want to try the sentences on their own. An alliterative English sentence might be "The big boa bit the berry." A Spanish sentence might be "La boa boba tragó una bola (o bolita)."

DAY 5

Letter Knowledge

English

- Have the children find and circle a specific letter in newspapers and magazines.

Spanish

- Have the children find and circle the letter *g* in newspapers and magazines.

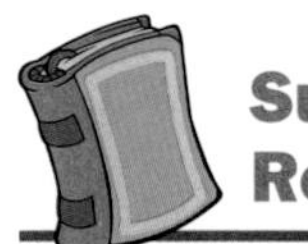

Suggested Reading

Are You My Mother? by P.D. Eastman
About Birds by Cathryn P. Sill

Anthology Support

"Two Little Blackbirds"
"Dos mirlos"
"Five Little Ducks"
"Los cinco patitos"
"There Was a Little Turtle"
"Había una tortuguita"

Scaffolding Strategies

More Help Read nonfiction books about reptiles and/or birds.

Extra Challenge Invite the children to draw pictures of Freddie/Braulio in all his different shapes.

Reflect/Assess

- *What are some differences between birds and reptiles?*
  ¿Qué diferencias hay entre los pájaros y los reptiles?
- *Can you tell me some names of birds you know?*
  ¿Me pueden decir los nombres de algunos animales que conocen?

Literacy Circle

Storytime 1

- Read the "My Very Own Pet"/"Mi propia mascota" flannel board story. Discuss why Austin's mother would not let him have any of the zoo animals for pets.

Storytime 2

- Reread *Edward the Emu/Eduardo el emú*. Discuss what kind of animal Edward/Eduardo is and where he would live in a zoo.

Content Connection

Science

Objectives
To participate in creating and using simple data charts
To describe properties of objects and characteristics of living things

Vocabulary
climb, fly, jump, run, swim
trepar, volar, saltar, correr, nadar

Materials to Gather
butcher paper, magazines

Activity 1

- Divide a piece of butcher paper into five sections. Label the sections *swim, fly, jump, climb,* and *run*. Make or use a magazine picture for each verb. For example, for the climb section, use a mountain climber.
- Have the children create an animal mural by drawing animals that perform each action listed on the butcher paper. They may also use pictures from magazines. Display their work in your classroom or in the hallway.

Activity 2

- Play a riddle game. Provide several clues allowing the children to rule out some animals in order to identify a specific animal. For example, say "Miguel saw three animals at the zoo: a giraffe, an emu, and a monkey. He likes them all, but one is his favorite. His favorite animal has four legs (this rules out the emu), two eyes, and a long neck (this rules out the monkey)." Ask: *Which animal is Miguel's favorite?*
  ¿Cuál animal era el favorito de Miguel?

DAY 5

Objectives

- To combine, separate, and name "how many" concrete objects and record findings
- To use a variety of software packages with audio, video, and graphics to enhance learning experiences

Vocabulary

add	sumar
adding	sumar
number names	nombres de los números

DLM Materials

- Rafita and Pepita/Rafita y Pepita puppets
- *Math Resource Guide*
  Cube Trains/Trenes de cubos
- See Day 1
- *DLM Math* software
- *Diez deditos* CD
- *Where Is Thumbkin?* CD
- *Teacher's Resource Anthology*
  Duck, Duck, Goose/Pato, pato, ganso

Materials to Gather

- connecting cubes
- crayons in colors matching the cubes
- See Day 1
- stickers (optional)

MATH

Focus

- Ask the children to help Rafita and Pepita count big numbers. Have them make mistakes like skipping or repeating numbers. Catch their mistakes, correct them, and then count with them to help them get it right.
- Discuss the Counting Jar. Examine the children's displayed recordings of how many items are in the Counting Jar. Do they remember how many of each type? Dump the objects and count them to check.

Develop

- Have the children make numbers with their fingers. Ask the children to show you 6. Then ask them to show you 6 using some fingers on each hand. Ask a volunteer to describe what he or she has done.
- Next, ask the children to show you 6 using the same number of fingers on each hand. Ask a volunteer to describe what he or she has done.
- Finally, ask the children to show you 6 with just one hand. Have a volunteer describe why he or she can't do that.

Practice

- Invite the children to work with Rafita and Pepita to help them learn to count.
- Assign the children a number and have them create Number Pictures/Dibujos de números. (See Day 1.)
- Invite the children to make Cube Trains/Trenes de cubos.
- Encourage the children to play Off and On/Apaga y prende and record their tosses.
- Invite the children to work on Number Pictures and any other activity they wish.

Reflect/Assess

- Computer Show: Have children show their number pictures on the computer. *How did you describe your pictures with numbers?*
  ¿Cómo describieron sus dibujos con números?
- *How did you know that Rafita and Pepita were not counting correctly?*
  ¿Cómo supieron que Rafita y Pepita no estaban contando correctamente?

Music and Movement

- Play Duck, Duck, Goose/Pato, pato, ganso.
- Play "Sun, sun, ba, ba, e" from the *Diez deditos* CD. You might choose "Crocodile Song" from the *Where Is Thumbkin?* CD instead.

Suggested Reading

Curious George Visits the Zoo by H. A. Rey

Content Connection

Science

Objectives

To sort objects and organisms into groups and begin to describe how groups were organized

To describe properties of objects and characteristics of living things

DLM Materials

Oral Language Cards 6–22

Teacher's Resource Anthology

"Party at Daisy's"/"Fiesta en casa de Daisy" flannel board story

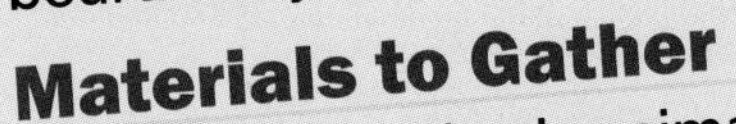

Materials to Gather

berry baskets, plastic animals

Activity 1

- Encourage play in the Blocks Center by giving the children some math problems to work on. Tell the children that you have 4 giraffes. Ask them how you could arrange the giraffes into 2 cages. Have the children work with you to find all the combinations.

Activity 2

- Give the children Oral Language Cards 6–22. Have the children use the cards to make a graph on the floor of fast-moving and not-fast-moving animals. Invite the children to think of other ways to graph the animals.

Reflect on the Day

- *What have you learned about zoo animals this week?*
  ¿Qué aprendieron esta semana sobre los animales del zoológico?
- *What animal sign language do you remember from this week?*
  ¿Qué lenguaje animal por señas recuerdan de esta semana?

Looking Ahead

Connecting to the Theme: Farm Animals

During this theme, the children will learn not only about animals encountered on a farm but about life on a farm. The study of animals should help the children develop an awareness of how to treat and care for animals properly.

	Objectives	DLM Materials	Materials to Gather
DAY 1	• To become increasingly sensitive to the sounds of spoken words • To enjoy listening to and discussing storybooks and information books read aloud • To participate in creating and using real and pictorial graphs • To sort objects into groups by an attribute and to begin to explain how the grouping was done	• *The Farm/La granja* • magnetic letters • *Teacher's Resource Anthology* • pattern blocks • *Math Resource Guide* • *DLM Math* software • *Esta es mi tierra* CD	• tape of animal sounds • farmer's attire • empty food containers • bristle brush • toothpicks (10 per child) • connecting cubes • cups • envelopes or plastic bags (one per child)
DAY 2	• To listen for different purposes • To begin to break words into syllables or clap along with each syllable in a phrase • To sort objects into groups by an attribute and to begin to explain how the grouping was done • To combine, separate, and name "how many" concrete objects	• *The Farm/La granja* • magnetic letters • Oral Language Cards 15 & 16 • *Teacher's Resource Anthology* • pattern blocks • *Math Resource Guide* • *Making Music with Thomas Moore CD* • dinosaur counters	• rubber ducks • farm animal puzzles • feathers • animal sounds tape and cards (see Day 1) • duck, chicken, and turkey puzzles • feathers • spoon • envelopes or plastic bags (one per child)
DAY 3	• To listen with increasing attention • To listen for different purposes • To sort objects into groups by an attribute and to begin to explain how the grouping was done • To combine, separate, and name "how many" concrete objects	• magnetic letters • *Teacher's Resource Anthology* • pattern blocks • *Math Resource Guide* • *DLM Math* software • Oral Language Cards 6–22	• character name necklaces • canned biscuits • sausage • toaster oven • cotton • yarn
DAY 4	• To connect information and events in books to real-life experiences • To begin to retell some sequences of events in stories • To begin to use scientific words and phrases to describe objects, events, and living things • To sort objects into groups by an attribute and to begin to explain how the grouping was done	• Oral Language Cards 9, 13, & 14 • My Sick Little Donkey sequence cards • *The Farm/La granja* • *Teacher's Resource Anthology* • *Math Resource Guide* • *DLM Math* software • pattern blocks	• farm animal puzzles • baby food jars • whipping cream • salt • crackers • plank of wood • berry baskets • plastic animals
DAY 5	• To show appreciation of repetitive language patterns • To connect information and events in books to real-life experiences • To sort objects into groups by an attribute and to begin to explain how the grouping was done • To imitate pattern sounds and physical movements	• *SRA Book of Animals/SRA El libro de los animales* • *The Little Red Hen/La gallinita roja* • *The Farm/La granja* • Oral Language Cards 52 & 53 • *Teacher's Resource Anthology* • *Math Resource Guide* • *DLM Math* software • pattern blocks	• class animal sounds book • animal sounds tape • balance beam or masking tape • beanbag • yarn • duck-shaped sponges • yellow tempera paint

(See individual lesson pages for complete lists of materials.)

Learning Centers

CONSTRUCTION

Create a Farm

Objective
To begin to create or re-create stories, moods, or experiences through dramatic representations

Materials to Gather
ground cover, silo, plastic and rubber animals, tractors, trucks, green and brown paint

Develop
Turn the block center into a farm. Make ground cover from an old sheet that you have sprayed with a mixture of green and brown paint to look like farmland. Make a silo out of an oatmeal box. Use construction paper to make a cone roof on the silo. Use a shallow pan or a piece of blue construction paper for a pond. Add plastic and rubber farm animals, as well as tractors and trucks. Have the children role-play a farmer and his or her animals.

Reflect/Assess
Would you like to live on a farm?
¿Les gustaría vivir en una granja?
If you lived on a farm, what kinds of animals would you have?
Si vivieran en una granja, ¿qué tipo de animales les gustaría tener?

DISCOVERY

Farm Food

Objective
To understand the basic human needs of all people for food, clothing, and shelter

Materials to Gather
empty food containers and cartons

Develop
Place several empty food containers and cartons from products produced on farms. For example, use egg cartons, milk cartons, ice-cream containers, cottage cheese containers, and so on. During the week, help the children sort the containers according to which animal supplies which product. If possible, provide real food samples during the week for the children to try.

Reflect/Assess
What is your favorite farm food?
¿Cuál es su comida de granja favorita?
What other kinds of foods come from farms?
¿Qué otros tipos de alimentos provienen de las granjas?

DRAMATIC PLAY

Farm Dress Up

Objective
To begin to engage in dramatic play with others

Materials to Gather
farmer's attire, farm kitchen attire

Develop
Provide farm clothing in the center. Include clothing for the farmer such as overalls, gloves, sun hats, bandanas, and boots. Provide farm kitchen clothing like an apron and props like hot pads, pots and pans, and so on. Encourage the children to be farmers and cooks during the week. Be sure you suggest overlapping the role of the farmer and the role of the cook.

Reflect/Assess
Do you like the clothes that farmers wear?
¿Les gusta la ropa que usan los granjeros?
Would you rather be the farmer or the cook, or both?
¿Les gustaría más ser el granjero o el cocinero o ambos?

What Research Suggests

Eggs are an important food for the brain because they are high in protein. Produce, such as spinach and broccoli, is an excellent source of selenium and boron, which are also important to brain functions. The natural sugars found in most fruits and carrots are important to brain functions because they stimulate and aid the memory.

DAY 1

Begin the Day

- Bring to the Morning Circle some objects commonly used by farmers (such as a hoe, scarecrow, or toy tractor). Tell the children that the items are clues to what they will be studying this week. Tell them that you are going to give them another clue. Sing "Old MacDonald"/"El viejo MacDonald." Ask the children if they can guess what they will be studying this week.
  ¿Pueden adivinar lo que van a estudiar esta semana?
- Use one of the suggestions for Morning Circle in the front of this *Teacher's Edition.*

Objectives

- To become increasingly sensitive to the sounds of spoken words
- To enjoy listening to and discussing storybooks and information books read aloud

Vocabulary

farm	granja
farmland	terreno de cultivo
farmer	granjero, agricultor
farm animals	animales de granja
ducks	patos
chickens	pollos
cows	vacas
horses	caballos
pigs	cerdos
sheep	ovejas
lambs	corderos
onomatopoeia	onomatopeya

DLM Materials

- *The Farm/La granja*
- magnetic letters
- *SRA Photo Library* software
- *Teacher's Resource Anthology*
  farm animal card patterns
  "Old MacDonald"/"El viejo MacDonald"
  "The Farm"/"La granja"
  Farm Animal Concentration

Materials to Gather

- tracing paper
- tempera paint
- tape of animal sounds
- index cards
- farmer's attire

Focus

- Sing "The Farm"/"La granja." Ask the children again what they know about farms.
  ¿Qué saben sobre las granjas?
- Tell them that today we will be learning about animal life on the farm.
  Hoy vamos a aprender de los animales que viven en una granja.

Develop

One Way to Develop the Lesson

- Show the children the cover of the book *The Farm/La granja*. Ask if they can predict what the book will be about. Tell the children that the book is based on a traditional song.
- Read the book. Invite the children to read with you as they catch on to the predictable text of the song.
- When you have finished reading the story, ask the children to help you make a list of all the farm animals mentioned in the story. Next to an animal's name, write the sound that animal makes in the book. Ask if anyone can remember what the term is for words that sound like the word they describe. If they don't remember, remind them of the term *onomatopoeia*.

Another Way to Develop the Lesson

- Tell the children that you are going to tell them another story about farm animals. Present the "Old MacDonald"/"El viejo MacDonald" flannel board story.
- When you have finished telling the story, ask the children to recall the animals mentioned in the story. Discuss the farmer. *Is anyone surprised that Old MacDonald is a woman?*

  ¿Le sorprendió a alguien saber que el viejo MacDonald era una mujer?
- Make a list of the animals and their sounds.

Practice

- Place *The Farm/La granja* book and the listening tape in the Listening Center.
- Place the flannel board story in the Language Center. Invite the children to retell the story or to create a new story.
- Place the word cards in the Writing Center and let the children trace them, copy them with magnetic letters, or copy them using crayons or pencils.
- Invite the children to play the Farm Animal Concentration game.
- Encourage the children to draw or paint a farm.
- Provide a tape with animal sounds and a set of the farm animal card patterns. Invite the children to sequence the animal patterns according to the order of their sounds on the tape.
- Encourage the children to find the farm animals in the Animals category on the *SRA Photo Library* software.

Preparation

- Make the flannel board story.
- Gather farmer's attire.
- Make two copies of the farm animal card patterns. Color them, cut them out, and laminate them.
- Make word cards. Write the names of the farm animals on index cards.
- Make a tape of animal sounds and copies of the farm animal card patterns to go with the tape. You will want to color, cut out, and laminate the copies of animal pictures.

Scaffolding Strategies

More Help Arrange a field trip to a farm. Invite the children to make animal sounds during the day. For example, ask that everyone who is ready to go outside bark like dogs.

Extra Challenge Invite the children to think and discuss what an elephant might do on a farm.

DAY 1

Letter Knowledge

English

- Read any of the letter stories in the *English Phonics Resource Guide*.

Spanish

- Introduce the letter *x* using the story "México" in the *Spanish Phonics Resource Guide*.

Second Language Learners

Onomatopoetic words represent the sounds of objects, based on the sound system of the language. For example:

Roosters say *cock-a-doodle-doo*./Los gallos hacen *kikirikí*.

Ducks say *quack quack*./ Los patos hacen *cuá cuá*.

Cows say *moo*./Las vacas hacen *muuu*.

Sheep say *baa*./Las ovejas hacen *bee*.

As the children listen to actual sounds of animals, ask if they can tell why people imitate the sounds the way they do. Do these sounds resemble the sounds of the animals?

Anthology Support

"Three White Mice"
"Los tres ratones blancos"
"Henny-Penny"
"Gallinita-Nita"
"The Ant and the Grasshopper"
"La hormiguita y el grillo"

Reflect/Assess

- *Which farm animal do you think is interesting?*
  ¿Qué animal de granja creen que es interesante?
- *Would you like to be a farmer? Why? Why not?*
  ¿Quisieran ser granjeros? ¿Por qué? ¿Por qué no?

Literacy Circle

Storytime 1

- Read *The Farm/La granja* again. Invite the children to read it with you or to try singing it.

Storytime 2

- Present the "Old MacDonald"/"El viejo MacDonald" flannel board story. Sing it this time. Compare this story to *The Farm/La granja*.

Content Connection

Social Studies/Math

Objectives

To understand the basic need of all people for food, clothing, and shelter

To participate in creating and using real and pictorial graphs

DLM Materials

- *Teacher's Resource Anthology*
- farm animal card patterns

Materials to Gather

empty food containers, bristle brush

Activity 1

- Talk about farm animals and their products (cow-milk/vaca-leche; chicken-eggs/pollo-huevos; pig-bristles/cerdo-cerdas). Use empty food containers and a bristle brush to demonstrate the products.

Activity 2

- Make a large floor graph. Make three columns: one each for the chicken, the pig, and the cow. Use the pictures from the farm animal card patterns to illustrate each column. Encourage the children to classify the examples of animal products by placing them below the picture of the animal that provides each product. Place the graph in the Discovery Center so the children can continue to use it all week.

Pongan los productos debajo de los dibujos de animales a los que pertenecen.

DAY 1

Objectives

- To combine, separate, and name "how many" concrete objects and record findings
- To use a variety of input devices, such as mouse, keyboard, voice/sound recorder, or touch screen

Vocabulary

add sumar
adding sumar

DLM Materials

- *Math Resource Guide*
  Cube Trains/Trenes de cubos
  Places Scenes: Number Parts version (farm background)
  Estimating Jar (previously Counting Jar)
- *DLM Math* software
- *Esta es mi tierra* CD
- *Teacher's Resource Anthology*
  "Farmer in the Dell"/"El granjero en la cañada"
- See Zoo Animals, Day 1

Materials to Gather

- connecting cubes
- crayons in colors matching the cubes
- See Zoo Animals, Day 1

Preparation

- Fill the Estimating Jar (previously the Counting Jar) with a collection of 8 identical plastic farm animals or counters.
- Make a special box for the chil-

MATH

Focus

- Ask if anyone knows what an estimate is. Discuss different situations in which people make estimates, such as picking up a stack of papers to hand out to the class or when filling crackers in a bowl for a snack.
- Show a collection of 5 to 10 toy farm animals. Ask the children to estimate how many there are. Count to check.
- Show the Estimating Jar and explain that it was called the Counting Jar. Tell them that there is a cover on the jar that will not come off until Friday. So, they will be estimating the contents, not counting it.

Develop

- Tell the children they will continue to work on their Number Books this week. Tell them we will add Places Scenes: Number Parts version to the center activities so that they can record numbers for their books. Explain that they will place farm animals or counters on the 2 work areas of the farm background, and then remove the counters and replace them with stickers or color the places where the counters were.
- Reintroduce the computer activity Number Pictures, with saving. Encourage the children to make a number picture and save their favorites for their Number Books. Tell them that they can then work on any activity they wish, such as Double Trouble, Level 6 (Free Explore) or any other activity.

Practice

- Invite the children to work on and record a Places Scenes: Number Parts version background.
- Encourage the children to make an estimate of the items in the Estimating Jar and to record their estimates. Have them place their recordings in the box you have prepared.
- Have the children continue to work on last week's Practice activities.

Reflect/Assess

- *How did you figure out how many were in your number picture?*
  ¿Cómo determinaron cuántos había en sus dibujos numéricos?

Content Connection

Physical Development/Fine Arts

Objectives
To begin to participate in group games involving movement
To begin to show interest in the artwork of others

Vocabulary
farm animal names, counting words
nombres de animales de granja, palabras para contar

DLM Materials
The Farm/La granja
Teacher's Resource Anthology
"Farmer in the Dell"/ "El granjero en la cañada"

Activity 1

- Play "Farmer in the Dell"/"El granjero en la cañada." Have the children count and add 1 more as the children join the farmer.

Activity 2

- Have the children look at the illustrations in *The Farm/La granja*. Discuss the animals on each page. Count them. Ask: *How many do you see?*
  ¿Cuántos ven?

Reflect on the Day

- *What did you learn about farm life today?*
  ¿Qué aprendieron sobre la vida en la granja hoy?
- *Tell me the names of some animals you find on a farm.*
  Díganme los nombres de algunos animales que hay en una granja.

Music and Movement

- Have the children dance to "Farmer in the Dell"/"El granjero en la cañada."
- Sing "Old MacDonald"/ "Juancho Pancho" from the *Esta es mi tierra* CD.

Suggested Reading

Old MacDonald Had an Apartment House by Judi Barrett
Big Red Barn by Margaret Wise Brown

What Research Suggests

Learning to communicate mathematically is just as important as learning about numbers.

Begin the Day

- Sing "Five Fat Turkeys Are We"/"Somos los cinco pavos gordos." Discuss how we use turkeys in our daily lives.
- Use one of the suggestions for Morning Circle in the front of this *Teacher's Edition.*

Objectives

- To listen for different purposes
- To begin to break words into syllables or clap along with each syllable in a phrase

Vocabulary

chicken	pollo
duck	pato
turkey	pavo

DLM Materials

- *The Farm/La granja*
- magnetic letters
- Oral Language Development Cards 15 & 16
- *SRA Photo Library* software
- *Teacher's Resource Anthology*
  "Five Fat Turkeys Are We"/"Somos los cinco pavos gordos"
  "Six White Ducks"/"Los seis patos blancos"
  "Los pollitos"/"The Baby Chicks"
  Farm Animal Concentration game
  farm animal card patterns (duck, chicken, turkey)
  "Silly Nellie: The Story of One Funny Turkey"/"Clotilde Bobilde: La historia de una pavita muy divertida"
  "Henny-Penny"/"Gallinita-Nita"
  plastic bag book
  animal sounds tape and cards

Materials to Gather

- rubber ducks
- feathers
- duck, chicken, and turkey puzzles

LITERACY

Focus

- Sing "Six White Ducks"/"Los seis patos blancos."
- Tell the children that today we will be learning about ducks, chickens, and turkeys on the farm.

  Hoy aprenderemos sobre los patos, los pollos y los pavos de la granja.

Develop

One Way to Develop the Lesson

- Show Oral Language Development Cards 15 and 16. Use the suggestions on the backs of the cards to stimulate discussion. If you have pictures of a turkey and a duck, show those pictures as well. You can use the book *The Farm/La granja* to help with pictures.
- Discuss the sounds that each animal makes. *What term is used for these sounds?*

  ¿Qué término se usa para estos sonidos?

  Tell the children that they are going to write their own book about animal sounds. Everyone will help. They will collect illustrations for the book each day this week.
- Write *chickens, ducks,* and *turkeys* on a piece of chart paper. Read the words to the children. Have the children clap out the syllables of each animal name.
- Ask the children to help you list the products that come from each animal.

Another Way to Develop the Lesson

- Invite the children to participate in the action rhyme "Los pollitos"/"The Baby Chicks." Do the rhyme a couple of times. *What sound do the baby chicks make? What does the mother feed them? How does the mother keep the babies warm?*

  ¿Qué sonido hacen los pollitos? ¿Qué les da de comer la mamá? ¿Cómo la mamá mantiene abrigados a los pollitos?

Practice

- Place the *The Farm/La granja* book and listening tape in the Listening Center.
- Place the word cards in the Writing Center and let the children trace them, copy them with magnetic letters, or copy them using crayons or pencils.
- Invite the children to play the Farm Animal Concentration game.
- Give the children copies of the chicken, duck, and turkey from the farm animal card patterns. Encourage them to color the animals of their choice. Provide feathers to glue on the animals. Help them make speech bubbles above their animals. Ask them what sounds their animals make and then write them in the bubbles. Tell the children that they will be collecting illustrations all week for the animal sounds book they are making.
- Give the children the animal sounds tape and the farm animal card patterns to arrange.
- Provide rubber ducks for the water table.
- Invite the children to work on the duck, chicken, and turkey puzzles.
- Encourage the children to find the duck, turkey, and chicken in the Animals category on the *SRA Photo Library* software.

Preparation

- Make the flannel board story.
- Make and enlarge copies (one per child) of the duck, chicken, and turkey from the farm animal card patterns.
- Make enlarged copies of the duck, the turkey, and the chicken from the farm animal card patterns. Color them, cut them out, laminate them, and cut them into puzzle pieces.
- Make a plastic bag book to hold the illustrations you are collecting for the class animal sounds book.

Scaffolding Strategies

More Help Have the children answer you in animal sounds like they did yesterday. Today, use chicken, duck, and turkey sound responses.

Extra Challenge Ask the children to think about and respond to the question *Do ducks that live in Japan sound different from ducks that live in America?*

¿Los patos que viven en Japón suenan diferente de los patos que viven en Estados Unidos?

DAY 2

Letter Knowledge

English

- Read selections from the *SRA Alphabet Book*. You may want to read "Quack, Quack!" or "Ducks in the Rain" today.

Spanish

- Read "Máximo" from *Los niños alfabéticos.*

Second Language Learners

After telling the flannel board story "Henny-Penny"/"Gallinita-Nita," place it in the Language Center. Invite children to tell the story in pairs. A child who is proficient in the language can work with a second language learner. Note the language the second language learner uses. Does the proficient child help the second language learner by asking questions and providing important details? During the proficient child's story, does the second language learner also interact? In what ways?

Anthology Support

"Five Little Ducks"
"Los cinco patitos"
"She'll Be Comin' 'Round the Mountain"
"Little Ducky Duddle"
"El patito Tito"

Suggested Reading

Make Way for Ducklings by Robert McCloskey
Quack and Honk by Allan Fowler

Reflect/Assess

- *Which of the three animals we studied today do you think makes the funniest sound? Why do you think that sound is funny?*

  ¿Cuál de los tres animales que estudiamos hoy creen que hace el sonido más cómico? ¿Por qué?
- *How are the animals alike? How are they different?*

  ¿En qué se parecen los animales? ¿En qué se diferencian?

Literacy Circle

Storytime 1

- Present the "Silly Nellie: The Story of One Funny Turkey"/"Clotilde Bobilde: La historia de una pavita muy divertida" flannel board story.

Storytime 2

- Present the "Henny-Penny"/"Gallinita-Nita" flannel board story. *What was Henny-Penny's life on the farm like? Which other animals that we discussed today are in the story?*

  ¿Cómo era la vida de Gallinita-Nita en la granja? ¿Qué otros animales de los cuales hablamos hoy se mencionan en el cuento?

Content Connection

Physical Development

Objective
To explore moving in space

Vocabulary
race, contestant, champion
carrera o competencia, concursante, campeón o ganador

Materials to Gather
feathers, spoon

Activity 1

- Remind the children that the lesson today was about ducks, turkeys, and chickens, all of which have feathers.
- Invite the children to play Keep the Feather in the Air. Give two children each a lightweight feather. Encourage them to toss the feathers in the air and blow under them to keep them aloft. The one whose feather stays up the longest is the champion and can face a new contestant.

  ¿Quién quiere jugar? Lancen las plumas al aire y sóplenlas por debajo para mantenerlas flotando. El ganador será el que logre mantener la pluma flotando por más tiempo.

Activity 2

- Invite the children to play Pass the Feather. Have the children stand in a circle. Place a feather on a spoon and have the children pass the spoon around the circle without dropping the feather.

  ¿Quién quiere jugar? Pónganse en un círculo y pasen la cuchara con la pluma sin que se caiga.

DAY 2

Objectives
- To combine, separate, and name "how many" concrete objects and record findings
- To sort objects into groups by an attribute and begin to explain how the grouping was done

Vocabulary

add	sumar
adding	sumar
number names	nombres de números

DLM Materials
- *Math Resource Guide*
  Cube Trains/Trenes de cubos
  Number Cookies/Galletas numéricas
  Estimating Jar (previously Counting Jar)
- See Zoo Animals, Day 1
- *DLM Math* software
- *Making Music with Thomas Moore* CD
- *Teacher's Resource Anthology*
  Fruit Salad Game/Juego de la ensalada de frutas

Materials to Gather
- construction paper
- light and dark brown construction paper
- large sheets of white construction paper (1 per child)
- See Zoo Animals, Day 1

Preparation
- Cut cookies from the light brown construction paper and small chips from the dark brown construction paper.

MATH

Focus
- Discuss all the things the children have learned about numbers this year. Ask them if they would have been able to describe 4 so well at the beginning of the year.
  ¿Creen que hubieran podido describir el 4 tan bien al comienzo del año?
- Discuss their ability to count higher and better and their ability to put numbers together. Encourage them to show some of the recordings they are saving for their Number Books.

Develop
- Introduce Number Cookies/Galletas numéricas. Show the children how to place paper chips on paper cookies in different arrangements. For example, you can place 7 chips on a cookie and make a smiley face, a numeral 7, or a pattern of rows. Use a flannel board to demonstrate or use a large cookie cut from construction paper. Tell the children that they will record this activity for their Number Books.

Practice
- Invite the children to make Number Cookies/Galletas numéricas. Give the children construction paper cookies and chips and assign them a number. Have them decorate their cookies with chips in different arrangements and then glue the chips in place. Have them glue their cookies on a cookie sheet (large sheet of white construction paper).
- Invite the children to play Places Scenes: Number Parts version. Remind them to record their number combinations.
- Have the children make an estimate of the items in the Estimating Jar and record their estimates. Have them place their estimates in the box you have prepared.
- Have the children continue to work on last week's Practice activities.
- Invite the children to work on Number Pictures and any other activity they wish. Use informal assessments at the computer, using the combinations that children are building. Do they see the connections?

Reflect/Assess

- *If you went home and sorted the people in your home by girls and boys, what numbers would you have for each?*

  Si fueran a sus casas y clasificaran a las personas de sus casas en niñas y niños, ¿qué números tendrían de cada uno?

Content Connection

Personal and Social Development/Physical Development

Objectives

To begin to share and cooperate with others in group activities

To begin to participate in group games involving movement

DLM Materials

dinosaur counters

Math Resource Guide

Counting cards

More or Less game/Más o menos

Teacher's Resource Anthology

Duck, Duck, Goose/Pato, pato, ganso

Activity 1

- Play the More or Less game/Más o menos. Give each player a handful of counters and a Counting card.
- Have them empty their hands and estimate if there are more, fewer, or the same number of counters as dots on their cards.

Activity 2

- Invite the children to play Duck, Duck, Goose/Pato, pato, ganso. When the game is over and all the children have had a chance to be a goose, graph them according to the month in which they were born.

Music and Movement

- Invite the children to do the "Chicken Dance" from the *Making Music with Thomas Moore* CD.
- Have the children play Chickens Fly Away/Pollitos voladores as you would the Fruit Salad game/ Juego de la ensalada de frutas.
- Have the chickens (children) stand in the 4 corners of the barnyard (playground or classroom) near their nest (a piece of brown construction paper). Appoint a child to be the fox. The fox stands in the center and calls *Chickens, fly away*. The chickens must then change the corner they are standing in and find a nest in another corner. If the fox catches them before they find a new nest, they become the fox. Observe the children's reactions to this free-movement activity to assess how well they are able to compose themselves.

Reflect on the Day

- *What did you learn about chickens, ducks, and turkeys today?*

  ¿Qué aprendieron sobre los pollos, los patos y los pavos hoy?
- *What information can you share with your family?*

  ¿Qué información pueden compartir con su familia?

Begin the Day

- Sing "Mary Had a Little Lamb"/"María tenía una corderita."
- Use one of the suggestions for Morning Circle in the front of this *Teacher's Edition.*

Objectives

- To listen with increasing attention
- To listen for different purposes

Vocabulary

sheep	oveja
lamb	cordero
ram	carnero
ewe	oveja hembra

DLM Materials

- magnetic letters
- *SRA Photo Library* software
- *Teacher's Resource Anthology*
  "Mary Had a Little Lamb"/"María tenía una corderita"
  "Baa, Baa, Sweet Sheep"/"Be, ba, oveja buena"
  "The Three Billy Goats Gruff"/"Los tres chivitos Gruff"
  Farm Animal Concentration game
  farm animal card patterns (pig)
  "The Ram in the Chile Patch"/"El carnero en el sembrado de chiles"
  "The Three Little Pigs"/"Los tres cerditos"

Materials to Gather

- character name necklaces
- canned biscuits
- sausage
- toaster oven
- red and white finger paint
- recorder and tape
- tracing paper
- word cards

LITERACY

Focus

- Sing "Baa, Baa, Sweet Sheep"/"Be, ba, oveja buena." Ask the children to describe sheep they have seen.
  ¿Han visto ovejas alguna vez?
- Tell the children that today we will be learning about goats, sheep, and pigs that live on farms.
  Hoy aprenderemos sobre los chivos, las ovejas y los cerdos de la granja.

Develop

One Way to Develop the Lesson

- Ask the children to make the animal sounds for goats, sheep, and pigs. Show the children any pictures you may have of any of these animals.
- Ask the children questions about each of the animals. *What do they eat? Where do they live? How do they move? How do they act?*
  ¿Qué comen? ¿Dónde viven? ¿Cómo se mueven? ¿Cómo actúan?
  Let the children demonstrate movements. Explain that ewes are female sheep, rams are male sheep, and lambs are baby sheep.
- Write the name of each animal on chart paper. Read the names of the animals to the children and ask them to clap out the syllables in each animal name.
- Ask the children to help you list products that come from these animals. They probably need more help with these animals. Your list should include cheese, milk, wool, meat, and clothing.

Another Way to Develop the Lesson

- Present the "The Three Billy Goats Gruff"/"Los tres chivitos Gruff" flannel board story.
- Ask the children if they think the billy goats live on a farm. It is quite possible that they do.

  ¿Creen que los tres chivitos viven en una granja?
- Encourage the children to role-play the story. Provide character name necklaces with the character's names and pictures.

Practice

- Place the flannel board story in the Language Center and invite the children to retell the story or make up a new story.
- Invite them to play the Farm Animal Concentration game.
- Place red and white finger paint on the tabletop and see if the children can figure out how to make pink pigs.
- Have the children record pig and sheep sounds.
- Make Pigs in a Blanket. Wrap canned biscuits around breakfast sausages and bake in a toaster oven for twelve minutes.
- Give the children copies of the pig from the farm animal card patterns. Encourage them to color the pig. Help them make a speech bubble above the pig. Ask them what sound the pig makes and then write it in the bubble. Tell them that you will add today's animal to the animal sounds book they are making.
- Give the children the word cards and encourage them to trace the words, copy the words with magnetic letters, or copy the words with crayons or pencils.
- Encourage the children to find the goat, sheep, and pig in the Animal category on the *SRA Photo Library* software.

Preparation

- Make the flannel board stories, if not already made.
- Make a name necklace for each of the characters in "The Three Billy Goats Gruff"/"Los tres chivitos Gruff." Use the character illustrations from the flannel board story to add a picture to each name card.
- Make enlarged copies of the pig in the farm animal card patterns (one per child).

Scaffolding Strategies

More Help Invite the children to respond to their names today by using the animal sounds for goats, sheep, or pigs.

Extra Challenge Ask the children which of the animals discussed today is somewhat different from the others, and have them explain how it is different.

¿Cuál de los animales que estudiamos hoy se parece menos a los demás?

Second Language Learners

Encourage the children to name the farm animals they uncover as they play the Farm Animal Concentration game. This will help them recall the location of the animal on the next trial and pro-

DAY 3

Letter Knowledge

English

- Invite the children to shape the letters of the alphabet with play dough.

Spanish

- Invite the children to shape the letter *x* with play dough.

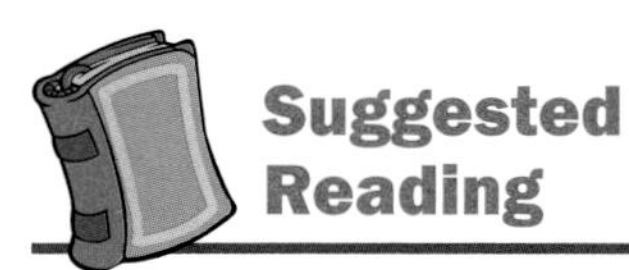

Suggested Reading

The Shepherd Boy by Kristine L. Franklin
El niño pastor by Kristine L. Franklin
El chivo en la huerta by Lada J. Kratky

Anthology Support

"Little Bo Peep"
"La pequeña Lolita"
"Mary Had a Little Goat"
"María tenía una cabrita"

Technology Support

If your schedule permits, take the children to *www.sra4kids*.com and help them navigate using the computer's mouse. You might provide hints to guide them.

Reflect/Assess

- *Tell me something you learned today about pigs.*
  Díganme algo que hayan aprendido hoy sobre el cerdo.
- *How are a lamb and a ram alike? How are they different?*
  ¿En qué se parecen el cordero y el carnero? ¿En qué se diferencian?

Storytime 1

- Read the "The Ram in the Chile Patch"/"El carnero en el sembrado de chiles" flannel board story. Remind the children that a ram is a male sheep.
  Un carnero es una oveja macho.

Storytime 2

- Tell "The Three Little Pigs"/"Los tres cerditos" flannel board story. *How are the pigs in the story like real pigs? How are they different?*
  ¿En qué se parecen los cerdos del cuento a los cerdos de verdad? ¿En qué se diferencian?

Content Connection

Fine Arts/Physical Development

Objective

To use different colors, surface textures, and shapes to create form and meaning

Materials to Gather

construction paper, cotton, art paper, white finger paint, yarn, tempera paint

Activity 1

- Invite the children to make hand print sheep. Make white handprints on construction paper (fingers make the legs and the thumb makes the neck and face), and then cover the body and head with cotton.

  Vamos a dibujar en cartulina una oveja a partir de un calco de nuestras manos.

Activity 2

- Provide art paper (creased down the middle), yarn, and tempera paints. Invite the children to dip yarn in the paint, then arrange it in a design on one side of their papers. Fold the papers along the creases and press. Pull the yarn out and open the papers to reveal designs. Remind the children that some yarn is made from wool.

  Pongan el estambre en la pintura, luego hagan un diseño en uno de los lados de la hoja del papel. Doblen la hoja en el pliegue y presionen. Halen el estambre y abran la hoja para que vean el diseño.

DAY 3

Objectives

- To combine, separate, and name "how many" concrete objects and record findings
- To sort objects into groups by an attribute and begin to explain how the grouping was done

Vocabulary

add	sumar
adding	sumar

DLM Materials

- *Math Resource Guide*
  Fingers Game/Juego con los dedos
  Cube Trains/Trenes de cubos
  Number Cookies/Galletas numéricas
  2 Estimating Jars
- See Zoo Animals, Day 1
- *DLM Math* software
- *Teacher's Resource Anthology*
  plastic bag books
  "Little Bo Peep"/"La pequeña Lolita"
  "Little Boy Blue"/"Pequeño pastor"

Materials to Gather

- construction paper
- light and dark brown construction paper
- large sheets of white construction paper (1 per child)
- yarn (optional)
- chenille wires
- See Zoo Animals, Day 1

Preparation

- Make a second Estimating Jar with 10 identical items inside it.
- Make an 8-page plastic bag book for each child using the large size plastic bags.

MATH

Focus

- Play the Fingers Game/Juego con los dedos. Tell the children to show you 4. Then ask them to show you 4 using the same number of fingers on each hand. Repeat with other even numbers.

Develop

- Read and discuss the children's recorded estimates of how many items are in the Estimating Jar. Show an identical jar and, along with the children, count 5 identical objects into that jar. Hold up both jars so the children can compare them. Let them identify the jar they believe has more in it.
- Count out 5 more (i.e., start counting at 6) into the identical jar and compare again. Tell them that they will make new estimates today.
- Tell the children that they will start putting their Number Books together today.

Practice

- Set up a book-making area. Let the children make their final selections for their Number Books and then help them assemble the books. You can slip their work into plastic bag books or you can punch holes in the items and tie the pages together with yarn.
- Invite the children to make Number Cookies/Galletas numéricas.
- Have the children make and record an estimate of the items in the Estimating Jar. Put out a different color of paper for the children to use to record their new estimates. This can be used as an informal assessment.
- Have the children continue to work on the Practice activities from last week.
- Invite the children to work on Number Pictures and any other activity they wish. Encourage the children to use physical shapes next to the computer to help them think of new, creative, number pictures.

Reflect/Assess

- *How did you describe your pictures with numbers?*
  ¿Cómo describieron sus dibujos con números?

Content Connection

Science

Objectives
To compare objects and organisms and identify similarities and differences
To sort objects and organisms into groups and begin to describe how groups were organized

DLM Materials
Oral Language Cards 6–22

Materials to Gather
yarn, index cards, construction paper

Activity 1

- Ask the children to think about which animals they usually see on a farm and which they see at a zoo. Make a *Zoo* sign and a *Farm* sign out of construction paper. Have them sort the animal cards by the signs, *Zoo* and *Farm*. Count the number of animals in each stack.

Activity 2

- Make 2 yarn circles on the floor. Overlap the circles in the middle to create a Venn diagram. Place the *Zoo* and *Farm* signs in the circles and write both words on a third card and place it in the center space. Ask the children to sort the animal pictures according to where they are found: farm, zoo, or both places.
- Count and record how many animals are in each circle and how many are in the middle.

Music and Movement

- Make curly pigtails from large chenille wires and pin them to the back of the children's clothing. Put on some music and invite the children to do a pig jig.
- Have the children act out "Little Bo Peep"/ "La pequeña Lolita" or "Little Boy Blue"/ "Pequeño pastor."

Suggested Reading

Big Red Barn by Margaret Wise Brown
Barnyard Dance! by Sandra Boynton

Reflect on the Day

- *What did you learn today about sheep, lambs, goats, and pigs?*
  ¿Qué aprendieron hoy sobre las ovejas, los corderos, las cabras y los cerdos?
- *Who can help me spell the word* pig?
  ¿Quién me puede ayudar a deletrear la palabra cerdo?

Begin the Day

- Sing "Old Gray Mare."
- Use one of the suggestions for Morning Circle in the front of this *Teacher's Edition*.

Objectives

- To connect information and events in books to real-life experiences
- To begin to retell some sequences of events in stories

Vocabulary

horse	caballo
donkey	burro
cow	vaca
real	real
make-believe	imaginario

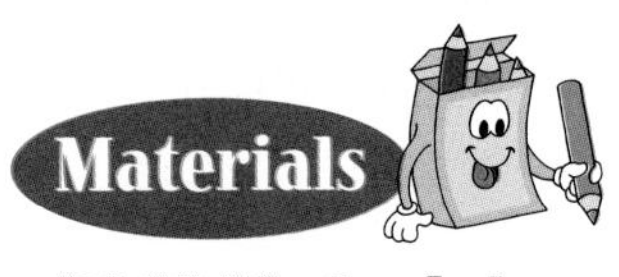

DLM Materials

- Oral Language Development Cards 9, 13, 14
- My Sick Little Donkey sequence cards
- *The Farm/La granja*
- *SRA Photo Library* software
- *Teacher's Resource Anthology*
  "Old Gray Mare"
  "Sweetly Sings the Donkey"/"Dulcemente canta el burro"
  "El burrito enfermo"/"My Sick Little Donkey"
  Farm Animal Concentration game
  farm animal card patterns
  baggie ice cream
  "The Farm"/"La granja"
  "Old MacDonald"/"El viejo MacDonald"

Materials to Gather

- chart paper
- poster board
- farm animal puzzles

LITERACY

Focus

- Sing "Sweetly Sings the Donkey"/"Dulcemente canta el burro."
- Tell the children that today we will be learning about horses, donkeys, and cows on the farm.

Develop

One Way to Develop the Lesson

- Show Oral Language Cards 9, 13, and 14. Use the suggestions on the backs of the cards to stimulate conversation.
- Ask about each of the animals. *What sounds do they make? What are their behaviors? How do they move? What do they eat? Where do they live on the farm?*

  ¿Qué sonidos hacen? ¿Cómo se comportan? ¿Cómo se mueven? ¿Qué comen? ¿En qué parte de la granja viven?
- List each animal's name on a piece of chart paper. Read each name to the children. Have them clap out the syllables of each animal name.
- Discuss the roles the animals play on the farm. *How is the cow's role different from the horse's role and donkey's role? What products do we get from cows? How do donkeys and horses help the farmer?*

  ¿En qué se diferencia el papel que cumple la vaca del papel que cumplen el caballo y el burro? ¿Qué productos obtenemos de la vaca? ¿Cómo ayudan el burro y el caballo al granjero?

Another Way to Develop the Lesson

- Tell the children that you are going to tell them a story about a donkey. Present "El burrito enfermo"/"My Sick Little Donkey." *Is this story real or make-believe? How do you know? How do you think a farmer would really care for a sick donkey?*

  ¿El cuento es de verdad o imaginario? ¿Cómo lo saben? ¿Cómo creen que un granjero cuidaría de un burro enfermo?
- Show the children the My Sick Little Donkey/El burrito enfermo sequence cards. Ask them to help put the cards in the correct sequence.

Preparation

- Make the flannel board stories.
- Make enlarged copies of the horse and cow from the farm animal card patterns (one per child).
- Gather ingredients for baggie ice cream.

Practice

- Place the flannel board story in the Language Center and encourage the children to retell the story or make up a new story.
- Give them the farm animal puzzles to work on.
- Invite the children to play Farm Animal Concentration.
- Give them copies of the horse and cow from the farm animal card patterns. Encourage them to color the animals of their choice. Help them make speech bubbles above their animals. Ask them what sounds their animals make and then write them in the bubbles. Remind them that these are the illustrations for the class animal sounds book they are making.
- Ask the children to write a story about meeting, riding, or owning a horse.
- Let the children experiment with sand combs. Compare the troughs made by the combs to those made by a plow pulled by a horse.
- **(Allergy Warning)** Make baggie ice cream with the children. Call attention to the milk in the ice cream. Remind the children that milk comes from cows.
- Encourage the children to find the horse, cows, and donkey in the Animals category on the *SRA Photo Library* software.

Scaffolding Strategies

More Help Read books about cows, horses, and donkeys to the children.

Extra Challenge Encourage the children to create a Venn diagram of horses and donkeys.

Second Language Learners

Compare horses and cows. Use vocabulary describing appearances and habits. If the children describe the characteristics of only one of the animals, ask: "Does the horse have (four legs) as the cow does? Yes? Oh, then the horse AND the cow have four legs." If they point out a difference, reply, "Oh, you say the horse has a THICK tail, BUT the cow has a THIN tail." Stress key vocabulary to describe the animals.

DAY 4

Letter Knowledge

English

- Invite the children to think of ways to make letters with their bodies. Use the Think, Pair, Share game with this activity.

Spanish

- Invite the children to think of ways to make the letter *x* with their bodies. Use the Piensa, aparea, comparte game with this activity.

Anthology Support

"Pancho and Sky"
"Pancho y Cielo"
"Three Wishes"
"Tres deseos"

Suggested Reading

What a Wonderful Day to Be a Cow by Carolyn Lesser
The Cow That Went Oink/La vaca que decía oink by Bernard Most

Reflect/Assess

- *How are horses and donkeys alike? How are they different?*
  ¿En qué se parecen los caballos y los burros? ¿En qué se diferencian?
- *Which of the animals that we discussed today would you prefer to ride?*
  ¿Cuáles animales que estudiamos hoy preferirían montar?

Literacy Circle

Storytime 1

- Read or sing *The Farm/La granja*. Try dividing the class into four reading groups. Give each group a copy of the small book and tell them that they can read the book by themselves. The predictable language and the illustrations make this a feasible task. Celebrate their accomplishment of reading on their own. *Which of the animals we discussed today are in the story?*
  ¿Cuáles animales de los que hablamos hoy se mencionan en el cuento?

Storytime 2

- Tell or sing the "Old MacDonald"/"El viejo MacDonald" flannel board story. *Which of the animals we discussed today are in the story?*
  ¿Cuáles animales de los que hablamos hoy se mencionan en el cuento?

Content Connection

Science

Objectives
To begin to use scientific words and phrases to describe objects, events, and living things
To begin to demonstrate safe practices and appropriate use of materials

Vocabulary
change of state, liquid, solid, sound
cambio de estado, líquido, sólido, sonido

Materials to Gather
baby food jars, whipping cream, salt, crackers, plank of wood, blocks

Activity 1

- **(Allergy Warning)** Let the children make butter. Give each child a baby food jar. Measure two tablespoons of whipping cream (at room temperature) into each jar. Remind the children that cream comes from the milk of a cow. Call attention to the fact that what you have poured into the jars is a liquid. Now have the children shake the jars until the liquid turns into a solid. Add a pinch of salt and enjoy the butter on a cracker. Explain to the children that when the cream portion of milk is churned or mixed well it will turn into butter.
  Vamos a hacer mantequilla. Agiten los frascos hasta que el líquido se convierta en sólido. Cuando la parte cremosa de la leche se agita bien, se convierte en mantequilla.

Activity 2

- Provide several different types of blocks and a plank of wood. Invite the children to experiment with the blocks to get the best "clopping" sound. *Does the noise sound like a horse walking on pavement?*
  ¿Suena como un caballo galopando sobre el pavimento?

DAY 4

Objectives

- To combine, separate, and name "how many" concrete objects and record findings
- To sort objects into groups by an attribute and begin to explain how the grouping was done

Vocabulary

add	sumar
adding	sumar
number names	nombres de números

DLM Materials

- pattern blocks (triangles, squares, blue rhombuses, and trapezoids)
- *Math Resource Guide*
  Fingers Game/Juego con los dedos
  Cube Trains/Trenes de cubos
  Number Cookies/Galletas numéricas
  Estimating Jar
- See Zoo Animals, Day 1
- *DLM Math* software
- *Teacher's Resource Anthology* plastic bag books

Materials to Gather

- construction paper
- light and dark brown construction paper
- large sheets of white construction paper (1 per child)
- See Zoo Animals, Day 1

Focus

- Play the Fingers Game/Juego con los dedos. Ask the children to show you 4 using the same number of fingers on each hand. Repeat with other even (2, 6, 8, 10) and odd (1, 3, 5, 7, 9) numbers until they are convinced you can't do it with odd numbers. Invent your own finger game challenges.

Develop

- Have 5 children stand up. Then have them sort themselves by a new attribute such as blue eyes and not blue eyes, or wearing red and not wearing red. Record the number combinations. Repeat with 5 new children.

Practice

- Help the children to finish assembling their Number Books (see Day 3).
- Invite the children to make Number Cookies/Galletas numéricas.
- Have the children continue to work on Practice activities from the previous week.
- Have the children make an estimate of the items in the Estimating Jar and record them.
- Invite the children to work on Number Pictures and any other activity they wish. Ask the children if they can think of a way to describe or label their number pictures in a different way from the way the computer does it.

Reflect/Assess

- *How can you figure out which numbers could be hidden inside 6?*
  ¿Cómo determinaron qué números se podían esconder dentro de 6?

Music and Movement

- Teach the children to run, gallop, and trot like horses.
- Invite the children to play a game of horseshoes.

Content Connection

Science

Objective
To sort objects and organisms into groups and begin to describe how groups were organized

Vocabulary
counting words
palabras para contar

Materials to Gather
berry baskets, plastic animals

Activity 1

- Visit the farm in the Blocks Center. Encourage dramatic play by posing problem-solving scenarios. Tell the children you have 5 chickens (or whatever animal you have). Ask them how you could arrange the chickens into 2 cages (or chicken coops).
- Have the children work with you to find all the combinations.

Activity 2

- Tell the children that you have 6 cows (or whatever animal you have). Ask them how you could arrange the cows into 2 areas.
- Have the children work with you to find all the combinations.

Suggested Reading

Rosie's Walk by Pat Hutchins

Reflect on the Day

- *Who remembers what products we get from cows?*
  ¿Quién recuerda los productos que obtenemos de las vacas?
- *What can you share with your family about horses, cows, and donkeys?*
  ¿Qué pueden compartir con sus familias sobre los caballos, las vacas y los burros?

Home Connection

Send four children home with a take-home book pack.

Begin the Day

- Sing "Three White Mice"/"Los tres ratones blancos."
- Use one of the suggestions for Morning Circle in the front of this *Teacher's Edition*.

Objectives

- To show appreciation of repetitive language patterns
- To connect information and events in books to real-life experiences

Vocabulary

cats	gatos
dogs	perros
mice	ratones

DLM Materials

- *SRA Book of Animals/SRA El libro de los animales*
- *The Little Red Hen/La gallinita roja*
- *The Farm/La granja*
- Oral Language Development Cards 52 & 53
- *SRA Photo Library* software
- *Making Music with Thomas Moore* CD
- *Teacher's Resource Anthology*
  "Three White Mice"/"Los tres ratones blancos"
  "Bingo"/"Bingo"
  "El gato y los ratones"/"The Cat and the Mice"
  Farm Animal Concentration game
  farm animal card patterns (dog, cat)
  dog and bone match patterns
  story map
  "The Little Red Hen"/"La gallinita roja"

Materials to Gather

- class animal sounds book
- fine-tip markers
- animal sounds tape

LITERACY

Focus

- Sing "Bingo"/"Bingo." Ask the children if they think farm dogs are different from city dogs. You might want to have the children sing along to the instrumental version on the *Making Music with Thomas Moore* CD.

  ¿Creen que los perros de una granja son diferentes de los perros de una ciudad?
- Tell them that today we will be talking about dogs, cats, and mice on the farm.

Develop

One Way to Develop the Lesson

- Show the children Oral Language Development Cards 52 and 53. Although these pets don't look exactly like farm animals, use the cards to stimulate conversation.
- Ask the children what roles they think dogs and cats play on the farm. *Do we get any products from dogs or cats? Do they do any work on the farm? Are they pets?*

  ¿Los perros o los gatos nos dan algún producto? ¿Ellos hacen algún trabajo en la granja? ¿Son mascotas?
- For the most part, dogs and cats on farms are pets. However, dogs also keep wolves away from the livestock, and cats catch the mice that are in barns.
- Have the children select a five-letter name for a cat, such as *Boots,* and sing "Bingo"/"Bingo" using the new name.

Another Way to Develop the Lesson

- Read "Mice"/"Ratones" in the *SRA Book of Animals/SRA El libro de los animales*.
- Tell the story "El gato y los ratones"/"The Cat and the Mice." Embellish the story by making the location of the story an old barn instead of a town or village. *What was the cat looking for? Why were the mice frightened? How did the cat trick the mice? Do you think that this is the way it is on a farm? Do you think the mice are afraid of the farm cat?* *¿Qué buscaba el gato? ¿Por qué tenían miedo los ratones? ¿Cómo el gato engañó a los ratones? ¿Creen que así es en la granja? ¿Creen que los ratones le tienen miedo al gato de la granja?*

Practice

- Invite the children to play Farm Animal Concentration.
- Let the children listen to the animal sounds tape again and sequence the farm animal card patterns by the sounds on the tape.
- Give the children dog or cat pictures to color. Draw speech bubbles above their animals' heads. Ask the children what sounds their animals make and write them in the bubbles. Add the final pictures to the class animal sounds book so it will be ready to read at storytime. Be sure to make a list of the authors and illustrators.
- Provide finger paints and let the children make thumbprint mice. Use a fine-tip marker to add details. Encourage the children to name their mice.
- Invite the children to play the Dog and Bone Match game. Print letters on the dogs' name tags and matching letters on the bones.
- Encourage the children to find the dog, cat, and mouse in the Animals category on the *SRA Photo Library* software.

Preparation

- Be ready to complete the class animal sounds book after selecting a few illustrations from today's lesson.
- Make five copies of the dog and bone match patterns to create a matching game. Print the letters of Bingo's name on the collar tags and on the bones.

Scaffolding Strategies

More Help Discuss dogs and cats the children know. These might be their pets or pets that belong to friends or extended family members.

Extra Challenge Invite the children to make up a song about a mouse using "Bingo"/"Bingo" as a model. They will need to select a five-letter name for the mouse. *Can a mouse be a pet?* *¿Un ratón puede ser una mascota?*

Letter Knowledge

English

- Invite the children to find and circle a specific letter of the alphabet in newspapers and magazines.

Spanish

- Invite the children to find and circle the letter *x* in newspapers and magazines.

Second Language Learners

Ask parents to send pictures of their children's pets. Using the pictures as a guide, ask each child to tell a story about his or her pet or a classroom pet. Ask questions for clarification and further detail, and encourage the other children to ask questions. Ask each child to dictate a sentence or two to create a class story about the pets. Clearly enunciate each sound as you write it. Then invite the children to read with you. Attach the photos to the story, or ask children to draw pictures of the pets in the story.

Anthology Support

"My Dog Rags"
"Mi perra Perla"
"Cat and Mouse"
"El gato y el ratón"
"My Very Own Pet"
"Mi propia mascota"

Suggested Reading

The Puppy Who Wanted a Boy by Jane Thayer
Loudmouse by Richard Wilber

Reflect/Assess

- *Which farm pet would you prefer, a dog or a cat?*
  ¿Qué animal de granja preferirían, un perro o un gato?
- *Which animal might have to do more work on the farm: the cat catching mice or the dog watching over the other animals?*
  ¿Qué animal tendría que trabajar más en la granja: el gato cazando ratones o el perro cuidando a los otros animales?

Literacy Circle

Storytime 1

- Read "The Little Red Hen"/"La gallinita roja." *Who are the characters in the story? Do they work hard or do they not work at all?*
  ¿Cuáles son los personajes del cuento? ¿Trabajan mucho o no hacen nada?
- Make a story map for this story.

Storytime 2

- Read the class animal sounds book the children have been working on this week. *How similar is the class book to* The Farm/La granja?
  ¿En qué se parece el libro de la clase a La granja/The Farm?

Content Connection

Physical Development

Objectives

To explore moving in space

To move within a space of defined boundaries, changing body configurations to accommodate the space

Materials to Gather

balance beam or masking tape, beanbag, butcher paper, yarn

Activity 1

- Discuss the cat's incredible sense of balance. Let the children walk a balance beam like a cat. If you don't have a balance beam, just place a strip of masking tape on the floor. Encourage the children to walk the balance beam with beanbags on their heads.

  Caminen por la barra de equilibrio con una bolsa de frijoles en su cabeza.

Activity 2

- Draw a cat without a tail on a piece of butcher paper. Make a tail out of yarn. Let the children play Pin the Tail on the Cat.

DAY 5

Objectives

- To combine, separate and name "how many" concrete objects and record findings
- To imitate pattern sounds and physical movements

Vocabulary

add sumar
adding sumar

DLM Materials

- *Math Resource Guide*
  Cube Trains/Trenes de cubos
  Number Cookies/Galletas numéricas
  Listen and Copy/Escucha e imita
  Estimating Jar
- *DLM Math* software
- *Teacher's Resource Anthology*
  plastic bag books
  "Old Gray Cat"/"El viejo gato gris"
  Whose Dog Are Thou?/¿De quién son esos perros?
  "Farmer in the Dell"/"El granjero en la cañada"

Materials to Gather

- construction paper
- light and dark brown construction paper
- large sheets of white construction paper (1 per child)

MATH

Focus

- Read and discuss the children's recorded estimates of how many items there are in the Estimating Jar. Some children might notice that after seeing the 5 and 10 benchmarks that their estimates were closer.
- Dump the objects and count them to check.
- Discuss how their estimates changed after seeing the second Estimating Jar and counting the benchmark objects.

Develop

- Play Listen and Copy/Escucha e imita. Clap and count. Have the children copy your *aaabb* pattern: clap (one), clap (two), clap (three), slap (one), slap (two), and so forth.
- Ask the children how many claps they hear and how many slaps they hear. Then ask how many claps and slaps in all.
- Repeat with a new pattern.
- Remind the children that today will be the last day to prepare their Number Books. We will share them at the end of the day.

Practice

- Help the children to finish assembling their Number Books (see Day 3).
- Invite the children to make Number Cookies/Galletas numéricas.
- Have the children make an estimate of the items in the Estimating Jar and record them.
- Have the children continue to work on last week's Practice activities.
- Invite the children to work on Number Pictures and any other activity they wish.

Reflect/Assess

- Computer Show: Have the children show their number pictures on the computer and in their books.
- Book Show: Invite the children to show their favorite number pictures or number combination recordings in their Number Books.

Music and Movement

- Have the children perform the story "Old Gray Cat"/"El viejo gato gris."
- Play Whose Dog Are Thou?/¿De quién son ésos perros? or "Farmer in the Dell"/"El granjero en la cañada."

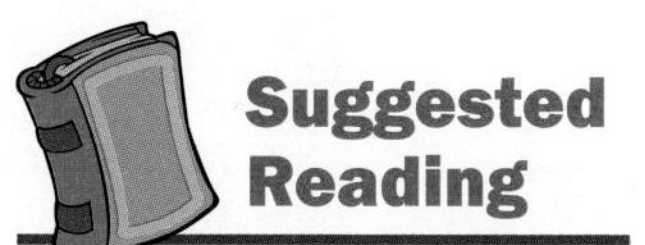

Suggested Reading

Rosie's Walk by Pat Hutchins

Content Connection

Science

Objective

To sort objects and organisms into groups and begin to describe how groups were organized

DLM Materials

Teacher's Resource Anthology farm animal card patterns

Materials to Gather

sticky notes, green and blue construction paper, duck-shaped sponges, yellow tempera paint

Activity 1

- Invite the children to vote for their favorite farm animals. Use the pictures from the farm animal card patterns to illustrate each column. Encourage them to place a sticky note in the column that represents their favorite animal. Make a more concrete graph by having them stand in lines that correspond to their votes.

Activity 2

- Tape a piece of blue construction paper and green construction paper together to make a pond and a yard. Give the children duck sponges and yellow tempera paint. Have them make 4 ducks, some in the pond and some in the yard. Ask them to describe their pictures. *How many ducks are in the pond? How many ducks are in the yard? How many ducks in all?*

Reflect on the Day

- *What did you learn this week about farm animals?*
  ¿Qué aprendieron esta semana sobre los animales de granjas?
- *Which of this week's stories was your favorite? Why?*
  ¿Cuál fue su cuento favorito de esta semana? ¿Por qué?

Looking Ahead

Connecting to the Theme: Ocean Life

The children have progressed in their study of animals from the zoo to the farm, and now to the ocean as they discover animals that make their homes in bodies of water. The children will learn about the world's oceans and what things can be found in them in the course of this theme. Some of the focus creatures include starfish, sea horses, dolphins, whales, and octopuses.

	Objectives	DLM Materials	Materials to Gather
DAY 1	• To listen for different purposes • To understand and follow simple oral directions • To observe and describe properties of rocks, soil, and water • To put together puzzles of increasing complexity • To start, use, and exit software programs • To begin to participate in group games involving movement	• *Fish Wish/Deseos de un pez* • *The Zebra on the Zyder Zee/Una aventura en alta mar* • *Teacher's Resource Anthology* • *Math Resource Guide* • *DLM Math* software • *Four Baby Bumblebees* CD • *Esta es mi tierra* CD	• globe or map • funnel • mineral oil • plastic cups • salt • beach ball • beanbags • blue food coloring • Epsom salts • nature tapes of ocean sounds • small, clean, clear liter bottles • green food coloring
DAY 2	• To refine and extend understanding of known words • To link new learning experiences and vocabulary to what is already known about a topic • To begin to perform simple investigations • To recognize, describe, and name shapes • To begin to investigate and predict the results of putting together two or more shapes	• *Fish Wish/Deseos de un pez* • Oral Language Development Card 67 • *Teacher's Resource Anthology* • pattern blocks • *Math Resource Guide* • *DLM Math* software	• star templates • tweezers • washers • coat hanger tube • building blocks • tub for water • large clear sequins • yarn sea horse and fish puzzles • corks with nails through the centers • sheets of colored acetate (transparencies) • books showing dancers
DAY 3	• To show appreciation for repetitive language patterns • To connect information and events in books to real-life experiences • To begin to make size comparisons between objects • To put together puzzles of increasing complexity • To begin to recognize when a shape's position or orientation has changed	• *Fish Wish/Deseos de un pez* • *Blue Cat/Gato azul* • *Teacher's Resource Anthology* • pattern blocks • *Math Resource Guide* • *DLM Math* software • *SRA Photo Library* software	• shallow box • magnets • building blocks • yarn • dolphin and whale puzzles • geoboards and rubber bands (optional) • light source with sets of translucent shapes (optional) • sheets of colored acetate (transparencies)
DAY 4	• To ask questions and make comments related to the current topic of discussion • To use sentences of increasing length (three or more words) and grammatical complexity in everyday speech • To begin to perform simple investigations • To begin to recognize, describe, and name shapes • To put together puzzles of increasing complexity	• *Fish Wish/Deseos de un pez* • *SRA Book of Animals/SRA El libro de los animales* • *Teacher's Resource Anthology* • Rafita and Pepita/Rafita y Pepita puppets • pattern blocks • *Math Resource Guide* • *DLM Math* software	• octopus puzzles • magnets • squirt bottles • suction cups • basters • balloons • straw • yarn or string • objects to pick up with suction cups • colored glue in a squirt bottle • geoboards and rubber bands (optional) • sheets of colored acetate (transparencies)
DAY 5	• To begin to attend to the beginning sounds in familiar words by identifying that the pronunciations of several words all begin the same way • To begin to put together puzzles of increasing complexity • To follow basic oral or pictorial cues for operating programs successfully	• *Teacher's Resource Anthology* • pattern blocks • *Math Resource Guide* • *DLM Math* software • *Four Baby Bumblebees* CD • *Esta es mi tierra* CD	• ocean puzzles • seashells • sponges • fine sand • tablespoon • large blue sheet • beach ball • sandpaper • poster board • green tissue paper • collection of items found in the sea • fishing game (Day 2)

(See individual lesson pages for complete lists of materials.)

Learning Centers

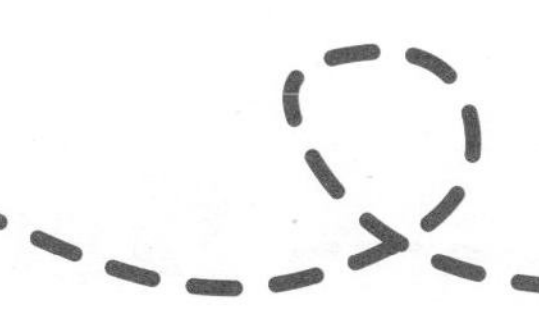

DRAMATIC PLAY

Let's Go Fishing

Objective
To begin to engage in dramatic play with others

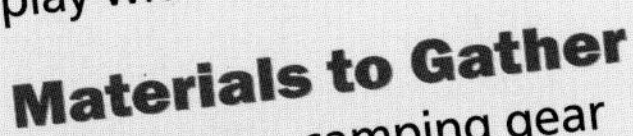

Materials to Gather
fishing gear, camping gear

Develop
Set up a fishing camp. Fill the center with props for fishing. Make a small boat out of a large cardboard box. Provide several fishing poles made from coat hanger tubes and yarn. Tie a magnet on some of them. Provide sun hats, a tackle box, a net, a raincoat, and some fish to catch. Make sure you have a pretend log fire and a pan to fry up the daily catch. You may want to add snorkel gear or scuba gear. You can make air tanks from two-liter soda bottles. Encourage the children to fish and then cook their dinner over the fire.

Reflect/Assess
Have you ever been to the ocean with your family? Did you fish?
¿Alguna vez han ido a la playa con su familia? ¿Pescaron?

SCIENCE

Exploring the Ocean

Objective
To observe and describe properties of rocks, soil, and water

Materials to Gather
ocean and sea materials

Develop
Fill the center with maps, globes, ocean pictures and books, fish pictures, seashells, rocks, and sand. Encourage the children to explore the materials throughout the week.

Reflect/Assess
What do you like best that comes from the ocean?
¿Qué creen que es la cosa más curiosa que proviene del mar?

BLOCKS

Ships and Harbors

Objective
To begin to engage in dramatic play with others

Materials to Gather
blue paper, small boats, pictures of harbors, blocks

Develop
Encourage the children to build a harbor. Provide plastic boats. Use blue paper to create water. Show the children how to build a dock with the blocks. Provide pictures of harbors. Provide information daily about what goes on in harbors, since the children will probably have limited experiences with them. Discuss the types of boats that seek shelter in harbors. *How are things loaded and unloaded from boats?*
¿Cómo cargan y descargan los barcos?
Midweek, you may want to expand play concepts by adding trains and trucks to take supplies from the boats to other locations.

Reflect/Assess
Do you think it would be fun to live near a harbor? Why?
¿Creen que sería divertido vivir cerca de un puerto? ¿Por qué?

What Research Suggests

Repetition is an important part of learning. It strengthens children's understandings of patterns and often helps clarify information for them. Repetition should be routine in your teaching.

DAY 1

Begin the Day

- Sing "There's a Hole in the Middle of the Sea"/"Hay un hueco en el medio del mar."
- Use one of the suggestions for Morning Circle in the front of this *Teacher's Edition*.

Objectives

- To listen for different purposes
- To understand and follow simple oral directions

Vocabulary

ocean	océano
sea	mar
map	mapa
globe	globo terráqueo
seawater	agua de mar
salt water	agua salada

DLM Materials

- *Fish Wish/Deseos de un pez*
- *The Zebra on the Zyder Zee/Una aventura en alta mar*
- *SRA Photo Library* software
- *Teacher's Resource Anthology*
  "There's a Hole in the Middle of the Sea"/"Hay un hueco en el medio del mar"
  "A Sailor Went to Sea"
  "I Saw a Ship A-Sailing"/"Yo vi un barco navegando"
  "My Bonny Lies Over the Ocean"/"Mi conejito flota en el océano"

Materials to Gather

- globe or map
- Epsom salts
- black construction paper
- word cards
- nature tapes of ocean sounds
- bags

LITERACY

Focus

- Sing "A Sailor Went to Sea" or say the rhyme "I Saw a Ship A-Sailing"/"Yo vi un barco navegando." Ask the children to tell you about their experiences at the ocean or the beach.
- Tell the children that this week they will learn about the ocean and sea life.

Develop

One Way to Develop the Lesson

- Display a globe or a map. Tell the children that the blue they see is ocean. There is much more water than there is land on Earth's surface. Water covers nearly three-fourths of Earth.
  Todo lo azul que ven en el globo terráqueo es océano. Hay más agua que tierra en nuestro planeta. El agua cubre casi tres cuartas partes de la Tierra.
- Write the word *ocean* on a piece of chart paper and circle it. Use it as the center of a word web. Encourage the children to tell you what they know about oceans. It is fine if they mention inhabitants today, but they will focus on animal life tomorrow.
- Make sure the children list the following facts: the ocean and the sea are salty; seas are smaller than oceans; there are four oceans on Earth (the Pacific, the Atlantic, the Indian, and the Arctic); there are coral reefs in the oceans.

Another Way to Develop the Lesson

- Tell the children that you are going to play a listening game. Show them the chart on which you have written the first verse to "My Bonnie Lies Over the Ocean"/"Mi conejito flota en el océano." Tell them that first they will learn the song and then they will play the game.
- Teach "My Bonnie Lies Over the Ocean"/"Mi conejito flota en el océano." Point to the words as you sing the song. Ask a volunteer to show you the words in the first three lines that are the same. *Which word in the first three lines is different?*

  ¿Qué palabra en las primeras tres líneas es diferente?

  Tell the children that one reason the song is so easy to learn is because the lines are almost identical.
- Teach the second verse to the song and then play the game. Tell the children that they will have to listen carefully. Have them stand up and sit down every time they hear the word *bonnie*.

  Deben prestar atención. Cada vez que oigan la palabra conejito, *deben levantarse y sentarse.*

Practice

- Make a word card for *ocean*. Place it in the Writing Center and encourage the children to copy the word using sticks to write in a pan of damp sand.
- Let the children paint with a mixture of Epsom salts and water on black construction paper.
- Provide nature tapes of ocean sounds.
- Put large rocks in the water play table and let the children create a shoreline. Provide boats as well.
- Fill the Library Center with books about the ocean and encourage the children to browse the books.
- Give each child a bag and let him or her collect five items from around the classroom. Encourage the children to find as many items that float as possible. Let them experiment with their items.
- Encourage the children to find the ocean and coral reef in the Earth category on the *SRA Photo Library* software.

Preparation

- Gather Epsom salts.

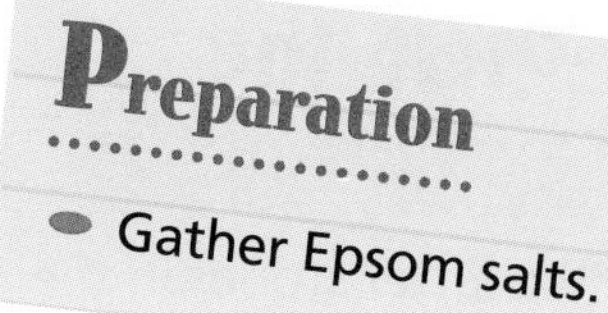

Scaffolding Strategies

More Help Ask the children questions about smaller bodies of water they may have seen, such as lakes and streams. *What did you see there? What did you do?*

¿Qué vieron allí? ¿Qué hicieron?

Extra Challenge Encourage the children to compare oceans and rivers or oceans and ponds, depending on their experiences.

Second Language Learners

Ask parents to send pictures of a trip to the seashore or objects from the shore (such as shells, sand, or starfish), or bring these items yourself. Using the pictures or objects as a guide, ask the children to talk about the seashore and the ocean. After each child has finished, ask questions for clarification and further detail, and encourage the other children to ask questions too. Use this discussion to develop the word web.

Anthology Support

"Row, Row, Row Your Boat"
"Rema, rema tu canoa"
"I Saw a Ship A-Sailing"
"Yo vi un barco navegando"
"I Love the Ocean"
"Amo el océano"

DAY 1

Letter Knowledge

English

- Read any of the letter stories in the *English Phonics Resource Guide*.

Spanish

- Introduce the letter *k* using the letter story "Katie" in the *Spanish Phonics Resource Guide.*

Suggested Reading

Oceans by Seymour Simon

Technology Support

Encourage the children to find the ocean animals in the Animal category on the *SRA Photo Library* software.

Reflect/Assess

- *How are oceans and seas different? How are they the same?*

  ¿En qué se diferencian los océanos y los mares? ¿En qué se parecen?
- *What is the most interesting thing you learned about the ocean?*

  ¿Qué fue lo mejor que aprendieron del océano?

Literacy Circle

Storytime 1

- Read *Fish Wish/Deseos de un pez*. Stop occasionally and let the children look at the wonderful sea creatures.

Storytime 2

- Read *The Zebra on the Zyder Zee/Una aventura en alta mar. How long do you think it took the zebra and his friends to cross the sea? Look on the map. Which sea might he have been crossing?*

  ¿Cuánto tiempo creen que le tomó a la cebra cruzar y sus amigos el mar? Miren el mapa. ¿Qué mar pudiera estar cruzando?

Content Connection

Science

Objective
To observe and describe properties of rocks, soil, and water

Vocabulary
ocean, salt water
océano, agua salada

Materials to Gather
funnel; small, clean, clear liter bottles (one per child); water; mineral oil; blue and green food coloring; plastic cups; salt; straws

Activity 1

- Help the children make wave machines. Show them how to use funnels to fill their bottles half full of water. Tell them to add eight drops of blue food coloring to each bottle. (You may want to add a few drops of green food coloring as well.) Help the children fill the rest of their bottles with mineral oil. Show them how to glue the lids on their bottles. Then let them rock the bottles back and forth to create waves.

Activity 2

- Invite the children to make an ocean in a cup. Have them each pour a cup of warm water into a plastic cup and add a teaspoon of salt. Tell them to stir their cups of water with straws and then touch the straws to their tongues. Warn them not to drink the water. Tell the children that this is what seawater tastes like and that it is not good to drink.

DAY 1

Objectives

- To put together puzzles of increasing complexity
- To start, use, and exit software programs

Vocabulary

side	lado
all shape names	nombres de todas las figuras

Materials

DLM Materials

- pattern blocks
- *Math Resource Guide*
  Building Straws
  Shape Set
  Shape Step/Paso de figuras
  Tangram Puzzles
  Pattern Block Puzzles (26–32)
  Estimating Jar
- *DLM Math* software
- *Four Baby Bumblebees* CD
- *Esta es mi tierra* CD
- *Teacher's Resource Anthology*
  "Counting Rhyme"
  "Pin uno"

Materials to Gather

- building blocks
- large blue sheet
- beach ball

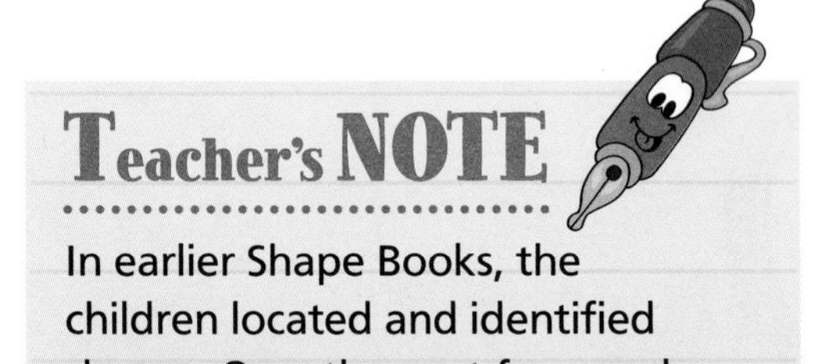

Teacher's NOTE

In earlier Shape Books, the children located and identified

MATH

Focus

- Say the "Counting Rhyme" or "Pin uno."

Develop

- Play Shape Step/Paso de figuras. Ask the children to touch a shape with 4 sides with their toes. Count the sides of shapes together. This activity will help the children correct any wrong choices they make.
- Gather the children around the computer. In Create-a-Scene, the children will pick a background and create a scene by putting shapes together. Show the children the special tools to magnify, shrink, break apart, and glue together shapes, and the color palette they can use to color them.
- This is the most complicated set of tools the children will use, but the most powerful for learning mathematics. Take your time introducing the tools, showing how they work, and discussing how they might be useful in combining shapes.
- In the second activity, Memory—Geometry, Level 5, the children match combinations of shapes.
- Remind them that these pictures and all the pictures and designs they make in the center go in their Shape Books.

Practice

- Encourage the children to play Shape Step/Paso de figuras.
- Invite children to make shapes with Building Straws or building blocks.
- Ask the children to choose and complete Pattern Block Puzzles.
- Have the children complete Tangram Puzzles.
- Encourage the children to record their estimates of the number of items in the Estimating Jar. Have them place their estimates in the box you prepared last week.
- Invite the children to work on Create-a-Scene (no level assigned).

Reflect/Assess

- *How did you figure out which parts of shapes are sides and which are corners?*
  ¿Cómo determinaron qué partes de figuras son lados y cuáles son esquinas?

Music and Movement

- Take a large blue sheet and a beach ball outside. Have the children stand around the perimeter of the sheet and hold it off the ground. Put a beach ball on the sheet. Encourage them to make waves with the sheet and bounce the ball on the "water."
- Sing "On the Good Ship Lollipop" from the *Four Baby Bumblebees* CD or sing "Esta es mi tierra" from the *Esta es mi tierra* CD.

Suggested Reading

Blue Sea by Robert Kalan
Across the Big Blue Sea: An Ocean Wildlife Book by Jakki Wood

Content Connection

Physical Development

Objectives
To explore moving in space
To begin to participate in group games involving movement

DLM Materials
Math Resource Guide
Shape Step/Paso de figuras
Making Music with Thomas Moore CD (optional)

Materials to Gather
ocean tape (optional), shapes from the math lesson, beanbags

Activity 1

- Invite the children to play Ocean Shape Step, a variation of Shape Step/Paso de figuras. Use the shapes you taped to the floor for the math lesson. Play a tape of ocean sounds or some music from the *Making Music with Thomas Moore* CD and have the children pretend to be fish swimming in the ocean.
- Ask them to swim to the shape that is called or to the attribute of the shape named (for example, "Swim to the shape that has 4 sides" or "Swim to a corner").

Activity 2

- Give the children beanbags and have them toss them onto the shapes taped to the floor as you call out attributes or shape names.

Reflect on the Day

- *What did you learn about oceans today?*
  ¿Qué aprendieron sobre los océanos hoy?
- *Which activity did you most enjoy? Why?*
  ¿Qué actividad disfrutaron más? ¿Por qué?

Home Connection

Send a note home to families letting them know that their child will need a shoe box for a project we will be doing next week.

Begin the Day

- Say "Counting Rhyme" or "Pin uno."
  Has anyone ever caught a fish?
  ¿Alguno de ustedes ha pescado un pez?
- Use one of the suggestions for Morning Circle in the front of this *Teacher's Edition.*

Objectives

- To refine and extend understanding of known words
- To link new learning experiences and vocabulary to what is already known about a topic

Vocabulary

fish	pez
starfish	estrella de mar
sea horse	caballito de mar

DLM Materials

- *Fish Wish/Deseos de un pez*
- Oral Language Development Card 67
- *SRA Photo Library* software
- *Teacher's Resource Anthology*
  "Counting Rhyme"
  "Pin uno"
  "Swimming, Swimming"/"Nadar y nadar"
  ocean card patterns
  "Fish"/"Pececitos"
  Ocean Concentration game
  "Fish Games"/"Juegos de peces"
  "Sammy the Rodeo Sea Horse"/
  "Omar, el caballito de mar"

Materials to Gather

- coat hanger tube
- construction paper
- star templates
- yarn sea horse and fish puzzles
- large clear sequins
- tweezers
- word cards

LITERACY

Focus

- Sing "Swimming, Swimming"/"Nadar y nadar."
- Tell the children that today the class is going to talk about fish and small ocean creatures, such as starfish and sea horses.
  Hoy vamos a hablar sobre los peces y las criaturas marinas pequeñas como las estrellas de mar y los caballitos de mar.

Develop

One Way to Develop the Lesson

- Show the fish, sea horse, and starfish from *Fish Wish/Deseos de un pez.* Ask if the children have ever seen any of these creatures.
  ¿Alguna vez han visto estas criaturas?
- Make a word web for ocean creatures. Ask the children to list creatures they know and creatures they learned about in *Fish Wish/Deseos de un pez.*
- Share some of the following facts about fish and sea horses with the children.
  - Fish come in all sizes. Fish breath though gills and will die if they are taken out of the water. They move by swishing their tails from side to side.
  - Sea horses look like tiny horses without legs. They have eyes that can move independently of each other. They use their tails like hands. They grow up to 8 inches long. (Demonstrate this with yarn.) The males give birth to the babies.

- Starfish are fish. They usually have five arms, but can have up to fifty. They are yellow, orange, pink, red, or variations thereof. If they lose an arm, they can grow a new one. They can be as small as 1/2 inch in diameter or as large as 3 feet. They are soft in the water but get brittle when they die. Display Oral Language Card 67. Encourage the children to discuss the starfish in the picture.
- Show the children the sea horse and the starfish in the Animals category on the *SRA Photo Library* software. Use the definitions of the creatures to provide additional information to the children.

Another Way to Develop the Lesson

- Read the poem "Fish"/"Pececitos." Tell the children that they are going to pretend to be fish. Go over the words slowly and ask a volunteer to demonstrate the movements.
- Read the poem a second time and have the children act out the words that describe the fish's movements.

Practice

- Place the *Fish Wish/Deseos de un pez* book and listening tape in the Listening Center.
- Add a word card for *fish* to your ocean word cards. Encourage the children to use tweezers to move clear sequin scales to cover the letters.
- Provide large clear sequins and a fish shape. Encourage the children to glue the sequins on the fish to make scales.
- Provide a fishing pole made from a coat hanger tube with a yarn line and attached magnet. Provide fish with alphabet letters on them. Encourage the children to catch the fish. After they have caught a few fish, have them see if they can make a word with the letters they caught.
- Invite the children to play the Ocean Concentration game.
- Encourage the children to work on sea horse and fish puzzles.
- Give the children star templates to trace to make starfish. Have them color their starfish yellow, red, pink, or orange.
- Have the children find the starfish and sea horse in the Animal category on the *SRA Photo Library* software.

Preparation

- Make two photocopies of the ocean card patterns. Color them, cut them out, and laminate them to make an Ocean Concentration game.
- Make enlarged copies of the fish and the sea horse ocean card patterns. Color them, cut them out, laminate them, and cut them into puzzle pieces.
- Cut fish out of construction paper. Write an alphabet letter on each fish. Put a paper clip on the nose of each fish.
- Add *fish* to the word cards.

Scaffolding Strategies

More Help Read books about sea animals to the children.

Extra Challenge Encourage the children to compare the life of a goldfish in a fishbowl with that of an ocean fish.

Second Language Learners

Encourage the children to name the ocean creatures and objects they uncover as they play Ocean Concentration. This will help them to recall the location of the objects on the next trial and will promote vocabulary development.

DAY 2

Letter Knowledge

English

- Read selections from the *SRA Alphabet Book.*

Spanish

- Read "Katia de Kenia" in *Los niños alfabéticos.*

Suggested Reading

Swimmy by Leo Lionni
Rainbow Fish by Marcus Pfister
Nadarín by Leo Lionni
Turquesita by Silvia Dubovoy

Anthology Support

"Pescadito lindo"
"Five Little Fishes Swimming in the Sea"
"Cinco pecicitos nadando en el mar"

Reflect/Assess

- *How are fish and sea horses alike? How are they different?*
  ¿En qué se parecen los peces y los caballitos de mar? ¿En qué se diferencian?
- *What do you think it would be like to live in the ocean?*
  ¿Cómo creen que sería vivir en el océano?

Literacy Circle

Storytime 1

- Read the listening story "Fish Games"/"Juegos de peces." *Which of the games mentioned in the story are similar to games you like to play?*
  ¿Cuáles de los juegos mencionados en el cuento son parecidos a los juegos que les gusta jugar?

Storytime 2

- Read the listening story "Sammy the Rodeo Sea Horse"/"Omar, el caballito de mar." *What is Sammy's favorite thing to do? Do you think Sammy would make a good rodeo horse?*
  ¿Qué es lo que más le gusta hacer a Omar? ¿Creen que Omar sería un buen caballo de rodeo?

Content Connection

Health and Safety/Science

Objectives

To know about safe behavior around bodies of water

To begin to perform simple investigations

Materials to Gather

corks with nails through the centers, tub for water, washers

Vocabulary

sink, float, safety

hundir, flotar, seguridad

Activity 1

- Discuss water safety with the children. Help them make a list of safe behavior around bodies of water. Be sure your list includes things such as not going near water without adult supervision, not running on wet surfaces, and entering the water feet first.

Activity 2

- Provide a tub of water and several corks that have small nails driven through their centers. Encourage the children to stack washers on the nails until the corks sink.
- Discuss what causes the cork to sink.

DAY 2

Objectives

- To begin to recognize, describe, and name shapes
- To begin to investigate and predict the results of putting together two or more shapes

Vocabulary

all shape names — nombres de todas las figuras

DLM Materials

- pattern blocks
- *Math Resource Guide*
  Snapshots: Shape Parts version/ Instantáneas: versión partes de figuras
  Shape Transparencies
- See Day 1
- *DLM Math* software
- *Teacher's Resource Anthology*
  Duck, Duck, Goose/Pato, pato, ganso

Materials to Gather

- overhead projector
- sheets of acetate (transparencies)
- white construction paper

Preparation

- Use the first page of the Shape Transparencies to cut shapes from sheets of acetate (transparency paper). Cut the shapes apart *near* the black lines, not on them. Use the other pages as models for the children.

MATH

Focus

- Play Snapshots: Shape Parts version/Instantáneas: versión partes de figuras. Give the children a small set of Building Straws. Secretly make a shape, such as a rectangle, and cover it. Tell them to watch carefully and make a snapshot in their heads of what they see.
- Show your straw shape for 2 seconds. Have the children build the same shape. Show your shape for 2 more seconds. Have them check their shapes, changing them if necessary. Reveal your shape and have them describe what they saw and how they built their own. Repeat with other shapes.

Develop

- Introduce the Shape Transparencies by showing the children how they can combine the shapes to make many different designs by placing transparencies on top of one another on white paper. You may want to demonstrate on the overhead projector so it will be easier for all the children to see. This activity is optional and is not recorded for the Shape Books.
- Review the use of the tools in Create-a-Scene.

Practice

- Invite the children to combine shapes using the Shape Transparencies. Have them work on white paper or an overhead projector.
- Encourage the children to play Shape Step/Paso de figuras.
- Invite the children to make shapes from parts using the Building Straws or building blocks.
- Ask the children to choose and complete Pattern Block Puzzles.
- Have the children complete Tangram Puzzles.
- Encourage the children to record their estimates of the number of items in the Estimating Jar. Have them place their estimates in the box you prepared last week.

Reflect/Assess

- *How are you using the computer tools to make your pictures in Create-a-Scene?*

  ¿Cómo usan las herramientas de computadora para hacer dibujos en Create-a-Scene?
- *How did you figure out which Building Straws to use to make the snapshot shapes?*

  ¿Cómo determinaron cuáles pajitas de construcción usar para hacer las figuras instantáneas?

Music and Movement

- Play Fish, Fish, Starfish/Pez, pez, estrella de mar as you would Duck, Duck, Goose/Pato, pato, ganso.
- Invite the children to swim like fish to a variety of tempos of music. Have them swim like happy fish, grumpy fish, frightened fish, and tired fish.

Content Connection

Fine Arts

Objective
To participate in classroom music activities

Vocabulary
ocean life
vida marina

DLM Materials
Fish Wish/Deseos de un pez
Math Resource Guide
Building Straws

Materials to Gather
books showing dancers

Activity 1

- Teach the children a few dance positions such as first through fifth positions, or an arabesque. Discuss the angles of the body in these positions.

Activity 2

- Show the children the illustrations in *Fish Wish/Deseos de un pez*. Encourage them to identify shapes that make up ocean life.
- Invite them to re-create the shapes with Building Straws.

Suggested Reading

Color Dance by Ann Jonas
How Can You Dance? by Rick Walton
Song and Dance Man by Karen Ackerman
The Ballet Book: The Young Performer's Guide to Classical Dance (National Ballet School)

What Research Suggests

Creating a *scene* and a context for learning helps children remember what they have learned.

Reflect on the Day

- *What activity did you like best today?*

  ¿Qué actividad les gustó más hoy?
- *What can you share with your family about fish and sea horses?*

  ¿Qué pueden compartir con su familia sobre los peces y los caballitos de mar?

Begin the Day

- Sing "My Bonnie Lies Over the Ocean"/"Mi conejito flota en el océano." Stand and then sit again when the word *bonnie* is said.
- Use one of the suggestions for Morning Circle in the front of this *Teacher's Edition.*

Objectives

- To show appreciation of repetitive language patterns
- To connect information and events in books to real-life experiences

Vocabulary

whales	ballenas
dolphins	delfines

DLM Materials

- *Fish Wish/ Deseos de un pez*
- *Blue Cat/Gato azul*
- *SRA Photo Library* software
- *Teacher's Resource Anthology*
  "My Bonnie Lies Over the Ocean"/"Mi conejito flota en el océano"
  "Swimming, Swimming"/"Nadar y nadar"
  Ocean Concentration game
  ocean patterns (dolphin, whale)
  "Going on a Whale Watch"/"Vamos a mirar ballenas"
  "Five Dancing Dolphins"/"Cinco delfines bailarines"
  play dough

Materials to Gather

- dolphin and whale puzzles
- word cards
- tracing paper
- shallow box
- magnets
- gray tempera paint
- yarn

LITERACY

Focus

- Sing "Swimming, Swimming"/"Nadar y nadar."
- Tell the children that today they will discuss whales and dolphins.

Develop

One Way to Develop the Lesson

- Show the whale and the dolphins from the book *Fish Wish/Deseos de un pez.* Ask if the children have seen either of these creatures in real life.
  ¿Alguna vez han visto alguna de estas criaturas?
- Make a Venn diagram for dolphins and whales. Use the information that the children know about these animals and the facts below to fill in the diagram.
- Whales are mammals. They are among the most intelligent of all creatures. They have no sense of taste or smell and they have very poor eyesight. A whale experiences its surroundings by using touch and sound. Unlike fish, whales have lungs and must come to the surface to breath. Their tail fins move up and down instead of side to side like a fish. The blue whale is the largest living animal. It can measure up to 100 feet long.
- Dolphins are small whales. They are also mammals and are highly intelligent. The have lungs like the whale and must come to the surface to breathe. Dolphins range in size from 4 feet to 30 feet. Demonstrate 30 feet with a piece of yarn.

Another Way to Develop the Lesson

- Tell the children that you are going to read them a fanciful story about a whale and several other animals. Tell them that this is a book that they can read with you.
- Read *Blue Cat/Gato azul.* Encourage the children to chime in as soon as they pick up the pattern. *Is this book fiction or nonfiction? Does any one remember what a nonfiction book is? Which animals in the book belong in the ocean and which ones do not belong there? Were you surprised by the ending of the story? Could this story actually happen?*

  ¿Este libro es ficción o no ficción? ¿Alguien recuerda qué es un libro de no ficción? ¿Cuáles animales del libro pertenecen al mar y cuáles no? ¿Les sorprendió el final del cuento? ¿Este cuento podría realmente suceder?
- Read the book a second time, then let the children read it to you.

Practice

- Place the *Blue Cat/Gato Azul* book and listening tape in the Listening Center.
- Invite the children to play the Ocean Concentration game.
- Encourage the children to work the dolphin and whale puzzles.
- Add *dolphin* and *whale* to your word cards. Let the children use tracing paper to trace the names.
- Have the children find the dolphin and whale in the Animal category on the *SRA Photo Library* software.
- Draw a reef maze on the bottom of a box. Make a copy of the whale in the ocean card patterns and glue a magnet on the back of it. Invite the children to hold a second magnet beneath the box to guide the whale through the maze.
- Provide gray paint and encourage the children to paint whales and dolphins.

Preparation

- Make the flannel board story.
- Make enlarged copies of the dolphin and whale from the ocean card patterns. Color them, cut them out, and laminate them. Cut them into puzzle pieces.
- Add *dolphin* and *whale* to the word cards.
- Draw a coral reef maze on the bottom of a shallow box. Copy the whale from the ocean card patterns. Cut it out and glue a magnet to the back of it.

Scaffolding Strategies

More Help Ask the children about movies they may have seen about dolphins and/or whales. Read them stories about dolphins and whales.

Extra Challenge Ask the children why they think there are no animals as large as whales on land.

Second Language Learners

Tell the "Five Dancing Dolphins"/ "Cinco delfines bailarines" flannel board story twice. First pantomime each activity in the story. Children can then pantomime the actions while you describe what they are doing. Be sure to use language from the story. Then tell the story using the flannel board figures. Place the flannel board and figures in a learning center, and encourage children to tell the story alone or with a friend. Note the language used.

DAY 3

Letter Knowledge

English

- Invite the children to shape letters with play dough.

Spanish

- Invite the children to shape the letter *k* with play dough.

Suggested Reading

Whales by Seymour Simon
Going on a Whale Watch by Bruce McMillan
Qué hay bajo el océano by Janet Palazzo-Craig
Angelita, la ballena pequeñita by Lolo Rico

Anthology Support

"There's a Hole in the Middle of the Sea"
"Hay un hueco en el medio del mar"
"A Sailor Went to Sea"

Reflect/Assess

- *Do you think a whale would fit in a swimming pool? Why? Why not?*
  ¿Creen que una ballena cabría en una piscina? ¿Por qué sí o por qué no?
- *What do whales and dolphins have in common with fish?*
  ¿En qué se parecen las ballenas y los delfines a los peces?

Literacy Circle

Storytime 1

- Invite the children to participate in the action rhyme "Going on a Whale Watch"/"Vamos a mirar ballenas." *Would you like to go on a whale watch? Why? Why not?*
  ¿Les gustaría ir a mirar ballenas? ¿Por qué sí o por qué no?

Storytime 2

- Present the "Five Dancing Dolphins"/"Cinco delfines bailarines" flannel board story. *If the dolphins called someone else to join them, who do you think it might be?*
  Si los delfines llamaran a alguien más para que se unieran a ellos, ¿quién creen que sea?
- Write a new verse for the story.

Content Connection

Math/Science

Objectives

To begin to make size comparisons between objects

To use simple measuring devices to learn about objects and organisms

Vocabulary

longer, longest

más largo, el (la) más largo(a)

Materials to Gather

yarn (from Literacy lesson)

Activity 1

- Have the children stretch the yarn on the playground to demonstrate the length of a dolphin. Have all the children stand along the yarn holding hands. *Which is longer, their line or the yarn?*

  ¿Cuál es más largo, su línea o el estambre?

Activity 2

- Compare yarn that represents the whale's length to the yarn that represents the dolphin's length. *Which is longer?*

  ¿Cuál es más largo?

DAY 3

Objectives

- To put together puzzles of increasing complexity
- To begin to recognize when a shape's position or orientation has changed

Vocabulary

angle	ángulo
length	longitud, largo
puzzle	rompecabezas
line	línea, recta
horizontal	horizontal
vertical	vertical
slanted	inclinada
all shape names	nombres de todas las figuras

DLM Materials

- *Math Resource Guide*
  Shape Set
  2 Estimating Jars
- See Days 1 and 2
- *DLM Math* software
- *Teacher's Resource Anthology*
  Pin the Nose on the Pumpkin/Pega la nariz en la calabaza
  Red Rover/Pirata rojo

Materials to Gather

- sheets of acetate (transparencies)
- white construction paper
- See Days 1 and 2

Preparation

- Make a second Estimating Jar. Place 10 objects identical to those in the original Estimating Jar.

MATH

Focus

- Read and discuss the children's recorded estimates of how many items there are in the Estimating Jar. Show the identical jar and, along with the children, count 5 identical objects into that jar. Hold up both jars so children can compare them. Let the children identify the jar they believe has more in it.
- Count out 5 more objects (i.e., start counting at 6) into the identical jar and compare again. Tell them that they will make new estimates today.
- Play Shape Step/Paso de figuras focusing on rectangles.

Develop

- Teach the children to make Body Shapes/Figuras corporales. Have them make squares with their bodies. Encourage them to lie down with friends to make the shapes or to get into positions that require using their arms, hands, and fingers. They can make a rectangle by using their arms and hands or by using their thumbs and pointer fingers.
- Challenge them to make differently shaped rectangles, such as a longer rectangles. They might do it with their own bodies, or join with friends.
- Challenge the children to make a shape like each shape in the Shape Set. They can use these shapes as models.

Practice

- Invite the children to combine shapes using the Shape Transparencies. Give them a sheet of white paper to work on or allow them to work on an overhead projector.
- Have the children continue to work on the Practice activities from Day 1.
- Invite the children to work on Create-a-Scene (no level assigned) and Memory—Geometry, Level 5. To help children think of ideas, lay out physical shapes next to the computer for them to use.

Reflect/Assess

- *How did you figure out how to make a rectangle with your body?*
  ¿Cómo determinaron cómo hacer un rectángulo con su cuerpo?
- *How do you know what shapes to step on that are not rectangles?*
  ¿Cómo saben qué figuras pisar que no sean rectángulos?

Music and Movement

- Play Pin the Tail on the Whale/Ponle la cola a la ballena as you would Pin the Nose on the Pumpkin/Pega la nariz en la calabaza
- Play Blue Whale/Ballena azul as you would Red Rover/Pirata rojo.

Suggested Reading

The Sea by Marie Aubinais
Hello Fish: Visiting the Coral Reef by Sylvia A. Earle

Content Connection

Science

Objectives

To describe properties of objects and characteristics of living things
To begin to use scientific words and phrases to describe objects, events, and living things

DLM Materials

SRA Photo Library software
Teacher's Resource Anthology
ocean card patterns

Materials to Gather

finger paint

Activity 1

- Show the pictures of the ocean animals on the *SRA Photo Library* software. Have the children look at 2 animals, a large one and a small one, and ask the children to estimate how many times bigger one animal is than the other. Ask them how many sharks it would take in a line to be as long as the whale.

Activity 2

- Make slightly enlarged copies of the fish in the ocean card patterns and give 1 to each child. Have them estimate how many thumbprints (scales) they can make inside the fish. Give the children finger paint and let them test their estimates.

Reflect on the Day

- *What did you learn about whales and dolphins today? How are they alike? How are they different?*
  ¿Qué aprendieron sobre las ballenas y los delfines hoy? ¿En qué se parecen? ¿En qué se diferencian?
- *What can you tell your family about whales and dolphins?*
  ¿Qué le pueden decir a su familia sobre las ballenas y los delfines?

Begin the Day

- Read "Octopus." Discuss the funny use of language and help the children see the humor.

  Tell me, O Octopus, I begs,
  Is those things arms, or is they legs?
  I marvel at thee, Octopus;
  If I were thou, I'd call me Us.
- Use one of the suggestions for Morning Circle in the front of this *Teacher's Edition.*

Objectives

- To ask questions and make comments related to the current topic of discussion
- To use sentences of increasing length (three or more words) and grammatical complexity in everyday speech

Vocabulary

octopus pulpo

DLM Materials

- *Fish Wish/Deseos de un pez*
- *SRA Book of Animals/SRA El libro de los animales*
- *SRA Photo Library* software
- *Teacher's Resource Anthology*
  "Swimming, Swimming"/"Nadar y nadar"
  Ocean Concentration game
  ocean card patterns (octopus)

Materials to Gather

- octopus puzzles
- magnets
- tracing paper
- colored glue in a squirt bottle
- squirt bottles
- suction cups
- objects to pick up with suction cups
- basters
- word cards
- chart paper

Focus

- Sing "Swimming, Swimming"/"Nadar y nadar."
- Tell the children that today they will learn about octopuses.

Develop

One Way to Develop the Lesson

- Show the picture of the octopus in *Fish Wish/Deseos de un pez.* Ask if any of the children have seen an octopus before. If so, where?

  ¿Alguno de ustedes ha visto un pulpo anteriormente? ¿Dónde?
- Let the children help make a list on chart paper of things they have learned this week about sea creatures that would apply to the octopus.
- Explain that the octopus has eight "arms," called tentacles, and that the bottom of each arm is lined with suction cups that help the octopus hold on to objects.
- Tell the children that octopuses have no bones, just a very thick skin that gives them their body shape. Most octopuses are the size of a fist. However, the largest octopus can measure 28 feet across from the tip of one tentacle to the tip of the opposing tentacle.
- Encourage each child to say one thing that amazes him or her about the octopus.

Another Way to Develop the Lesson

- Discuss what it would be like to have eight arms. *What would you do with eight arms?*

  ¿Qué harían con ocho brazos?
- Demonstrate having eight arms. Ask four children to crouch back-to-back to form a small circle. Ask them to wave their eight arms around and pretend to be an octopus. Then have the children lock their arms together at the elbow and try to walk using their eight legs. *What happens?*

  ¿Qué sucede?

Practice

- Place the *Fish Wish/Deseos de un pez* book and listening tape in the Listening Center.
- Invite the children to play the Ocean Concentration game.
- Encourage the children to work the octopus puzzles.
- Add *octopus* to your word cards. Let the children copy the word using tracing paper, then have them go over their letters with colored glue in a squirt bottle.
- In the Water and Sand Center, provide suction cups and items that the children can pick up using the suctions cups. Also provide squirt bottles and basters so the children can explore the force of the water.
- Take the children outdoors. Draw a circle that is 28 feet in diameter. Invite the children to try to fill the circle. They can stand in it, sit in it, or even lie in it. Can they fill it?
- Have the children find the octopus in the Animals category on the *SRA Photo Library* software.
- Use the reef maze you created yesterday with the octopus today.

Preparation

- Make enlarged copies of the octopus from the ocean card patterns. Color them, cut them out, laminate them, and cut them into puzzle pieces.
- Make a copy of the octopus from the ocean card patterns. Cut it out and glue a magnet to the back of it.
- Add *octopus* to your word cards.

Scaffolding Strategies

More Help Read books about octopuses to the children.

Extra Challenge Encourage the children to think of another animal that has eight legs. *How are spiders and octopuses alike? How are they different?*

¿En qué se parecen las arañas y los pulpos? ¿En qué se diferencian?

Second Language Learners

Compare pictures of an octopus and a spider, or provide models of the animals for description and comparison. If children describe the characteristic of only one of the animals, ask: *Does the octopus have many legs, as the spider does (or vice versa)? Yes? Oh, then the octopus AND the spider have many legs. Let's count them.* If they point out a difference, reply: *Oh, you say the octopus has a BIG head, BUT the spider has a LITTLE head.* Stress key vocabulary to

DAY 4

Letter Knowledge

English

- Invite the children to make letters with their bodies. Use the Think, Pair, Share/Piensa, aparea, comparte game with this activity.

Spanish

- Invite the children to make the letter *k* with their bodies. Use the Think, Pair, Share/Piensa, aparea, comparte game with this activity.

Suggested Reading

My Very Own Octopus by Bernard Most
Octopus by Carol Carrick

Anthology Support

"There's a Hole in the Middle of the Sea"
"Hay un hueco en el medio del mar"
"A Sailor Went to Sea"
"Pescadito lindo"

Reflect/Assess

- *What do you like best about octopuses?*
  ¿Qué les gusta más sobre los pulpos?
- *Would you like to have eight arms? How would you use them?*
  ¿Les gustaría tener ocho brazos? ¿Cómo los usarían?

Literacy Circle

Storytime 1

- Read "The Hermit Crab"/"El cangrejo ermitaño" from the *SRA Book of Animals/SRA El libro de los animales. How are hermit crabs different from the octopus? Are the octopus and the hermit crab alike in any way?*
  ¿En qué se diferencian los ermitaños de los pulpos? ¿Los pulpos y los ermitaños se parecen de alguna manera?

Storytime 2

- Reread *Fish Wish/Deseos de un pez*. Read some of the factual information in the back of the book. *How many of the animals mentioned in the back of the book have we studied this week?*
  ¿Cuántos de los animales nombrados en la parte posterior del libro hemos estudiado esta semana?

Content Connection

Science

Objectives
To begin to use scientific words and phrases to describe objects, events, and living things
To begin to perform simple investigations

Vocabulary
thrust
empujar, impeler

Materials to Gather
balloons, straw, yarn or string, tape

Activity 1
- Explain that an octopus can only move backwards. It moves by drawing water into its body and squeezing it out through an opening under its head. To demonstrate, fill a balloon with air and let go of it. The balloon will fly around the room, propelled by air shooting out of it. Explain to the children that an octopus can move slower than the balloon. Make sure the children handle balloons in a safe manner.

Activity 2
- To help children better understand thrust, hang a piece of string or yarn from the ceiling to the floor. Blow up a balloon and put a clamp on the opening. Tape a straw to the side of the balloon and string the yarn through the straw. Remove the clamp and watch the balloon shoot upward.

DAY 4

Objectives

- To begin to recognize, describe, and name shapes
- To put together puzzles of increasing complexity

Vocabulary

angle	ángulo
length	longitud, largo
puzzle	rompecabezas
line	línea, recta
horizontal	horizontal
vertical	vertical
slanted	inclinada
all shape names	nombres de todas las figuras

DLM Materials

- Rafita and Pepita/Rafita y Pepita puppets
- *Math Resource Guide*
  Shape Set
- See Days 1 and 2
- *DLM Math* software
- *Teacher's Resource Anthology*
  One Elephant/Un elefante

Materials to Gather

- See Days 1 and 2

MATH

Focus

- Ask the children to use their bodies to make simple shapes that replicate a shape you hold up from the Shape Set. Ask them to explain how they made the sides and angles they needed to make the shapes.

Develop

- Play Shape Step/Paso de figuras with Rafita and Pepita/Rafita y Pepita. Have one of the puppets confuse the side of a trapezoid with its corner. Ask the children to help the puppet by explaining what is a side and what is a corner.
- Next, have the other puppet step on shapes that are close to the right shape, but not correct. Help the children describe the specific attribute that confused the puppet.

Practice

- Invite the children to combine shapes using the Shape Transparencies.
- Have the children continue to work on the Practice activities from Day 1.
- Call attention to situations that naturally occur during the day when children might see shapes in body positions. For example, when children place their hands on their hips, the result is a triangle. When the children are sitting crossed-legged on the floor, their legs might make overlapping triangles.
- Invite the children to work on Create-a-Scene (no level assigned) and Memory—Geometry, Level 5.

Reflect/Assess

- *How can you explain to Rafita and Pepita/Rafita y Pepita why this shape* (show a trapezoid) *is not a rectangle?*

  ¿Cómo pueden explicarles a Rafita y Pepita/Rafita and Pepita por qué esta figura (show a trapezoid) *no es un rectángulo?*

Content Connection

Science

Objectives

To show an interest in investigating unfamiliar objects, organisms, and phenomena

To begin to perform simple investigations

Materials to Gather

yarn

Activity 1

- Have the children make shapes using the 30-foot piece of yarn from Day 3. Have 4 volunteers stand up. While holding a section of the yarn, have them stand in the shape of a square, adjusting the yarn as they move. Next, have them form a rectangle. Have 1 volunteer let go of the yarn while the others reposition themselves to form a triangle. Ask the children to evaluate each of the shapes by having them name the shapes and their corresponding number of sides. Ask them to explain the difference between the rectangle and the square.

Activity 2

- Show the children the 30-foot piece of yarn you used yesterday to represent the length of a large dolphin and a 4-foot piece of yarn you cut today to represent the length of a small dolphin. Ask the children to estimate how many small dolphins it would take to equal the length of the large dolphin. Check their estimates.

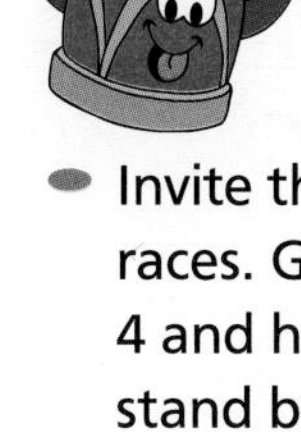

Music and Movement

- Invite the children to hold octopus races. Group the children into sets of 4 and have them lock arms as they stand back-to-back in a small circle. Mark off a starting line and a line where the octopuses must change direction and return to the starting line. This way, half of the members of each octopus group will experience moving backwards as the octopus does.
- Play One Octopus/Un pulpo as you would One Elephant/Un elefante. Instead of a spider web, have them play on a coral reef.

Suggested Reading

Somewhere in the Ocean by Jennifer Ward

Reflect on the Day

- *What was your favorite activity today?*

  ¿Cuál fue su actividad favorita hoy?
- *What surprised you most about octopuses?*

  ¿Qué les sorprendió más sobre los pulpos?

Home Connection

Send home a take-home book pack with four children.

Begin the Day

- Read "I Love the Ocean"/"Amo el océano."
- Use one of the suggestions for Morning Circle offered in the front of this *Teacher's Edition.*

Objectives

- To become increasingly sensitive to the sounds of spoken words
- To begin to attend to the beginning sounds in familiar words by identifying that the pronunciations of several words all begin the same way

Vocabulary

sand	arena
jewelry	joyas
sponges	esponjas
seashells	conchas
seaweed	algas

DLM Materials

- *Teacher's Resource Anthology*
  "I Love the Ocean"/"Amo el océano"
  "Swimming, Swimming"/"Nadar y nadar"
  "Sister Susie"
  "Going for a Swim"/"Voy a nadar"
  "Summer at the Beach"/"Verano en la playa"
  ocean card patterns

Materials to Gather

- ocean puzzles
- seashells
- fishing game (Day 2)
- sponges
- word cards
- collection of items found in the sea
- chart paper
- paint

LITERACY

Focus

- Sing "Swimming, Swimming"/"Nadar y nadar."
- Tell the children that today they will discuss gifts that come from the ocean and ways people enjoy the ocean.
  Hoy vamos a hablar de los regalos que provienen del océano y también sobre cómo disfrutamos del océano.

Develop

One Way to Develop the Lesson

- Discuss the many gifts people get from the sea. Show any of the following things: a natural sponge, a piece of coral, a shell or pearl necklace or another piece of jewelry, a shaker of salt, something made from sand, a can of oil, and a fish (construction paper cutout). Talk about each of the items and let the children describe how the items are used.
- Discuss the fact that fish are the primary food source for some people in the world.
- Discuss the pleasure people feel when swimming and boating. Many people enjoy walking on the beach and listening to the waves.
- Have the children make a list of gifts from the sea, such as shells, sponges, food, and sand.

Another Way to Develop the Lesson

- Present the "Sister Susie" tongue twister.
- Ask the children to find the words that start with the same letter. Underline them as the children point them out. Ask if anyone remembers what it is called when several words in a row start with the same letter sound. (alliteration)

  Busquen palabras que empiecen con la misma letra. ¿Quién recuerda cómo decimos cuando varias palabras seguidas comienzan con la misma letra?
- Remind the children that shells are gifts from the sea.

Practice

- Encourage the children to work all of the puzzles you have used this week.
- Let the children copy the word cards from the week in a tray of damp sand, using craft sticks as writing instruments.
- Put out the fishing game you made on Day 2.
- Encourage the children to draw pictures of their favorite gifts from the sea.
- Place seashells in the water table and encourage the children to wash them.
- Invite the children to sponge paint or to use sponges to wash classroom tables. Remind the children that sponges are gifts from the sea.

Preparation

- Write the words to the "Sister Susie" tongue twister on chart paper.

Second Language Learners

Practice alliterative tongue twisters using pictures of a hermit crab. Speak slowly and pantomime or point to the corresponding pictures as you say the tongue twister. Stress the initial sounds as you say them. Then encourage children to repeat the sentences with you several times. Some may then want to try the sentence on their own.
English: The crab climbs into a cozy conch and curls up for a nap.
Spanish: La concha es la casa del cangrejo. ¡Qué cosa!

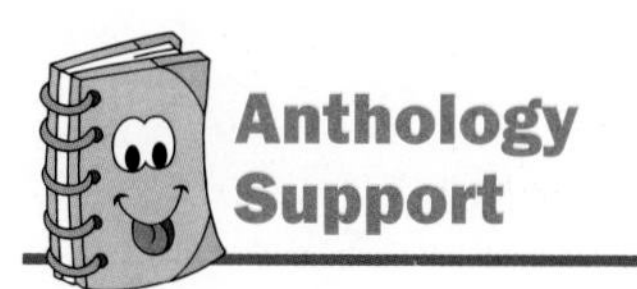

Anthology Support

"Five Little Fishes Swimming in the Sea"
"Cinco pececitos nadando en el mar"
"Fish"
"Pececitos"
"Los pececitos"

DAY 5

Letter Knowledge

English/Spanish

- Invite the children to find and circle a specific letter in newspapers and magazines.

Suggested Reading

Fish Is Fish by Leo Lionni
Coral Reef by Norman S. Barrett
El barco de Camila by Allen Morgan
Dentro del arrecife de coral by Katy Muzik

Reflect/Assess

- *Which of the gifts from the ocean do you like best?*
  ¿Cuál de los regalos del océano creen que es el mejor?
- *What will you look for the next time you go to the beach?*
  ¿Qué buscarán la próxima vez que vayan a la playa?

Literacy Circle

Storytime 1

- Invite the children to participate in the action rhyme "Going for a Swim"/"Voy a nadar."

Storytime 2

- Read the listening story "Summer at the Beach"/"Verano en la playa" or "I Love the Ocean"/"Amo el océano." *What is your favorite thing about the ocean?*
  ¿Qué es lo que más les gusta del océano?

Content Connection

Personal and Social Development/Fine Art

Objectives

To begin to share and cooperate with others in group activities
To begin to show interest in the artwork of others

Materials to Gather

white butcher paper, seashells, green tissue paper, construction paper, fine sand, tempera paint (light blue and other colors), powdered drink mix, sponges, tablespoon

Activity 1

- Make an underwater mural on white butcher paper that you have lightly washed in blue tempera paint and water. Give the children sponges to dip into the tempera paint and use to make coral formations. Provide shells to glue on and strips of green tissue paper to attach as seaweed. Encourage the children to draw some of the sea creatures they have learned about this week.

Activity 2

- Put three tablespoons of fine sand into each of several small containers (salt shakers work well). Blend one teaspoon of powdered drink mix into each container of sand. Let the children squeeze glue onto construction paper. While the glue is still wet, have them pour or shake out the sand, one color at a time. Shake off the excess sand and let the paintings dry.

MATH

Objectives

- To put together puzzles of increasing complexity
- To follow basic oral or pictorial cues for operating programs successfully

Vocabulary

angle	ángulo
length	longitud, largo
puzzle	rompecabezas
line	línea, recta
all shape names	nombres de todas las figuras

DLM Materials

- *Math Resource Guide* Snapshots: Shape Parts version/ Instantáneas: versión partes de figuras
- See Days 1 and 2
- *DLM Math* software
- *Four Baby Bumblebees* CD
- *Esta es mi tierra* CD

Materials to Gather

- See Days 1 and 2
- large blue sheet
- beach ball

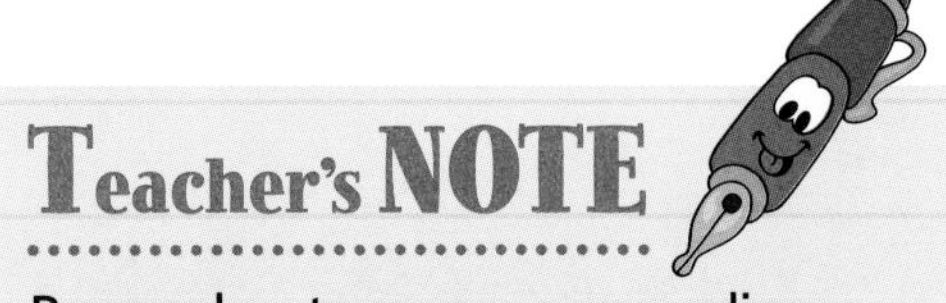

Remember to save any recordings the children have made for the Shape Books.

Focus

- Read and discuss the children's recorded estimates of how many items there are in the Estimating Jar. Dump the objects and count them to check.
- Compare the children's first estimates with those after the benchmarks were shown. Discuss with the children how their estimates changed. Congratulate them for doing a great job of estimating.
- Play Snapshots: Shape Parts version/Instantáneas: versión partes de figuras. Give the children a small set of Building Straws. Challenge them to copy your trapezoid or other shapes after you show it for only 2 seconds. Challenge them to make 1 of each of the shapes from the Shape Set.

Develop

- Have several children share a favorite puzzle they completed or a favorite shape they made from parts.
- Complete a computer task with the children. Discuss the different shapes in the pictures and how to solve the puzzle. Emphasize how and why the shapes fit.

Practice

- Invite the children to combine shapes using the Shape Transparencies.
- Encourage the children to play Shape Step/Paso de figuras with each other.
- Invite the children to make shapes from parts using the Building Straws or building blocks.
- Ask the children to choose and complete Pattern Block Puzzles.
- Have the children complete Tangram Puzzles.
- Invite the children to work on Create-a-Scene (no level assigned) and Memory—Geometry, Level 5. Ask the children if the combinations of shapes in Memory—Geometry, Level 5 help them think of good combinations for their work with Create-a-Scene.

Reflect/Assess

- *How did you know which straw or block to use to make the shape you made?*
  ¿Cómo supieron qué pajita o bloque usar para hacer la figura que hicieron?
- *How did you figure out how to make a whole picture with the shapes and tools?*
  ¿Cómo determinaron cómo hacer un dibujo completo con las figuras y herramientas?

Music and Movement

- Take a large blue sheet and a beach ball outdoors. Invite the children to stand around the perimeter of the sheet and hold it off the ground. Put a beach ball on the sheet. Have the children make waves with the sheet and bounce the ball on the "water."
- Sing "On the Good Ship Lollipop" from the *Four Baby Bumblebees* CD or sing "Esta es mi tierra" from the *Esta es mi tierra* CD.

Content Connection

Fine Arts

Objective
To use a variety of materials to create original work

Materials to Gather
seashells, sandpaper, glue, poster board, crayons

Activity 1

- Encourage the children to take a close look at a seashell. What geometric shapes do they see? What patterns do they see?
- Invite the children to arrange the seashells into designs and glue them to a piece of lightweight poster board.

Activity 2

- Cut geometric shapes out of sandpaper and let the children make crayon rubbings of the shapes. Discuss the origin of sandpaper.
- Encourage the children to put shapes together.

Suggested Reading

Look Again! by Tana Hoban

Reflect on the Day

- *What have you learned about the ocean this week?*
  ¿Qué aprendieron sobre el océano esta semana?
- *Which activity this week did you most enjoy? Why?*
  ¿Qué actividad disfrutaron más esta semana? ¿Por qué?

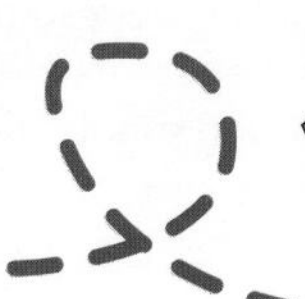

Home Connection

Remind families that their children will need a shoe box by Thursday of next week.

Looking Ahead

Connecting to the Theme: Big Things

Expanding the concept of opposites, the lessons in this theme encourage the children to think about and examine objects using large size as the determining attribute. The lesson also helps the children develop their critical thinking skills by leading them to realize that sometimes knowing what something *is not* allows us to better understand something about what it *is*.

	Objectives	DLM Materials	Materials to Gather
DAY 1	To enjoy listening to and responding to books To listen for different purposes To begin to perform simple investigations To use simple measuring devices to learn about objects and organisms To begin to investigate and predict the results of putting together two or more shapes To start, use, and exit software programs	*Sing a Song of Opposites/Canta una canción de opuestos* *The Dragon's Coming After You/El dragón te está persiguiendo* *Teacher's Resource Anthology* pattern blocks *Math Resource Guide* *DLM Math* software	basket coffee can measuring tape or yardstick toothpicks (10 per child) straws sheets of colored acetate large envelopes or plastic baggies graham crackers
DAY 2	To refine and extend understanding of known words To show a steady increase in listening and speaking vocabulary To begin to recognize when a shape's position or orientation has changed To begin to recognize, describe, and name shapes	*Who Is the Beast?/¿Quién es la bestia?* *Teacher's Resource Anthology* pattern blocks *Math Resource Guide* *DLM Math* software *De Colores/De colores*	black and orange ribbon or crepe paper box magazines yarn toothpicks (10 per child) straws sheets of colored acetate
DAY 3	To select books to read based on personal criteria To connect information and events in books to real-life experiences To begin to investigate and predict the results of putting together two or more shapes To begin to recognize, describe, and name shapes	*Teacher's Resource Anthology* pattern blocks *Math Resource Guide* *DLM Math* software	lima beans newspaper toothpicks (10 per child) attribute blocks unused plunger marigold height graphs plastic eggs rope
DAY 4	To use sentences of increasing length (three or more words) and grammatical complexity in everyday speech To use language for a variety of purposes To begin to investigate and predict the results of putting together two or more shapes To participate in creating and using simple data charts	Oral Language Development Cards 33 & 43–45 *Teacher's Resource Anthology* pattern blocks *Math Resource Guide* *DLM Math* software *Four Baby Bumblebees* CD *Diez deditos* CD	Big Things Concentration game big things puzzles books about big things made by humans shoe boxes yarn toys that the children have brought to school/additional toys for children who didn't bring a toy to school
DAY 5	To understand that writing is used to communicate ideas and information To begin to understand cause-and-effect relationships To begin to investigate and predict the results of putting together two or more shapes To begin to recognize, describe, and name shapes	*Teacher's Resource Anthology* *Animals That Build Their Homes/Animales que construyen sus nidos* *Sing a Song of Opposites/ Canta una canción de opuestos* *DLM Math* software *Four Baby Bumblebees* CD *Diez deditos* CD	poster board graham crackers miniature marshmallows peanut butter clay straws attribute blocks white felt

(See individual lesson pages for complete lists of materials.)

Learning Centers

CONSTRUCTION

Building Big!

Objective
To begin to share and cooperate with others in group activities

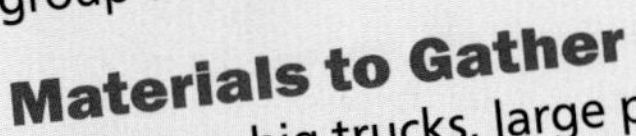

Materials to Gather
big boxes, big trucks, large paper bags, newspaper, wrapping paper tubes

Develop
Make big blocks by stuffing large paper bags about three quarters full with crumpled newspaper. Fold the tops closed into squares and tape to secure. Encourage the children to cooperate with one another to build a large structure using the various materials.

Reflect/Assess
Did you use more than one person's idea for the structure?
¿Usaron más de una idea de una persona para la estructura?

DRAMATIC PLAY

Too Big, Too Small

Objectives
To begin to engage in dramatic play with others

Materials to Gather
adult-sized clothing, infant-sized clothing

Develop
Place adult and infant sized clothes in the center. Try to include big accessories such as hats, scarves, and shoes. Have the children try on the adult clothing to see how it fits. On the next day of play, have them experiment with infant clothing (they should realize that these items do not fit them). Discuss and contrast sizes with the children.

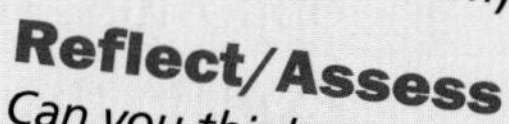

Reflect/Assess
Can you think of any ways to make the larger clothing items fit you?
¿Pueden pensar en alguna manera de hacer que las prendas de vestir más grandes les sirvan?

DISCOVERY

What's My Size?

Objective
To begin to order two or three objects by size

Materials to Gather
small, medium, and large brushes; crayons; and paper

Develop
Place a variety of items in graduated sizes (for example: small, medium, large or big, bigger, and biggest) in the center. Help the children explore the sizes and place the materials in certain size orders. Discuss the sizes and how they recognize each size.

Reflect/Assess
How do you know if you are smaller or bigger than another object?
¿Cómo saben si son más pequeños o más grandes que otro objeto?

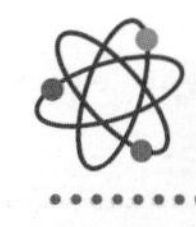

What Research Suggests

Comparisons help brains organize information. Children should understand the concept of *big* more thoroughly after they have experience with the concept of *small* and vice versa.

Begin the Day

- Present "Five Huge Dinosaurs"/"Cinco enormes dinosaurios." Help the children name things that are big.
- Use a suggestion for Morning Circle found in the front of this *Teacher's Edition.*

Objectives

- To enjoy listening to and responding to books
- To listen for different purposes

Vocabulary

big	grande
bigger	más grande
biggest	el (la) más grande

DLM Materials

- *Sing a Song of Opposites/Canta una canción de opuestos*
- *The Dragon's Coming After You/El dragón te está persiguiendo*
- *Teacher's Resource Anthology*
  "Five Huge Dinosaurs"/"Cinco enormes dinosaurios"
  "Big and Small"/"Soy alto, soy bajito"
  "Goldilocks and the Three Bears"/ "Goldilocks y los tres osos"
  "The Ram in the Chile Patch"/"El carnero en el sembrado de chiles"

Materials to Gather

- basket
- index cards
- items in sets of three in graduated sizes
- various writing implements in different sizes
- small and large pieces of paper

Literacy

Focus

- Say the "Big and Small"/"Soy alto, soy bajito" chant. Explain that *tall* and *big* are the opposites of *small* and *little.* Tell the children that sometimes things are easier to understand when they are aware of opposites. For example, using the concept of *small* helps clarify *big.*
- Explain that the children will be studying things that are big all week. Tell them that they will be looking at different versions of an object to determine which object is bigger.

Develop

One Way to Develop the Lesson

- Read *Sing a Song of Opposites/Canta una canción de opuestos.* As you begin, instruct the children to listen carefully to identify the pairs of opposites. Discuss their responses.
- Review the book and do a picture talk. Help the children identify the attributes in the pictures that determine why items are opposites.
- Have the children share other things that fit into each category. For example, big (bus), little (dime), tall (tree), and short (baby). Review how knowing a thing's opposite helps a person understand it better.

Another Way to Develop the Lesson

- Show the children item pairs from your basket. Ask which items are bigger. Have them arrange the items in size order (small, medium, large).
- Write the words *big, bigger,* and *biggest* on index cards. Ask the children to help you place a word card next to an item it describes.
- Divide the class in half. Instruct each member of one group to find a child in the other group who is taller than he or she is; have the children stand next to each other. Have everyone return to their groups. Repeat the activity in reverse (have members find shorter classmates). Conclude by having groups, consisting of three children, stand in size order. Explain that people describe size based on people to whom they are compared.

Practice

- Place the *Sing a Song of Opposites/Canta una canción de opuestos* book and listening tape in the Listening Center.
- Give the children your basket of object sets and the *big, bigger,* and *biggest* cards. Encourage them to sort and label the items.
- Place various sized writing implements in the Writing Center. For example, small and large crayons, broad and fine tipped pens, and short and long pencils. Encourage the children to experiment by writing or drawing with each implement. Help them compare their results and discuss each implement's lines using correct vocabulary.
- Provide each child with a small piece of paper (one by two inches) and a large piece of paper (eight by ten inches). Help them print their names on each paper. Ask: *Which paper is it easier to fit your name on? Why?* *¿En qué hoja es más fácil que quepa tu nombre? ¿Por qué?*
- Make the "Goldilocks and the Three Bears"/"Goldilocks y los tres osos" flannel board story available to the children. Have them sort the bears' things into small, medium, and large categories.

Preparation

- Make the flannel board stories, if necessary.
- Gather sets of three items in graduated sizes (blocks, books, crayons, and so on).

Scaffolding Strategies

More Help Provide various sized manipulatives for the children to experiment with until they are familiar with size attributes.

Extra Challenge Increase how many items the children need to compare.

Second Language Learners

As the children work in the Discovery Center with items that are bigger and smaller than a coffee can, talk with them about how they know an item is bigger or smaller. Use language to describe the relationships: "The bread box is TOO BIG to fit in the coffee can. The bread box is BIGGER than the coffee can." After several examples, ask the children to find another object that is bigger than the coffee can. Then have them find objects that are not bigger (the same size or smaller).

DAY 1

Letter Knowledge

English

- Read any of the letter stories from the *English Phonics Resource Guide.*

Spanish

- Discuss the letter *w* using "Wendy" from the *Spanish Phonics Resource Guide.*

Suggested Reading

Is It Larger? Is It Smaller? by Tana Hoban
Willy and Hugh by Anthony Hugh
Enanos y gigantes by Max Bollinger
La giganta y el chiquitín by Dip Ayala

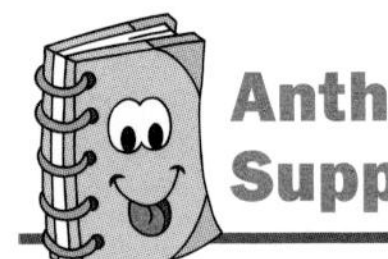

Anthology Support

"Three Bears Rap"
"El rap de los tres osos"
"The Elf and the Dormouse"
"El duende y el lirón"
"Big and Small"
"Soy alto, soy bajito"

Reflect/Assess

- *What are some items in the room that are smaller than I am?*
  ¿Cuáles son algunos objetos del salón de clases que son más pequeños que yo?
- *Who is the tallest person in your family?*
  ¿Quién es la persona más alta de su familia?

Literacy Circle

Storytime 1

- Read *The Dragon's Coming After You/El dragón te está persiguiendo.* Discuss the dragon's size. Ask: *Is the dragon bigger than the things that are hiding from it?*
  ¿El dragón es más grande que las cosas que se esconden de él?

Storytime 2

- Present "The Ram in the Chile Patch"/"El carnero en el sembrado de chiles" flannel board story. Review size as it relates to the story.

Content Connection

Science

Objectives

To begin to perform simple investigations

To use simple measuring devices to learn about objects and organisms

Materials to Gather

coffee can, containers in graduated sizes, measurable items, measuring tape or yardstick

Vocabulary

bigger, less, more, smaller

más grande, menos, más, más pequeño

Activity 1

- Place a coffee can and several items that can be measured in the Discovery Center. Some items should be bigger and some should be smaller than the can. Have the children sort the items based on whether or not they think the items will fit into the can. Help them check the items to see how many they identified correctly.

Activity 2

- For use in the Water and Sand Center, provide containers in graduated sizes (small, medium, large). Allow the children to measure and compare how much water or sand each container can hold.

DAY 1

Objectives

- To begin to investigate and predict the results of putting together two or more shapes
- To start, use, and exit software programs

Vocabulary

all shape names — nombres de todas las figuras

DLM Materials

- pattern blocks
- *Math Resource Guide*
  - Shape Step/Paso de figuras
  - Building Straws
  - Tangrams from Shape Set
  - Tangram Puzzles
  - Pattern Block Puzzles (26–32)
  - Pattern Block Cutouts
  - Estimating Jar
- *DLM Math* software

Materials to Gather

- toothpicks (10 per child)
- construction paper
- straws
- large envelopes or plastic baggies
- balls

Preparation

- Fill Estimating Jar with 5 to 15 dinosaur counters.
- Write the children's names on the envelopes or plastic bags for them to use to store their book pages.
- Make construction paper copies of the Tangram Puzzles and the Tangrams from the Shape Set.

MATH

Focus

- Have the children play Shape Step/Paso de figuras (see Ocean Life).

Develop

- Tell the children that all the pictures and designs they make this week will go in their Shape Books.
- Introduce Memory—Geometry, Level 6. The children will match cards showing different combinations of shapes. This is a snapshot version. One group of cards shows for only 2 seconds. The children can use the *peek again* button to see the card again.
- Review the directions for Create-a-Scene (see Ocean Life, Day 1).

Practice

- Invite the children to make shapes with Building Straws and toothpicks, and record and label their favorite designs or pictures. Provide additional straws for the children to glue onto construction paper to replicate their Building Straws designs.
- Encourage the children to choose and complete the Pattern Block Puzzles and glue down Pattern Block Cutouts to record their work.
- Have the children work on Tangram Puzzles. They can record their solutions by pasting copies of the puzzle pieces onto pieces of construction paper.
- Have the children make a picture with either pattern blocks or a Shape Set. Then they can choose their favorite picture to copy with the Pattern Block Cutouts.
- Encourage the children to estimate how many items are in the Estimating Jar and to record their estimates.
- Invite the children to work on Create-a-Scene (no level) and Memory—Geometry, Level 6. If they have more time, encourage them to play Dinosaur Shop, Level 5 (Free Explore).

Reflect/Assess

- *Did you know the names of all the shapes at the beginning of the year? Which did you learn?*

  ¿Sabían los nombres de todas las figuras al comienzo del año? ¿Cuáles aprendieron?

Music and Movement

- Have the children play catch with a large and a small ball (they may roll the balls instead). Ask: *Which ball is easier to catch (roll)?*

  ¿Cuál pelota es más fácil de atrapar (rodar)?
- Invite the children to walk around the perimeter of the playground taking small steps, and then have them repeat using large steps. Discuss differences with them. This can be an indoor activity also.

Suggested Reading

Rainbow Fish and the Big Blue Whale by Marcus Pfister

Content Connection

Social Studies

Objectives

To cooperate with others in a joint activity

To share ideas and take turns listening and speaking

DLM Materials

Teacher's Resource Anthology

"Smart Cookie's Best Friend, Gabby Graham"/"Gabby Graham, la mejor amiga de Smart Cookie"

Materials to Gather

graham crackers

Activity 1

- Give the children a whole graham cracker. Have them break it in half and then in fourths. As they break the cracker, ask them about the shape and size of the pieces. Ask them which rectangle is larger.

  ¿Cuál rectángulo es más largo?
- Invite the children to eat their crackers.

Activity 2

- Present the "Smart Cookie's Best Friend, Gabby Graham"/"Gabby Graham, la mejor amiga de Smart Cookie" flannel board story. Ask questions. *What shape is each of the cookies? Which other shapes are mentioned in the story?*

Reflect on the Day

- *What did you learn about things that are big today?*

  ¿Qué aprendieron sobre las cosas que son grandes hoy?
- *Is it easier to take small or large steps as you walk?*

  ¿Es más fácil dar pasos pequeños o grandes al caminar?

Home Connection

Notify families that their children need to bring a toy to school on Wednesday.

Begin the Day

- Say "Five Huge Dinosaurs"/"Cinco enormes dinosaurios." You might allow the children to act out the rhyme today.
- Use one of the suggestions for Morning Circle found in the front of this *Teacher's Edition.*

Objectives

- To refine and extend understanding of known words
- To show a steady increase in listening and speaking vocabulary

Vocabulary

big	grande
bigger	más grande
biggest	el (la) más grande
lion	león
tiger	tigre

DLM Materials

- *Who Is the Beast?/¿Quién es la bestia?*
- *SRA Photo Library* software
- *Teacher's Resource Anthology*
  "Five Huge Dinosaurs"/"Cinco enormes dinosaurios"
  "Three Terrifying Tigers"
  "Tres tristes tigres"
  Big Things Concentration game
  "The Lion and the Mouse"/"El león y el ratón agradecido"
  "The Lion's Haircut"/"El corte de pelo del león"
  zoo card patterns
  big things card patterns

Materials to Gather

- black and orange ribbon or crepe paper
- black and orange tempera paint
- box
- magazines
- paintbrushes in various sizes
- yarn

LITERACY

Focus

- Say the "Three Terrifying Tigers" chant or the "Tres tristes tigres" rhyme.
- Tell the children that they will continue to learn about big things today. Ask them to recall what big thing was part of the song or chant.

Develop

One Way to Develop the Lesson

- Make a big thing word web. Help the children think of and name big things. List categories (animals, transportation, nature, and things that people build) in different colors and write the items in each category in the corresponding color. Review and discuss each category and the items in it.
- Help the children name large things local to your area. Ask them to explain what makes these things big. Provide size prompts such as height, length, volume, depth, how people can fit inside, and so on.

Another Way to Develop the Lesson

- Show the cover of *Who Is the Beast?/¿Quién es la bestia?* Have a volunteer point out the story's big thing. You might review the location and name of the author/illustrator on the cover.
- Read *Who Is the Beast?/¿Quién es la bestia?* Remind the children that they learned about tigers while studying zoo animals. Ask: *Why did the animals run from the tiger?*

  ¿Por qué los animales huyeron del trigre?
- Review the book's other animals. Discuss how they compare in size to the tiger. Ask: *Can someone name an animal larger than a tiger?*

  ¿Alguien me puede decir el nombre de un animal más pequeño que el tigre?

Practice

- Place the *Who Is the Beast?/¿Quién es la bestia?* listening tape and book in the Listening Center. Encourage the children to review the story.
- Have the children paint with various sized brushes. Discuss the size and shape variations of the paintings. Suggest that they paint tiger stripes.
- Invite the children to complete the lion and tiger puzzles.
- Play Catch a Tiger by the Tail. Put the tails in a box with small pieces hanging over the edge. Have a child choose a tail and try to name the letter attached to it. If a child says the correct letter, he or she keeps the tail. If not, the tail goes back in the box. The child with the most tails wins!
- Allow the children to search for big and little things in magazines.
- Have the children play Big Things Concentration.
- Encourage the children to find big animals in the Animals category on the *SRA Photo Library* software.

Preparation

- Make "The Lion's Haircut"/"El corte de pelo del león" prop story.
- Enlarge copies of the lion and the tiger zoo animal patterns. Color them, laminate them, and cut them into puzzles.
- Make tiger tails. Twist 36-inch pieces of orange and black ribbon or crepe paper together and attach cards with alphabet letters on them.
- Make two copies of the big things card patterns. Color them, laminate them, and cut them out.

Scaffolding Strategies

More Help Read a book such as *Is It Larger? Is It Smaller?* by Tana Hoban.

Extra Challenge Name a pair of objects and have the children tell you which object is larger.

Second Language Learners

Encourage the children to name the big things they uncover as they play Big Things Concentration. This will help them recall the locations of the objects on the next trial and promote vocabulary development.

DAY 2

Letter Knowledge

English

- Read a selection from the *SRA Alphabet Book.*

Spanish

- Read "La W" from *Los niños alfabéticos.*

Suggested Reading

The Biggest Animal Ever by Allan Fowler
Amos and Boris by William Steig
Huge Harold by Bill Peet
Amos y Boris by William Steig
El animal más grande del mundo by Allan Fowler

Anthology Support

"Peanut, the Teeniest, Tiniest Pup on the Planet"
"Maní, el perrito más pequeñito del planeta"
"Going on a Bear Hunt"
"Vamos a cazar un oso"
"Animal Fair"

Reflect/Assess

- *What is the biggest thing in our room?*
  ¿Cuál es la cosa más grande de nuestro salón de clases?
- *What is the biggest animal you have ever had as a pet?*
  ¿Cuál es el animal más grande que han tenido como mascota?

Literacy Circle

Storytime 1

- Present "The Lion and the Mouse"/"El león y el ratón agradecido" listening story. Ask: *How big do you think the lion appeared to the mouse?*
  ¿Qué tan grande creen que el león le parecía al ratón?

Storytime 2

- Tell "The Lion's Haircut"/"El corte de pelo del león" prop story. Ask: *Was the lion big at the beginning of the story? What size was he at the end of the story?*
  ¿El león era grande al comienzo del cuento? ¿De qué tamaño era al final del cuento?

Content Connection

Personal and Social Development/Social Studies

Objectives

To begin to express thoughts, feelings, and ideas through language as well as through gestures and actions

To begin to examine a situation from another person's perspective

Vocabulary

helpful

útil

DLM Materials

Teacher's Resource Anthology

"The Lion and the Mouse"/"El león y el ratón agradecido"

Activity 1

- Discuss the moral of "The Lion and the Mouse"/"El león y el ratón agradecido" (Storytime 1). Help the children think of times when someone or something small helped someone or something big (for example, a child helping an adult, a pigeon carrying a message for a person, a bee pollinating a flower, and so on).

Activity 2

- Building on Activity 1, ask the children to help you make a list of helpful things people can do for others without being tall or big (for example, doing certain chores, reading books, listening, and so on).

DAY 2

Objectives

- To begin to recognize when a shape's position or orientation has changed
- To begin to recognize, describe, and name shapes

Vocabulary

side	lado
corner	esquina
angle	ángulo
all shape names	nombres de todas las figuras

DLM Materials

- *Math Resource Guide*
  Shape Transparencies
- See Day 1
- *DLM Math* software
- *Teacher's Resource Anthology*
  "Going on a Whale Watch"/"Vamos a mirar ballenas"
  One Elephant/Un elefante

Materials to Gather

- white paper
- sheets of acetate (transparencies)
- See Day 1

Preparation

- Use the first page of the Shape Transparencies to cut shapes from sheets of acetate (transparencies). Cut the Shapes apart *near* the black lines, not on them. Use the other pages as models for the children.

MATH

Focus

- Encourage the children to show one of the book pages they made yesterday.

Develop

- Give the children 6 toothpicks and challenge them to make a rectangle. Ask them how many toothpicks they used on each side and how many in all.
- Repeat with a triangle, a square, and a hexagon. Is it possible to make each of these shapes using all 6 toothpicks? Repeat the activity using 8 toothpicks.
- Encourage the children to make these shapes any way they can. Some advanced students will accept the implicit rule to use all 6 toothpicks and say that some shapes (i.e., squares) are not possible without breaking the toothpicks. Others will simply use 4 toothpicks.
- Invite the children to use the shapes they make for their Shape Books.

Practice

- Invite the children to combine shapes using the Shape Transparencies to make different designs. Give them a sheet of white paper to work on or allow them to work on an overhead projector. This activity is optional and is not recorded for their Shape Books.
- Encourage the children to estimate how many items are in the Estimating Jar and to record their estimates.
- Have the children continue to work on the Practice activities from Day 1.
- Invite the children to work on Create-a-Scene (no level) and Memory—Geometry, Level 6. The glue tool really enhances the unit-of-units idea. Encourage children to make shapes by combining other shapes.

Reflect/Assess

- Encourage the children to show some of their Shape Book pages they made today.

Music and Movement

- Have the children participate in the "Going on a Whale Watch"/ "Vamos a mirar ballenas" action rhyme. Remind them of how large a whale is.
- Sing the song and play the game One Elephant/Un elefante. Remind the children that elephants are the largest land animals.

Suggested Reading

Picture Pie 2 by Ed Emberley
A Pig Is Big by Douglas Florian

Content Connection

Physical Development

Objectives
To begin to hold writing tools with fingers instead of with a fist
To begin to use scissors

Materials to Gather
drawing paper, scissors, crayons

Vocabulary
circular, triangular, rectangular
circular, triangular, rectangular

Activity 1

- Have the children draw a picture of their favorite big animal on a paper plate. Encourage them to cut their plates into fourths (4 pie wedges) to make a puzzle. Discuss the original shape of the pictures and then the shape of the puzzle pieces.

Activity 2

- Ask the children to fold a rectangular piece of drawing paper into 4 parts. Encourage them to unfold their papers and then draw a picture of a dinosaur. When they have finished drawing, have them cut their papers on the fold lines to create a 4-piece puzzle. *What shape is the puzzle? What shape are the puzzle pieces?*
  ¿Qué figura tiene el rompecabezas? ¿Qué figuras tienen las piezas del rompecabezas?

Reflect on the Day

- *What was your favorite activity today? Why?*
  ¿Qué actividad fue su favorita hoy? ¿Por qué?
- *What do you have at home that is big in size?*
  ¿Qué tienen en su casa que sea grande?

Home Connection

Remind the children and their families that they need to bring a toy to school tomorrow.

Begin the Day

- Sing "Sing a Song of Opposites"/"La canción de los opuestos." Sing it with a normal voice, and then sing it big and loud.
- Use a suggestion for Morning Circle from the front of this *Teacher's Edition.*

Objectives

- To select books to read based on personal criteria
- To connect information and events in books to real-life experiences

Vocabulary

big	grande
giant	gigante

DLM Materials

- *Teacher's Resource Anthology*
  "Sing a Song of Opposites"/"La canción de los opuestos"
  "Three Bears Rap"/"El rap de los tres osos"
  "There Once Were Three Brown Bears"/"Había una vez tres osos café"
  "Jack and the Beanstalk"/"Jaime y los frijoles mágicos"
  "The Great Big Turnip"/"El nabo gigante"
  "Peanut, the Teeniest, Tiniest Pup on the Planet"/"Maní, el perrito más pequeñito del planeta"
  "The Three Billy Goats Gruff"/"Los tres chivitos Gruff"
  story map

Materials to Gather

- box
- gold and green paint
- lima beans
- newspaper
- plastic eggs

Literacy

Focus

- Sing the "Three Bears Rap"/"El rap de los tres osos" or "There Once Were Three Brown Bears"/"Había una vez tres osos café."
- Explain that today the class will discuss stories about big things.

Develop

One Way to Develop the Lesson

- Make a list of stories about big things.
- Present the "Jack and the Beanstalk"/"Jaime y los frijoles mágicos" flannel board story.
- Review the story. Ask the children: *Do you think the giant was big or small? Was the beanstalk smaller than Jack? How would the story be different if the giant was an elf?*
  ¿Creen que el gigante era grande o pequeño? ¿El tallo de frijoles era más pequeño que Jaime? ¿Cómo cambiaría el cuento si el gigante fuera un duende?
- Discuss what the word *giant* means.
- Make a story map for "Jack and the Beanstalk"/"Jaime y los frijoles mágicos."

Another Way to Develop the Lesson

- Tell the "The Great Big Turnip"/"El nabo gigante" flannel board story. Ask: *What is the big thing is this story?*

  ¿Cuál es la cosa grande de este cuento?
- Continue discussing the story. Ask: *Do you think the turnip could fit in our classroom? Where could the turnip fit?*

  ¿Creen que el nabo cabría en nuestro salón de clases? ¿Dónde podría caber el nabo?
- To connect the events of the story to everyday life, have the children show you something in your room comparable to the turnip in size. If there are incorrect responses, help them decide if what they selected is actually smaller or larger than the turnip.
- Let the children perform the story. Have them decide what to use to represent the turnip. Change the story's characters to Charlie's gang or another group of children familiar to your class.

Practice

- Place both flannel board stories in the Language Center. Encourage the children to retell the stories or to make up new stories using the flannel board pieces.
- Have the children draw big things based on a familiar story.
- Paint lima beans green or gold to represent magic beans. Print a letter of the alphabet on one side of each bean. Help the children spell their names using the beans. Have them drop a few beans into a box. As they remove the beans, ask them to name the letters. Ask: *Did you choose any letters that are part of your name?*

  ¿Eligieron cualquier letra que deletree su nombre?
- Paint a few plastic eggs gold. Put the name of a big thing in each egg to use as a story starter. For example, "On the way home from school, I saw a huge dinosaur taking a nap . . ."
- Play Drop the Golden Egg. Give the children a plastic egg painted gold. With newspaper, make three nests on the floor. Put a *big, bigger,* or *biggest* word card on each nest. Have a child name the nest into which he or she will drop the egg and then drop the egg.

Preparation

- Make the flannel board stories, if necessary.
- Copy one of the story maps.
- Paint lima beans green or gold. Write alphabet letters on them.
- Paint plastic eggs gold. Put story starters in some eggs and leave a few for the Drop the Golden Egg game.

Scaffolding Strategies

More Help Allow the children to look for big things in library books.

Extra Challenge Have the children search for books about big things.

Second Language Learners

As you present "The Three Billy Goats Gruff"/"Los tres chivitos Gruff," clearly stress the differences in the goats' voices and movements. Place the flannel board story in the Language Center afterward, and note whether the children also change their voices and movements as they play different-sized goats.

Anthology Support

"The Elf and the Dormouse"
"El duende y el lirón"
"The Great Big Pumpkin"
"La calabaza gigante"
"Cat and Mouse"
"El gato y el ratón"

DAY 3

Letter Knowledge

English

- Have the children shape letters with play dough.

Spanish

- Have children shape the letter *w* with play dough.

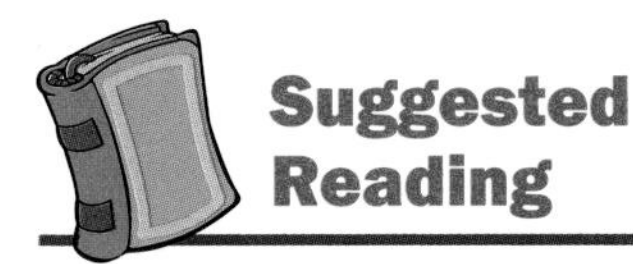

Suggested Reading

Jack and the Beanstalk by Cooper Eden
Abiyoyo by Pete Seeger
Las semillas mágicas by Joseph Jacobs
Ya vienen los gigantes by Angelina Gatell

Reflect/Assess

- *Which of today's stories is your favorite story about a big thing? Why?*
  ¿Cuál de los cuentos de hoy sobre algo grande es su favorito? ¿Por qué?
- *Can you name a book about something little?*
  ¿Pueden nombrar un libro sobre algo pequeño?

Literacy Circle

Storytime 1

- Review and discuss "Peanut, the Teeniest, Tiniest Pup on the Planet"/"Maní, el perrito más pequeñito del planeta." Ask: *How small was Peanut at the beginning of the story? How big was Peanut at the end of the story?*
  ¿Qué tan pequeño era Maní al comienzo del cuento? ¿Qué tan grande era Maní al final del cuento?

Storytime 2

- Present "The Three Billy Goats Gruff"/"Los tres chivitos Gruff" flannel board story. Ask: *Who are the big characters? Which characters have big or loud voices?*
  ¿Quiénes son los personajes grandes? ¿Cuáles personajes tienen voces fuertes o intensas?

Content Connection

Physical Development

Objectives

To become more able to move from one space to another in different ways

To begin to participate in group games involving movement

Vocabulary

creep

arrastrarse

DLM Materials

Teacher's Resource Anthology

"Jack and the Beanstalk"/"Jaime y los frijoles mágicos"

Materials to Gather

rope

Activity 1

- Review different ways that Jack moved in the story (for example, walking with the cow, climbing up the beanstalk, creeping around the castle, and running away from the giant). Have the children demonstrate these movements as you call them out.

Activity 2

- Divide the children into teams to have a tug-of-war. Discuss whether rope tugging reminds them of anything from one of today's stories.

DAY 3

Objectives

- To begin to investigate and predict the results of putting together two or more shapes
- To begin to recognize, describe, and name shapes

Vocabulary

side	lado
corner	esquina
angle	ángulo
all shape names	nombres de todas las figuras

DLM Materials

- Rafita and Pepita puppets
- *Math Resource Guide*
  Shape Transparencies
  Shape Step/Paso de figuras
  More or Less game/Más o menos
  Counting cards
- See Day 1
- *DLM Math* software
- *Teacher's Resource Anthology*
  "Rafita and Pepita: Dance of Opposites"/"Rafita y Pepita: un baile de opuestos"

Materials to Gather

- counters
- attribute blocks
- small ball
- unused plunger
- See Day 1

MATH

Focus

- Read and discuss the children's recorded estimates of how many items there are in the Estimating Jar. Show an identical jar and, along with the children, count 5 identical objects into that jar. Hold up both jars so the children can compare them. Let them identify the jar they believe has more in it.
- Count out 5 more objects (i.e., start counting at 6) into the identical jar and compare again. Tell them that they will make new estimates today.

Develop

- Play Shape Step/Paso de figuras with attribute blocks. Name a block such as a triangle and have a small group of children step just on triangles. If you use plastic shapes, tape them down and have safety rules, such as touching the shape with your toe, so the children do not fall.
- Repeat with different groups of children and with more complicated attributes: red shapes, shapes with straight sides, shapes that are circles and blue, shapes that are square but not small, shapes that are not green triangles, and so on. Practice at various times throughout the day.
- Remember to play the More or Less game/Más o menos during short transition times (see the Content Connection in Farm Animals, Day 2).

Practice

- Invite the children to continue combining shapes using the Shape Transparencies. Give them a sheet of white paper to work on or allow them to work on an overhead projector.
- Encourage the children to estimate how many items are in the Estimating Jar and to record their estimates.
- Have the children continue to work on the Practice activities from Day 1.
- Invite the children to work on Create-a-Scene (no level) and Memory—Geometry, Level 6. The glue tool really enhances the unit-of-units idea. Suggest that the children choose big thing themes for their pictures.

Reflect/Assess

- Encourage the children to show and describe one of their Shape Book pages.

Content Connection

Social Studies/Science

Objectives
To recognize changes in the environment over time
To begin to categorize time intervals using words

Vocabulary
height, length, measure, week
altura, alto; longitud, largo; medir, medida; semana

DLM Materials
De Colores/De colores

Materials to Gather
connecting cubes, marigold height graphs

Activity 1

- One final time, have the children measure their marigolds with connecting cubes and add to their weekly graphs.
- Discuss the graphs and what they show about how much the plants grew over time.

Activity 2

- Read *De Colores/De colores* to the children. Stop on each page, looking for shapes in the illustrations. Look specifically at growing things. Discuss the changes in the illustrations from the beginning to the end of the book.

Reflect on the Day

- *What did you learn about opposites today?*
  ¿Qué aprendieron sobre opuestos hoy?
- *Which story will you tell your family tonight?*
  ¿Qué historia le contarán a su familia esta noche?

Music and Movement

- Using the Rafita and Pepita/Rafita y Pepita puppets, do the "Rafita and Pepita: Dance of Opposites"/"Rafita y Pepita: un baile de opuestos."
- Challenge the children to catch a small ball in an unused plunger.

Suggested Reading

Flower Garden by Eve Bunting
Planting a Rainbow by Lois Ehlert

What Research Suggests

Children in preschool learn to recognize common shapes such as squares and circles, but are just as interested in and capable of learning about many other shapes.

Begin the Day

- Sing the "Little Red Caboose"/"La furgonita roja" song. Explain what a caboose is and where it is on a train. Ask: *Has anyone ever seen a caboose? Was it big or small?*

  ¿Alguien ha visto una furgonita? ¿Era grande o pequeña?
- Use a suggestion for Morning Circle from the front of this *Teacher's Edition.*

Objectives

- To use sentences of increasing length and grammatical complexity in everyday speech
- To use language for a variety of purposes

Vocabulary

ball field	campo de pelota
bus	autobús
hot air balloon	globo aerostático
jet	avión
ship	barco
skyscraper	rascacielo
stadium	estadio
train	tren

DLM Materials

- Oral Language Development Cards 33, 43–45
- *SRA Photo Library* software
- *Teacher's Resource Anthology*
  "Little Red Caboose"/"La furgonita roja"
  "Wheels on the Bus"/"Ruedas del bus"
  "Engine Ninety-Nine"/"La máquina noventa y nueve"
  big things card patterns
  Big Things Concentration game

Materials to Gather

- big things puzzles
- books about big things made by humans
- butcher paper
- shoeboxes
- fasteners or staples

LITERACY

Focus

- Sing the "Wheels on the Bus"/"Ruedas del bus" song. Ask the children: *Is a bus a big thing?*

  ¿Un autobús es algo grande?
- Explain that today the class will study big things built by humans.

Develop

One Way to Develop the Lesson

- Display Oral Language Card 33. Use the suggestions on the back of the card to stimulate conversation.
- Help the children brainstorm a list of big things that people build. The list could include stadiums, airports, malls, and so on.

Another Way to Develop the Lesson

- Show Oral Language Cards 43, 44, and 45. Use the suggestions on the backs of each card for additional activity ideas.
- Brainstorm another list of big transportation items (such as trains, cruise ships, helicopters, trucks, and tanks).
- Help the children think about a place that they would like to visit. Ask: *What type of transportation would you use?*

  ¿Qué tipo de transporte usarían?

  You might suggest arriving at a local place in a stretch limousine (provide a limousine photograph if possible).

Practice

- Review what a skyscraper is. Give each child a shoe box and have them make skyscrapers. Suggest drawing windows and doors. Provide additional art materials. Save the skyscrapers for tomorrow.
- Have the children build sandcastles in the sand table.
- Fill the Library Center with books about big things built by people.
- Invite the children to play the Big Things Concentration game.
- Have the children work on the hot air balloon, skyscraper, ship, and airplane puzzles. You might have them put the items in size order.
- Give each child his or her copy of *My Little Book of Big Things*. Have them draw pictures of big things on each page. Ask them to dictate a label or sentence for each picture. Encourage the children (authors) to write their names on the covers.
- Encourage children to find big things in the Structures category and Transportation category on the *SRA Photo Library* software.

Preparation

- Make the flannel board story, if necessary.
- Make enlarged copies of the airplane, hot air balloon, skyscraper, and ship big things patterns. Color them, cut them out, mount them onto construction paper, laminate them, and cut them into puzzle pieces.
- Make each child a My Little Book of Big Things. Bind blank pages with yarn, fasteners, or staples (with tape covering the sharp edges). Leave space on the cover for them to write their names.

Scaffolding Strategies

More Help Take the children on a walk around the school and discuss big things that you see.

Extra Challenge Ask the children to describe big things from their neighborhoods. You might discuss whether or not people built them.

Second Language Learners

On the walk around the school, take pictures of some of the big things the children identify. If there is more than one of the same item, such as trees, ask which is the BIGGER tree. Display the photos in the room after the trip.

DAY 4

Letter Knowledge

English

- Use the Think, Pair, Share/ Piensa, aparea, comparte game to help the children make letters with their bodies.

Spanish

- Use the Think, Pair, Share / Piensa, aparea, comparte game to help the children create the letter *w* with their bodies.

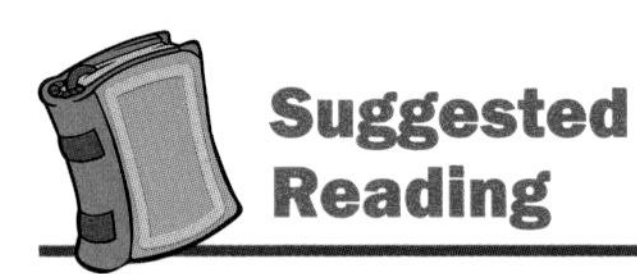

Suggested Reading

Skyscrapers by Joy Richardson
Freight Train by Donald Crews

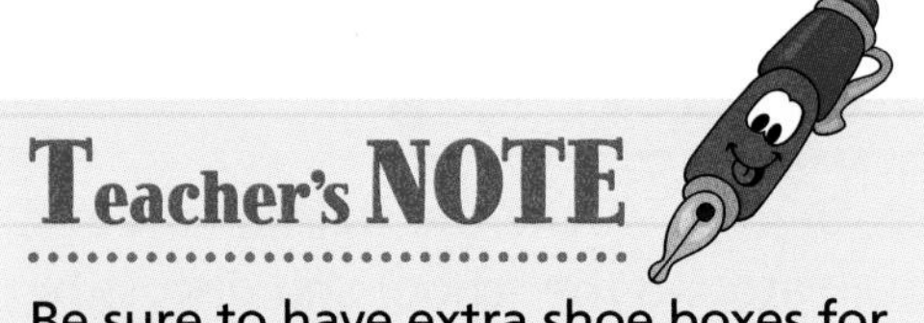

Teacher's NOTE

Be sure to have extra shoe boxes for children who may not have their own.

Anthology Support

"The Airplane"
"Steam Shovel
"Avión, avión"
"Submarino"

Reflect/Assess

- *What is the largest means of transportation you have used to travel?*
  ¿Cuál es el medio de transporte más grande que hayan usado para viajar?
- *What is the biggest thing you have seen built by people?*
  ¿Cuál es la cosa más grande que hayan construido las personas?

Literacy Circle

Storytime 1

- Tell the "Wheels on the Bus"/"Ruedas del bus" flannel board story. Encourage the children to retell the story using complete sentences.

Storytime 2

- Read the "Engine Ninety-Nine"/"La máquina noventa y nueve" listening story. Ask: *What was the last thing that the people did to complete Engine Ninety-Nine? How big do you think the engine is?*
  ¿Cuál fue la última cosa que hicieron las personas para completar la Máquina noventa y nueve? ¿De qué tamaño creen que es la máquina?

Content Connection

Social Studies/Fine Arts

Objectives

To create simple representations of home, school, or community through drawings or block constructions

To begin to show interest in the artwork of others

Vocabulary

skyscrapers
rascacielos

DLM Materials

Oral Language Development Card 33

Materials to Gather

butcher paper, construction paper, shape templates

Activity 1

- Prepare shape templates of a circle, a square, a rectangle, and a triangle. Place the templates on a table. Review the shape names with the children.
- Display Oral Language Card 33. Invite the children to find the template shapes in the structures shown on the card.

Activity 2

- Invite the children to draw different shapes on construction paper using the templates and then cut them out. Explain that the shapes will be used for buildings. Have them glue the shapes onto butcher paper to create a skyline mural. They may continue to decorate the mural with trees, clouds, birds, and so forth using a crayon.

DAY 4

Objectives

- To begin to investigate and predict the results of putting together two or more shapes
- To begin to recognize, describe, and name shapes

Vocabulary

side	lado
corner	esquina
angle	ángulo
all shape names	nombres de todas las figuras

DLM Materials

- *Math Resource Guide*
  - Feely Box
  - Shape Set (trapezoid and rectangle)
  - Toothpick Shapes/Figuras de palillos de dientes
  - Guess My Shape/Adivina mi figura
  - Shape Transparencies
- See Day 1
- *DLM Math* software
- *Four Baby Bumblebees* CD
- *Diez deditos* CD

Materials to Gather

- toothpicks (12 per child)
- attribute blocks
- See Day 1

MATH

Focus

- Invite the children to make Toothpick Shapes/Figuras de palillos de dientes. Give the children 12 toothpicks and challenge them to make a rectangle. Ask them how many toothpicks they used on each side and how many they used in all. Repeat with an equilateral triangle, a square, and a hexagon.
- Repeat with 4 toothpicks. Encourage the children to use the shapes they make for their Shapes Books.

Develop

- Demonstrate the Feely Box. Show a trapezoid and a rectangle from the Shape Set. Hide them both and secretly place one in the Feely Box. Show a second, identical trapezoid and rectangle.
- Have one child guess which shape you hid by touching it in the Feely Box and describing it, using the displayed shapes as an aid to identification.
- Challenge the children with shapes such as a rectangle and parallelogram, a right isosceles triangle and an equilateral triangle, and different rhombuses. Repeat these pairs, sometimes hiding the other shape as you see fit.

Practice

- Encourage the children to play Guess My Shape/Adivina mi figura. The children challenge each other to guess the shape they have placed in the Feely Box.
- Invite the children to combine shapes using the Shape Transparencies.
- Have the children continue to work on the Practice activities from Day 1.
- Invite the children to work on Create-a-Scene (no level) and Memory—Geometry, Level 6.

Reflect/Assess

- *How did you tell one rhombus from another in the Feely Box?*
  ¿Cómo diferenciaron un rombo del otro en la Feely Box?
- *How do you remember where the matching cards are in Memory—Geometry?*
  ¿Cómo recuerdan dónde están las tarjetas de emparejar en Memory—Geometry?

Music and Movement

- Sing "On the Good Ship Lollipop" from the *Four Baby Bumblebees* CD. Encourage the children to dance to the music.
- Sing "Las ruedas del camión" from the *Diez deditos* CD. Invite the children to develop motions to match the song's words.

Content Connection

Science

Objectives

To compare objects and organisms and identify similarities and differences

To participate in creating and using simple data charts

Vocabulary

names of attributes

nombres de atributos

Materials to Gather

toys the children have brought to school, additional toys for children who didn't bring one, paper for graphing

Activity 1

- Have the children briefly show the toys they brought to school.
- Work with the group to sort them by various attributes including shapes (2-dimensional shapes on their faces or 3-dimensional shapes), colors, and so on.

Activity 2

- Make a graph of the results of 1 or more of the toy sorts.
- Count how many toys are in each category.

Suggested Reading

Changes, Changes by Pat Hutchins

Reflect on the Day

- *What big objects did you learn about today?*
  ¿Qué objetos grandes aprendieron hoy?
- *Which activity today did you enjoy the most? Why?*
  ¿Qué actividad disfrutaron más hoy? ¿Por qué?

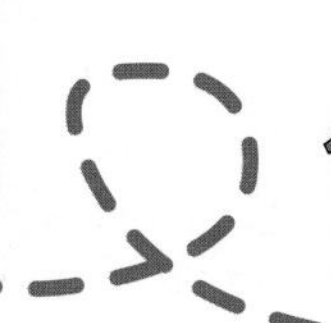

Home Connection

Send four children home with a take-home book pack.

Begin the Day

- Sing "Wheels on the Bus"/"Ruedas del bus." Discuss what happens to the song as each new verse is added.
- Use one of the suggestions for Morning Circle found in the front of this *Teacher's Edition.*

Objectives

- To understand that writing is used to communicate ideas and information
- To begin to dictate words, phrases, and sentences to an adult recording on paper

Vocabulary

big — grande
bigger — más grande

DLM Materials

- *Teacher's Resource Anthology*
  "Wheels on the Bus"/"Ruedas del bus"
  One Elephant/Un elefante
  "Down by the Bay"/"Junto a la bahía"
  "Henny-Penny"/"Gallinita-Nita"
  "Five Dancing Dolphins"/"Cinco delfines bailarines"
  giant puzzle
  Big Things Concentration game

Materials to Gather

- blocks
- chart paper
- big things puzzles
- art materials
- poster board
- graham crackers
- miniature marshmallows
- peanut butter

LITERACY

Focus

- Sing One Elephant/Un elefante. Ask: *What happens to the line when a new elephant joins it?*
  ¿Qué le pasa a la línea cuando llega un elefante nuevo?
- Explain that today the class will discuss things that get bigger as they add to them.

Develop

One Way to Develop the Lesson

- Give each child a block. Have the children stack the blocks one at a time in the circle area's center. Ask: *What happens as each block is added?*
  ¿Qué sucede cuando se agrega cada bloque?
- Help the children add verses to the song "Down by the Bay"/"Junto a la bahía" (this song is also on the *Where Is Thumbkin?* CD). Write the new song verses on chart paper or the board. Explain that the song gets longer or bigger with each verse that is added.
- Help the children brainstorm a list of things that grow bigger as people add to them such as cakes, clay models, block structures, and so on.

Another Way to Develop the Lesson

- Help the children write a story about a growing city using predictable text for the story's structure. For example:

  Samuel built a skyscraper, but it stood alone.
  Jeanne marched a skyscraper over to Samuel's.
  So the city grew.
  José danced a skyscraper over to the city.
  So the city grew.
  Ginny skipped a skyscraper over to the city.
  So the city grew.
  Linda crawled a skyscraper over to the city.
  So the city grew.
- Have each child get his or her shoebox skyscraper from yesterday. Allow them to construct a city in your room using their skyscrapers.
- Let each child choose a safe action to get his or her skyscraper to the city. They should participate one at a time so they can watch the city grow. Other action suggestions include gliding, racing, jumping, hopping, twirling, snaking, oozing, and trucking. Discuss how the city began and how it grew. You might compare it to the story's growth.

Practice

- Place the story chart (from the Second Develop) in the Art Center and allow the children to illustrate it.
- Give each child three blocks. Have groups of four children work together to build a structure. When they have finished, ask: *What happens as blocks are added to the structure?*

  ¿Qué sucede a medida que se agregan los bloques?
- Allow the children to play the Big Things Concentration game.
- Provide the children with the big things puzzles you made this week.
- Give each child a piece of the giant puzzle and crayons. Have them color their pieces any color, as long as they completely cover any white areas.
- **(Allergy Warning)** Invite the children to make a big snack. Have them make a triple-decker snack by spreading peanut butter on three graham crackers and stacking them with miniature marshmallows between the crackers.

Preparation

- Make the flannel board stories, if necessary.
- Write the words to this lesson's song on chart paper.
- Make a giant puzzle.
- Gather ingredients for big things snacks.

Scaffolding Strategies

More Help Work with the children one-on-one as they put crayons in a box or stack paper cups.

Extra Challenge Discuss how a person grows.

Second Language Learners

With the aid of photographs or drawings, ask the children to compare big objects. Make a rebus predictable story with the pictures they identify. Write the words ahead of time on a chart, and ask the children to paste the pictures in the appropriate spaces. Make sure all the letters are at least 2" high. Sample text: "This (tree) is big but this (tree) is bigger. This (house) is big but this (house) is bigger. These are big things." Read the rebus story, pointing to each word as you read it. Ask the children to find words in the story that look the same.

DAY 5

Letter Knowledge

English

- Have the children find and circle a specific letter in newspapers and magazines.

Spanish

- Have the children find and circle the letter *w* in newspapers and magazines.

Anthology Support

"Old MacDonald"
"El viejo MacDonald"
"La granja"
"The Farm"
"This Old Man Is Rockin' On"
"El señor"
"Johnny Works with One Hammer"
"Juan trabaja con un martillo"
"El circo"

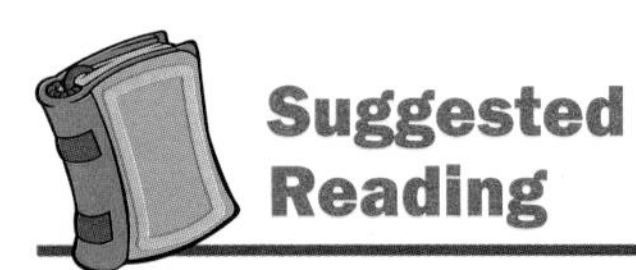

Suggested Reading

If You Give a Mouse a Cookie by Laura Joffe Numeroff
The Magic Porridge Pot by Paul Galdone
Stone Soup by Marcia Brown
El cumpleaños de Moira by Robert Munsch
La oruga muy hambrienta by Eric Carle

Technology Support

To review the concepts of greater than and less than, type problems for the children to solve using (>) or (<). For example: 5 _ 8, 10 _ 3, 6 _ 2.

- Let the children put the giant puzzle together. Have them turn their pieces over to look at the numbers on the back. Say the numbers aloud (starting with one and stopping before or at 24); the numbers go left to right. Nine starts the second puzzle line and seventeen starts the third line. When done, discuss how the puzzle became so big.

Reflect/Assess

How did we make the "Down by the Bay"/"Junto a la bahía" song longer?

¿Cómo hicimos más larga la canción "Junto a la bahía"/"Down by the Bay"?

- *What did we do to make our city big?*

  ¿Qué hicimos para hacer más grande nuestra ciudad?

Storytime 1

- Tell the "Henny-Penny"/"Gallinita-Nita" flannel board story. Ask the children: *What happens to the group of animals' size on their way to see the king?*

  ¿Qué le sucede al grupo de tamaños de animales al ir a ver al rey?

Storytime 2

- Present the "Five Dancing Dolphins"/"Cinco delfines bailarines" flannel board story. Discuss what happens to the dolphins as the story continues.

Content Connection

Social Studies/Science

Objectives
To begin to understand cause-and-effect relationships
To begin to observe changes in size, color, position, weather, and sound

Vocabulary
big, nature
grande, naturaleza

DLM Materials
Animals That Build Their Homes/Animales que construyen sus nidos
Sing a Song of Opposites/Canta una canción de opuestos

Materials to Gather
clay

Activity 1
- Discuss big things in nature. Show the children the tall trees from *Sing a Song of Opposites/Canta una canción de opuestos.* Display the tall termite tower from *Animals That Build Their Homes/Animales que construyen sus nidos.*
- Talk about large homes that animals build (spider webs) and large homes where animals live (bear caves). Discuss how the homes are made or what causes them to develop. Allow the children to share other examples.

Activity 2
- Help the children brainstorm a list of big things in nature. Invite them to dictate their answers so they understand how their thoughts translate to written words on paper. Possible responses include oceans, mountains, volcanoes, roads, trees, and icebergs. You might explain how a melting iceberg contributes to the size of an ocean.
- Provide clay for the children to shape volcanoes and mountains.

DAY 5

Objectives

- To begin to investigate and predict the results of putting together two or more shapes
- To begin to recognize, describe, and name shapes

Vocabulary

side	lado
corner	esquina
angle	ángulo
all shape names	nombres de todas las figuras

DLM Materials

- *Math Resource Guide*
  Feely Box
  Guess My Shape/Adivina mi figura
  Shape Transparencies
- See Day 1
- *DLM Math* software
- *Four Baby Bumblebees* CD
- *Diez deditos* CD

Materials to Gather

- toothpicks (12 per child)
- attribute blocks
- See Day 1

Scaffolding Strategies

More Help Use building blocks in the Feely Box.

Extra Challenge Give several *not* clues for the Feely Box, such as *this shape does not have any straight sides.*

MATH

Focus

- Read and discuss the children's recorded estimates of how many items there are in the Estimating Jar. Dump the objects and count them to check.
- Compare the children's first estimates with those after the benchmarks were shown. Discuss how their estimates changed. Congratulate them on a great job of estimating.
- Play Guess My Shape/Adivina mi figura. Have a child secretly put 1 of the shapes from the Shape Set in the Feely Box. Challenge the children to identify what shape you are feeling. Describe the sides and angles of the shape you are feeling. Give other hints as needed.
- After the children have guessed, pull the shape out to check. Repeat with new shapes.

Develop

- Have several children share a favorite puzzle they completed or a favorite shape they made from parts.
- Complete a task from Memory—Geometry, Level 6, with the children. Talk about the different ways to solve, and to figure out how to solve the puzzle, emphasizing how and why shapes fit.

Practice

- Encourage the children to play Guess My Shape/Adivina mi figura. The children challenge each other to guess the shape they have placed in the Feely Box.
- Invite the children to combine shapes using the Shape Transparencies.
- Have the children continue to work on the Practice activities from Day 1.
- Invite the children to work on Create-a-Scene (no level) and Memory—Geometry, Level 6.

Reflect/Assess

- Computer Show: *How did you figure out how to make a whole picture with the shapes and tools?*
  ¿Cómo determinaron cómo hacer un dibujo completo con las figuras y herramientas?

Music and Movement

- Sing "Green Bottles" from the *Four Baby Bumblebees* CD. Discuss the size of an elephant compared to the size of a spider's web.
- Sing "La tía Mónica" from the *Diez deditos* CD.

Content Connection

Science

Objective
To begin to use scientific words and phrases to describe objects, events, and living things

DLM Materials
- *Teacher's Resource Anthology*
- play dough

Materials to Gather
white felt, flannel board

Activity 1
- Discuss the size and shape of the moon. Use a flannel board and white felt cut into appropriate sizes to show the moon when it is full, half, and quarter size.
- Encourage the children to use the moons and white stars cut from felt to make a night sky.

Activity 2
- Use play dough to demonstrate whole/part relationships. Divide a ball of play dough into halves, thirds, and fourths. Roll each part into a new ball. Discuss the changes in size of the balls as you create more of them. Recombine the balls to make 1 large ball.
- Let the children explore making large and small balls out of play dough.

Suggested Reading

Moon Rope: A Peruvian Folktale by Lois Ehlert
Un lazo a la luna: una leyenda peruana by Lois Ehlert

Reflect on the Day

- *What have you learned this week about things that are b*
  ¿Qué aprendieron esta semana sobre cosas que son grandes?
- *What will you share with your families about size?*
  ¿Qué compartirán con sus familias sobre el tamaño?

Home Connection

Send a note home asking families if they can donate unwanted or old summer clothing, sunglasses, sun visors, and empty sunscreen containers for next week's lessons.

Looking Ahead

Connecting to the Theme: Summer Fun

As the school year draws to a close, what better theme to conclude with than summertime fun! Even if the class you have now ends during another season, children can still learn about summer. They can also review their school year experiences. Lessons will discuss typical summer activities, clothing, and weather.

	Objectives	DLM Materials	Materials to Gather
DAY 1	• To refine and extend understanding of known words • To link new learning experiences and vocabulary to what is already known about a topic • To begin to recognize, describe, and name shapes • To begin to use words that indicate where things are in space	• Oral Language Development Card 58 • *De Colores/De colores* • Rafita and Pepita puppets • *Teacher's Resource Anthology* • *DLM Math* software • *Where Is Thumbkin?* CD • *Diez deditos* CD	• summer puzzles • flowers • leaves • sponges • books about summertime • toothpicks (10 per child) • straws
DAY 2	• To listen to and engage in several exchanges of conversations with others • To begin to recognize, describe, and name shapes • To begin to use words that indicate where things are in space • To begin to manipulate play objects that have fine parts	• Oral Language Cards 58 & 59 • *Insect Picnic/El picnic de los insectos* • *Teacher's Resource Anthology* • Rafita and Pepita puppets • pattern blocks • *Math Resource Guide* • *DLM Math* software • *Where Is Thumbkin?* CD	• summer puzzles (see Day 1) • books about summer • sand • summer clothing • tray • word cards • toothpicks (10 per child) • straws
DAY 3	• To understand that different text forms are used for different functions • To understand that print carries a message by recognizing labels, signs, and other print forms in the environment • To understand attributes of shapes by building them from parts	• Oral Language Development Card 58 • *Insect Picnic/El picnic de los insectos* • *Teacher's Resource Anthology* • Rafita and Pepita puppets • pattern blocks • *Math Resource Guide* • *DLM Math* software	• summer puzzles • milk • picnic supplies • vanilla • sun hats • ice • lemons • picnic basket • rock salt • sunglasses • self-sealing plastic bags (large and small) • sunscreen (allergy warning)
DAY 4	• To understand that illustrations carry meaning but cannot be read • To begin to recognize the association between spoken and written words by following the print as it is read aloud • To begin to recognize, describe, and name shapes • To begin to use words that indicate where things are in space	• Oral Language Cards 13–20, 29, 30, 41–45 • *The Little Ants/Las hormiguitas* • *Sara Sidney* • *Teacher's Resource Anthology* • pattern blocks • *Four Baby Bumblebees* CD • *Diez deditos* CD	• index cards • bug puzzles • word cards • toothpicks (10 per child) • glue • straws • counters • crepe paper or lightweight scarves
DAY 5	• To use new vocabulary in everyday communication • To refine and extend understanding of known words • To begin to use scientific words and phrases to describe objects, events, and living things • To begin to recognize, describe, and name shapes	• *Teacher's Resource Anthology* • *DLM Math* software	• balloons • water hose • bubble wands • mini pie tins • plastic utensils • spray bottles • tongue depressors • sponges • sprinkler

(See individual lesson pages for complete lists of materials.)

Learning Centers

DRAMATIC PLAY

Beach Picnic

Objective

To begin to create or re-create stories, moods, or experiences through dramatic representations

Materials to Gather

basket, blanket, beach ball, beach towels, empty food containers, empty sunscreen bottles, plastic eating utensils, plastic plates, sand buckets, sand shovels, shells, sunglasses

Develop

Make the center into a beach for the first part of the week. During this time, invite the children to pretend they are swimming, sunning, building sandcastles, playing volleyball, and so on. During the last part of the week, change the center into a picnic area. Suggest that the children pretend they are eating and playing games with friends. You might combine the scenes for a picnic on the beach.

Reflect/Assess

Do you prefer going to the beach or having a picnic?

¿Prefieren ir a la playa o hacer un picnic?

ART

Summer Scenes

Objectives

To use a variety of materials to create original work

To use different colors, surface textures, and shapes to create form and meaning

Materials to Gather

chalk, construction paper, crayons, markers, tempera paint, tissue paper

Develop

Encourage the children to experiment with different art materials each day. Have them use primarily summer colors such as yellows, oranges, pinks, greens, blues, and white. Help them think of summer themes such as festivals, amusement parks, baseball, swimming, and so on. Create a Step Up to Summertime Fun bulletin board by displaying the children's summertime artwork.

Reflect/Assess

Which materials do you like to use to show your ideas?

¿Qué materiales les gusta usar para mostrar sus ideas?

SCIENCE

Summer Observations

Objectives

To gather information using simple tools such as a magnifying lens and an eyedropper

To compare objects and organisms and identify similarities and differences

Materials to Gather

bug specimens, flowers, leaves, magnifying lens, nonfiction summer books, summer photos

Develop

Fill the center with flowers, various leaves or tree foliage, bug specimens, and summer photographs. Place nonfiction books about summer in the center for reference. If you can safely supply live bugs for the children to examine, it will add to the center's appeal. Release the live bugs outdoors as soon as possible. Encourage the children to use a magnifying lens to observe the summertime items.

Reflect/Assess

What do you like or dislike about examining outdoor items?

¿Qué les gusta o disgusta de examinar los objetos de afuera?

What Research Suggests

Make sure the children are drinking enough water. In order to hydrate the brain properly, they need to drink water at least every hour and a half throughout the day. Water nourishes the brain and will help the children stay alert and think.

Begin the Day

- Read "Counting My Blessings."
- Use a suggestion for Morning Circle found in the front of this *Teacher's Edition.*

Objectives

- To refine and extend understanding of known words
- To link new learning experiences and vocabulary to what is already known about a topic

Vocabulary

summer verano

DLM Materials

- *Fall/El otoño*
- Oral Language Development Card 58
- *De Colores/De colores*
- Rafita and Pepita puppets
- magnetic letters
- *SRA Photo Library* software
- *Teacher's Resource Anthology*
  summer card patterns
  "Counting My Blessings"
  "Summer Is Coming"/"Ya viene el verano"
  summer observation bottles
  Summer Concentration game

Materials to Gather

- summer puzzles
- brown and green paint
- flowers
- leaves
- magnifying lens
- sponges
- books about summertime

LITERACY

Focus

- Sing "Summer Is Coming"/"Ya viene el verano."
- Explain that the children will be talking about summer this week.

Develop

One Way to Develop the Lesson

- Help the children create a word web about summer. Write the word *summer* in the center of a piece of paper and circle it.
- Ask the children to share what they know about summer (for example, sports, nature, wildlife, water activities, carnivals, and so on). Record their responses on lines surrounding *summer.*
- Using Rafita and Pepita, discuss the signs of summer. Ask: *What colors are the leaves on trees? Does the weather feel warm or cool? What activities do we do in the summer?*

  ¿De qué color son las hojas de los árboles? ¿El clima es frío o cálido? ¿Qué actividades hacemos en el verano?
- You might also discuss any summer birthdays or summer holidays. Add new information to your word web during the discussion. Keep the web available throughout the week so you can include additional summertime discoveries.

Another Way to Develop the Lesson

- Display Oral Language Card 58. Use the suggestions on the back of the card to continue your discussion.
- If the school year is ending, help the children review some of the things they have learned (new words, beginning to write and read, spelling their names, safety, cooperation, and so on). Allow them to share what they will miss about school.
- Conclude by having the children share any special plans for summer. Because many families may not be able to vacation, you might ask: *What would you like to do this summer?* or *Where would you like to go this summer?*

  ¿Qué les gustaría hacer este verano? ¿Dónde les gustaría ir este verano?

Practice

- Provide brown paint, green paint, and some sponges. Instruct the children to paint a tree trunk and to use the sponges to make leaves. Next, have the children draw themselves involved in summer activities. Finally, have each child dictate a sentence about his or her artwork for you to write on the bottom or back of his or her picture.
- Write the word *summer* on a piece of paper. Allow the children to copy the word using magnetic letters.
- Place books about summer in the Library Center. Invite the children to use the books to explore what other people do in the summer.
- Allow the children to play the Summer Concentration game.
- Give the children summer puzzles to complete.
- Provide summer observation bottles for the children to examine. Answer any questions they might have about what they see.
- Have the children use a magnifying lens to look closely at summer leaves and flowers. Please note any allergies or safety concerns.
- Encourage the children to find the summer pictures in the Earth category on the *SRA Photo Library* software.

Preparation

- Make two copies of the summer card patterns. Color, laminate, and cut them out.
- Make enlarged copies of the summer card patterns. Color, cut, mount on construction paper, laminate, and cut into puzzle pieces.
- Make summer observation bottles.

Scaffolding Strategies

More Help Have the children look out a window to find signs of summer.

Extra Challenge Have the children draw a tree for each season.

Second Language Learners

Encourage the children to describe the pictures they uncover as they play Summer Concentration. This will help them recall the locations of the pictures on the next trial and promote vocabulary development.

Anthology Support

"Mister Sun"

"Señor Sol"

"She Waded in the Water"

DAY 1

Letter Knowledge

English

- Read any of the letter stories from the *English Phonics Resource Guide.*

Spanish

- Read any of the letter stories from the *Spanish Phonics Resource Guide*.

Suggested Reading

Summer by Ron Hirschi
Time of Wonder by Robert McCloskey

Reflect/Assess

- *How is summer similar to spring?*

  ¿En qué se parece el verano a la primavera?
- *How is summer different from spring?*

  ¿En qué se diferencia el verano de la primavera?

Literacy Circle

Storytime 1

- Read *De Colores/De colores*. You might want to quickly review each of the seasons. Ask: *Which scenes in the story look like they take place in summer?*

  ¿Qué escenas del cuento parecen verano?

Storytime 2

- Read *Fall/El otoño*. Discuss the differences between summer and fall.

Content Connection

Science/Fine Arts

Objectives

To begin to observe changes in size, color, position, weather, and sound

To begin to use art as a form of self-expression

Vocabulary

green, summer

verde, verano

Materials to Gather

masking tape

Activity 1

- Take the children outdoors for a summer walk. Before venturing out, make a nature bracelet for each child. Place a band of masking tape with the adhesive side out on each child's wrist. Encourage them to pick up safe summer treasures to attach to their bracelets.
- Help the children look for natural signs that it is summer. Discuss weather, animals, colors, temperature, and so on. Make sure to address any issues that are specific to the region where you live.

Activity 2

- Have the children use their bracelets to make individual summer collages. If they collected enough materials, you might make a class summer mural instead.

DAY 1

MATH

Objectives

- To begin to recognize, describe, and name shapes
- To begin to use words that indicate where things are in space

Vocabulary

side	lado
corner	esquina
angle	ángulo
length	longitud, largo
puzzle	rompecabezas
line	línea, recta
horizontal	horizontal
vertical	vertical
slanted	inclinada
all shape names	nombres de todas las figuras

DLM Materials

- pattern blocks
- *Math Resource Guide*
  - Building Straws
  - Shape Set
  - Tangrams from Shape Set
  - Tangram Puzzles
  - Pattern Block Puzzles (26–32)
  - Pattern Block Cutouts
  - Estimating Jar
- *DLM Math* software
- *Where Is Thumbkin?* CD
- *Diez deditos* CD

Materials to Gather

- toothpicks (10 per child)
- construction paper
- straws
- plastic liter bottles
- plastic coffee can lids

Focus

- Ask the children if they remember how, at the beginning of the year, they showed how old they were on their fingers. Ask them to show their age now on their fingers.
- Have them show their age with some fingers on each hand. Ask them to tell about the numbers they made.

Develop

- Give each child a set of Building Straws and ask them to show you the shapes they can make. Ask them what shapes they can make with 2 short straws and 2 long straws that are the same length. Ask them what shape they can make with 4 straws that are all the same length.
- Show the children the Estimating Jar. Let them choose (or vote) on the items to place in the Estimating Jar for this final week. Offer items that relate to summer fun such as chalk or jacks. Remind them to record their estimates.

Practice

- Invite the children to make shapes with Building Straws or toothpicks and record and label their favorite designs or pictures.
- Encourage the children to choose and complete the Pattern Block Puzzles and use Pattern Block Cutouts to record their work.
- Have the children work Tangram Puzzles. Have them record their solutions.
- Have the children make a picture with either pattern blocks or a Shape Set. Have them choose their favorite picture to copy with the Pattern Block Cutouts.
- Encourage the children to estimate how many items are in the Estimating Jar and to record their estimates.
- Invite the children to work on Create-a-Scene (no level). Encourage children to make their favorite Summer Fun scene or character. Remind them to use the tools to make interesting scenes.

Reflect/Assess

- *How did you figure out which parts of shapes are sides and which are corners?*
  ¿Cómo determinaron qué partes de las figuras son lados y cuáles son esquinas?

Music and Movement

- Play Horseshoes/Herraduras. Use weighted plastic litre bottles for stakes and cut the centers out of plastic coffee can lids for horseshoes.
- Sing "Down by the Bay" from the *Where Is Thumbkin?* CD or "En nuestra tierra tan linda" from the *Diez deditos* CD.

Content Connection

Literacy

Objectives

To enjoy listening to and responding to books
To demonstrate an interest in books and reading through body language and facial expressions

Vocabulary

shape names
nombres de figuras

DLM Materials

Teacher's Resource Anthology
"Freddie the Snake"/"Braulio, la culebra"
"Tillie Triangle"/"El Triángulo Tilín"

Materials to Gather

yarn

Activity 1

- Present the "Freddie the Snake"/"Braulio, la culebra" flannel board story. Give the children pieces of yarn to use to make the snake's shapes as you tell the story. *What lesson did Freddie/Braulio learn?*
  ¿Qué lección aprendió Braulio/Freddie?

Activity 2

- Read the chalk story, "Tillie Triangle"/"El Triángulo Tilín" to the children. *What lesson did Tillie learn?*
  ¿Qué lección aprendió Tilín?
- Have the children compare "Tillie Triangle"/"El Triángulo Tilín" to "Freddie the Snake"/"Braulio, la culebra."

Suggested Reading

One Hot Summer Day by Nina Crews

Reflect on the Day

- *What did you learn about summer today?*
  ¿Qué aprendieron sobre el verano hoy?
- *Which activity did you most enjoy? Why?*
  ¿Qué actividad disfrutaron más? ¿Por qué?

Home Connection

Send home the Water Fun letter to let families know that, weather permitting, Friday's lesson will focus on outdoor water play.

Begin the Day

- Sing "Mister Sun"/"Señor Sol."
- Use one of the suggestions for Morning Circle offered in the front of this *Teacher's Edition.*

Objectives

- To listen with increasing attention
- To listen to and engage in several exchanges of conversations with others

Vocabulary

hot caliente
warm tibio

DLM Materials

- Oral Language Development Card 56, 58
- *Insect Picnic/El picnic de los insectos*
- *SRA Photo Library* software
- *Teacher's Resource Anthology*
  "Mister Sun"/"Señor Sol"
  "This Is the Way We Dress for Summer"/"Así nos vestimos en verano"
  "Dress-Me-Bears for Summer"/ "Vísteme para el verano"
  "Dress-Me-Bears for Spring"/ "Vísteme para la primavera"
  Summer Concentration game
  "The Wind and the Sun"/"El viento y el sol"
  Dress-Me-Bears patterns

Materials to Gather

- summer puzzles (see Day 1)
- books about summer
- index cards
- sand
- summer clothing
- tray
- word cards

LITERACY

Focus

- Sing "This Is the Way We Dress for Summer"/"Así nos vestimos en verano." Discuss what kinds of clothes people typically wear in the summer. Ask: *What is happening to the weather? How does the weather influence the clothes we wear?*

  ¿Qué le sucede al clima? ¿Cómo el clima influye en la ropa que usamos?
- Explain that today the class will discuss summer weather and summer clothing.

Develop

One Way to Develop the Lesson

- Discuss what summer is like in your part of the country. Help the children understand that different places may experience seasons differently. For example, summer in the Midwest is different from summer in Alaska, Florida, or on the West Coast.
- Talk about typical summer weather. Ask: *How is summer different from spring? How is summer different from winter?*

  ¿En qué se diferencia el verano de la primavera? ¿En qué se diferencia el verano del invierno?
- Present the "Dress-Me-Bears for Summer"/"Vísteme para el verano" flannel board story. Discuss the clothing that the bears choose to wear.

Another Way to Develop the Lesson

- You might want to review what spring is like in your part of the country. Allow the children to ask questions about spring and/or summer, especially if spring and summer are similar in your region.
- Present the "Dress-Me-Bears for Spring"/"Vísteme para la primavera" flannel board story. Discuss the bears' springtime clothing and how summer clothing is different from spring clothing. Ask: *How are summer clothes similar to spring clothes? How are summer clothes different from winter clothes?*

  ¿En qué se parecen los objetos de verano a los de primavera? ¿En qué se diferencia la ropa de verano de la de invierno?

Practice

- Provide copies of the Dress-Me-Bears. Have the children color typical summer clothing on their own Dress-Me-Bears.
- Give the children the "Dress-Me-Bears for Summer"/"Vísteme para el verano" and the "Dress-Me-Bears for Spring"/"Vísteme para la primavera" flannel board stories. Invite them to retell the stories or to make up new stories using the flannel board pieces.
- Add typical and appropriate summer clothing to the Dramatic Play Center. Have the children sort through various clothing items, deciding if they are appropriate for summer or another season.
- Fill your library with books about summer. Suggest that the children pay attention to what the characters are wearing and to the weather depicted in books.
- Give the children summer puzzles.
- Allow the children to play the Summer Concentration game.
- Using the *summer* word card and a tray of sand, encourage the children to copy the word in the sand using their fingers or craft sticks.
- Encourage the children to find summer clothes in the clothing category on the *SRA Photo Library* software.

Preparation

- Make flannel board stories.
- Make copies of the Dress-Me-Bears patterns (one per child).
- Write the word *hot* on an index card to add to your word cards.

Scaffolding Strategies

More Help Work with children individually to examine characteristics of typical summer clothing.

Extra Challenge Help the children think of clothing that people can wear year round.

Second Language Learners

As children sort summer and winter clothes, talk with them to find out what they know. Do they know the names of all the clothes? Can they describe parts of the clothing (for example sleeves/mangas, buttons/botones, collars/cuello)? Do they use concept words to describe the clothing, such as "short sleeves/"mangas cortas"and "long sleeves/"mangas largas"? Describe unfamiliar objects to help children learn new vocabulary.

DAY 2

Letter Knowledge

English

- Read a selection from the *SRA Alphabet Book.*

Spanish

- Read a selection from *Los niños alfabéticos.*

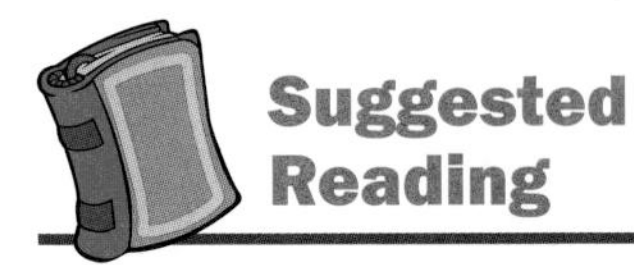

Suggested Reading

Earth Circles by Sandra Griffin
Flowy, Snowy, Blowy by Nancy Tafuri

Anthology Support

"You Are My Sunshine"
"Tú eres mi luz del sol"
"Ice Cream Chant"
"La canción del helado"
"De colores"
"The Colors"
"Summer Is Coming"
"Ya viene el verano"

Reflect/Assess

- *Are some of your spring outfits too warm to wear in the summer?*
  ¿Algunas de sus prendas de vestir de primavera son demasiado calientes para usarlas en el verano?
- *What do you like to wear in the summer?*
  ¿Qué les gusta usar en el verano?

Literacy Circle

Storytime 1

- Read "The Wind and the Sun"/"El viento y el sol" listening story. Ask: *Do you ever wear a jacket and decide it is too hot to wear?*
  ¿Alguna vez han tratado de usar una chaqueta y deciden que es muy caliente para usarla?

Storytime 2

- Read *Insect Picnic/El picnic de los insectos.* Ask: *What kind of clothing do the characters in the story wear?*
  ¿Qué tipo de ropa usan los personajes del cuento?

Content Connection

Social Studies

Objective
To recognize changes in the environment over time

Vocabulary
fall, seasons, summer
otoño, estaciones, verano

DLM Materials
Oral Language Development Cards 56 & 58

Materials to Gather
chart paper

Activity 1

- Make a word web on a piece of chart paper or the board for summer. Write the word *summer* and draw a circle around it. Draw lines that extend from the circle; this is where you will record the children's responses.
- Have the children tell you what they know about summer. Provide suggestions for their brainstorming such as clothing, food, animals, activities, or weather. Write appropriate answers on the web lines.
- Make another word web for fall. Write the word *fall* in the center and circle it. Draw several lines from the circle. You might discuss that fall has another name, *autumn*. Ask the children to share what they know about fall. You might initiate the discussion by reviewing what the weather in fall is like in your part of the country.
- When you have completed both word webs, help the children draw conclusions about similarities and differences between the two seasons.

Activity 2

- Display Oral Language Card 58. Use the suggestions on the back of the card to continue the class discussion of summer. Ask: *Have you learned anything new about summer?*

  ¿Han aprendido algo nuevo sobre el verano?
- Show the children Oral Language Card 56. Review the back of the card for additional activity suggestions. Discuss any new fall information that the children have learned.
- After you have examined each card, help the children consider similarities and differences between the two seasons.

DAY 2

Objectives

- To begin to recognize, describe, and name shapes
- To begin to use words that indicate where things are in space

Vocabulary

side	lado
corner	esquina
angle	ángulo
length	longitud, largo
puzzle	rompecabezas
line	línea, recta
horizontal	horizontal
vertical	vertical
slanted	inclinada
all shape names	nombres de todas las figuras

DLM Materials

- Rafita and Pepita/Rafita y Pepita puppets
- *Math Resource Guide*
- See Day 1
- *DLM Math* software
- *Where Is Thumbkin?* CD
- *Teacher's Resource Anthology* "Weather"/"El tiempo"

Materials to Gather

- See Day 1

MATH

Focus

- Have 5 children stand up. Then have them sort themselves into those wearing shorts and those not wearing shorts (or any other attribute). Record the number combinations.
- Repeat the activity with 5 new children.

Develop

- Give each child a set of Building Straws. Include Rafita and Pepita/Rafita y Pepita in today's activity. Let them demonstrate some of the straw shapes to illustrate how much they have learned. Ask them to show you the shapes they can make with 3 straws of the same length. Then ask them to show you the shapes they can make with 2 straws of the same length and 1 other straw of a different length. Next, ask the children to show you a shape they can make with 8 straws all of the same length.
- Children often start by making only rectangles. Challenge them to be creative!

Practice

- Invite the children to make shapes with Building Straws or toothpicks and record and label their favorite design or picture.
- Encourage the children to choose and complete the Pattern Block Puzzles and use Pattern Block Cutouts to record their work.
- Have the children work Tangram Puzzles and record their solutions.
- Have the children make a picture with either pattern blocks or a Shape Set. Then have them copy their favorite picture with the Pattern Block Cutouts.
- Encourage the children to estimate how many items are in the Estimating Jar and record their estimates.
- Invite the children to work on Create-a-Scene (no level). After they finish a scene, remind them that they can explore any activity they enjoyed during the year.

Reflect/Assess

- *How did you figure out which shapes to use for the puzzles?*
  ¿Cómo determinaron qué figuras usar para los rompecabezas?

Content Connection

Physical Development

Objectives
To begin to manipulate play objects that have fine parts
To begin to participate in group games involving movement

DLM Materials
 *Teacher's Resource Anthology*
bubble soap

Materials to Gather
masking tape, chenille wire

Activity 1
- Use masking tape to make large shape outlines on the floor. Play music and encourage the children to march around the shapes on the floor.

Activity 2
- Invite the children to bend wire or chenille wire into different shapes to make bubble wands. Provide bubble soap and encourage the children to try out their wands. Is anyone surprised that the bubble shapes don't change?
  ¿Les sorprende que las figuras de burbujas no cambian?

Reflect on the Day

- *What did you learn about clothing today?*
  ¿Qué aprendieron sobre la ropa hoy?
- *How does the weather change what we wear?*
  ¿Cómo el clima cambia lo que debemos usar?

Music and Movement

- Sing "Crocodile Song" from the *Where Is Thumbkin?* CD.
- Invite the children to participate in the "Weather"/"El tiempo" action story. Ask them: *How do we know what clothes to wear outdoors? What should we wear in the rain? Sun? Snow?*
  ¿Cómo sabemos qué ropa debemos usar para estar afuera? ¿Qué debemos usar en la lluvia? ¿Bajo el sol? ¿En la nieve?

Suggested Reading

Knots on a Counting Rope by Bill Martin Jr and John Archambault
Las tres mellizas, Blancanieves y los siete enanitos by Wilhelm and Jacob Grimm

Begin the Day

- Sing "This Is the Way We Dress for Summer"/"Así nos vestimos en verano."
- Use a suggestion for Morning Circle from the front of this *Teacher's Edition.*

Objectives

- To understand that different text forms are used for different functions
- To understand that print carries a message by recognizing labels, signs, and other print forms in the environment

Vocabulary

summer activities — actividades de verano

DLM Materials

- Oral Language Development Card 58
- *Insect Picnic/El picnic de los insectos*
- *Teacher's Resource Anthology*
  "This Is the Way We Dress for Summer"/"Así nos vestimos en verano"
  "The Ants Go Marching"/"Las hormiguitas marchan"
  baggie ice cream
  baggie ice cream rebus
  Summer Concentration game
  "Going for a Swim"/"Voy a nadar"
  "Summer at the Beach"/"Verano en la playa"

Materials to Gather

- ice
- small and large self-sealing plastic bags
- lemons
- milk
- picnic basket and supplies
- rock salt
- vanilla

LITERACY

Focus

- Sing "The Ants Go Marching"/"Las hormiguitas marchan." Ask: *Do ants look like they are marching? Do ants move fast or slow?*

  ¿Parece que las hormigas están marchando? ¿Las hormigas son rápidas o lentas?
- Explain that today the class will discuss summertime activities.

Develop

One Way to Develop the Lesson

- Help the children list summer activities. The list might include games, trips, visits to special places (museums, concerts), family visits, swimming, the beach, picnics, cookouts, camping, bike riding, and so on. Allow the children to share their favorite activities.
- Review Oral Language Card 58. Use the photo to continue your class conversation about activities people enjoy in the summer months.
- When the list is complete, ask: *Which of these things would you like to do this summer? Is anyone going to a new place?*

  ¿Cuáles de estas cosas les gustaría hacer este verano? ¿Alguien va a un lugar nuevo?
- To help reinforce that print conveys a message, read the activity list aloud. Instruct the children to raise their hands if they think the activities you read are things they might do.

Another Way to Develop the Lesson

- Bring a picnic basket full of picnic supplies to the circle area. Supplies might include paper plates, plastic eating utensils, a blanket or sheet, empty food containers, storage containers, paper cups, napkins, and so on. Do not show supplies to the children yet.
- Tell the children that you are pretending to get ready for a picnic. Have them help you create a packing list. Ask: *What items should we pack for the picnic? What are some good picnic foods to take?*

  ¿Qué cosas debemos empacar para el picnic? ¿Cuáles son algunos alimentos para picnic buenos de llevar?

  You might also discuss taking games to play.
- One at a time, compare the items in your basket with the items on the list. Ask: *Are we missing anything from the list? Do we have any items in the basket that are not on the list?*

  ¿Nos falta algo de la lista? ¿Hay algo en la canasta que no esté en la lista?

Practice

- Place the *Insect Picnic/El picnic de los insectos* book and tape in the Listening Center. Allow the children to review the story.
- Place the picnic supplies in the Dramatic Play Center. Invite the children to pack the basket and go on a pretend picnic. Post your list from the second Develop in the center.
- Have the children draw pictures of activities that they plan to do this summer.
- Supply several summer related word cards to trace.
- Help the children make lemonade to enjoy during snacktime.
- Use the baggie ice cream rebus card to make ice cream with the class.
- Invite the children to play the Summer Concentration game.
- Allow the children to complete the summer puzzles.

Preparation

- Make copies of the baggie ice cream rebus card.
- Gather ingredients for baggie ice cream and lemonade.
- Pack the picnic basket.
- Write the word *picnic* on an index card and add it to your word cards.

Second Language Learners

Create a rebus card for children to follow as they make lemonade. Describe the steps as you demonstrate the process, referring to the card as you go. After the children drink the lemonade, ask them to describe the process using the rebus card, so they can make lemonade at home. If possible, send home a rebus sheet so children can describe the process to their families.

"Ice Cream Chant"
"La canción del helado"
"Summer Is Coming"
"Ya viene el verano"
"Take Me Out to the Ballgame"
"She Waded in the Water"
"Down by the Bay"
"Junto a la bahía"

DAY 3

Letter Knowledge

English

- Have the children shape letters with play dough.

Spanish

- Have the children shape letters with play dough.

Suggested Reading

Bubble Bubble by Mercer Mayer
On My Beach There Are Many Pebbles by Leo Lionni

Technology Support

In summary to the children's first year of school, allow each child to type his or her name and age into the computer.

Reflect/Assess

- *What are you looking forward to this summer?*
  ¿Qué es lo que más desean hacer este verano?
- *What do we do in the summer that we cannot do in the winter?*
  ¿Qué hacemos en el verano que no podemos hacer en el invierno?

Literacy Circle

Storytime 1

- Have the children participate in the "Going for a Swim"/"Voy a nadar" action story.

Storytime 2

- Read the "Summer at the Beach"/"Verano en la playa" listening story. Allow the children to share any beach experiences.

Content Connection

Health and Safety

Objectives
To become aware of routine healthy behaviors
To begin to follow health-promoting routines

Vocabulary
sun protection, sunscreen
protección solar, protector solar

Materials to Gather
sun hats, sunglasses, sunscreen
(Allergy Warning)

Activity 1
- Discuss how people can protect themselves from the sun. Explain that, even though the sun may feel good, it is important not to burn one's skin or to harm one's eyes.
- Have a show and tell for each of the following items: sunscreen (please note any allergies), sun hats, and sunglasses. Address each item's importance. You might use yourself as an example of how to apply sunscreen. Explain that people can be safe and have fun at the same time!

Activity 2
- Allow the children to try on various hats from the Dramatic Play Center. You might discuss which hats would best protect them from too much sun.
- Provide a variety of sunglasses for the children to explore. Review the importance of protecting eyes from overexposure to the sun.

DAY 3

Objectives

- To begin to recognize, describe, and name shapes
- To begin to use words that indicate where things are in space

Vocabulary

angle	ángulo
length	longitud, largo
puzzle	rompecabezas
line	línea, recta
horizontal	horizontal
vertical	vertical
slanted	inclinado
all shape names	nombres de todas las figuras

DLM Materials

- Rafita and Pepita puppets
- *Math Resource Guide*
  Shape Set
- See Day 1
- *DLM Math* software
- *Teacher's Resource Anthology*
  plastic bag books
  Hopscotch/Rayuela

Materials to Gather

- plastic flying discs
- See Day 1

Preparation

- Make plastic bag books for the children to use for Shape Books. Use the gallon size plastic bags.

MATH

Focus

- Read and discuss the children's recorded estimates of how many items there are in the Estimating Jar. Show an identical jar and, along with the children, count 5 identical objects into that jar. Hold up both jars so the children can compare them. Let them identify the jar they believe has more in it.
- Count out 5 more objects (i.e., start counting at 6) into the identical jar and compare again. Tell them that they will make new estimates today.

Develop

- Have Rafita and Pepita/Rafita y Pepita count the sides of, and name, the hexagon from the Shape Set. Have them get mixed up again today (e.g., counting 8 instead of 6 and calling it an octagon). Ask the children to help the puppets get it straight.
- Tell the children that they will assemble their Shape Books today.

Practice

- Set up a center for constructing the Shape Books. Have materials available for the children to create book covers.
- Have the children work in pairs to determine which shapes are in the Feely Box.
- Encourage the children to make a new estimate of the number of items in the Estimating Jar based on the benchmark counters. Change the color of the paper they are using for recording.
- Have the children continue to work on the Practice activities from Day 1.
- Invite the children to work on Create-a-Scene (no level).

Reflect/Assess

- *What is your favorite shape? Why?*
  ¿Cuál es su figura favorita? ¿Por qué?
- *What are some ways you can tell if shapes will go together?*
  ¿Cuáles son algunas formas de decir si las figuras encajarán?

Music and Movement

- Take plastic flying discs outdoors to play catch. You might also use a safe ball to throw. Or, have the children safely chase bubbles you blow.
- Allow the children to play Hopscotch/Rayuela.

Content Connection

Science

Objectives

To begin to use scientific words and phrases to describe objects, events, and living things

To share observations and findings with others through pictures, discussions, or dramatizations

Materials to Gather

die cut objects, crayons, drawing paper

Activity 1

- Use the die cut machine to cut out several objects—some that are symmetrical and can be cut in half, and some that are asymmetrical and cannot be cut in half. Ask the children to determine which objects can be cut in half and help them determine why.

Activity 2

- Take the children to the playground and have them stand in a place where they cast shadows on the ground. Discuss the shapes they make on the ground and then discuss the symmetry of their shadows and their bodies.
- Encourage the children to draw pictures of themselves and their shadows.

Suggested Reading

Gator Pie by Louise Mathews

Munia y la luna by Asun Balzola

Reflect on the Day

- *What did you learn about summer activities today?*
  ¿Qué aprendieron sobre las actividades de verano hoy?
- *What will you share with your family about summer activities?*
  ¿Qué compartirán con su familia sobre las actividades de verano?

Begin the Day

- Sing "Five Little Speckled Frogs"/"Cinco ranitas manchadas." Allow the children to share any of their frog experiences.
- Use one of the suggestions for Morning Circle located in the front of this *Teacher's Edition.*

Objectives

- To understand that illustrations carry meaning but cannot be read
- To begin to recognize the association between spoken and written words by following the print as it is read aloud

Vocabulary

ants	hormigas
butterflies	mariposas
fireflies	luciérnagas
flies	moscas
mosquitoes	mosquitos

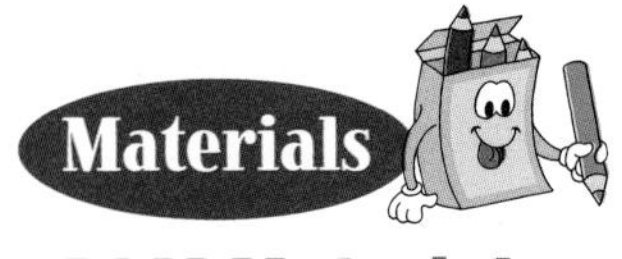

DLM Materials

- Oral Language Development Cards
- *The Little Ants/Las hormiguitas*
- magnetic letters
- *SRA Photo Library* software
- *Teacher's Resource Anthology*
  bug card patterns
  animal card patterns
  farm animal card patterns
  "Five Little Speckled Frogs"/"Cinco ranitas manchadas"
  "The Ants Go Marching"/"Las hormiguitas marchan"
  "Ms. Bumblebee Gathers Honey"/"La avispa Zumbi lleva miel"
  "The Ant and the Grasshopper"/"La hormiguita y el grillo"

Materials to Gather

- index cards
- bug puzzles
- word cards

LITERACY

Focus

- Sing "The Ants Go Marching"/"Las hormiguitas marchan" again. Ask: *Do you remember this song? What are the ants doing in the song? Has anyone ever seen ants like these?*

  ¿Recuerdan esta canción? ¿Qué hacen las hormigas en la canción? ¿Alguien ha visto unas hormigas como éstas?
- Help the children understand that the song's lyrics written down are identical to the words they are singing.
- Tell the children that today they will discuss summer animals.

Develop

One Way to Develop the Lesson

- Initiate a discussion about summertime insects and animals. Encourage the children to describe what they see during the summer. Answers will vary depending on where you live. Focus on insects and animals with which the children are familiar.
- Spend time discussing each insect and animal that the children name. Ask: *Where have you seen [insert name of insect or animal]? What does it live in? Does it fly? Can it bite? Does it make a special noise? How does it move?*

  ¿Dónde han visto [insert name of insect or animal]? ¿En qué vive? ¿Vuela? ¿Puede morder? ¿Hace un ruido especial? ¿Cómo se mueve?
- Display any appropriate summer animal and insect Oral Language Cards to assist with brainstorming.
- Invite the children to imitate any insect or animal noises and/or movements.

Another Way to Develop the Lesson

- Tell the children that you have a story about a summer insect. Show them the cover of *The Little Ants/Las hormiguitas.* Ask: *What is this insect called?*

  ¿Cómo se llama este insecto?
- Help the children understand that, even though they know what the story is about by looking at the cover illustration, the picture has meaning independent of words or written language. You might show another book cover to reinforce this idea.
- Read *The Little Ants/Las hormiguitas.* When the children catch on to the story's predictable language, invite them to join you. Ask questions about the story: *Is it a true story? Is it a make-believe story? Do ants actually dance?*

  ¿Es una historia real? ¿Es una fantasía? ¿Las hormigas realmente bailan?
- Explain that this book is based on a traditional Mexican song.
- Read or sing the story again and allow the children to perform it.

Practice

- Place *The Little Ants/Las hormiguitas* book and tape in the Listening Center for the children to review.
- Give the children the animal card patterns. Instruct them to sort the cards into those they see in the summer and those they do not. Repeat this activity with the farm animal and bug pattern cards.
- Have the children draw pictures of their favorite summer insects or animals. You might change this activity and have them draw their least favorite insects or animals.
- Provide the bug puzzles for the children to complete.
- Write the word *bug* on an index card and add it to your word cards. You might also include an *insect* word card. Have the children use magnetic letters to copy appropriate word cards from this week.
- Have the children find the summer insects and animals in the Animal category on the *SRA Photo Library* software.

Preparation

- Make copies of the animal, bug, and farm animal card patterns. Color, laminate, and cut out.
- Make enlarged copies of the bug pattern cards. Color, cut out, mount on construction paper, laminate, and cut into puzzle pieces.

Scaffolding Strategies

More Help Take the children outdoors to look for animals and insects.

Extra Challenge Help the children make a list of insects and animals that we do not see during the winter months.

Second Language Learners

Talk about living and nonliving things as the children sort the Oral Language Development Cards. Can they name all the objects on the cards? Do they understand why the things are living or nonliving? Note the language they use.

DAY 4

Letter Knowledge

English/Spanish

- Use the Think, Pair, Share/ Piensa, aparea, comparte game to help the children think of ways to make letters with their bodies.

Suggested Reading

The Very Hungry Caterpillar by Eric Carle
La oruga muy hambrienta by Eric Carle
Fireflies in the Night by Judy Hawes
La Mariposa by David Cutts

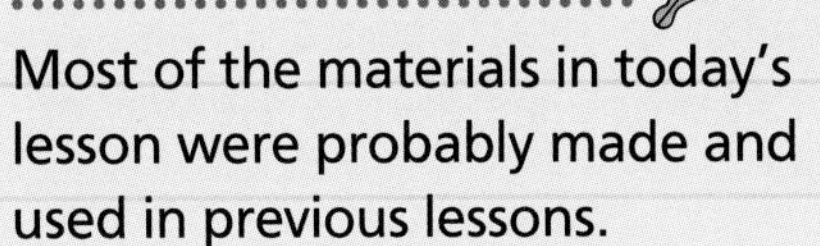

Teacher's NOTE

Most of the materials in today's lesson were probably made and used in previous lessons.

Anthology Support

"The Caterpillar"
"La oruga"
"A Fuzzy Caterpillar"
"Una oruga peluda"
"Baby Bumblebee"
"Abejorro bebé"
"Big Brown Bee"
"Little Ducky Duddle"
"El patito Tito"

Reflect/Assess

- *Which summer insects do you see most often? Where do you see them?*
  ¿Qué insectos de verano ven más a menudo? ¿Dónde?
- *What do ants build? Do they cooperate with each other?*
  ¿Qué construyen las hormigas? ¿Cooperan unos con otros?

Literacy Circle

Storytime 1

- Present the "Ms. Bumblebee Gathers Honey"/"La avispa Zumbi lleva miel" puppet and prop story. Allow the children to share any bee stories and discuss where bees live.

Storytime 2

- Read the "The Ant and the Grasshopper"/"La hormiguita y el grillo" listening story. If you saved the firefly story that the children created on Day 2 of Week 30, you might also read that here.

Content Connection

Science

Objectives

To identify animals and plants as living things

To group organisms and objects as living and nonliving and begin to identify things people have built

DLM Materials

Oral Language Development Cards 1, 14–20, 41–45, living things card patterns, nonliving things card patterns

Vocabulary

living, nonliving

vivo, no vivo

Activity 1

- Prepare copies of the living and nonliving things card patterns. Color, laminate, and cut out if you have not already done so.
- Define what living things and nonliving things are. You might provide examples to reinforce the children's comprehension. Help them look out a window for an example of each.
- Display Oral Language Cards 1, 14–20, and 41–45. Instruct the children to tell you each card's proper classification as a living or nonliving thing.

Activity 2

- Allow the children to sort the Oral Language Cards into living and nonliving categories. You might repeat this activity with the pattern cards. Be sure to correct any mistakes and clarify what is incorrect.
- Have the children draw living and/or nonliving things. Label them.

DAY 4

Objectives

- To begin to recognize, describe, and name shapes
- To begin to use words that indicate where things are in space

Vocabulary

side	lado
corner	esquina
angle	ángulo
length	longitud, largo
puzzle	rompecabezas
line	línea, recta
horizontal	horizontal
vertical	vertical
slanted	inclinada
all shape names	nombres de todas las figuras

DLM Materials

- *Math Resource Guide*
  Dot cards
  More or Less Game/Más o menos
- See Day 1
- *DLM Math* software
- *Four Baby Bumblebees* CD
- *Diez deditos* CD
- *Teacher's Resource Anthology*
  "Ten in the Bed"/"Diez en una cama"
- counters

Materials to Gather

- crepe paper or lightweight scarves
- See Day 1

MATH

Focus

- Do the "Ten in the Bed"/"Diez en una cama" finger play.
- Have children who have finished their Shape Books share them.

Develop

- Play the More or Less Game/Más o menos. Give each player a handful of counters and a Dot card.
- Have them empty their hands and estimate if there are more, fewer, or the same number of counters as dots on their cards.
- Encourage the children to match the counters to the dots to make a one-to-one correspondence. Were they right?
- Encourage the children to complete their Shape Books.

Practice

- Have the children finish assembling their Shape Books.
- Invite the children to make shapes with Building Straws or toothpicks and record and label their favorite designs or pictures.
- Encourage the children to choose and complete the Pattern Block Puzzles and use Pattern Block Cutouts to record their work.
- Have the children work Tangram Puzzles and have them record their solutions.
- Have the children work in pairs to determine which shapes are in the Feely Box.
- Encourage the children to make a new estimate of the number of items in the Estimating Jar based on the benchmark counters. Change the color of the paper they are using for recording.
- Invite the children to work on Create-a-Scene (no level).

Reflect/Assess

- Discuss what the children have learned about shapes.

Content Connection

Social Studies

Objectives
To identify common features in the home and school environment
To create simple representations of home, school, or community through drawings or block constructions

Vocabulary
shape names, line names
nombres de figures, nombres de líneas/rectas

DLM Materials
Sara Sidney: The Most Beautiful Iguana in the World/Sara Sidney: la iguana más bella del mundo

Materials to Gather
crayons, paper

Activity 1

- Show the children the plans of Sara Sidney's house in the book *Sara Sidney: The Most Beautiful Iguana in the World/Sara Sidney: la iguana más bella del mundo.* Ask them to discuss the shapes of the rooms.
- Have the children draw a plan of their house or their bedroom.

Activity 2

- Draw a plan of the classroom with the children or if the children are able, a plan of the school. Compare this drawing to those you made earlier in the year.

Reflect on the Day

- *What did you learn about summer animals today?*
  ¿Qué aprendieron sobre los animales de verano hoy?
- *Which summer insect do you like the best?*
  ¿Qué insecto de verano les gusta más?

Music and Movement

- Give the children crepe paper streamers or lightweight scarves. Play classical music and have them dance around like butterflies.
- Sing "Bringing Home a Baby Bumblebee" from the *Four Baby Bumblebees* CD or "Sun, sun, ba, ba, e" from the *Diez deditos* CD.

Suggested Reading

Building a House by Byron Barton (1990)
Barcos, barcos, barcos by Joanna Ruane

Home Connection

Remind families that tomorrow is outdoor water day. Children will need swimsuits, towels, sunscreen, and waterproof sandals if possible.

Begin the Day

- Sing "Summer Is Coming"/"Ya viene el verano."
- Use a suggestion for Morning Circle offered in the front of this *Teacher's Edition.*

Objectives

- To use new vocabulary in everyday communication
- To refine and extend understanding of known words

Vocabulary

mud pies — pasteles de lodo
water play — juegos con agua

DLM Materials

- *Teacher's Resource Anthology*
  "Summer Is Coming"/"Ya viene el verano"
  "Sing Me a Rainbow"/"Cántame un arco iris"
  bubble soap

Materials to Gather

- balloons
- basket
- bubble wands
- butcher paper
- chalk
- cookie cutters (optional)
- mini pie tins
- plastic utensils
- sponges
- spray bottles
- sprinkler
- tempera paint
- tongue depressors
- water hose

LITERACY

Focus

- Allow the children to select a favorite song for the class to sing.
- Weather permitting, tell the children that this is a special day because all of the class activities will be done outdoors.

Develop

One Way to Develop the Lesson

- Help the children think about outdoor safety. Make a list of outdoor rules for the day. Your list should include not running in wet and slippery areas or near the road, using sunscreen (please note any allergies), waiting for their turns, staying on school property, and so on.
- Remind the children to be cooperative with and considerate of others. If you have lunch outdoors, discuss any additional rules that apply.
- Discuss any new vocabulary that might have been introduced while developing the outdoor rules list.

Another Way to Develop the Lesson

- Describe the games and activities that you have set up outdoors. Assign the children to areas where they should start their play. Monitor each area to help keep the class orderly and in manageable groups.
- Adapt your activities for the classroom if the weather is not agreeable. This would be a good time for the children to use their outdoor imaginations indoors. You might also update your rule list from the first Develop.

Practice

- Explain what a mud pie is. Stress the fact that a mud pie is not a pie to eat. Invite the children to make mud pies. Provide pie tins, plastic utensils (for mixing and building, not for eating), and some water. Encourage them to use natural ingredients in their mud pies (twigs, leaves, grass, and so on) without harming anything.
- Hand out the sponge puppets you made. Encourage the children to work together to tell a story or put on a play with the puppets.
- Provide spray bottles filled with liquid tempera paint. Put a piece of butcher paper on the ground. (You may weight it down with rocks or other safe heavy objects.) Allow the children to spray paint a masterpiece.
- If possible, supply a sprinkler in which the children can play. You might also show them how to make a rainbow with spray from the hose.
- Using small water balloons and a basket, challenge the children to toss the balloons into the basket. Warn them that the balloons might break.
- Give the children bubble soap and wands and have them blow and catch bubbles.
- Provide chalk to make sidewalk art. Be sure to clean up afterward.

Preparation

- Make bubble soap.
- Set up specific areas for outdoor activities and label them with signs.
- Fill spray bottles and balloons with liquid tempera paint.
- Make puppets by cutting animals and people out of sponges. Glue them to tongue depressors. You might use cookie cutters as guides.

Second Language Learners

Using an instant camera, photograph each child as he or she plays in the water. Afterward, ask each child to dictate a description to write on the bottom of his or her picture. Read it with the child, pointing to each word as you read. Send the picture home.

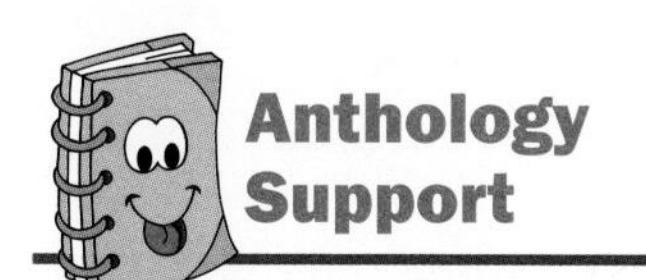

Anthology Support

"She Waded in the Water"
"The Ants Go Marching"
"Las hormiguitas marchan"
"Mister Sun"
"Señor Sol"

DAY 5

Letter Knowledge

English

- Allow the children to find and circle a specific letter in newspapers and magazines.

Spanish

- Allow the children to find and name letters hidden in the sand.

Suggested Reading

Summer by Robert Hirsh
The Kissing Hand by Audrey Penn
Time of Wonder by Robert McCloskey

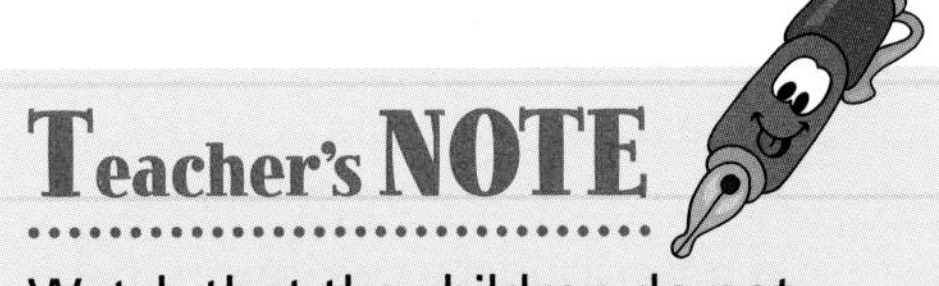

Teacher's NOTE

Watch that the children do not get too much sun, and be sure to provide drinking water.

Reflect/Assess

- *How do today's activities compare with our activities on a routine day?*
  ¿En qué se parecen las actividades de hoy a las de un día común y corriente?
- *What is fun about learning outdoors?*
  ¿Qué tiene de divertido aprender sobre la vida al aire libre?

Literacy Circle

Storytime 1

- Hold storytime outdoors. Present the "Sing Me a Rainbow"/ "Cántame un arco iris" flannel board story. Review anything from the story that is related to today's outdoor activities.

Storytime 2

- Hold storytime outdoors. Read one of the class's favorite stories. If applicable, allow the children to act out the story. Ask: *Why do you like this story? Did we learn any new words from the story?*
  ¿Por qué les gusta este cuento? ¿Aprendimos palabras nuevas de este cuento?

Content Connection

Science

Objectives
To observe and describe properties of rocks, soil, and water
To begin to use scientific words and phrases to describe objects, events, and living things

Materials to Gather
buckets, paintbrushes, sand, water

Vocabulary
dams, erosion, evaporation
represas, erosión, evaporación

Activity 1

- Explain what a dam is. You might use beaver dams as an example and/or show pictures of well-known dams built by people.
- Show the children how to make dams with sand. Review how a dam works. Have them build a dam in the sand table.
- Define erosion as it relates to dams. Try to model what erosion is using the dam they built. You might show pictures. Discuss how dirt areas can be washed away or weakened by the flow of water.

Activity 2

- Using buckets of water and clean paintbrushes, have the children pretend to paint a fence or the sidewalk. Discuss what happens as the water dries. You might explain how the sun makes paint and some colors fade over time (similar to erosion).

DAY 5

Objectives

- To begin to recognize, describe, and name shapes
- To follow basic oral or pictorial cues for operating programs successfully

Vocabulary

sorting	ordenar
classifying	clasificar
recording	anotar

DLM Materials

- *DLM Math* software

Materials to Gather

- Shape Books

Patterning is at the heart of mathematics. Some define mathematics as the science of patterns in number and shape.

MATH

Focus

- Read and discuss the children's recorded estimates of how many items there are in the Estimating Jar. Dump the objects and count them to check.
- Discuss how they have progressed in their ability to make good estimates.

Develop

- Have the children finish sharing their Shape Books.

Practice

- Have the children clean up and put the materials neatly away in the Math Center.
- Invite the children to work on Create-a-Scene.

Reflect/Assess

- Computer Show and Book Show: Have the children show their work on the computer and in their books. *How did you describe your pictures with shapes? With numbers?*

  ¿Cómo describieron sus dibujos con figuras? ¿Con números?

Music and Movement

- Have the children play shadow tag. The players should try to catch opponents by stepping on their shadows before someone steps on theirs.
- Play music while the children safely explore outdoors.

Content Connection

Physical Development

Objectives

To move within a space of defined boundaries, changing body configurations to accommodate the space

To begin to participate in group games involving movement

DLM Materials

Teacher's Resource Anthology

Square Dance/Baile de figuras

Activity 1

- Have 8 children stand in a square (2 children on each side). Add a third child to each side of the square. Ask them, *What happens?*

  ¿Qué pasa?

  Continue adding children as long as you have an even number to add.
- Reverse the activity by taking children away from each side of the square. Ask them, *What happens?*

  ¿Qué pasa?

Activity 2

- Invite the children to do a Square Dance/Baile de figuras. Discuss the starting position for the dance.

Suggested Reading

Shapes and Things by Tana Hoban

Amigos by Alma Flor Ada

Reflect on the Day

- *Do you like being indoors or outdoors? Why?*

  ¿Les gusta estar adentro o afuera? ¿Por qué?
- *What will you remember most about your first year of school?*

  ¿Qué recordarán más sobre el primer año escolar?

Home Connection

Send home with the children a note that contains a few ideas that families can use to keep their children learning over the summer.

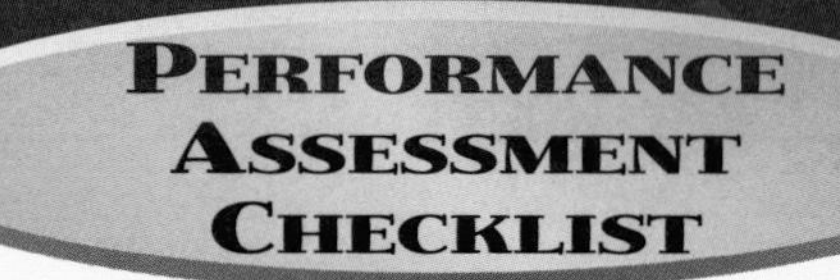

Assessment in the Prekindergarten Classroom

Performance Assessment Checklist

The objectives in ***The DLM Early Childhood Express*** cover a wide range of skills that young children develop. Of course, all children do not acquire these skills in the same manner or in the same time frame. It is, however, reasonable to assume that over the course of a school year, most of the objectives will have been accomplished.

You informally observe your children every day. You know what each child is able to do. In order to help you turn the knowledge you gain from observing the children into a tangible assessment of the skills development of each child, the objectives from ***The DLM Early Childhood Express*** are arranged in a Performance Assessment Checklist. You can use this checklist to fit your needs. For example, combined with samples of children's work and/or your anecdotal notes, it can provide parents with specific information about their children's skills-development progress.

It is recommended that you observe each child over three time spans during the year. You do not necessarily have to look for each skill on the same day; the observation period can cover whatever time span you desire. Allow enough time between observations so that growth can be seen, possibly observing at the beginning, in the middle, and toward the end of the school year.

To use the checklist, make a copy for each child. You might choose to keep each child's checklist in a separate folder. You might want to divide the list into smaller sections, such as Literacy, Math, and so on, and keep those lists in notebooks near the places you are most likely to observe the children interacting with the various content areas.

Enter each child's name on his or her Performance Assessment Checklist(s), and note the dates of the observation period(s). For the skills being assessed, indicate a child's progress using the following scale. Once a skill has been mastered, no further observation for that particular skill is required.

N: not currently performing

O: occasionally performing

C: consistently performing

Portfolio Assessment

In addition to observing children's performances on an informal and ongoing basis, many teachers want to provide documentation of the children's progress. Keeping a portfolio for each child is a wonderful way to document progress for parents. You can use the contents of the portfolio to support the Performance Assessment Checklist. The article following the checklist will help you understand and set up a portfolio assessment system that works for you and your class.

Performance Assessment Checklist

OBSERVATION PERIODS			
1st	Fall	______ to	______
2nd	Winter	______ to	______
3rd	Spring	______ to	______

KEY
N: not currently performing
O: occasionally performing
C: consistently performing

NAME ____________________

Literacy

I. LANGUAGE AND EARLY LITERACY DEVELOPMENT

A. Listening Comprehension

		1st	2nd	3rd
1.	Listens with increasing attention			
2.	Listens for different purposes (e.g., to learn what happened in a story, to receive instructions, to converse with an adult or a peer)			
3.	Understands and follows simple oral directions			
4.	Enjoys listening to and responding to books			
5.	Listens to and engages in several exchanges of conversations with others			
6.	Listens to tapes and records, and shows understanding through gestures, actions, and/or language			
7.	Listens purposefully to English-speaking teachers and peers to gather information and shows some understanding of the new language being spoken by others (ESL)			

B. Speech Production and Speech Discrimination (Oral Language Development)

		1st	2nd	3rd
1.	Perceives differences between similar sounding words (e.g., "coat" and "goat," "three" and "free," [Spanish] "juego" and "fuego")			
2.	Produces speech sounds with increasing ease and accuracy			
3.	Experiments with new language sounds			
4.	Experiments with and demonstrates growing understanding of the sounds and intonation of the English language (ESL)			

C. Vocabulary (Oral Language Development)

		1st	2nd	3rd
1.	Shows a steady increase in listening and speaking vocabulary			
2.	Uses new vocabulary in everyday communication			
3.	Refines and extends understanding of known words			
4.	Attempts to communicate more than current vocabulary will allow, borrowing and extending words to create meaning			
5.	Links new learning experiences and vocabulary to what is already known about a topic			
6.	Increases listening vocabulary and begins to develop a vocabulary of object names and common phrases in English (ESL)			

D. Verbal Expression (Oral Language Development)

		1st	2nd	3rd
1.	Uses language for a variety of purposes (e.g., expressing needs and interests)			
2.	Uses sentences of increasing length (three or more words) and grammatical complexity in everyday speech			
3.	Uses language to express common routines and familiar scripts			
4.	Tells a simple personal narrative, focusing on favorite or most memorable parts			
5.	Asks questions and makes comments related to the current topic of discussion			
6.	Begins to engage in conversation and follows conversational rules (e.g., staying on topic and taking turns)			
7.	Begins to retell the sequence of a story			
8.	Engages in various forms of nonverbal communication with those who do not speak his/her home language (ESL)			
9.	Uses single words and simple phrases to communicate meaning in social situations (ESL)			
10.	Attempts to use new vocabulary and grammar in speech (ESL)			

Performance Assessment Checklist

Name ______________________

E. Phonological Awareness

		1st	2nd	3rd
1.	Becomes increasingly sensitive to the sounds of spoken words			
2.	Begins to identify rhymes and rhyming sounds in familiar words, participates in rhyming games, and repeats rhyming songs and poems			
3.	Begins to attend to the beginning sounds in familiar words by identifying that the pronunciations of several words all begin the same way (e.g., "dog," "dark," and "dusty," [Spanish] "casa," "coche," and "cuna")			
4.	Begins to break words into syllables or claps along with each syllables in a phrase			
5.	Begins to create and invent words by substituting one sound for another (e.g., bubblegum/gugglebum, [Spanish] calabaza/balacaza)			

F. Print and Book Awareness

		1st	2nd	3rd
1.	Understands that reading and writing are ways to obtain information and knowledge, generate and communicate thoughts and ideas, and solve problems			
2.	Understands that print carries a message by recognizing labels, signs, and other print forms in the environment			
3.	Understands that letters are different from numbers			
4.	Understands that illustrations carry meaning but cannot be read			
5.	Understands that a book has a title and an author			
6.	Begins to understand that print runs from left to right and top to bottom			
7.	Begins to understand some basic print conventions (e.g., the concept that letters are grouped to form words and that words are separated by spaces)			
8.	Begins to recognize the association between spoken and written words by following the print as it is read aloud			
9.	Understands that different text forms are used for different functions (e.g., lists for shopping, recipes for cooking, newspapers for learning about current events, letters and messages for interpersonal communications)			

G. Letter Knowledge and Early Word Recognition

		1st	2nd	3rd
1.	Begins to associate the names of letters with their shapes			
2.	Identifies 10 or more printed alphabet letters			
3.	Begins to notice beginning letters in familiar words			
4.	Begins to make some letter/sound matches			
5.	Begins to identify some high-frequency words (age 4)			

H. Motivation to Read

		1st	2nd	3rd
1.	Demonstrates an interest in books and reading through body language and facial expressions			
2.	Enjoys listening to and discussing storybooks and information books read aloud			
3.	Attempts to read and write independently			
4.	Shares books and engages in pretend-reading with other children			
5.	Enjoys visiting the library			

I. Developing Knowledge of Literary Forms

		1st	2nd	3rd
1.	Recognizes favorite books by their cover			
2.	Selects books to read based on personal criteria			
3.	Understands that books and other print resources (e.g., magazines, computer-based texts) are handled in specific ways			
4.	Becomes increasingly familiar with narrative form and its elements by identifying characters and predicting events, plot, and the resolution of a story			
5.	Begins to predict what will happen next in a story			
6.	Imitates the special language in storybooks and story dialogue, and uses it in retellings and dramatic play (such as "Once upon a time...")			
7.	Asks questions and makes comments about the information and events from books			
8.	Connects information and events in books to real-life experiences			
9.	Begins to retell some sequences of events in stories			

NAME ______________________

J. Written Expression

		1st	2nd	3rd
1.	Attempts to write messages as part of playful activity			
2.	Uses known letters and approximations of letters to represent written language (especially meaningful words like his/her name and phrases such as "I love you" or [Spanish] "Te quiero")			
3.	Attempts to connect the sounds in a word with its letter forms			
4.	Understands that writing is used to communicate ideas and information			
5.	Attempts to use a variety of forms of writing (e.g., lists, messages, stories)			
6.	Begins to dictate words, phrases, and sentences to an adult recording on paper (e.g., "letter writing," "story writing")			

Math

II. MATHEMATICS

A. Number and Operations

		1st	2nd	3rd
1.	Arranges sets of concrete objects in one-to-one correspondence			
2.	Counts by ones to 10 or higher			
3.	Counts concrete objects to five or higher			
4.	Begins to compare the numbers of concrete objects using language (e.g., "same" or "equal," "one more," "more than," or "less than")			
5.	Begins to name "how many" are in a group of up to three (or more) objects without counting (e.g., recognizing two or three crayons in a box)			
6.	Recognizes and describes the concept of zero (meaning there are none)			
7.	Begins to demonstrate part of and whole with real objects (e.g., an orange)			
8.	Begins to identify first and last in a series			
9.	Combines, separates, and names "how many" concrete objects			

B. Patterns

		1st	2nd	3rd
1.	Imitates pattern sounds and physical movements (e.g., clap, stomp, clap, stomp,...)			
2.	Recognizes and reproduces simple patterns of concrete objects (e.g., a string of beads that are blue, blue, yellow, blue, blue)			
3.	Begins to recognize patterns in their environment (e.g., day follows night, repeated phrases in storybooks, patterns in carpeting or clothing)			
4.	Begins to predict what comes next when patterns are extended			

C. Geometry and Spatial Sense

		1st	2nd	3rd
1.	Begins to recognize, describe, and name shapes			
2.	Begins to use words that indicate where things are in space (e.g., "beside," "inside," "behind," "above," "below")			
3.	Begins to recognize when a shape's position or orientation has changed			
4.	Begins to investigate and predict the results of putting together two or more shapes			
5.	Puts together puzzles of increasing complexity			
6.	Puts together shapes to make new shapes and designs			
7.	Identifies horizontal and vertical lines			

D. Measurement

		1st	2nd	3rd
1.	Covers an area with shapes (e.g., tiles)			
2.	Fills a shape with solids or liquids (e.g., ice cubes, water)			
3.	Begins to make size comparisons between objects (e.g., taller than, smaller than)			
4.	Begins to use tools to imitate measuring			
5.	Begins to categorize time intervals and uses language associated with time in everyday situations (e.g., "in the morning," "after snack")			
6.	Begins to order two or three objects by size (seriation) (e.g., largest to smallest) (age 4)			

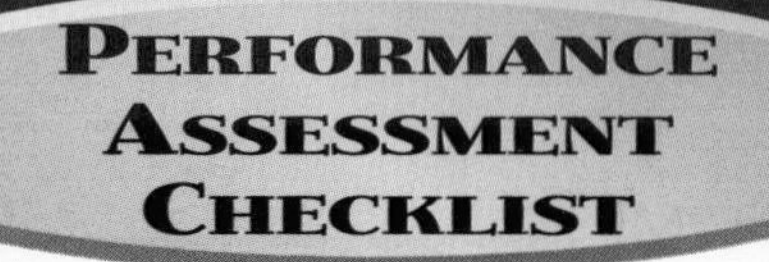

NAME ______________________

E. Classification and Data Collection

		1st	2nd	3rd
1.	Matches objects that are alike			
2.	Describes similarities and differences between objects			
3.	Sorts objects into groups by an attribute and begins to explain how the grouping was done			
4.	Participates in creating and using real and pictorial graphs			

Science

III. SCIENCE

A. Science Processes

		1st	2nd	3rd
1.	Begins to demonstrate safe practices and appropriate use of materials			
2.	Asks questions about objects, events, and organisms			
3.	Shows an interest in investigating unfamiliar objects, organisms, and phenomena			
4.	Uses one or more senses to observe and learn about objects, events, and organisms			
5.	Describes observations			
6.	Begins to perform simple investigations			
7.	Gathers information using simple tools such as a magnifying lens and an eyedropper			
8.	Explores by manipulating materials with simple equipment (e.g., pouring from a cup and using a spoon to pick up sand or water)			
9.	Uses simple measuring devices to learn about objects and organisms			
10.	Compares objects and organisms and identifies similarities and differences			
11.	Sorts objects and organisms into groups and begins to describe how groups were organized			
12.	Begins to offer explanations, using his or her own words			
13.	Predicts what will happen next based on previous experience			
14.	Solves simple design problems (e.g., making a box into a little house for a storybook character, toy, or pet)			
15.	Participates in creating and using simple data charts			
16.	Shares observations and findings with others through pictures, discussions, or dramatizations			

B. Science Concepts

		1st	2nd	3rd
1.	Observes and describes properties of rocks, soil, and water			
2.	Describes properties of objects and characteristics of living things			
3.	Begins to observe changes in size, color, position, weather, and sound			
4.	Identifies animals and plants as living things			
5.	Groups organisms and objects as living or nonliving and begins to identify things people have built			
6.	Begins to recognize that living things have similar needs for water, food, and air			
7.	Begins to identify what things are made of (e.g., distinguishing a metal spoon from a plastic spoon)			
8.	Uses patterns (such as growth and day following night) to predict what happens next			
9.	Identifies similarities and differences among objects and organisms			
10.	Begins to use scientific words and phrases to describe objects, events, and living things			

NAME ____________________

Social Studies

IV. SOCIAL STUDIES

A. Individual, Culture, and Community

		1st	2nd	3rd
1.	Shares ideas and takes turns listening and speaking			
2.	Cooperates with others in a joint activity			
3.	Identifies and follows classroom rules			
4.	Participates in classroom jobs and contributes to the classroom community			
5.	Identifies similarities among people like himself/herself and classmates as well as among himself/herself and people from other cultures			
6.	Begins to examine a situation from another person's perspective			

B. History

		1st	2nd	3rd
1.	Identifies common events and routines (e.g., snack time, storytime)			
2.	Begins to categorize time intervals using words (e.g., "today," "tomorrow," "next time")			
3.	Recognizes changes in the environment over time (e.g., growth, seasonal changes)			
4.	Connects past events to current events (e.g., linking yesterday's activity with what will happen today)			
5.	Begins to understand cause-and-effect relationships (e.g., if one goes outside in the rain, one will get wet)			

C. Geography

		1st	2nd	3rd
1.	Identifies common features in the home and school environment (e.g., the library, the playground)			
2.	Creates simple representations of home, school, or community through drawings or block constructions			
3.	Begins to use words to indicate relative location (e.g., "front," "back," "near," "far")			
4.	Identifies common features of the local landscape (e.g., houses, buildings, streets)			
5.	Labels common features in familiar environments			

D. Economics

		1st	2nd	3rd
1.	Understands the basic human needs of all people for food, clothing, and shelter			
2.	Understands the roles, responsibilities, and services provided by community workers			
3.	Becomes aware of what it means to be a consumer			

Fine Arts

V. FINE ARTS

A. Art

		1st	2nd	3rd
1.	Uses a variety of materials (e.g., crayons, paint, clay, markers) to create original work			
2.	Uses different colors, surface textures, and shapes to create form and meaning			
3.	Begins to use art as a form of self-expression			
4.	Shares ideas about personal artwork			
5.	Begins to show interest in the artwork of others			

B. Music

		1st	2nd	3rd
1.	Participates in classroom music activities			
2.	Begins to sing a variety of simple songs			
3.	Begins to play classroom instruments			
4.	Begins to respond to music of various tempos through movement			
5.	Begins to distinguish among the sounds of several common instruments			

NAME ____________________

C. Dramatic Play

		1st	2nd	3rd
1.	Expresses feelings through movement			
2.	Begins to create or re-create stories, moods, or experiences through dramatic representations			
3.	Begins to engage in dramatic play with others			

Health/Safety

VI. HEALTH AND SAFETY

A. Health

		1st	2nd	3rd
1.	Becomes aware of routine healthy behaviors (e.g., brushing teeth)			
2.	Begins to follow health-promoting routines (e.g., washing hands)			
3.	Begins to understand the need for exercise and rest			
4.	Refines use of eating utensils			
5.	Begins to recognize and select healthy foods			
6.	Prepares simple healthy snacks			
7.	Demonstrates an understanding of basic health and safety rules			

B. Safety

		1st	2nd	3rd
1.	Recognizes the danger of fire and learns to treat fire with caution			
2.	Responds appropriately during a fire drill			
3.	Knows how to seek help in an emergency			
4.	Knows how to cross a street safely			
5.	Recognizes the symbol for poison			
6.	Knows never to eat substances that are not food			
7.	Recognizes the danger of poisonous substances, including drugs			
8.	Knows not to talk to, accept rides from, or take treats from strangers			
9.	Knows how to get help from a parent and/or trusted adult when made to feel uncomfortable or unsafe by another person/adult			
10.	Knows never to take medicine unless it is administered by a trusted adult			
11.	Knows about safe behavior around bodies of water (e.g., pools, lakes)			
12.	Knows about safe behavior around bugs and insects			
13.	Understands about safe behavior in potentially dangerous places			

Personal/Social

VII. PERSONAL AND SOCIAL DEVELOPMENT

A. Personal Development

		1st	2nd	3rd
1.	Develops a sense of personal space			
2.	Expresses interest and self-direction in learning			
3.	Begins to show self-control by following classroom rules			
4.	Begins to be responsible for individual behavior and actions			
5.	Begins to show greater ability to control intense feelings (e.g., anger)			

B. Social Development

		1st	2nd	3rd
1.	Begins to share and cooperate with others in group activities			
2.	Respects other people's space and personal belongings			
3.	Begins to develop friendships with others			
4.	Begins to express thoughts, feelings, and ideas through language as well as through gestures and actions			
5.	Responds to the suggestions of others			

Physical

VIII. PHYSICAL DEVELOPMENT

A. Physical Movement

		1st	2nd	3rd
1.	Explores moving in space			
2.	Shows an awareness of name, location, and relationship of body parts			
3.	Moves within a space of defined boundaries, changing body configurations to accommodate the space			
4.	Becomes more able to move from one space to another in different ways (e.g., running, jumping, hopping, skipping)			
5.	Becomes more able to move in place (e.g., axial movements such as reaching, twisting, turning, and bending)			
6.	Begins to move in rhythm			
7.	Begins to participate in group games involving movement (e.g., Duck, Duck, Goose)			

B. Gross-Motor Development

		1st	2nd	3rd
1.	Begins to throw or kick an object in a particular direction			
2.	Begins to play catch with a bean bag or a large ball			
3.	Bounces a large ball and catches it			
4.	Begins to coordinate arms and legs (e.g., swinging, stretching)			

C. Fine-Motor Development

		1st	2nd	3rd
1.	Begins to develop pincer control in picking up objects (e.g., weaving, touching small objects)			
2.	Begins to practice self-help skills (e.g., zipping, buttoning)			
3.	Begins to hold writing tools with fingers instead of with a fist			
4.	Begins to manipulate play objects that have fine parts			
5.	Begins to use scissors			
6.	Begins to coordinate finger activities and clapping exercises			

Technology

IX. TECHNOLOGY APPLICATIONS

		1st	2nd	3rd
1.	Starts, uses, and exits software programs			
2.	Uses a variety of input devices, such as mouse, keyboard, voice/sound recorder, or touch screen			
3.	Begins to use technical terminology, such as "mouse," "keyboard," "printer," "CD-ROM"			
4.	Follows basic oral or pictorial cues for operating programs successfully			
5.	Enjoys listening to and interacting with storybooks and information texts (e.g., multimedia encyclopedia) in electronic forms			
6.	Uses a variety of software packages with audio, video, and graphics to enhance learning experiences (e.g., improving vocabulary, increasing phonological awareness)			

Promoting Authentic Assessment:

Portfolios in Early Childhood Education

Beverly J. Irby, Ed.D., Professor
Genevieve Brown, Ed.D., Professor

Department of Educational Leadership and Counseling
Sam Houston State University
Huntsville, Texas

Student assessment and evaluation are too often based on standardized tests. These assessment or evaluation measurements are limited and provide little information that teachers, parents, and students can use to gain a comprehensive picture of academic, linguistic, social, or developmental progress. Recognizing the limitations of such assessment methods, teachers have begun to restructure student assessment to include authentic, or performance-based, methods in which students actively participate in assessing their own learning.

Using the portfolio process facilitates authentic assessment and provides multiple opportunities for learning. The portfolio is a collection of thoughtfully selected work samples, or artifacts, and accompanying reflections indicative of the child's learning experiences, effort, and progress toward and/or attainment of established curriculum goals. As children choose work samples for their portfolios, they become involved in their own learning and assessment. They begin to have a notion of evaluating their own work, thus initiating the development of reflective, self-assessment skills.

How Can Portfolios Help?

One of the greatest advantages of the portfolio is that using it allows teachers, parents, and children to follow the children's progress in order to identify areas of growth and necessary improvement. Through reviewing children's portfolio artifacts and listening to children's reflections on their work, teacher are able to:
(1) keep track of children's accomplishments,
(2) address state and local accountability factors, (3) align instruction and assessment, and (4) facilitate parent-teacher conferences.

According to teachers, portfolios are beneficial to children in the following ways. Using portfolios:

- Involves children in the learning process
- Highlights student strengths as opposed to weaknesses
- Initiates the skill of reflective practice among children
- Encourages curiosity and creativity
- Promotes organizational skills
- Motivates children as they review their own progress
- Promotes oral language development as they articulate their reflections
- Enhances children's self-confidence
- Addresses learning styles, language proficiencies, and ethnic backgrounds of students

Not only does the use of portfolios benefit children, but teachers also report benefits. They say that the portfolio process helps them to:

- Promote reflection on classroom pedagogy among teachers
- Maintain a focus on student performance
- Provide concrete examples of the child's work to pass on to special teachers or to the next year's teacher
- Offer an easily understood document for parents as teachers conduct parent-teacher conferences
- Promote authentic assessments based on classroom experiences
- Plan curriculum that is individualized and developmentally appropriate for each child
- Assist in identification of needed curriculum resources
- Capitalize on teacher observations of children in daily classroom activities